Decentralized Governance and Accountability

At the end of the twentieth century, academics and policymakers welcomed a trend toward fiscal and political decentralization as part of a potential solution for slow economic growth and poor performance by insulated, unaccountable governments. For the past two decades, researchers have been trying to answer a series of vexing questions about the political economy of multilayered governance. Much of the best recent research on decentralization has come from close collaborations between university researchers and international aid institutions. As the volume and quality of this collaborative research have increased in recent decades, the time has come to review the lessons from this literature and apply them to debates about future programming. In this volume, the contributors place this research in the broader history of engagement between aid institutions and academics, particularly in the area of decentralized governance, and outline the challenges and opportunities to link evidence and policy action.

Jonathan A. Rodden is a professor of political science at Stanford University, a senior fellow at the Hoover Institution, and founder of the Stanford Spatial Social Science Lab. He is the author of an award-winning book, *Hamilton's Paradox: The Promise and Peril of Fiscal Federalism*, as well as a new book on political geography, *Why Cities Lose: The Deep Roots of the Urban-Rural Political Divide*.

Erik Wibbels is the Robert O. Keohane professor of political science at Duke University and the co-general editor of the Cambridge Studies in Comparative Politics series. His research focuses on development, redistribution, and political geography and has been published by Cambridge University Press, *World Politics, International Organization, American Journal of Political Science, American Political Science Review*, and other journals. He is also the co-director of DevLab@Duke, which works with bilateral and multilateral donors to improve the design and evaluation of governance programming.

Decentralized Governance and Accountability

Academic Research and the Future of Donor Programming

Edited by

JONATHAN A. RODDEN
Stanford University

ERIK WIBBELS
Duke University

CAMBRIDGE
UNIVERSITY PRESS

CAMBRIDGE
UNIVERSITY PRESS

University Printing House, Cambridge CB2 8BS, United Kingdom

One Liberty Plaza, 20th Floor, New York, NY 10006, USA

477 Williamstown Road, Port Melbourne, VIC 3207, Australia

314-321, 3rd Floor, Plot 3, Splendor Forum, Jasola District Centre, New Delhi - 110025, India

103 Penang Road, #05-06/07, Visioncrest Commercial, Singapore 238467

Cambridge University Press is part of the University of Cambridge.

It furthers the University's mission by disseminating knowledge in the pursuit of education, learning and research at the highest international levels of excellence.

www.cambridge.org
Information on this title: www.cambridge.org/9781108708869
DOI: 10.1017/9781108615594

First published 2019
First paperback edition 2022

A catalogue record for this publication is available from the British Library

Library of Congress Cataloging in Publication data
NAMES: Rodden, Jonathan, editor. | Wibbels, Erik, 1972– editor.
TITLE: Decentralized governance and accountability : academic research and the future of donor programming / edited by Jonathan A. Rodden, Stanford University, California, Erik Wibbels, Duke University.
DESCRIPTION: Cambridge, United Kingdom ; New York, NY, USA : Cambridge University Press, 2018. | Includes bibliographical references and index.
IDENTIFIERS: LCCN 2018049104 | ISBN 9781108497909 (alk. paper)
SUBJECTS: LCSH: Decentralization in government – Developing countries. | Government accountability – Developing countries. | Corruption – Developing countries – Prevention. | Economic assistance – Developing countries.
CLASSIFICATION: LCC JF60 .D435 2019 | DDC 320.9172/4–dc23
LC record available at https://lccn.loc.gov/2018049104

ISBN 978-1-108-49790-9 Hardback
ISBN 978-1-108-70886-9 Paperback

We dedicate this volume to all the world's citizens suffering at the hands of capricious governments, and to those struggling to hold those governments accountable, including our colleagues in the development industry who have helped us think about the conditions under which outsiders might help make things better.

Contents

Figures and Tables

Contributors

Kate Baldwin, Yale University

Gary Bland, RTI International

Derick W. Brinkerhoff, RTI International

Christopher L. Carter, UC Berkeley

Fotini Christia, Massachusetts Institute of Technology

Thad Dunning, UC Berkeley

Guy Grossman, University of Pennsylvania

Gianmarco León, Pompeu Fabra University, Barcelona GSE, and IPEG

Edmund Malesky, Duke University

Jan H. Pierskalla, The Ohio State University

Alison E. Post, UC Berkeley

Pia Raffler, Harvard University

Jonathan A. Rodden, Stanford University

Leonard Wantchekon, Princeton University and African School of Economics

Anna Wetterberg, RTI International

Erik Wibbels, Duke University

Acknowledgments

This volume would not have been possible without the generous support and vision of the leadership of USAID's Center of Excellence on Democracy, Human Rights, and Governance, especially Morgan Holmes, Nick Higgins, Mike Keshishian, and Corinne Rothblum. We would also like to thank the dozens of development professionals at USAID and beyond who have listened to us, taught us, and helped build bridges between the academic and policy worlds.

I

Introduction

Jonathan A. Rodden and Erik Wibbels

For much of the twentieth century, many developing countries were governed by insulated, unaccountable, and often corrupt officials in their capital cities. It was clear that, at least in part, anemic economic growth and woeful provision of public services were attributable to poor performance by these governments. Thus many academics and policymakers welcomed the trend toward fiscal and political decentralization at the end of the twentieth century as part of a potential solution to the twin challenges of poor governance and lagging economic development. Aid agencies sought ways to strengthen and support decentralization initiatives around the world.

The intuitive appeal of decentralization was simple. Ideally, after breaking the central government's monopoly on authority and resources, heterogeneous populations could choose policies to fit local preferences and circumstances. Corrupt or lazy officials could be monitored and punished by local citizens at the voting booth, through local social sanctioning, or by moving.

However, it quickly became clear that decentralization in practice bore little resemblance to optimistic theories from welfare economics. It turned out that there were a variety of ways in which local officials could ignore local demands and avoid accountability from local voters and from higher-level governments. Academics and practitioners began to learn a variety of lessons about clientelism, patronage, and capture by powerful local interests. They discovered that under some conditions, decentralization frees up dominant local groups to take the lion's share of resources for themselves and to exclude traditionally oppressed groups. It became clear that the structure of taxation and intergovernmental finance shapes officials' incentives in powerful and often unfortunate ways. It turns out not to be so simple to rely on local citizens, who face a basic collective action problem and often profound resource constraints, to monitor local officials, especially when responsibilities and fiscal flows are opaque. All of these challenges are even greater in the presence of social heterogeneity and a recent history of conflict.

For the past two decades, the academic literature on decentralization in developing countries has been grappling with these and related issues, and trying to answer a series of vexing questions about the political economy of multilayered governance. Meanwhile, local governments and intergovernmental relations have become crucial to much of the work being done by international agencies such as the United States Agency for International Development (USAID), the World Bank, the Department for International Development (DFID), and many others. For many aid programs, the difference between success and failure often lies in issues like local capture, clientelism, corruption, and weak incentives for monitoring and accountability. This is most obviously true for governance projects, but it is increasingly clear that these same challenges are central for any attempt to improve health, education, legal, and policing systems, as well as regulatory environments for local businesses. In short, key features of local governance condition the efficacy of a large share of donor programming.

Thus academics and aid practitioners have considerable potential gains from exchange. University-based researchers are making advances in theory, measurement, data analysis, and causal inference that can be applied to the questions of interest for aid practitioners. Aid agencies have immeasurable experience working with central and local governments as well as civil society groups and local citizens in developing countries around the world. They are also often in a position to assemble data that would be extremely valuable to researchers, and to build experimental or quasi-experimental features into their programming. Increasingly, donors and academics are engaged across these shared interests, but considerable room for improvement remains.

Collaboration and information exchange between aid agencies and academics in the fields of public administration and public policy have a long pedigree. In studies of decentralization, the research output has often taken the form of analytical case studies of specific countries. More recently, political scientists have become deeply engaged in studies of decentralization and governance. This is quite natural, since many of the vexing challenges facing aid agencies and the governments and citizens with whom they partner are political in nature. As in the field of development economics, political scientists working in this area have come to embrace a largely quantitative approach to evidence, and have developed a strong focus on causal inference.

At the same time, aid practitioners have been seeking to move beyond an exclusive reliance on analytical narratives and case studies and to build a base of knowledge about decentralization from quantitative studies. Moreover, aid agencies have become active participants and collaborators in many of these studies. In our view, much of the best research on decentralization over the past two decades has come from close collaborations between university-based researchers and institutions like the World Bank and USAID. Sometimes this takes the shape of cooperation in designing studies using quantitative observational data or qualitative field research. Increasingly, it also involves collaboration between academics, development agencies, and governments on experiments and quasi-experiments that are built into the design of decentralization programs from the beginning. This work sets out not to replace but rather to supplement the familiar analytical case studies of the past.

Given that the volume and quality of this collaborative research have increased in recent decades, the time is right to review what we have learned about decentralized governance from this literature, and to assess how these lessons might inform future programming. As studies have become more exacting and careful in their approach to causal identification, they can also become more context-dependent. For instance, a decentralization program might appear to produce positive health outcomes in Uganda, while a largely similar program in Ghana produces no discernable results. The development community and academics alike are left wondering whether the difference stems from small tweaks or mistakes in the design of the program (or the evaluation), or whether there is something distinctive about each context. In light of existing research, can we say anything beyond the bromide that "context matters"?

The answer, as provided by these chapters, is a resounding "yes." In developing this volume, we worked in close collaboration with USAID's Center of Excellence on Democracy, Human Rights and Governance (DRG Center) to identify the most important thematic questions for both academics and development professionals. The DRG Center sought this thematic input as it begins the process of revising its strategy on decentralization. We hope this thematic approach serves the interests of policymakers and note that it distinguishes this book from the more common case study approach in edited volumes.

After settling on these key themes, our strategy was to recruit some of the most successful empirical researchers working on political and fiscal aspects of decentralization, with the hope that they would step outside the usual research process, think bigger thoughts from a distinctive angle, and reflect on the past and future of the lines of inquiry with which they have engaged. Empirical researchers in political science and economics do not generally face incentives to address the difficult questions that plague the policy world. They face incentives to write rigorous papers drawing on a particular context that will withstand the exacting process of peer review. Beyond the need to write a perfunctory literature review, they are not often asked to make thoughtful assessments of the "big picture" in their line of inquiry. Thus, we encouraged the authors not only to be reflective, but more important, to be prospective in a way that would help shape the agenda for future aid programming and research. More broadly, the authors assess whether scholars are asking the right questions and designing studies suited to answer them.

The authors pay special attention to the prospects for enhanced collaboration between academics and aid agencies in carrying out an innovative quantitative research agenda. As such, their reviews are less attuned to important work in applied policy research than some might like. We recognize this approach has a cost, but we note that many of the chapters draw extensively on reviews of relevant policy research. While our approach is distinctive, our goal is to supplement the insights of other broad contributions to the study of decentralization and development, including Connerly, Eaton, and Smoke (2010), Dickovick and Wunsch (2014), and Fauget and Pöschl (2015). We hope that what we sacrifice in disciplinary coverage we gain in analytical insight.

The ten substantive chapters cover some of the most crucial intellectual terrain for researchers and practitioners alike. Some of the topics have been at the center of the literature for years: fiscal decentralization, the integrity and efficacy of local elections, post-conflict peace building, social accountability, and local economic development. Others are just as crucial but have not yet received the academic attention they deserve: for instance, the proliferation of subnational jurisdictions, the infrastructure needs of booming cities, and the important role of traditional leaders in local governance.

To balance the academic voices, three excellent applied researchers from RTI International – Derick Brinkerhoff, Anna Wetterberg, and Gary Bland – provide a concluding chapter, appropriately titled a "practical postscript." The authors place the volume in the broader history of engagement between USAID and academics, particularly in the area of decentralized governance, and outline the challenges and opportunities to link evidence and policy action.

In the thematic chapters, each author has attempted to extract lessons not only about the practice of decentralization, but wherever possible, also about the involvement of aid agencies and other multilateral institutions. They have also been asked to look for areas in which the collaboration between academics and practitioners might be improved. In some of these cases – i.e., booming cities – there is a great deal of donor programming, but little academic research to guide it; in other cases – i.e., traditional leaders – there is an emergent body of academic research, but as yet, little donor programming. We hope to draw attention to both types of lacunae and to promote work on both sides of the donor/academic partnership. In what follows, we briefly review some of the key substantive lessons, which we have clustered into five categories, and conclude with some lessons about ways to improve the partnership in the years ahead.

THE EFFECT AND EFFICACY OF LOCAL ELECTIONS

The earliest proponents of political decentralization emphasized local elections as a means to promote accountability. Initially, however, claims of the superiority of local elections (versus the appointment of local officials by higher-level authorities) largely rested on untested claims and faith. At this point, we have a good deal of evidence on the pros and cons of elections as a mechanism to select local officials. As Grossman discusses in Chapter 3 of this volume, local elections appear to generate better outcomes than appointment, particularly in environments with extensive political competition, a robust media market, low levels of social and economic inequality, and strong national political parties. There are some narrow conditions under which the appointment of local officials may have advantages – such as when the success of national officials is closely tied to local output and a corporate party structure can induce yardstick competition via promotions and retention – but the overarching message is that local elections often do provide stronger incentives for local officials to be responsive.

At the same time, there are many conditions under which local elections may not live up to their potential. As León and Wantchekon explain in Chapter 10 of this volume, the integrity of decentralized elections is often threatened by clientelistic practices, i.e., the targeting of public resources to citizens in exchange for their votes. Where clientelism is pervasive, it favors short-term benefits at the expense of broad policy considerations. This has important costs to social welfare, transparency, and accountability.

Researchers have learned a good deal about the processes that underpin clientelism. Poor voters are more responsive to clientelistic appeals. For clientelistic exchange to work, parties have to be able to monitor how voters (or groups of voters) vote. Additionally, local vote brokers are crucial intermediaries between parties and voters/clients. Clear attention to the institutions and incentives that produce clientelism also provides some insight into tools for reducing it. First, election monitoring can help by limiting the extent to which parties can compromise the privacy of the vote. Second, meritocratic appointment and promotion procedures and forceful, transparent central oversight of key public resources can limit officials' ability to use them to engage in patronage politics. Third, local policy deliberation that involves citizens can help commit politicians to postelection policy agendas at the expense of patronage politics. Other factors that shape the incentives for clientelism, such as the institutional rules at work within political parties, are usually beyond the purview of practitioners working on decentralization, but they are important nonetheless.

The chapters by Grossman, León and Wantchekon, and Dunning point out ways in which practitioners, in collaboration with academics, might pay closer attention to the key details of electoral and party institutions' structures. Grossman points to key features of elections – partisan versus nonpartisan contests, "at-large" versus single-member districts, and term limits – where we have some accumulated insights from developed democracies but a dearth of evidence from decentralized settings in the developing world. León and Wantchekon emphasize how careful attention to the role of local citizens in decentralized settings could enrich what we know about the demand side of clientelism. Dunning points to the role of hierarchical links within political parties that mobilize local politicians as part of their own national-level electoral strategy. Program designers and academics alike should focus on how the hierarchical organization of parties shapes local officials' incentives to be responsive to local citizens versus clientelistic machines.

LOCAL FORMS OF ACCOUNTABILITY

For many, decentralization is desirable to the extent it promotes local accountability, and most attention has focused on the formal institutions of decentralized governments. Yet as Baldwin and Raffler make clear in Chapter 4 of this volume, in many settings – and particularly where the state is weak – traditional tribal, religious, and caste leaders play a crucial role in local governance. Though many practitioners and academics have voiced skepticism about traditional leaders, Baldwin and Raffler point to growing evidence that such leaders are often socially accountable, have long time horizons and serve as "development brokers." Particularly where they are politically and socially embedded in their communities, they can have incentives to govern well even in the absence of elections.

Indeed, Christia's chapter in this volume (Chapter 9) shows that the support of traditional leaders is one of the crucial ingredients of successful post-conflict community-driven development and decentralization initiatives. Given the importance of traditional leaders, and our growing body of knowledge about the conditions under which they face good incentives, donors may wish to give them a more prominent role as they develop programming strategies in some societies with strong traditional leaders.

One key message from the Baldwin and Raffler chapter is that the social context in which traditional leaders are embedded has important implications for the quality of local governance. Reflecting on social accountability programming, Wibbels's chapter in this volume (Chapter 2) emphasizes the importance of understanding local context through the lenses of social and political networks. While donor programming and accompanying impact evaluations focus resources on mobilizing civil society and "social accountability" so that citizens might become better participants in politics, they are rarely systematically designed with the diverse capacities and organization of decentralized communities in mind.

Yet local citizens live in highly varied social contexts even in a single city or county. Experiences with social accountability theory and programming to date suggest several recurring weaknesses, such as overreliance on transparency, poorly specified theories of change, and lack of attention to local context – weaknesses that could be at least partially addressed by paying more attention to research on social networks. Such research provides a rigorous means of thinking about and measuring social capital, the density of civil society, social trust, information diffusion, social coordination, and collective action – and therefore the conditions under which social accountability initiatives are likely to work and how they might be precisely tailored to specific local contexts. There are exciting opportunities for collaboration between academics and the aid community in conducting rigorous explorations of social networks.

SOCIAL HETEROGENEITY AND CONFLICT

The chapter by Thad Dunning focuses on the impact of decentralization in societies that are divided by strong ethnic, religious, or other social cleavages, and the chapter by Fotini Christia examines the extent to which decentralization might be part of the solution in the aftermath of conflict generated by such divisions. Both authors argue that the success of decentralization, and much of the aid and donor programming related to it, depends on ethnic geography, the salience of ethnicity, and the ways in which parties and political institutions shape the incentives of elites.

The presence of geographically segregated social groups is often part of the basic logic of decentralization, which can allow different local groups to offer their desired forms of religious or language training to schoolchildren, for example, rather than forcing a "one-size-fits-all" policy. Yet decentralization does not often take place in settings where each district or village is internally homogenous. In fact, decentralization often takes place in areas that are locally heterogeneous, e.g., the Indian villages and towns discussed by Dunning and the large urban centers discussed by Carter and Post (Chapter 8).

These chapters begin to address important questions about how local officials deal with ethnic and social heterogeneity. Under what conditions might long-standing patterns of discrimination and social exclusion by dominant groups be upended? Under what conditions might migration to urban city centers lead to a decline in ethnic identities, and under what conditions might these identities serve as building blocks for urban political entrepreneurs? Among other things, Dunning argues that the answers often lie in the structure of political parties, and the ways in which central-level partisans from the government and opposition attempt to bring local elites into their own networks of patronage and clientelism. Pierskalla (Chapter 6) also points to the role of changing jurisdiction structures in overturning time-honored patterns of dominance by certain local groups over others.

Christia examines scenarios in which decentralization is viewed as part of a potential post-conflict settlement. She points out a number of constraints facing reformers, including the demands of those whose positions have improved through war, and the incentives of those who hope to profit from skimming funds to ex-combatants. Unfortunately, post-conflict decentralization is often a form of gamesmanship, and does little to forestall the return of fighting. She pays special attention to the role of foreign aid in post-conflict environments, which is often distributed at the local level. She reviews evidence suggesting that aid is most successful when there is a negotiated settlement in which all parties have a stake in decentralization, and where the means exist to build capable and accountable local governments. She argues that donors must find a way to align the interests of the central government, local government, and traditional authorities.

Christia further provides a careful assessment of post-conflict community-driven development programs. She reviews a cluster of studies that demonstrate relatively consistent positive effects of such programs on service delivery, but weaker effects for socioeconomic well-being, no long-term effects for governance, and very context-dependent effects regarding the return of violence.

THE STRUCTURE OF JURISDICTIONS

One of the striking dynamics across the developing world is the proliferation of local governance units in many countries. Pierskalla's chapter makes clear that this often occurs through the splitting of districts or counties, but as Carter and Post explain, this also results from the proliferation of often-overlapping special-purpose districts in burgeoning cities across the developing world. There are reasonable arguments in favor of making decentralized governments small. Most important, they can provide representation for marginalized, geographically concentrated groups who otherwise might struggle to find influence in larger districts. But as Pierskalla explains, this increased representation often comes at the cost of weakened administrative capacity and more corruption, and the logic that typically drives district proliferation derives from political-strategic considerations rather than concerns with minority representation or the efficiency of the public sector. While academics have considerable work to do in order to understand the causes and consequences of proliferating units of governance, donors and implementers should be aware of this trend, and the potential role of the aid community in contributing to it.

This point is reinforced in the chapter by Carter and Post, which explains that while much of the empirical work on decentralization in developing countries focuses on rural villages, cities are growing rapidly and face distinctive challenges associated with land titling, urban infrastructure, pollution, service delivery, and slum management. They review a largely policy-based body of work on urban public finance and public administration and explain that overlapping jurisdictions and the proliferation of special-purpose districts are an obstacle to coordination and accountability. These special-purpose districts, often designed to overcome or avoid popular opinion, serve to multiply the number of actors involved in the provision of services, which in turn makes it difficult to solve many urban problems, like infrastructure, environmental protection, and property regulation, that are inherently cross-sectoral.

On a more positive note, Carter and Post summarize studies showing that political competition, independent fiscal resources, and strong civil societies facilitate more democratic outcomes following decentralization to municipal authorities. They conclude that decentralization can help urban citizens to pressure more effectively for inclusion and access, but can also make it more difficult for policymakers to address metropolitan-level or long-run concerns regarding investments in basic infrastructure that are complicated by overlapping jurisdiction or lack of salience for voters.

FISCAL FEDERALISM AND ECONOMIC DEVELOPMENT

Part of the intuitive appeal of decentralization is the argument that local decision makers are in a better position than higher-level officials to tailor taxing and spending decisions to specific local circumstances and thereby promote local development. The chapter by Malesky (Chapter 7) explains that one of the biggest challenges in developing countries is the construction of a vibrant private sector in which business owners feel comfortable making long-term investments. Malesky explores the role of local governments in facilitating (or undermining) a good investment environment in developing countries, but he also shows that in many settings the underlying endowments are such that local development is very difficult to promote. He argues that economic geography is crucial. Decentralization often enhances local and regional inequality as labor and capital migrate to those few localities with labor market opportunities, wealthier consumers, and better services. The classic core-periphery dynamic emerges quite naturally. Rural-to-urban migration patterns and regional inequality introduce thorny challenges for governments and aid agencies.

Local-level inequality is reflected in the huge variation in decentralized governments' ability to collect taxes. A great deal of research and development programming has focused on local revenue mobilization. As Rodden shows in his chapter (Chapter 5), we now have a growing base of evidence that own-source revenues, as opposed to intergovernmental grants, are associated with less waste and better service provision. Nevertheless, the prospects for substantially improving the performance of the local public sector via enhanced local revenue collection are probably quite modest, above all because local tax bases are often extremely thin, especially in rural areas. Moreover, many typical decentralized taxes (e.g., head taxes and property taxes) are politically unpopular. And as explored in Dunning's chapter, revenue decentralization in some unequal and culturally heterogeneous settings can actually exacerbate conflict.

Thus, for the foreseeable future in many decentralized governments, central transfers will remain the most important source of local revenue, and the design of those transfers and their corresponding implications for local incentives needs more attention from both academics and policymakers. Moreover, Rodden's chapter reviews a set of recent collaborations between academics, donors, and governments that have potential to reveal basic insights about the impact of different types of taxes and transfers. This literature is only in its infancy, but it shows considerable potential.

CONCLUSIONS: ACADEMIC AND POLICY WORK IN THE SERVICE OF LEARNING

We believe the most crucial lesson from these chapters is that traversing the borders between practitioners and academics yields impressive benefits. Many of the significant advances in what we know about decentralized governance have emerged from the joint efforts of academics and development practitioners over the past two decades. These collaborations typically began in an ad hoc way, and the merging of the two cultures and institutional environments has been challenging. But experience is loosening the boundaries, and both sides of the relationship are better positioned than ever to work with the other.

From the experiences of the contributors to this volume we can cull a few basic principles that emerge from academic involvement in applied development work. Both Chapter 9 by Christia and the concluding chapter by Brinkerhoff, Wetterberg, and Bland provide additional details on a number of these points.

First, when designing programs, it is necessary to carefully articulate a program theory linking specific interventions to specific measurable outcomes. As noted in what follows, from the point of view of donors and implementers, clearer program theory often implies unbundling complex, multifaceted programs into smaller, better motivated, and more evaluable parts. Academics can help practitioners at this stage by stating their own theories clearly and helping to translate them for the policy world. This is particularly true of academic research on governance, where much of the theorizing is too vague and informal, and where academics have a responsibility to clearly state the key actors, the strategic environments in which they operate, and the scope conditions governing theoretical claims.

Second, the evaluation agenda must be considered as early as possible in the process of program design in order to find the clearest possible link between specific interventions and specific outcomes. Early coordination and careful pre-analysis planning are crucial. There are many successful cases in which academics, implementers, and donors coordinated rigorous evaluation late in the game, but we also know many cases of failure, i.e., when the interests of implementers and external evaluators have failed because evaluation was not considered in the technical design of projects. The USAID DRG Center's "clinics," whereby academics join country mission officers over several days to brainstorms projects with an eye toward evaluability, is an excellent model. Unfortunately, even as academic organizations like J-PAL and EGAP have helped greatly increase the salience of rigorous evaluation, our own sense is that rigorous monitoring and evaluation still play a starring role in the vast *minority* of development projects on decentralized governance.

Third, the ongoing evaluation agenda requires less complex program designs. This can be achieved by slicing off a smaller piece of a broader multiyear, multipronged project and providing a rigorous design and implementation that is subject to strict monitoring and evaluation standards. The prospects for this approach have improved as donor RFPs on decentralized governance have begun to emphasize a bit more the importance of evaluation and impact assessment. There are a number of exacting design options beyond randomized control trials of an entire program, and some of them (such as phased designs) have the advantage of making implementation easier.

Fourth, academics have made significant advances in data collection, measurement, and statistical modeling over the past decade. While some of those advances have been adopted in development work on decentralized governance, others have not. Large gains can be made by systematic engagement when designing data collection systems and analyzing the results. Some examples from the chapters include survey experiments to gather information on "sensitive" behaviors like corruption, geo-spatial analysis, and network analysis. But it is important to note that ongoing donor interest in "adaptive management" requires both rigorous designs *and* high-frequency data collection to know when programs require adaptation. With many academics working at the frontier of data collection technologies, this is an important place where the development industry and academics can work together.

Fifth, another important observation from the chapters is that there is a striking rural bias in academic work on decentralization. Largely because of our preoccupation with causal identification and randomization, we have become very comfortable with studies that use rural villages as the unit of analysis. At a time when developing countries are rapidly urbanizing, there is an urgent need to invest resources in evaluations and broader learning endeavors in urban environments. Development practitioners have been active in cities for decades, and now a small group of academics is catching up.

Sixth and perhaps most important, the scope for shared learning oftentimes transcends the details of a given evaluation. When academics are invited to conduct an evaluation of a program, they should be encouraged to exploit a variety of additional learning opportunities beyond merely "yes" or "no" answers to questions about the program's impact on service outcomes, political participation, or government effort. For instance, academics can study social and economic determinates of program uptake. They can learn about the role of traditional and other elites, the inclusion of women (or lack thereof), the nature of clientelism, and the structure of local social networks. They can exploit cross-village heterogeneity in ethnic fractionalization, clan structure, and network structure.

Impact evaluations are costly endeavors, and as long as teams of enumerators will be trooping through the countryside collecting data from households, such exercises can be tailored to answer a variety of basic questions raised in the chapters in this volume. Aid agencies, program implementers, and academics should be open to the development of synergies such that some aspects of the evaluation are parts of a broader learning agenda that reaches well beyond the question of whether a specific intervention "works." Particularly when academics and practitioners see beyond the immediate impact evaluation, the scope for broader, shared learning is often very large indeed.

In this way, the evaluation team can be seen not as a potentially hostile group that may bring bad news in the form of null or negative results, but as collaborators in a long-term learning agenda in which aid agencies and implementers have a stake. Even if the results suggest that a specific program had little or no impact, by probing further, the academic team might be able to shed light on some explanations. For instance, it might discover that program uptake is low in certain types of communities, or that elites interfered with the program in unanticipated ways. Such activities can lead to broader insights about decentralization and development.

From aid agencies' point of view, academics are not always easy to work with. Their concerns about statistical power might lead them to demand that an intervention be expanded to far more villages, neighborhoods, or facilities than the budget allows. They might insist that mid-course corrections be avoided in order to facilitate a clean end-line analysis. Or they might ask for what seem like excessively simple interventions in complex environments. Sometimes they deliver bad (or ambiguous) news to those who have invested years of work in programs that they believe to be effective. Sometimes this news is based on under-powered evaluations or data that are collected in a time frame that seems far too short. Added to all of this, academics have strange schedules that limit availability during the academic year, and the financial systems of the development and university industries do not always work well together.

Yet each of the academics participating in this project – and we represent a small tip of a growing iceberg – has gained a great deal from collaborating with donors over the years, and we hope this assessment is mutual. Many of us have become better attuned to the challenges of implementation, more adept at pitching rigorous designs without fancy language, and better able to negotiate solutions with our implementing partners. We understand we have a long way to go, even as we celebrate the growth of work across the increasingly porous academic/policy divide.

Going forward, we envision a transition from a rather narrow "evaluation" agenda to a broader collaborative learning agenda aimed at answering the questions raised but not fully answered in this volume. This will require additional flexibility on the part of aid agencies, implementers, and academics, but the potential payoff is substantial. If nothing else, we hope this volume demonstrates to the community of donors and lenders that the collaboration is worthy of renewal and expansion over the next twenty years.

REFERENCES

Connerly, Edward, Kent Eaton, and Paul Smoke. 2010. *Making Decentralization Work: Democracy, Development, and Security*. Boulder, CO: Lynn Reinner.

Dickovick, Tyler and James Wunsch. 2014. *Decentralization in Africa: The Paradox of State Strength*. Boulder, CO: Lynn Reinner.

Fauget, Jean-Paul and Caroline Pöschl. 2015. *Is Decentralization Good for Development? Perspectives from Academics and Policy Makers*. Oxford, UK: Oxford University Press.

2

The Social Underpinnings of Decentralized Governance

Networks, Technology, and the Future of Social Accountability

Erik Wibbels

Accountable governance is defined by four elements: first, the definition of the interests of citizens and citizen groups; second, the aggregation or accumulation of those interests via a "technology," whether an election, lobbying, or social media; third, the translation of those preferences into government actions; and fourth, a means for citizens to evaluate the quality of government actions.

Decentralization has the potential to impact each of these elements. Most of the rigorous thinking on how it does so has focused on institutions: how formal rules governing elections, leadership selection, fiscal federalism, etc. impact political accountability. Donor programming and accompanying impact evaluations, on the other hand, have focused less on institutions and more on mobilizing civil society and "social accountability" (SA), i.e., on approaches to informing and mobilizing citizens so that they might become better participants in politics. These programming efforts have progressed with considerable enthusiasm but without, for the most part, reference to recent academic breakthroughs on the social conditions for cooperative behavior and collective action. The goal of this chapter is to consider how recent innovations in the study of information flows and cooperation in social networks might inform donor programming on social accountability. Research on social networks provides insights into the relational characteristics of communities that are certain to impact the prospects for accountability, and it gives a rigorous underpinning to the frequent, if ambiguous, claim that "context matters."

The arguments in favor of decentralization are now abundantly familiar: it protects citizens against encroachment by the state, limits ethnic conflict, safeguards individual and communal liberty, allows for a tailoring of taxing and spending to local preferences, and offers citizens the opportunity to more closely monitor the behavior of public officials (see Rodden 2006; Beramendi

The author would like to thank Guy Grossman, Anna Wetterberg, Derick Brinkerhoff, and participants in the "Geospatial Data, Governance, and the Future of Development Aid" workshop for their helpful comments.

2007). In poor countries where the central state has limited capacity to implement, regulate, build, etc. across considerable territory, these arguments take on added salience because decentralized governments are often the *only* governments that materially impact the lives of citizens. In such settings, deconcentrating responsibilities is perhaps the only means of improving services for many citizens, but it also raises the stakes for understanding the conditions under which local social orders (as defined by social, political, and economic networks) are consistent with good governance.

While traditional arguments continue to support hundreds of millions of dollars of development aid aimed at decentralization, it has become clear that decentralization in itself is no panacea. It can promote elite capture (Véron et al. 2006; Mansuri and Rao 2013), obfuscate lines of government responsibility, and unnecessarily expand the size of the public administration. Thus while decentralization *can* help promote accountability when the proper mechanisms are in place (World Bank 2004), in many cases they are not. In the absence of accountability mechanisms, citizens cannot discipline decentralized officials. In the absence of such discipline, decentralization neither solves agency problems nor ensures that local bundles of public goods reflect local preferences. Indeed, for many analysts, decentralization's inability to hold local officials accountable and its tendency to produce local "elite capture" is at the very heart of its failures.[1] Unsurprisingly, the term "accountability" appears 105 times in USAID's 2009 "Democratic Decentralization Programming Handbook." It follows that identifying the key mechanisms of accountability and understanding how they work are key to promoting better donor programming on decentralized governance.

In this chapter, I review some of the key mechanisms of social accountability that support decentralization's capacity to fulfill its promise. In doing so, I rely on traditional notions of governance as characterized by a series of principal-agent problems, albeit with a recognition that in many settings there is no single principal, since citizens, public officials, and administrators have competing notions as to what constitutes the public good. I also emphasize that these principal-agent relationships can often be better understood as relational networks and that the characteristics of those networks are crucial to understanding the conditions under which social accountability is likely to exist or to emerge as a result of donor efforts.

There is, of course, a plethora of potential mechanisms that might promote political accountability. Several important formal institutions of accountability are dealt with in later chapters of this volume, including the role of elections (León and Wantchekon, Chapter 10) and rules governing the choice of decentralized leaders (Grossman, Chapter 3). Other key institutions through which citizens might hold officials accountable, such as the police and courts, have received too little comparative academic and policy research to produce a coherent body of knowledge and thus are not addressed. Likewise, the

---

[1] On elite capture, see Olken 2007, and Banerjee and Duflo 2006.

physical mobility that underpins classic Tieboutian notions of efficiency and that can promote accountability by inducing competition among decentralized governments is largely absent in the developing world, where migration is often driven by perceptions of improved job opportunities in cities rather than inter-jurisdictional shopping for public goods; to the extent rapid urbanization bears on decentralized governance, it is discussed in the chapter by Carter and Post (Chapter 8).

In lieu of formal institutions, I focus on the social underpinnings of accountability. By "social underpinnings," I refer not just to traditional notions of civil society, but more broadly to the interpersonal, social, and political networks in which citizens are embedded. My overarching claim is that current research and programming on social accountability would benefit from more systematic engagement with the evidence and analytical tools that have emerged from research on social networks. Experiences with SA theory and programming to date suggest several recurring weaknesses – such as overreliance on transparency, poorly specified theories of change, and lack of attention to local context – weaknesses that could be at least partially addressed by paying more attention to social networks. Such research provides a rigorous means of thinking about and measuring social capital, the density of civil society, social trust, and the conditions under which social accountability initiatives are likely to work.

To support this claim, the chapter addresses: a) the ongoing push to encourage "social accountability" by promoting citizen information on, engagement with, and oversight of local government; b) the emergent work on social networks as civil society in shaping the prospects for collective action and social accountability; and c) the role of new information and communication technologies (ICT) in promoting citizen information, broadening social networks and allowing for networked monitoring of government behavior and outputs. I also underscore how the tools of network analysis are particularly well suited for the kind of data that the promotion of ICT generates. This analysis follows a discussion of what is meant by "accountability" and what citizens are meant to hold their decentralized governments accountable for.

BASIC APPROACHES TO ACCOUNTABLE GOVERNANCE

The initial enthusiasm for decentralization among academics and workers in the development field was based on the notion that it would enhance the match between preferences and policies and reduce agency costs. This distinction delineates two basic approaches to understanding accountable governance, and hence two basic approaches to program design and evaluation. Both views build on naïve assumptions of an idealized Tocquevillian citizenry and the ease of cultivating such a citizenry where it does not already exist. Some straightforward attention to the structure of local social and political relations, i.e., network characteristics, would provide insight into the settings where such assumptions are warranted and, thus, where development workers might contribute to accountability.

In the first view, accountability occurs when government officials successfully implement what one might consider "the will of the people." The key challenge of governance, in this view, is to align the incentives of public officials such that they have reason and capacity to gather information on the citizens' wishes and translate them into policy. We have elsewhere called this "prospective accountability" (Rodden and Wibbels 2013), although it also goes under the guise of "responsiveness," "pre-election politics" (Persson and Tabellini 2002), etc. It is in the spirit of enhancing prospective accountability that donors have set out to encourage electoral turnout, civil society mobilization, attendance at meetings, participatory budgeting, and other forms of engagement with local government. The central notion is that poor governance thrives when the electorate is disengaged and inactive, and policies can better approximate the "collective will" when citizens take an active role in directing public officials.

An alternative view of accountability is born of skepticism that "the public good" can be uncovered, since citizens who vary by gender, age, income, ethnicity, religion, etc. often have competing preferences over what government should do, and procedures for aggregating those preferences can produce different outcomes (Riker 1982). Instead, this view relies on citizens' capacity to evaluate the past behavior of government. These retrospective evaluations can be difficult because reliable information about the choices facing public officials is hard to come by, and those officials often have incentives to hide information in order to protect their own interests. Since information is scarce, voters often use information shortcuts based on everyday experiences with the economy or service provision to judge how their government is performing (Fiorina 1981). When these indicators fall below some threshold, citizens can remove (or otherwise sanction) officials and give someone else the opportunity to do better. As long as public officials desire to retain office, this retrospective judgment can be an effective way of keeping them in check. I refer to this accountability mechanism as *retrospective accountability*. It is in the spirit of enhancing this kind of accountability that donors have promoted various technologies for improving citizen information, including scorecards, media campaigns, information sheets, comparative data on different officials or localities, and published audits.

Both the prospective and retrospective views of accountability are fundamentally rooted in a principal-agent model of governance. The key principal-agent relationships run from voters to local elected officials, from those officials to local service providers/implementers, and from service providers/implementers to the consumers of those services. Broadly speaking, the goal of donor programming aimed at promoting accountability in decentralized governance is to tighten up one or more of these agency relationships so that the agent has less scope for acting contrary to the principal's interests.

There are two serious shortcomings with this approach to donor programming, and jointly they represent a blind spot in social accountability initiatives: first, the principal-agent approach's emphasis on information asymmetries relies on idealized assumptions about social relations that rarely match reality. Just as important as information are the underlying power relations among citizens, officials, and service providers. Indeed, feeding information to citizens who are in a dependent or clientelistic relationship with local elites is unlikely to promote accountability. These principal-agent relationships are embedded in local social networks that shape the use of information and the prospects for social accountability. Second, the principal-agent approach assumes that citizens are a homogenous bunch that share underlying preferences over what government should do or what constitutes good performance. Of course, most citizens want a stronger economy, better schools, higher-quality health care, etc. – but they often have differing ideas about policy priorities, tax rates, and the like. Thus, in many settings there is no single principal, and features of social and political networks determine which principals matter more or less than others.

These twin shortcomings raise a whole range of challenging questions. What are the key features of local social, political, and economic networks? How do those features affect the likely success of social accountability initiatives? How can we promote accountability in heterogeneous local settings with diverse local networks? Might promoting citizen mobilization promote conflict rather than accountability in settings where they have divergent opinions? Are there means of conflict mediation that can promote local accountability and participation at the same time? I return to these issues in the section on "Frontiers for Policy and Learning on Accountability."

ACCOUNTABLE FOR WHAT? DECENTRALIZATION AND THE ALLOCATION OF RESPONSIBILITIES

The concept of accountability in local governance raises the question as to what it is that decentralized governments are to be held accountable for. There is abundant literature on the optimal allocation of responsibilities across levels of government.[2] It provides a handful of guiding principles (see Rodden's chapter in this volume for details, Chapter 5): 1) Expenditure decentralization should follow heterogeneous preferences across communities. 2) To the extent possible, revenue responsibilities should follow expenditure decentralization so as to minimize intergovernmental transfers, limit government exploitation of citizens' ignorance about taxation, and promote the accountable expenditure of tax dollars. 3) Government responsibilities with considerable range across jurisdictions – such as defense, environmental regulation and enforcement, and

---

[2] See Gadenne and Singhal (2014) for a recent review.

interpersonal redistribution (such as through CCTs) – should be centralized to prevent a race to the bottom across subnational jurisdictions.

These principles are systematically violated in most developing countries. This results largely from the fact that major revenue sources are centralized and most localities have thin tax bases. But as Gadenne and Singhal (2014) note, this has not prevented considerable decentralization of expenditure responsibilities over the past fifteen years, with the result being that fiscal gaps have grown. Thus, while regional, district, and local governments are playing an ever-larger role in the provision and/or oversight of basic services like education, health care, and infrastructure, they are doing so with revenues raised elsewhere. The donor community might well have exaggerated these fiscal gaps because of the push to decentralize functional responsibilities to lower levels of government, despite the absence of robust local tax bases and the ongoing reliance on community-driven development (CDD) programming in countries with weak state capacities.

The growth of expenditure decentralization has two big implications for accountability. First, the services that citizens rely on are increasingly the responsibility of decentralized governments. Whether that responsibility is thin – as when decentralized governments are responsible for implementing central government policies, schemes, and expenditures – or thick, local and district governments have more and more impact on the government outputs that most immediately affect citizens, including health care, education, infrastructure, and public security. Thus, understanding the heterogeneity across localities, and how context matters, becomes hugely important. As discussed later in this chapter, a networked approach to decentralized settings offers a distinctly rigorous means to analyze this variety of contexts.

Second, the large fiscal gaps produced by decentralization have exaggerated a problem inherent in overlapping jurisdictions, namely the difficulty (and, at least sometimes, the unfairness) of holding decentralized governments accountable for public services and other outputs that they are only partially responsible for. Williams (2015) provides a recent example from Ghana, where ongoing decentralization has left district governments responsible for a good deal of public infrastructure. He shows that one-third of the capital projects (representing one-fifth of total infrastructure expenditures) begun by district governments are never completed. Given that these investments include the rural clinics, schoolhouses, and markets that citizens rely on, this looks like a striking failure of decentralized governance. But a closer look shows that no small part of the problem is that central government revenue transfers often appear late, if at all, which results in districts unable to pay contractors. There is no doubt that citizens want the capital investments, that some district governments are inefficient and even corrupt, and that the central government's failure to deliver revenues on time makes district government planning very difficult. Who are Ghanaian citizens to hold accountable for the resulting outcomes? In cases like this, the potential increased responsiveness of district assemblies must be balanced against the agency problems generated by the process of decentralization and the corresponding misalignment between revenues and expenditures.

A DECADE OF SOCIAL ACCOUNTABILITY PROGRAMS

Institutional fixes aside, the most significant push toward promoting accountability has occurred via "social accountability" programming by international donors. Although these are not always tied to formal decentralization programs, they are inherently local, and most of the programming aims to affect the local clinics, schools, administrators, and elected officials who define most citizens' day-to-day experiences with the state.

Writing for the World Bank, O'Meally (2013: p. 5) defines social accountability as "the broad range of actions and mechanisms, other than voting, that citizens can use to hold the state to account as well as actions on the part of government, civil society, media and other actors that promote or facilitate these efforts." The wave of social accountability enthusiasm is built on a belief (and occasionally a well-developed theory) that the primary obstacles to accountable governance are poor citizen information (Pande 2011) and a lack of venues through which they can have input into governing processes. Much of it also builds on a well-developed body of work on "social capital" that emphasizes the key role of citizen engagement in promoting good governance (Putnam 1993; Ostrom 2001; Krishna 2007). As discussed in what follows, the often vague concept of social capital can become more explicit, rigorous, and operational when approached from a social network perspective.

Consistent with the ideas of retrospective accountability and prospective accountability, social accountability initiatives can be organized into those that aim to: 1) improve citizens' knowledge about the performance of the public sector and the behavior of government officials so that they can hold them retrospectively accountable; and 2) improve government officials' responsiveness by providing avenues for citizens to provide input into decision making and public sector management (i.e., prospective accountability). The former projects focus on publishing audit reports, scorecards, increasing transparency, etc. (Olken 2007; Peisakhin and Pinto 2010; Andrabi et al. 2014). The latter projects focus on promoting participatory modes of decision making (Bjorkman and Svensson 2009; Olken 2010).

There are now several extensive review papers on social accountability programming that the reader can consult for a more detailed and expansive discussion of the dozens of social accountability projects of the past decade.[3]

---

[3] See, for instance, Fox (2015), Brinkerhoff and Wetterberg (2016), and Williamson (2015). On the closely related topic of community-driven development and a broader look at efforts to promote participation, see Mansuri and Rao (2013).

In lieu of another such review, I offer several points organized around key themes in research on social networks, which I explore in the next section. Some of these are addressed in the accumulated wisdom expressed in the review papers, but others are not.

Theories of change need clear specification. Theoretical work on information flow, collective action, and coordination in social networks offers an important source of insights.

- Social accountability programs are not typically derived from clear theoretical principles. This results in a failure to specify precise mechanisms linking project activities to outcomes. A properly spelled out "theory of change" would specify who the principals and agents are, the kind of information available to them, and the nature of institutions structuring their relationship. As discussed in the following section, such a theory should consider that citizens are deeply embedded in local social, political, and economic networks.

- Rigorous impact evaluations of social accountability programs are often criticized for failing to specify the mechanisms through which they do or do not work (see, for instance, Devarajan et al. 2014). In some cases, this failure is seen as indicating a weakness of randomized control trials (RCTs) or other rigorous methods of evaluation. But the failure to specify the mechanisms through which a social accountability project is expected to impact outcomes is first and foremost a failure of theory rather than evaluation. If the "theory of change" is sufficiently precise about mechanisms, there is no reason impact evaluations cannot be designed to evaluate them.

- The scale of the most rigorous social accountability impact evaluations does not reflect our knowledge that localities within countries vary hugely in terms of their social organization, social capital, and collective action capacity. To the extent impact evaluations estimate average effects, they limit what we can learn from the heterogeneity across decentralized settings. The implication is not to do fewer rigorous impact evaluations. Instead, "theories of change" should aim to address the relationship between community characteristics and interventions such that the heterogeneity is not ignored.

Transparency and information are not enough. The flow of information and accountability among citizens and government are deeply conditioned by local social networks.

- Increasing citizen information is not, by itself, enough to promote accountability. There are certainly studies showing that providing more information on the performance of government and active citizen participation improves outcomes (Bjorkman and Svensson 2009; Andrabi et al. 2014), but many rigorous evaluations uncover no effects of increased information (Humphreys and Weinstein 2007; Banerjee et al. 2010; Keefer and Khemani

2012; Lieberman et al. 2014), and at least one shows that it can actually discourage participation (Chong et al. 2015). There are at least two issues: first, the information has to be relevant to local citizens, and we do not have a consistent evidence base on what information citizens care most about or how best to deliver it; and second, absent some clear accountability mechanism, it is not always clear how citizens can effectively use additional information.

- Consistent with this point, increasing information is more likely to work when it is combined with some means of impacting the incentives of government officials and government officials with the administrative capacity to respond (Fox 2015; Brinkerhoff and Wetterberg 2016). The provision of information alone runs into the fact that citizens are resource-constrained and cognitively limited. Absent a clear path between the information, citizen action, and a potential change in government action, the information will have little effect.

Complex demands limit the usefulness of social accountability. The capacity of social networks to solve problems declines as the complexity of the problems they have to solve increases.

- The more complicated the administrative, oversight, or implementation tasks, the harder it is for time- and attention-challenged individual citizens and citizen groups to efficiently and effectively complete them. Whether one considers citizen input into establishing priorities for the government or citizens' capacity to actively and productively monitor development projects (Olken 2007; Khwaja 2009), it is best to keep things simple.
- Even if a means for citizen participation were optimally designed, the need for simplicity points to inherent limits in the capacity of social accountability to promote democracy. Simple, highly involved modes of participation impose limits of scale and attention. To the extent some (perhaps many) failures of governance do not have local or decentralized roots, sustainable solutions almost certainly require mass democratic organizations, such as parties and interest groups, that can scale up and contribute to deliberative procedures beyond decentralized levels.

Context matters. Awareness of local context, as indicated by social network characteristics, is crucial to successful SA initiatives.

- Social accountability initiatives work best when they are designed in a context-relevant way that takes account of local communities' concerns. The easiest way to know what information, service needs, and priorities are relevant to local citizens and social groups is to ask them before programming begins and to design projects appropriately. This is a difficult task given how donor contracts are awarded and run, but as I describe in the conclusion to this chapter, the challenges are surmountable.

- Power relations among citizens condition the success of participatory procedures and the way citizens use new information provided via social accountability initiatives. High levels of social hierarchy or inequality contribute to the elite capture of participatory processes; they also militate against a sense of political efficacy that would encourage citizens to act on information initiatives. As discussed in the following section, research on political networks provides a systematic way to design social accountability programming that is reflective of local power relations.

SOCIAL NETWORKS, CIVIL SOCIETY, AND ACCOUNTABILITY

In recent decades, donors have laid a great deal of faith in the capacity of NGOs, and civil society in general, to redress local governance failures and promote accountability. The motivating impulse has been that a robust civil society offers the capacity to gather information on government behavior, provides a voice for citizen needs, and holds public officials accountable (Putnam 1993; Devarajan et al. 2014). Civic engagement is costly, of course, and individual self-interest can undermine it. As Ostrom (2001: p. 176) argues, "Somehow [citizens] must find ways of creating mutually reinforcing expectations and trust to overcome the perverse short-run temptations they face." Social capital provides the means and the motivation for individual citizens to contribute to accountable government, and Ostrom notes that it is more likely to occur via mutual learning and norm development in tight social networks.

To the extent decentralization brings government closer to "the people," efforts to promote civil society and decentralization have an obvious affinity. And to the extent social accountability initiatives rely on the mobilization of civil society, they implicitly rely on the capacity of local social networks to deliver collective action. Early, naïve assumptions about the capacity of local civil societies and civic associations to provide robust checks and balances on decentralized governments have given way to a recognition that communities are highly varied in their social organization and capacity for collective action. To date, programming on social accountability, civil society, and decentralization has proceeded without careful attention to that variation. A growing body of research on social networks – the persistent informational, social, and economic links between individuals – provides a rigorous basis for assessing the conditions under which communities of different types and at different scales might work to promote accountability.

Figure 2.1 gives some sense of the huge variation in the structure of local social networks even within a single city. The figure presents graphs of leadership networks across six slums in Bangalore, where colleagues and I have asked household respondents who the most important local leader is. Central nodes reflect leader names, and outer nodes the respondents who name

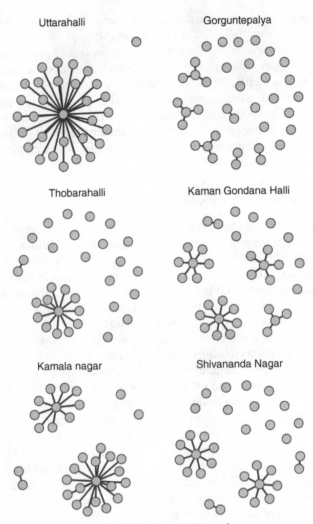

FIGURE 2.1 Leadership Networks in Six Slums in Bangalore

them. If social accountability requires a recognized leader and/or a locus for collective action, these network graphs indicate substantial variation in the capacity of these six slums to promote it. The slums range from environments of almost complete social anomie in which there is no recognized leader, to an almost fully centralized network where everyone recognizes a single leader, to bipolar networks, to everything in between. In a broader set of seventy-two slums, we have found evidence that centralized leadership networks facilitate the capacity of communities to coordinate votes and extract better public services in slums (Rojo, Jha, and Wibbels 2015; Wibbels, Krishna, and Sriram

2016). The main point, however, is that a one-size-fits-all social accountability program that pursues a standardized approach to information delivery, community meetings, and decision-making procedures with the aim of promoting collective decision making or oversight of local government is unlikely to work in the same way across these slums. Indeed, it seems clear that taking account of these differences could help tailor social accountability programming to local contexts.

Much of the work on social networks begins with the recognition that cooperative behavior and collective action, both crucial ingredients of a robust civil society, require some sort of deviation from narrow short-term self-interest. Frequent interactions between individuals are a well-known mechanism for overcoming collective action problems (Kranton 1996), but other characteristics of social networks are also important. Foremost, dense networks offer a host of advantages with regard to collective action (Greif 1993). First, they are associated with a high degree of shared preferences and expectations about what constitutes acceptable behavior. Second, they provide a monitoring technology that provides information on how members of the network behave. While it is very difficult for outsiders to know whether individuals are shirking or doing their share, it is much easier for close neighbors and local leaders who live in those communities to know these things about each other. Third and finally, dense social networks provide a mechanism for sanctioning community members who deviate from socially expected behavior. As discussed later in this chapter, dense networks can also suffer from serious problems, and there are conditions under which weak ties among citizens can facilitate information flow and accountability (Larson and Lewis 2016), but in many settings, the information and sanctioning that characterize dense networks provide the tools for overcoming collective action problems that are the heart of civil society activism.

Beyond these general features of social networks, we have also learned some of the factors that condition their capacity to generate consensus and collective action. Success tends to increase with the simplicity of the task (Khwaja 2009) and decline as the cost of communication within the network rises. As noted by Khwaja (2009), many important local decisions about service provision are technical in nature, and substantial participation by nonexperts can introduce inefficiencies. This insight is reflected in laboratory work, where task complexity and the number of potential solutions slow the capacity of networks to solve collective problems (McCubbins et al. 2013). Some straightforward implications for the design of social accountability initiatives follow.

First, *what* civil society will oversee and provide input into should be relatively straightforward; complex tasks of public administration (for instance, social audits) seem like poor candidates compared to simpler tasks. Second, while social accountability initiatives have focused a lot of effort on getting information into the hands of citizens as individuals, they

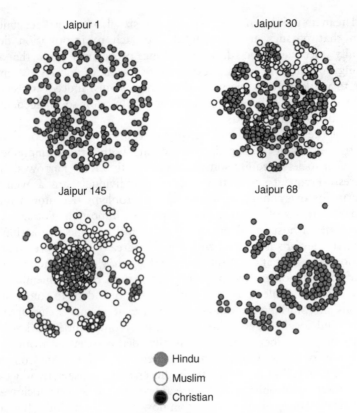

FIGURE 2.2 Four Alternative Social Networks

would benefit from more effort at lowering the cost of communication between citizens. I discuss this in greater detail in the next section.

A substantial body of work also shows that the structure of communication across members of a network can ease or complicate problemsolving, knowledge acquisition, consensus, and collective action (Golub and Jackson 2010; Banerjee et al. 2013; McCubbins et al. 2013). And here popular conceptions of a robust civil society at least potentially conflict with available research. Figure 2.2 presents network graphs from a full enumeration and survey of four slums in Jaipur, India, reported in Krishna, Spater, and Wibbels (2017). The figure shows the set of political relationships or ties among individuals in these four communities. Standard thinking would probably suggest that the community at the top right (Jaipur 30) represents an ideal decentralized citizenry – there are many citizens who are connected to many other citizens (the ties might reflect political conversations or requests for help), and there is limited hierarchy since no single individual is more central to the network than many others. Given the large number of connections (or edges), such networks can be slow and inefficient, however, and collective action can be difficult to mobilize; if this community has to coordinate on voting for a single candidate in order to achieve public services, for instance, it might have a hard time. The lower-left graph (Jaipur 145) shows an alternative network structure that solves these problems via some sort of leader, i.e., an actor who is central to the network. This focal-point person can coordinate others, facilitate problemsolving, and encourage collective effort. Relying on a huge study of social networks in dozens of Indian villages, Banerjee et al. (2013, 2014) have shown that such individuals diffuse information further and help social networks learn; Breza et al. (2015) show that such actors can also help promote cooperative behavior.[4] Obviously such a network is probably more brittle than the one in Jaipur 30, since it is more dependent on a single individual, and the lack of hierarchy in Jaipur 30 might make interpersonal interactions easier. In short, different network structures have different advantages.

Jaipur 1 at the top left represents a world of social anomie, and one that SA practitioners would like to improve. Jaipur 145 and Jaipur 30 present SA and civil society programmers with a set of difficult choices. They can promote resilience and mutual dependence (Jaipur 30) or collective action (Jaipur 145). And they can either aim to promote one of these network structures, which in some localities will involve attempts to disrupt and reconstruct existing networks, or they can take these network characteristics as given and promote SA initiatives that fit particular local contexts. Currently, it is not clear which program option is intended or why. Given that a lot of time and money is being spent on these programs, it is worth being intentional about them.[5]

Research also provides insight into some of the key obstacles to dense networks and the reasons that local communities might have trouble mobilizing collective responses to failures of accountability. Ethnic and religious heterogeneity are well-known characteristics that make coordinated social pressure more difficult, and there is recent micro-level evidence that information flows more freely in homogenous social networks (Larson and Lewis 2016).[6] Nevertheless, it is also worth noting that local heterogeneity does not preclude collective action or a robust civil society.[7] Beyond social

---

[4] Contrary to the emphasis on central actors to networks, there is at least some evidence that peripheral members of social networks play a key role in mobilizing collective action (Centola and Macy 2007).

[5] As McCubbins et al. (2013: 514) write: "legal and political environments are often intentionally designed, which means that it may be possible to build a structure of communication that encourages agreement."

[6] Though note that Larson and Lewis find that this information transmission occurs despite the fact that homogenous networks are not denser.

[7] I, for instance, am unable to uncover any relationship between slum-level caste- or religious-based heterogeneity and either the centralization of local leadership networks or indicators of local collective action in seventy-two slums in Bangalore and Udaipur, India.

identities, high levels of inequality and/or social hierarchy in local networks are associated with less cooperative behavior (Chandrasekhar et al. 2015). Macro-level evidence indicates a negative relationship between heterogeneity and public goods provision (Alesina et al. 1999), even if the precise mechanisms are not clear. At a more micro level, Bhavnani (2013) provides natural and survey experimental evidence of caste-based discrimination against candidates in India, and Grossman et al. (2016) exploit the random allocation of defendants to Israeli judicial panels to show that ethnicity has an important impact on outcomes. These individual-level results are echoed in Burgess et al.'s (2015) research on co-ethnic targeting of road projects in Kenya and elsewhere. Several possible mechanisms likely underpin these findings, including that identity provides an information shortcut and that it is difficult to sanction social cheaters across ethnic boundaries (Miguel and Gugerty 2005).

Any effort to build donor programming upon the growing evidence on social networks should recognize that network density comes with four potential problems. First, dense social networks and a mobilized civil society need not work in ways that are democratic or otherwise appealing. Dense social networks, for instance, have helped spread everything from Nazism (Berman 1997) to infectious diseases (Luke and Stamatakis 2012), and a whole host of negative behaviors are socially contagious. Second, dense networks can be quite closed and resistant to learning from the outside, and can thwart efforts to promote accountability. Brinkerhoff and Keener (2003), for instance, describe a situation in Madagascar where a small group of professional, tightly knit, decentralized administrators were closed to outside information and pressure:

Many of the SSDs [district health offices] are composed of a small group of profes-sionals who often have close family ties or multiple affiliations, thus providing room for degrading the effectiveness of internal oversight and auditing mechanisms or for benefits such as less formal sharing of resources. In terms of the kinds of checks and balances that support formal accountability, these informal interrelationships risk compromising the necessary separation, and open the door to collusion and mutual "back-scratching."

These underlying features seem prevalent in many bureaucracies across the developing world. Third, while centralized networks can promote collective action, they also may lend themselves to capture by elites. Fourth and finally, dense networks in heterogeneous settings can impede information flow because many social interactions occur with persons of "other" types with whom citizens are less likely to share important information (Larson and Lewis 2016).

To summarize, dense social networks can facilitate accountability by promoting information flow, building a shared sense of what a community needs, and facilitating collective action. Communities can thereby successfully generate prospective accountability even as they ease the sanctioning of corrupt or exploitative behavior. These benefits have to be weighed against the potential costs discussed above.

An important implication of these findings is that we already know a good deal about which communities are likely to be responsive to donor programming aimed at promoting accountability. This, however, leaves two challenges. First, donors need to develop the capacity to assess key characteristics of local social networks, including those individuals who are most central to them. As Banerjee et al. (2014) note, this is not as hard as it sounds, since members of a network can identify central individuals without knowing anything about the broader network structure. Second, we know very little about how dense (or other) social networks emerge, and this constrains outsiders' capacity to alter the civil underpinnings of accountable governance where it does not already exist. Nevertheless, even though we are not in a position to promote the emergence of local, participatory democratic orders where they do not exist, social accountability programming would benefit a great deal from recognizing in advance where it is unlikely to work, where tweaks of local programming are in order, and how local social context is likely to affect the impact of projects.

INFORMATION TECHNOLOGY, SOCIAL NETWORKS, AND ACCOUNTABILITY

A key element of the push toward social accountability has been a growing effort to use information communications technology (ICT) to promote citizen information, government transparency, and an avenue for citizen input into government processes (Peixoto and Fox 2016). Given citizens' difficulty in getting good, timely information on everything from the behavior of their politicians to the hours and drug stocks at local health clinics, cell-phone-based ICT offers huge potential. Potential efficiency gains aside (imagine the time saved by each person *not* walking to a closed clinic or one without drugs!), such information is obviously crucial for citizens' capacity to hold local officials accountable for their performance. It can also provide less time-consuming and more direct means for citizens to provide input into government decision making.

Participation, particularly in its traditional and more active forms – be it via school committees, budget meetings, or whatever – is demanding and can produce an elite bias (Dasgupta and Beard 2007; Alatas et al. 2013). ICT-based inputs, on the other hand, are less costly and have the benefit of anonymity. As a result (and as the boom in social networking applications makes clear), ICT has the potential to broaden networks among citizens and create new networks of accountability between citizens-as-service-consumers and governments-as-service-providers. In short, innovations in ICT offer the potential to keep citizens informed and to provide venues for feedback that require less effort. Indeed, the potential for ICT to improve accountability might be greatest in very poor countries, since cell phone ownership and usage is ubiquitous, even in many rural settings; civil society is often weak; and traditional forms of political accountability, such as courts, lobbying, elections, and a free press, are weak or missing. Indeed, inspired in no small part by the reported role of social media in the Arab Spring, the US government has funded similar efforts elsewhere,[8] and there is a great deal of optimism that ICT can address many of the challenges of governance in the developing world by developing networks of engaged citizens.

One growing branch of work on the relationship between ICT and politics explicitly focuses on the network characteristics inherent to cell phones, SMS, and social media (Sing et al. 2013; Pierskalla and Hollenbach 2013; Berger et al. 2015; Steinert-Threlkeld 2015; Lawrence 2017). Focused largely on the incidence of violence and repression, it provides insight not just into the correlation between cell phone coverage and violence but also into how usage changes before and during protest events.[9] At this point, the findings are inconclusive, with some results suggesting a positive association between protest activity and cell coverage (Pierskalla and Hollenbach 2013) and others not (Shapiro and Wedmann 2011). It is clear, however, that authoritarian regimes are well capable of using ICT to further their repressive aims (King et al. 2013; Rod and Weidmann 2015). To the extent protests and civil violence represent mechanisms of accountability, this work provides an entry into broader questions about the link between ICT and citizenship.

It is early to assess the impact of ICT on development programming, but some results are in from efforts to promote "digital democracy." In lieu of elections and polls, which provide some imperfect means of identifying a "public will," there have been several attempts to encourage citizens to communicate directly with public officials and administrators. One can think of these as attempts to create low-cost network ties between citizens and government officials. There is some evidence from a pilot project in Uganda that an SMS-based system can serve to promote participation, in particular by typically marginalized citizens (Ferrali et al. 2018), but a large follow-up study has found no such effect. The authors summarize that "uptake in treatment constituencies was low, marginalized populations largely refrained from using the ICT platform, and there was no price effect" (Grossman, Humphrey, and Sacramone-Lutz 2016: p. 3). Obviously, approaches such as this one are much more promising in more democratic settings where the social-network-enhancing features of ICT would find a more fertile context.

Short of feedback to politicians, efforts to promote the use of ICT by citizens to monitor government outputs and provide feedback on services abound. The ichangemycity.com platform in Bangalore is an SMS-based way for citizens to identify local service needs and vote them up (or not) in terms of importance; online platforms for commenting on proposed legislation in China;

---

[8] Ron Nixon, "U.S. Says It Built Digital Programs Abroad with an Eye to Politics." *New York Times*, April 25, 2014: www.nytimes.com/2014/04/26/world/us-ran-social-media-programs-in-afghanistan-and-pakistan.html?_r=4

[9] See Dafoe and Lyall (2015) and accompanying pieces for a review.

Web-based platforms for reporting corruption in Uganda and Kenya.[10] Many of these have not yet been subject to rigorous evaluation, but Grossman et al. (2015) provide evidence from a randomized control trial suggesting that a low-cost SMS-based attempt to elicit service feedback from citizens in Uganda doubled participation (albeit off a fairly low baseline). It is early in the lives of these efforts, but they offer the potential to promote networks of linked citizen-consumers who serve to provide government highly local information on how it is performing.

However, there are some reasons to doubt the capacity of ICT to fundamentally alter accountability relations. SMS systems, open budget initiatives, or other forms of direct digital democracy can be powerful tools for uncovering corruption and diffusing information about poor performance. But all the openness has costs too. It can serve to make bargaining more difficult, since side payments become public and bargaining gives way to posturing; likewise, all of the scrutiny associated with politics can dissuade entry by good and qualified potential leaders. And most of the ICT initiatives currently provide venues for *individual* action – the technology typically facilitates reporting and oversight by individuals who experience a failed irrigation pump or an act of corruption. If that is the case, technology does not solve the underlying social choice problems that plague any effort to divine citizens' preferences. More promising might be to link citizens into a network of government oversight. Such efforts might displace government from the central node of these ICT-based solutions in favor of promoting ties of oversight among citizens.

Yet if there are good reasons to doubt the capacity of ICT to improve fundamentally the nature of social choices, it does show remarkable promise for wringing efficiencies from systems of public administration. As technology and learning spread through the public sector, the costs of many important public goods are likely to go down. Government will know more and better about which roads need fixing, when and where drug stock-outs are occurring, which of its citizens need to visit a health care provider to prevent an emergency room visit, etc. Many of these benefits result from ICT's capacity to tighten the network ties between higher- and lower-level administrators, where principal-agent problems and absenteeism of frontline providers are endemic. Other benefits emerge from building on weak network ties among citizens and public officials, where the former can become important sources of information on the performance of very local public sectors. Where it wants to, government is likely to find big savings courtesy of extending technology into public administration and building stronger information networks between and among citizens, public officials, and service providers.

---

[10] See makingallvoicescount.org, a donor-funded program to develop e-platforms to improve governance.

FRONTIERS FOR POLICY AND LEARNING ON ACCOUNTABILITY

The most daunting challenges in the study of social networks are to understand 1) why they have the structure they do, and 2) whether they can be altered predictably from the outside. This has obvious implications for SA programming. Even if practitioners can already leverage research on social networks to understand the key features of local social contexts, it would be helpful to know when, and if, local networks are malleable, so that social accountability can be promoted. Here academic researchers and practitioners have very significant shared interests in working together. Researchers could embed their research on the adaptability of social networks into programming, and the learning could fuel better, more context-sensitive programming.

Beyond learning about social networks and their role in conditioning the prospects for social accountability, it is worth emphasizing that some of the key actors in decentralized settings across much of the developing world are left outside of traditional notions of accountability. Three actors are particularly important: 1) central governments, 2) private sector service providers; and 3) international NGOs and donors who play a prominent role in financing or delivering local services and infrastructure in many localities.

Central governments finance a large share of decentralized expenditures in many countries, and local governments serve largely to implement programs and priorities established by central governments. In these settings, local officials face incentives established by their national sponsors. Although bottom-up accountability of local officials is desirable, it is difficult to achieve if they are not elected or have few incentives to worry about the concerns of local citizens. In these situations, the best way to improve performance might be to strengthen mechanisms of hierarchical oversight rather than through programming aimed at enhancing local accountability. Likewise, where the private sector is an important service provider – as it is with water in a great many settings, and increasingly in both education and health care – promoting decentralized *political* accountability is unlikely to improve key services. Particularly where private providers are the only game in town, a robust system of government oversight is the first step in improving the services that local citizens hold dear. Finally, international NGOs and donors play a very large role in providing local infrastructure in many localities; in some cases, this provision is direct, while in others, it operates through budgetary support of decentralized governments. Though a nascent body of research indicates the citizens might have greater faith in the transparency and capacity of these outside providers (Findley et al. 2015; Wibbels et al. 2016), there are typically no means through which citizens might hold these outsiders accountable. And there is at least some possibility that by providing services directly, international actors erode accountability by weakening the link between governments and the governed. Echoing Gadenne and Singhal (2014: p. 597), how should we think about accountability if "a good local government is not one that builds schools but rather is successful at competing with other jurisdictions to attract an internationally funded NGO to build schools"? Each of these accountability relations – between central governments and local administrations, citizen-consumers and private sector service providers, and citizens and international actors – deserves additional academic and policy attention.

Most of the accountability mechanisms discussed earlier and in the broader body of work on political accountability emphasize the link between voters and elected officials. Yet it seems unlikely that citizens care much about the behavior of elected officials beyond the quality of the frontline services they get from government. One of the most important accountability relations, therefore, bears on the capacity of local politicians to induce good behavior on the part of unelected bureaucrats and service providers. Absenteeism and weak effort in the public sector are huge problems in many countries (Banerjee and Duflo 2006), and a small but important body of research and programming aims to understand the incentives of bureaucrats and frontline service providers (Muralidharan and Sundaraman 2009; Leonard 2010; Duflo et al. 2012; Hasnain et al. 2014; Khan et al. 2014). The evidence points to considerable variation in administrative responsiveness across agencies within countries; it also suggests that powerful incentives can promote better performance, although this may come with some social cost (Khan et al. 2014), and frontline bureaucrats are creative in finding ways around incentive schemes (Banerjee et al. 2008). Research and donor programming could explore alternative and less expensive means of promoting better employee performance. Work on corporate culture and workplace networks provides some foundation for thinking about how frontline agents might be motivated without relying on high-powered incentives.

Experimentation on administrative rules aside, accountability is particularly difficult to generate in decentralized settings where local administrators – be they teachers, health care workers, or police – are agents of the central government rather than of local voters. In these settings, the best way to combat absenteeism, corruption, and privilege-seeking might involve oversight and incentives from the central government rather than fostering distinctly local accountability (see the Grossman chapter in this volume). One of the more important avenues for improvement would be in the practices of local police and courts for many citizens, whose first (and perhaps only) experience with the state comes in the form of the local police officers and judges who are often to be avoided at all costs. Unfortunately, these agents of the rule of law have largely operated outside of academic research on accountability, even as donor programming recognized their importance for a while (USAID 2002). The recent boom in donor programming on these areas is viewed largely in terms of crime prevention rather than as a means of promoting accountable governance, but it is important that we learn how to promote professional and responsive frontline agents of the rule of law.

Finally, political accountability – be it decentralized or otherwise – is notoriously difficult to quantify. There are several large cross-national efforts to measure the quality of governance, including elements of accountability (Kaufmann and Kray 2008; Agrast et al. 2009). There are also related efforts to harmonize measurements of the quality of local governance, again with important elements of accountability thrown in (Bloom, Sunseri, and Leonard 2007). However, these tactics have not been widely adapted in the field. All such efforts are plagued with serious problems (Kaufmann and Kray 2008), none more serious than the atheoretical construction of indices from potentially unrelated underlying aspects of governance. Academics and donors are collecting a huge amount of data relevant to decentralized political accountability, but these efforts are uncoordinated and reflect the idiosyncratic needs of particular projects. As such, it is difficult to accumulate wisdom across research projects even as they aim to understand fairly similar accountability mechanisms. To the extent donor programming is aiming to improve accountability and to take part in the ongoing evaluation revolution, it is important that researchers and donors begin to coordinate their efforts to measure accountability. The challenge is conceptual (what are the key dimensions of accountability?), empirical (how to measure the key concepts appropriately across diverse settings?), and administrative (who will do the coordinating?). Addressing these challenges is even more pressing in light of the high profile that the UN's Sustainable Development Goals place on "accountable institutions."[11] USAID could play an important role in promoting a harmonized effort to measure decentralized accountability through its research support and programming on decentralization.

CONCLUSIONS

An awful lot of academic research on social capital, civil society, and community-driven development has assumed a common endpoint for a local, democratic order. Perhaps even more donor programming on social accountability has ignored local context in the expectation that a robust, participatory social order was an intervention away. In the face of mounting academic and policy frustration with these naïve and decontextualized notions of local political economies, it is important that researchers and the development community alike take a rigorous approach to learning about and programming for local social contexts and alternative means of promoting better local governance.

Luckily, while many of us interested in development were not paying attention, a host of formal theorists, sociologists, statisticians, and social networking analysts were developing a body of knowledge on what features of networks (i.e., of social context) matter for outcomes that we care about.

---

[11] See SDG #16: www.un.org/sustainabledevelopment/peace-justice/.

As Siegel (2011: p. 51) notes, "Networks may vary in importance by substantive topic and spatiotemporal setting, but their conceptualization is clear and constant." This chapter has provided a summary of some of the key insights of work on social networks and how they might instruct donor programming on social accountability, civil society promotion, and community-driven development.

Programming in a way that is consistent with what we know about social networks does require some practical change. At the point of project design, it requires a capacity to tailor interventions to local conditions so as to maximize the prospects for accountability. As noted earlier, this requires implementers to make a choice. Do they want to engineer local social networks that promote accountability, or do they want to take existing networks as given and design projects that reflect them? In either case, existing academic work provides some guidance. A networked approach to SA also requires some changes to monitoring and evaluation practices. Baseline, midline, and endline data (where they exist) are typically not relational and thus provide limited insight into network properties. If programming is to be responsive to local contexts, relational data have to be collected at baseline so as to inform that programming. Such data collection can be expensive, but technology is driving costs down, and innovations in sampling on networks offer savings. When it comes to monitoring and evaluation, there are tremendous gains to be had from cooperation between the development industry and academics. The former wants to know what works, and the latter specializes in figuring that out. Together, they can help build a rigorous learning agenda into social accountability programming.

The challenges of implementing this kind of programming are not trivial, but many of them have already been solved. Taking those solutions on board is crucial, because a relational, networked approach to decentralized social orders offers the potential to move beyond the trite notion that "context matters" to a rigorous understanding of when, where, and why social accountability exists. We are at a propitious moment: donor desire for systematic programming and evaluation, academic research interests, the technology of data collection, and citizen mobilization are all converging in such a way that we can make great progress in learning about these crucial issues.

REFERENCES

Agrast, Mark David, Juan Carlos Botero, and Alejandro Ponce. 2009. *The Rule of Law Index: Measuring Adherence to the Rule of Law around the World, Design and Implementation of the Index Country Profiles for 2009*. Washington, DC: World Justice Project.

Alatas, Vivi, Abhiji Banerjee, Rema Hanna, Benjamin Olken, Ririn Purnamasari, and Matthew Wai-Poi. 2013. "Does Elite Capture Matter? Local Elites and Targeted Welfare Programs in Indonesia." NBER Working Paper No. 18798.

Alesina, Alberto, Reza Baqir, and William Easterly. 1999. "Public Goods and Ethnic Divisions." *Quarterly Journal of Economics* 114: 1243–1284.

Andrabi, Tahir, Jishnu Das, and Asim Ijaz Khwaja. 2014. "Report Cards: The Impact of Providing School and Child Test-Scores on Educational Markets." HKS Working Paper No. RWP14-052.

Banerjee, Abhijit V., Rukmini Banerji, Esther Duflo, Rachel Glennerster, and Stuti Khemani. 2010. "Pitfalls of Participatory Programs: Evidence from a Randomized Evaluation in Education in India." *American Economic Journal: Economic Policy* 2(1): 1–30.

Banerjee, Abhijit, Arun Chandrasekhar, Esther Duflo, and Matthew Jackson. 2013. "Diffusion of Microfinance." *Science* 341(6144).

Banerjee, Abhijit, Arun Chandrasekhar, Esther Duflo, and Matthew Jackson. 2014. "Gossip: Identifying Central Individuals in a Social Network." NBER Working Paper 20422.

Banerjee, Abhijit, and Esther Duflo. 2006. "Addressing Absence." *Journal of Economic Perspectives* 20(1): 117–132.

Banerjee, Abhijit V., Esther Duflo, and Rachel Glennerster. 2008. "Putting a Band-Aid on a Corpse: Incentives for Nurses in the Indian Public Health Care System." *Journal of the European Economic Association* 6: 487–500.

Beramendi, Pablo. 2007. "Federalism." In Charles Boix and Susan Stokes, eds. *Oxford Handbook of Comparative Politics*. Oxford: Oxford University Press.

Berger, Daniel, Shankar Kalyanaraman, and Sera Linardi. 2015. "Violence and Cell Phone Communication: Behavior and Prediction in Cote D'Ivoire." Manuscript, University of Pittsburgh.

Berman, Sheri. 1997. "Civil Society and the Collapse of the Weimar Republic." *World Politics* 49: 401–429.

Bhavnani, Rikhil. 2013. "A Primer on Voter Discrimination against India's Lower Caste Politicians: Evidence from Natural and Survey Experiments." Working paper, University of Wisconsin.

Björkman, Martina, and Jakob Svensson. 2009. "Power to the People: Evidence from a Randomized Field Experiment on Community-Based Monitoring in Uganda." *Quarterly Journal of Economics* 124(2): 735–769.

Bloom, Evan, Amy Sunseri, and Aaron Leonard. 2007. *Measuring and Strengthening Local Governance Capacity: The Local Governance Barometer*. Washington, DC: USAID.

Breza, Emily, Arun Chandrasekhar, and Horacio Larreguy. 2015. "Network Centrality and Informal Institutions: Evidence from a Lab Experiment in the Field." Working Paper, Stanford University.

Brinkerhoff, Derick, and Sarah Keener. 2003. "District-Level Service Delivery in Rural Madagascar: Accountability in Health and Education." Report prepared for the World Bank under Contract No. 7124.

Brinkerhoff, Derick, and Anna Wetterberg. 2016. "Gauging the Effects of Social Accountability on Services, Governance, and Citizen Empowerment." *Public Administration Review* 76(2): 274–286.

Burgess, Robin, Remi Jedwab, Edward Miguel, Ameet Morjaria, and Gerard Padró i Miguel. 2015. "The Value of Democracy: Evidence from Road Building in Kenya." *American Economic Review* 105: 1817–1851.

Centola, Damon, and Michael Macy. 2007. "Complex Contagion and the Weakness of Long Ties." *American Journal of Sociology* 113: 702–734.

Chandrasekhar, Arun, Cynthia Kinnan, and Horacio Larreguy. 2015. "Social Networks As Contract Enforcement: Evidence from a Lab Experiment in the Field." Working paper, Stanford Department of Economics.

Chong, Alberto, Ana De La O, Dean Karlan, and Leonard Wantchekon. 2015. "Does Corruption Information Inspire the Fight or Quash the Hope? A Field Experiment in Mexico on Voter Turnout, Choice and Party Identification." *Journal of Politics* 77: 55–71.

Dafoe, Allan, and Jason Lyall. 2015. "From Cell Phones to Conflict? Reflections on the Emerging ICT–Political Conflict Research Agenda." *Journal of Peace Research* 52(3): 401–413.

Dasgupta, Anirruda, and Victoria Beard. 2007. "Community Driven Development, Collective Action and Elite Capture in Indonesia." *Development and Change* 38: 229–249.

Devarajan, Shantayanan, Stuti Khemani, and Michael Walton. 2014. "Can Civil Society Overcome Government Failure in Africa?" *World Bank Research Observer* 29(1): 20–47.

Duflo, Esther, Rema Hanna, and Stephen P. Ryan. 2012. "Incentives Work: Getting Teachers to Come to School." *American Economic Review* 1241–1278.

Ferrali, Romain, Guy Grossman, Melina Platas, and Jonathan Rodden. 2018. "Peer Effects and Externalities in Technology Adoption: Evidence from Community Reporting in Uganda." Working paper, Stanford University.

Findley, Michael, Adam Harris, Helen Milner, and Daniel Nielson. 2015. "Elite and Mass Support for Foreign Aid Versus Government Programs: Experimental Evidence from Uganda." AidData Working Paper #15.

Fiorina, Morris P. 1981. *Retrospective Voting in American National Elections*. New Haven, CT: Yale University Press.

Fox, Jonathan. 2015. "Social Accountability: What Does the Evidence Really Say." *World Development* 72: 346–361.

Gadenne, Luci, and Monica Singhal. 2014. "Decentralization in Developing Economies." *Annual Review of Economics* 6: 581–604.

Golub, Benjamin, and Matthew Jackson. 2010. "Naïve Learning in Social Networks and the Wisdom of Crowds." *American Economic Journal: Microeconomics* 2: 112–149.

Greif, Avner. 1993. "Contract Enforceability and Economic Institutions in Early Trade: The Maghribi Traders' Coalition." *American Economic Review* 83: 525–548.

Grossman, Guy, Oren Gazal-Ayal, Samuel D. Pimentel, and Jeremy M. Weinstein. 2016. "Descriptive Representation and Judicial Outcomes in Multiethnic Societies." *American Journal of Political Science* 60: 44–69.

Grossman, Guy, Macartan Humphreys, and Gabriella Sacramone-Lutz. 2016. "Information Technology and Political Engagement: Mixed Evidence from Uganda." Working paper, University of Pennsylvania.

Hasnain, Zahid, Nick Manning, and Jan Pierskalla. 2014. "The Promise of Performance Pay? Reasons for Caution in Policy Prescriptions in the Core Civil Service." *World Bank Research Observer* 29: 235–264.

Humphreys, Macartan, and Jeremy Weinstein. 2007. "Policing Politicians: Citizen Empowerment and Political Accountability in Uganda." Presented at the Annual Meeting of the American Political Science Association.

Kaufmann, Daniel, and Aart Kray. 2008. "Governance Indicators: Where Are We, Where Should We Be Going?" *World Bank Research Observer* 23: 1–30.

Keefer, Philip, and Stuti Khemani. 2012. "Do Informed Citizens Receive More ... Or Pay More? The Impact of Radio on the Government Distribution of Public Health Benefits." World Bank Policy Research Working Paper No. 5952.

Khan, Adnan, Asim Khwaja, and Benjamin Olken. 2014. "Experimental Evidence on Performance Pay for Tax Collectors." Working paper, MIT Department of Economics.

Khwaja, Asim Ijaz. 2009. "Can Good Projects Succeed in Bad Communities?" *Journal of Public Economics* 93(7–8): 899–916.

King, Gary, Jennifer Pan, and Margaret E. Roberts. 2013. "How Censorship in China Allows Government Criticism but Silences Collective Expression." *American Political Science Review* 107: 326–343.

Kranton, Rachel. 1996. "The Formation of Cooperative Relationships." *Journal of Law, Economics and Organization* 12: 214–233.

Krishna, Anirudh. 2007. "How Does Social Capital Grow? A Seven-Year Study of Villages in India." *Journal of Politics* 69: 941–956.

Krishna, Anirudh, Jeremy Spater, and Erik Wibbels. 2017. "Social, Political and Economic Networks in the Slums of India." Working paper, Duke University.

Larson, Jennifer, and Janet Lewis. 2016. "Ethnic Networks." Working paper, NYU Department of Politics.

Lawrence, Adria. 2017. "Repression and Activism among the Arab Spring's First Movers: Morocco's (Almost) Revolutionaries." *British Journal of Political Science.* 47(3): 699–718.

Leonard, David. 2010. "'Pockets' of Effective Agencies in Weak Governance States: Where Are They Likely and Why Does It Matter?" *Public Administration and Development* 30: 91–101.

Lieberman, Evan, Daniel Posner, and Lily Tsai. 2014. "Does Information Lead to More Active Citizenship? Evidence from an Education Intervention in Rural Kenya." *World Development* 60: 69–83.

Luke, Douglas, and Katherine Stamatakis. 2012. "Systems Science Methods in Public Health: Dynamics, Networks, and Agents." *Annual Review of Public Health* 33: 357.

Mansuri, Ghazala, and Vijayendra Rao. 2013. *Localizing Development: Does Participation Work?* Washington, DC: IBRD/The World Bank.

McCubbins, Mathew, Daniel Rodriguez, and Nicholas Weller. 2013. "Cheap, Easy or Connected: The Conditions for Creating Group Coordination." *California Law Review* 86: 495–516.

Miguel, Edward, and Mary Kay Gugerty. 2005. "Ethnic Diversity, Social Sanctions, and Public Goods in Kenya." *Journal of Public Economics* 89: 2325–2368.

Muralidharan, Karthik, and Venkatesh Sundararaman. 2009. "Teacher Performance Pay: Experimental Evidence from India." National Bureau of Economic Research. Working Paper No. w15323.

Olken, Benjamin A. 2010. "Direct Democracy and Local Public Goods: Evidence from a Field Experiment in Indonesia." *American Political Science Review* 104(2): 243–267.

Olken, Benjamin A. 2007. "Monitoring Corruption: Evidence from a Field Experiment in Indonesia." *Journal of Political Economy* 115(2): 200–249.

O'Meally, Simon C. 2013. "Mapping Context for Social Accountability: A Resource Paper." Washington, DC: World Bank.

Ostrom, Elinor. 2001. "Social Capital: A Fad or a Fundamental Concept?" In Partha Dasgupta and Ismail Serageldin, eds. *Social Capital: A Multifaceted Perspective.* Washington, DC: World Bank Publications.

Pande, Rohini. 2011. "Can Informed Voters Enforce Better Governance? Experiments in Low-Income Democracies." *Annual Review of Economics* 3: 215–237.

Peisakhin, Leonid, and Pablo Pinto. 2010. "Is Transparency an Effective Anti-Corruption Strategy? Evidence from a Field Experiment in India." *Regulation & Governance* 4: 261–280.

Peixoto, Tiago, and Jonathan Fox. 2016. "When Does ICT-Enabled Citizen Voice Lead to Government Responsiveness?" World Bank Background Paper.

Persson, Torsten, and Guido Enrico Tabellini. 2002. *Political Economics: Explaining Economic Policy*. Cambridge, MA: MIT Press.

Pierskalla, Jan H., and Florian M. Hollenbach. 2013. "Technology and Collective Action: The Effect of Cell Phone Coverage on Political Violence in Africa." *American Political Science Review* 107(2): 207–224.

Putnam, Robert. 1993. *Making Democracy Work: Civic Traditions in Modern Italy*. Princeton, NJ: Princeton University Press.

Riker, William H. 1982. *Liberalism against Populism: A Confrontation between the Theory of Democracy and the Theory of Social Choice*. Long Grove, IL: Waveland Press.

Rod, Espen Geelmuyden, and Nils B. Weidmann. 2015. "Empowering Activists or Autocrats? The Internet in Authoritarian Regimes." *Journal of Peace Research* 52: 338–351.

Rodden, Jonathan. 2006. "The Political Economy of Federalism." In Barry Weingast and Donald Wittman, eds., *Oxford Handbook of Political Economy*. Oxford: Oxford University Press.

Rodden, Jonathan, and Erik Wibbels. 2013. "Responsiveness and Accountability in Local Governance and Service Delivery: An Agenda for USAID Program Design and Evaluation." USAID Center of Excellence on Democracy, Human Rights, and Governance Evidence Review Paper.

Rojo, Guadalupe, Subhash Jha, and Erik Wibbels. 2015. "Political Networks, Clientelism and Public Goods: Evidence from Slums in Udaipur, India." Working paper, Duke University.

Siegel, David. 2011. "Social Networks in Comparative Perspective." *PS: Political Science & Politics* 44(1): 51–54.

USAID, Office of Democracy and Governance. 2002. "Achievements in Building and Maintaining the Rule of Law: MSI's Studies in LAC, E&E, AFR, and ANE." Occasional Paper Series.

Véron, René, Glyn Williams, Stuart Corbridge, and Manoj Srivastava. 2006. "Decentralized Corruption or Corrupt Decentralization? Community Monitoring of Poverty-Alleviation Schemes in Eastern India." *World Development* 34(11): 1922–1941.

Wibbels, Erik, Anirudh Krishna, and M. S. Sriram. 2016. "Land Title, Settlement Recognition and the Emergence of Property Rights: Evidence from 157 Slums." Working paper, Duke University.

Williams, Martin. 2015. "Policy Implementation, Institutions and Distributive Politics: Evidence from Unfinished Infrastructure in Ghana." Working paper, London School of Economics.

Williamson, Taylor. 2015. "Guide to Assessing Social Accountability Efforts across Sectors." RTI, International Development Group Working Paper Series No. 2015-04.

World Bank. 2004. *World Development Report 2004: Making Services Work for Poor People*. Washington, DC: World Bank Publications.

3

Leadership Selection Rules and Decentralized Governance

Guy Grossman

INTRODUCTION

This chapter explores the state of the academic knowledge regarding the effect of the institutional rules for selecting leaders at the subnational (regional and local) level. The starting point of this chapter is the distinction between administrative and fiscal decentralization on one hand, and political decentralization on the other. While the former forms of decentralization are primarily concerned with the roles and responsibilities of regional and local governments, the latter is concerned with the constitutional arrangements that govern how subnational leaders get selected into their position.

Following Falleti (2005), *administrative decentralization* is defined as the set of policies that transfer the administration and delivery of social services such as health care and education to subnational governments, while *fiscal decentralization* refers to the set of policies designed to increase the fiscal autonomy of subnational governments. By contrast, *political decentralization* is the set of institutions (e.g., constitutional and electoral reforms) designed to devolve political authority, especially electoral capacities, to subnational actors. Examples of this type of reforms are the popular election of governors, mayors, or village heads who previously were appointed to their positions.

One form of decentralization does not necessarily entail the other: countries can devolve greater administrative or fiscal responsibilities to subnational governments without reforming the rules for selecting key subnational officeholders. Interestingly, the literature debating the pros and cons of decentralization, to date, has focused almost exclusively on the trade-offs inherent to the devolution of fiscal and administrative responsibilities. With few exceptions, since the seminal work of Riker (1964) on fiscal federalism, the trade-offs inherent to the choice of institutions governing the selection of *subnational leaders* have received far less theoretical and empirical attention. Indeed, the growing theoretical literature on the trade-offs inherent in electoral institutions (for example, Persson and Tabellini [2005]) focuses almost exclusively on constitutional arrangements at the national level. This lacuna is problematic, since the effectiveness of administrative decentralization reforms is acutely tied to political institutions that shape the incentives of political actors at both national and local levels (Inman and Rubinfeld, 1997).

In this chapter, I address three related questions. I first explore the trade-offs associated with choosing between appointment systems on one hand and direct elections on the other at the regional or provincial level. Specifically, I examine the conditions under which each of the two leader selection rules might be more effective in securing positive development outcomes. I argue that at the regional (i.e., state or provincial) level, neither of the two leader selection rules – appointments from "above" and popular elections – unconditionally dominates the other. Instead, the relative effectiveness of leader selection rules is determined by local conditions. The effectiveness of popular elections increases with the constituency's level of political competition, the strength of national parties, and the quality of the media market. Appointment systems, by contrast, are more desirable when the central government's survival depends on local output, citizens are uninformed, political competition is low, and the center is controlled by a strong and cohesive party that can induce yardstick competition through promotions and retention.

I then move to examine the trade-offs between elections and appointments (both from "above" and by peers) at the local level. I argue that one cannot simply borrow from the fiscal decentralization literature, since the move to a more local context has important implications for the relative effectiveness of leader selection rules. I further argue that there are good theoretical reasons, and growing empirical evidence, that elections dominate both types of appointments at low levels of government. This is especially the case in high-information settings characterized by dense social ties and relatively low levels of inequality.

Finally, I discuss briefly how variation in electoral institutions might affect the responsiveness of democratic local governments. Specifically, I discuss the possible trade-offs involved in partisan vs. nonpartisan elections, "at-large" vs. district elections, and the presence of term limits. Given the dearth of literature regarding the effect of electoral institutions at the local level in the developing world, my main goal in this part of the chapter is to point to some recent findings (almost exclusively from developed countries) in order to help steer researchers (and donors) to address this disturbing gap.

Following this brief introduction, I discuss the theoretical and empirical literature regarding the impact of elections versus appointment at the provincial level, before moving to discuss the trade-offs associated with these leader selection rules in the context of local governments. In what follows, I discuss the implications of institutional design when holding elections at the local level.

LEADER SELECTION RULES AT THE STATE AND PROVINCE LEVELS

The key trade-off underlying the choice of elections versus appointments at the provincial level is between the benefits of *tailoring* against those of *harmonization*. On one hand, elections arguably strengthen local leaders' incentives to adopt policies that are tailored to local demands. On the other hand, subnational leaders appointed by the central government are better positioned to aid economic activity by leveraging technocratic expertise; providing more coherent, coordinated, and uniform policies; and supplying tighter control over how those policies are implemented (Amsden, 1992).

The Alleged Benefits of Political Decentralization (Elections)

Consider the set of arguments put forward by the "first generation" of fiscal federalism (Oates, 2005) in support of fiscal and administrative decentralizations – local, but not national, preference homogeneity (Oates, 1972), informational advantages (Hayek, 1948), and mobility that facilitates interjurisdictional competition (Tiebout, 1956). These criteria all assume that political institutions accompanying fiscal and administrative decentralization should be designed to maximize the extent to which local officeholders have incentives to respond to the needs and preferences of local populations. The literature, dating back to Riker (1964), assumed that under certain conditions (robust media market and high level of political competition), direct elections are more effective in securing this key goal.

Why are popular elections expected to increase the responsiveness of regional executive officeholders to the interests and preferences of their local constituents? Elections strengthen, on average, local political accountability, defined as the probability that the welfare of a given jurisdiction determines the (re)selection of an incumbent government (Seabright, 1996). However, the idea that political decentralization strengthens accountability does not rely on regional constituents having informational advantage over the central government in selecting candidates or in disciplining underperforming incumbents. In fact, when the local media market is weak, the central government likely has better information than voters with respect to the mapping between a local government's actions and outcomes.[1] It is also not always the case that the central government has a weaker incentive to discipline appointed subnational governors. When the survival of the central government depends on economic performance, it is likely to use its appointing authority to sanction and replace poorly performing agents in a fashion similar to voters (Blanchard and Shleifer, 2002).

---

[1] Gélineau and Remmer (2006), for example, demonstrate that uninformed Argentinian voters erroneously blame and reward subnational officials for national performance, leading to a very tenuous match between citizen preferences and the allocation of public resources.

Instead, the accountability argument rests mainly on change in what I term *responsive orientation*, which refers to the idea that leaders are expected to be more responsive to the preferences of the median voter of the group that selects them (Bueno de Mesquita and Smith, 2005). To the extent that the preferences and interests of a small number of appointers at the center are different from those of the average local constituency member, popular elections should better orient incumbents to be responsive to local preferences, needs, and conditions (Grossman, 2014).[2] To be clear, the alleged shift in responsive orientation from the center to local constituents should be associated with policies that more closely reflect local demands, even if the center and its appointed officials are well-meaning. In the absence of political decentralization, it is more likely that policies would fail to reflect multiple local preferences, needs, and conditions and produce a more uniform level of output. This is due to political considerations that typically constrain the central government from providing different (especially more generous) results in one jurisdiction than in another.

We had argued, following Persson and Tabellini (2000), that when elected regional leaders believe that their survival in office depends on local voters' approval, they are more likely to implement policies that satisfy their constituents. Indeed electoral accountability of public officials has been shown to powerfully motivate the adoption of growth-friendly policies and nurture an attractive investment environment (Besley and Case, 1995). There are, however, three conditions for this to be true.

First, the effectiveness of elections as a responsiveness-inducing device increases with the level of uncertainty that incumbents have about their reelection probability; i.e., when turnout is high and political competition is more intense (Beazer, 2015). When political competition and voter turnout are low, there is a greater concern that making public officials accountable to smaller constituencies would result in capture (i.e., theft of public assets) and corruption (Bardhan and Mookherjee, 2000). Using the case of Mexico, Careaga and Weingast (2003) find that higher levels of political competition result in policies with lower levels of corruption and greater provision of public goods.

Second, the effectiveness of popular elections in creating a responsive government increases with voters' level of information about the performance of their incumbent government, i.e., voters must be able to link incumbents' actions and outcomes. At the provincial level, the quality and availability of mass media are thus crucial for incentivizing elected governments to be responsive to their constituents' needs. For example, using data from the sixteen major Indian states for the period 1958–1992, Besley and Burgess

---

[2] For example, robust evidence suggests that the Russian central government under Putin judges provincial leaders, first and foremost, by the level of support they deliver for the ruling party, and not constituents' welfare (Nye and Vasilyeva, 2015). See also the variation in electoral orientation of appointed and elected officials in post-democracy Indonesia.

(2002) show that state governments are more responsive to drops in food production and crop flood damage via public food distribution and calamity relief expenditure not only where political competition is stiff but also where newspaper circulation is higher.

A relatively stable party system is a third condition for popular elections to effectively induce local political accountability. The more erratic the party system is, the greater the danger that elections at the provincial level would depress economic performance by creating a more volatile policy environment and a larger divergence between short-term and long-term incentives that deter investment (Nooruddin, 2010). Relatedly, Alesina and Perotti (1996) demonstrate theoretically and empirically that regulatory volatility is especially problematic when political turnover is high (i.e., weak incumbency advantage) and the electorate is fickle. Consistent with these arguments, Enikolopov and Zhuravskaya (2007) find – using data from seventy-five developing and transition countries over a twenty-five-year period – that when local elections are accompanied by strong national political parties (measured by the age of main parties and fractionalization of government parties), there is significant improvement of core outcomes of fiscal decentralization such as economic growth, quality of government, and public goods provision. Strong, stable, national political parties also allow the mitigation of the problem of interjurisdictional externalities, a point to which I return.

When voters feel that their local politicians are directly accountable to them – i.e., that the probability of an incumbent government's reelection is a function of its constituents' welfare – they are significantly more likely to contribute toward public goods. This theoretical argument has been substantiated both in laboratory and in observational studies. Using a series of novel laboratory experiments, Dal Bó, Foster, and Putterman (2010) show that a policy's effect on the level of cooperation is greater when the subjects democratically choose the policy. Similarly, using public goods experiments, Grossman and Baldassarri (2012) show that Ugandans are more likely to contribute to a common pot when the cooperation norm-enforcer is directly elected by subjects rather than appointed. Outside the laboratory, Fujiwara (2015) finds that an election reform that expanded enfranchisement and made state government officials more accountable also increased public goods provision.

The Alleged Benefits of Political Centralization (Appointments)

Notwithstanding the aforementioned benefits, several costs are associated with institutionalizing popular elections. First, by increasing the responsiveness of regional leaders to local preferences, popular elections may incentivize subnational politicians to overlook the interests of populations in other jurisdictions. The failure to internalize externalities, i.e., to consider issues and conditions from constituencies other than one's own, or from the nation, can completely undermine the benefits of decentralization (Rodden and Wibbels, 2002; Wibbels, 2006). For example, when regional governments are pressured to please local voters in order to win elections, they might adopt policies that undermine macroeconomic stability and increase budgetary deficits. Furthermore, due to local pressure and divergent interests, regional governments may fail to assist the central government in implementing policies that require coordination and harmonization across constituencies (Rodden, 2002; Rodden, Eskeland, and Litvack, 2003). The attempts of popularly elected governors in the United States to undermine the Affordable Care Act illustrates the difficulty in implementing national policies that require local buy-in from subnational executives who may not share the interests and preferences of the center.

Riker (1964) suggests that political centralization offers a viable solution in the face of grave interjurisdictional spillovers. Subordinating subnational leaders to an appointing center frees subnational governments from the pressure to consider the interests of their constituents above all. Reorienting accountability toward the center thus may mitigate the problem of interjurisdictional externalities as well as the difficulty in executing policies that require coordination and harmonization across jurisdictions. Comparing the rapid growth in China to the disappointing economic conditions in Russia during the 1990s, Blanchard and Shleifer (2002) argue that China's political centralization, i.e., the subordination of provincial leaders to the national center, is among the main reasons for the success of its fiscal and administrative decentralization reforms. The authors further argue that Russia's poor growth during that period owes much to its decision to subject governors to popular elections in the face of a weak national party system.

Central governments in an appointment system face an interesting and generally overlooked trade-off. On one hand, central governments, at least those that believe that their incumbency depends on economic performance, have an incentive to induce interregional competition, for example, by tying the promotion and retention of regional governors to the governors' performance. On the other hand, the more the center induces interjurisdictional competition, the more it undermines the alleged benefit of appointments in curbing externalities and in harmonizing policy.

Consider, for example, again, the case of provincial governors in China. Analyzing unique turnover data of senior provincial leaders between 1979 and 1995, Li and Zhou (2005) find that the likelihood of promotion increases with their economic performance, while the likelihood of termination decreases with their economic performance. Guo (2007) further demonstrates that even without popular election, a strong national party can induce yardstick competition between career-seeking provincial leaders.[3] On the other hand, a

---

[3] See Xu (2011) for a summary of the emerging literature on how the Communist Party in China holds regional leadership to account, using positions at the provincial level to groom, recruit, and screen capable leaders for national-level tasks.

recent study by Jia (2017) demonstrates how interregional competition in China is driving up pollution, a quintessential environmental externality. Similarly, Birney (2014) shows how the immense discretion that local officials have over which laws to implement makes it harder for the central government to detect corruption.

In sum, appointment systems must trade off between interregional *competition* and interjurisdictional *spillover*; it is hard to have both. An appointing central government may decide to limit interregional competition, solve the problem of interjurisdictional externalities, and prioritize cross-regional harmonization and coordination. Yet having central-level politicians reappoint only those local officials who are "well behaved" from the central officials' point of view undermines the benefits of fiscal federalism in the first place. The more appointed regional leaders are oriented to pleasing their bosses, the less they care for the preferences of the local population. There are no free lunches.

It is thus worth noting that elections might have a relative advantage at curbing interjurisdictional spillover, at least in the presence of strong national parties that compete locally, since such parties force regional government leaders to place nontrivial weight on the preferences of voters in other jurisdictions (Riker, 1964). Strong national parties are able to align the political incentives of locally elected politicians with national objectives by affecting the career concerns of local politicians. Unlike weak parties, strong parties have a high leverage over promotions of local politicians to national-level politics, and they are able to provide local politicians with valuable resources during local elections. Local politicians internalize the interjurisdictional externalities of their policies in the search for promotion and political support by their national governing party exactly because the party cares about national-level performance. This argument is substantiated by Enikolopov and Zhuravskaya (2007), who find that decentralized countries perform better under elections, but only in the presence of strong political parties.

Empirical Evidence at the Provincial Level

It is notoriously difficult to test the effects of political institutions at the subnational level since political units endogenously adopt rules for selecting officials. Cross-national analysis, such as that performed by Enikolopov and Zhuravskaya (2007), is valuable, but in the absence of exogenous variation in political institutions, it is difficult to rule out the possibility that unobserved conditions that contribute to the choice of a leader selection rule are also correlated with the outcome of interest.

Russia offers an interesting context in which to examine some of the above arguments. In 2005, Russia removed the direct election of regional governors in favor of gubernatorial appointments by the Kremlin. This allows for an interesting comparison of development outcomes before and after the reform. Using data on the election and appointment of Russian governors and regional economic indicators in eighty regions over the period 2003–2010, Beazer (2015) finds that political centralization improved economic performance, but only in regions where strong incumbent governors had previously depressed political competition.[4] When political competition was low, governors were able to collude with those representing narrow economic interests at society's expense. In this setting, the move to an appointment system was instrumental in reducing local capture.

By contrast, moving to an appointment system decreased economic performance in Russia's politically competitive regions. This is because political centralization has shifted local leaders' accountability away from voters, with their dominant interest in local economic concerns (Beazer, 2015). These findings are important in that they suggest that popular elections in decentralized settings can secure the beneficial effects described earlier, but only when incumbents are uncertain about the likelihood of their reelection. This conclusion is consistent with Ferraz and Finan (2011), who, using audit reports in Brazil, find significantly less corruption in municipalities where mayors can get reelected, as compared to municipalities in which the mayor is in her last term in office and thus is not constrained by reelection considerations.

Discussion

The foregoing discussion suggests that political decentralization (i.e., local elections) accompanying administrative decentralization frees provincial governors from their subordination to the central government and allows reorienting their attention toward their constituencies. However, whether they would use this freedom to advance the interests of their voters or to advance the interests of small powerful interest groups strongly depends on the constituency's level of political competition and on the quality of the media market. Robust media markets are important for providing citizens with benchmarked information on incumbents' performance. When citizens obtain such information they are less likely to select candidates based on ascriptive characteristics as compared to competence. Furthermore, even if elected governors are incentivized to advance the interests and preferences of their voters, elections might hurt economic outcomes due to interjurisdictional spillovers. Such externalities can be internalized in the presence of strong national parties that constrain local politicians through career incentives.

Strong cohesive national political parties are, however, hard to build in low-income countries, and the limited fiscal capacity of subnational units relying on

---

[4] Note that since the reform was implemented at the same time and across the board, and since some, but not all, appointed leaders have been previously elected to their position, the empirical strategy employed by Beazer (2015) does not allow for a clean causal identification.

central government transfers exacerbates externality problems stemming from external factors. Under such conditions, political centralization may seem appealing. Appointment systems, however, face their own set of trade-offs: the more they incentivize interjurisdictional competition, the less they are able to address interjurisdictional spillovers. The more appointment systems deliberately reduce interjurisdictional competition, the more standardized local outputs are, undermining the main benefits of administrative decentralization: outputs tailored to local conditions and local demand. Appointment systems are thus most effective when the central government's survival depends on local output, local media markets are weak (and thus citizens are uninformed), political competition is low, national parties are relatively weakly institutionalized, and the center is controlled by a cohesive party that can induce competition among political appointees through promotions and retention.

LEADER SELECTION RULE AT THE LOCAL LEVEL

I now move to discuss the trade-offs associated with the choice of leader selection rules at the more local level. Our starting point is the idea that "local" decentralized settings – e.g., villages, communes, counties, and even districts – differ from regional/state settings in several important ways.

First, the central government, at least in most developing countries, lacks the capacity for effective oversight of low levels of local governments (Bardhan, 2002), which is exacerbated by the fact that media outlets rarely report about very small administrative units. In addition, the state in most developing countries has a limited capacity to enforce laws against local leaders seeking to pad their coffers. Thus, in these environments local decision makers have considerable discretion, which makes it highly possible for local leaders to capture revenue. Lax monitoring and enforcement, it has been argued, allow for ample opportunities to embezzle public funds, misallocate program benefits, or collect bribes (Galasso and Ravallion, 2005; Keefer, 2007).

Second, citizens likely are better positioned to elicit the responsiveness of local leaders, as compared to provincial/state governors. At the local level, citizens have better information on local leaders and candidates (Casey, 2015), leaders have more information about their constituents (Alderman, 2002; Galasso and Ravallion, 2005), and citizens know that local leaders know their preferences and priorities. In addition, at the local level, leaders and citizens are embedded in relatively tight-knit social networks, allowing a greater role for norms of reciprocity (Baldassarri and Grossman, 2013) and for informal constraints on abuse of both de jure and de facto power (Tsai, 2007).

Third, the local level is characterized by decision making under preference heterogeneity. Whereas models of fiscal federalism assume homogenous preferences at the regional level as compared to the national (see, for example, Seabright [1996]), analysis of leader selection rules at the local level must grapple with heterogeneous preferences (Galasso and Ravallion, 2005). This is clearly the case when local officials are called upon to administer targeted transfer programs (Alderman, 2002), or when they need to make decisions over public goods investments, where different constituents prioritize different types of goods (Foster and Rosenzweig, 2001). Given these conditions, what are the benefits of elections and appointment institutions?

Theoretical Arguments

At the local level, public officials implement small-scale public goods projects, adjudicate disputes especially around land rights, and administer targeted programs. Much of the debate regarding leader selection rules at the local level is structured around an alleged trade-off between capture on one hand and accountability, legitimacy, and informational advantage on the other.

Proponents of appointment systems from "above" commonly make two main arguments. First, due to significant power asymmetries between local elites and local populations, local elites are well positioned to disproportionally steal development funds, or to implement projects that advance their interests at the expense of the larger community (Platteau and Abraham, 2002; Platteau and Gaspart, 2004). This power asymmetry stems not only from wealth and educational disparities (Baird, McIntosh, and Özler, 2013) but also from the fact that the relationship between local elites and followers is multifaceted.[5] In other words, villagers may be loath to challenge elites in one domain (governance), in order not to jeopardize relationships in other domains (e.g., access to credit).

Appointments ameliorate the problem of asymmetric power relations since local elites are allegedly more easily disciplined by external "higher-level" officials than by villagers or commune residents.[6] The second argument of appointment proponents is that, at the local level, elections suffer from the problem of free riding: compared to technocrats, elected local leaders have stronger incentives to exaggerate the severity of local conditions in an attempt to secure greater transfers from higher levels of government.

Proponents of direct (popular) elections make, in response, three main arguments. First, the disciplining capacity of the state can too easily be exaggerated. As mentioned earlier, the state might lack the information, reach, and capacity for judicial enforcement, to hold appointed leaders to account. More so, appointment systems can, in effect, reduce the incentive to

---

[5] Local leaders tend to also serve as money lenders, provide collateral for loans, adjudicate family disputes, etc.

[6] Consider the debate around targeted transfer programs; those arguing in favor of allocating responsibilities for such programs to appointed civil servants explicitly refer to the fear of capture, preferring to allocate benefits based on less precise, but less discretionary proxy-means test systems (Coady, Grosh, and Hoddinott, 2004).

support the formation of formal monitoring institutions due to familiarity between the appointing and appointed officials (Grossman, 2014). In other words, appointment by itself is not panacea against capture, and some bias in targeting transfer funds or in program selection, relative to programmatic ideal, should be expected.

Second, though elite capture could undoubtedly be a serious problem when citizens lack information about development funds (Reinikka and Svensson, 2004), it might not be as pervasive as the elite capture literature suggests. Specifically, elite capture is minimized when the conditions of a moral economy hold: a high-information environment, relatively low levels of inequality, and dense social ties (Scott, 1977). Schneider and Sircar (2018) explicitly argue that high information on candidates minimizes the problem of elite capture under direct elections, since citizens are expected to vote for candidates with pro-poor preferences. Similarly, Foster and Rosenzweig (2001) argue that under local democracy, an increase in the share of the poor should result in selection of leaders who support outcomes that are, *ceteris paribus*, more favorable to the poor, compared to different leader selection rules. Placing high value on those supporting local safety nets, risk sharing, and pro-poor preferences is, however, predicated upon relatively dense social networks, where each individual is reasonably socially connected to each other (Fafchamps, 1992).

Third, direct elections should be associated with other benefits. These include, for example, greater knowledge in the hands of local leaders, leading to better targeting and better alignment of development projects with local needs. In addition, direct elections imbue local leaders with greater legitimacy, leading to heightened willingness to contribute toward shared goals (Grossman and Baldassarri, 2012). Finally, by making community members responsible for holding officeholders to account, direct elections likely incentivize villagers to invest in obtaining information on the behavior of incumbents, in order to make an informed vote choice. In other words, direct elections lead to more robust informal monitoring institutions (Grossman, 2014).

In sum, it is far from clear a priori that capture by elected local leaders should be larger than capture by appointed civil servants who might lack strong ties to the community. In addition, the extent to which interjurisdictional "free riding" poses a serious concern at the local level is too an empirical question. Summarizing a growing body of evidence, described briefly in what follows, I argue that concerns about elite capture are likely overstated, the informational advantages of elected local leaders are substantial, and thus on average, the introduction of local elections results in better targeting and in a higher level of local public goods provision. I thus conclude that the case for institutionalizing elections is especially strong at the local level.

Empirical Findings

As discussed earlier, studying the effects of political institutions is fraught with great difficulties. In recent years, several studies have come up with innovative research designs, directly testing the relative efficiency of election and appointment rules.

First, as noted, there is growing empirical evidence that elite capture might be overemphasized. Focusing on targeted transfers that are especially prone to theft, recent studies have shown, using original survey data, that *within-village* distribution of antipoverty-targeting program resources is broadly pro-poor (Galasso and Ravallion, 2005; Bardhan and Mookherjee, 2006; Besley, Pande, and Rao, 2012). Consistent with the moral economy argument, Galasso and Ravallion (2005) show that local officials are more likely to improve targeting of antipoverty programs when land inequality is low. Most notably, in the context of a field experiment in Indonesia, Alatas et al. (2013) test explicitly for the presence of capture by local leaders in targeted transfer programs, in order to estimate whether such capture is quantitatively large enough to justify the attention it receives. Specifically, the authors test whether elite households are more likely to receive government benefits, conditional on their consumption levels. Alatas et al. (2013) find that elite capture was minimal, and at most had reduced the welfare gains from targeted transfer programs by less than 1%. Beyond targeted transfers, Fritzen (2007) and Dasgupta and Beard (2007) show that community leaders' rent-seeking behavior, in Indonesia, is reduced by introducing democratic arrangements. Similarly, Labonne and Chase (2009) show that inclusive participatory rules for selecting development projects in the Philippines resulted in equal representation of non-elite preferences.

Second, there is growing, robust, causal evidence that the introduction of elections at the local level is associated with a greater level of public goods provision, and more equitable outcomes (e.g., pro-poor prioritization of local public goods investment). Specifically, the introduction of direct elections at the village level in both China and India has allowed researchers to explore temporal variation in the introduction of elections to examine the causal effects of the rules for selecting local leaders. Consider the case of rural China, where during the 1980s and 1990s, village-level elections were introduced. Historically, Chinese village governments were comprised of two bodies appointed by the Communist Party: the Communist Party Branch and the Village Committee. The reform put the Village Committee – whose responsibilities included the provision of local public goods such as schooling, irrigation, or village roads – up for elections. Since the timing of the introduction of elections has been shown to be unrelated to village characteristics, researchers could take advantage of the staggered timing of the introduction of village elections, using a difference-indifference estimation strategy.

Notably, using different village samples, slightly different years of observation, and different measures of public goods provision, several different studies have reported very consistent results. Martinez-Bravo et al. (2017) construct a large-panel data set of village administrative records that allowed them to document the history of political reforms and economic policies for more than 200 villages. Martinez-Bravo et al. (2017) find the introduction of elections increased total local government expenditure on public goods by approximately 50%, and the frequency of positive expenditures by six percentage points. These figures strongly suggest that the newly introduced electoral institutions pushed officials to exert effort in providing public goods, which had been neglected under the appointment regime. The authors conclude that elections have shifted the accountability of local governments away from the party and toward villagers.

Similarly, using original survey data that includes information from more than 2,400 villages in rural China, Luo et al. (2010) find that the direct election of village leaders has led to increased public goods investment in the village. Furthermore, the authors find that when village leaders (who had been directly elected) implemented a larger number of public projects during their terms of office, they were more likely to be reelected in future elections. This finding strongly suggests that elections have indeed *reoriented responsiveness* away from the party bosses and toward the village members. Consistent with these findings, Wang and Yang (2010) find that elections substantially increased the share of public expenditures in village budgets.

Local elections not only increase the share of the budget that is devoted to public goods but also result in policies that are generally more pro-poor. Shen and Yao (2008) study how the introduction of village elections in China affected income distribution at the village level. They find that elections reduce the Gini coefficient by 4.3% of the sample average, and significantly increase the income shares of poorer portions of the population. Similarly, Zhang et al. (2004) find that the introduction of elections in rural China significantly shifted the distribution of taxation from individuals to enterprises, again suggesting a reorientation of accountability. Importantly, the results reported from China are consistent with the effect of introducing local elections in India. Foster and Rosenzweig (2001) use a unique-panel data set from 250 villages, describing village governance, public goods allocations, and economic circumstances in India in the years 1979–1999. They find that only when local leaders are directly elected, increasing the population weight of the poor induces public resource allocations that increase the welfare of the poor.

What are the mechanisms tying elections to both greater public goods provision and more pro-poor policies? The data at hand suggest that direct elections increase the legitimacy of local elites and thus the willingness of community members to contribute toward local public goods. Luo et al. (2010), for example, find that the introduction of local elections increased the overall contribution of villagers to their communities' public goods total investment by more than 50%. Similarly, Martinez-Bravo et al. (2017) have investigated the source of funds used to pay for village public goods and the amount of fees paid by households to the local government. They find that the increase in public goods expenditure is entirely financed by villagers, as the introduction of elections increased the amount of local fees paid by all households as a percentage of income. These results are consistent with Grossman (2014), which finds that the introduction of direct elections in Ugandan community organization has increased villagers' cooperative behavior, resulting in the provision of a wider range of group services.

Two recent lab-in-the-field experiments in India and Tanzania suggest an additional mechanism for the positive effects of elections at the local level. Schneider and Sircar (2018) demonstrate that voters, at least in the context of rural poverty, exhibit a preference for local leaders who target subsistence benefits to the poor. In a high-information village context, where voters and leaders know each other, they find that local elections lead to the selection of local leaders with pro-poor preferences over the distribution of these benefits. Similarly, Lierl (2018) uses a behavioral experiment with elected and nonelected village leaders in forty-eight Tanzanian villages, and finds that elections were remarkably effective at producing public-spirited leaders who are intrinsically motivated to refrain from siphoning funds.

Discussion

The growing evidence at hand suggests that, in local settings characterized by high levels of information, relatively tight-knit social networks, and relatively low levels of inequality, elections have an advantage in mitigating classical principal-agent problems: both moral hazard and adverse selection. In other words, not only do direct elections allow selecting candidates known to have pro-poor preferences but they also encourage the formation of local monitoring institutions that reduce the possibility of wrongdoing once in office. Future work should pay special attention to uncovering the conditions under which direct elections are more or less likely to produce desirable outcomes.

Finally, note that the aforementioned finding from a wide set of developing countries – that direct elections result in more responsive officeholders – is consistent with work in Organisation for Economic Co-operation and Development (OECD) countries, for example, on the trade-off between elected and appointed judges, between elected and appointed state regulators, and between directly elected mayors and appointed city managers.

For example, consumer price data suggest that elected state regulators produce more pro-consumer policies than appointed regulators, in areas as diverse as public utilities, telecommunications, and insurance (Besley and Coate, 2003). Similarly, Huber and Gordon (2004) find that elected judges become more punitive the closer they are to standing for reelection, independent of personal and ideological attributes. They interpret this as a sign that elections increase judges' responsiveness to the public. Moving to the choice between elected and appointed mayors, the dominant view among scholars is that cities with an elected mayor are more responsive to the views of their citizens than cities with a council-manager system (Sharp, 1997), though city managers might have a slight advantage in promoting efficiency (Stein, 1990). Future work in the developing world should pay closer attention to integrating knowledge accumulated over the past decades in governance studies of OECD countries.

VARIATION WITHIN DEMOCRATIC ELECTORAL INSTITUTIONS

In this section, I turn to discuss the implications of two institutional design choices, which are relevant where elections are used to elect representatives (e. g., city councilors) at the local level. First, I examine the trade-offs between holding partisan or nonpartisan local elections. Second, I examine briefly the pros and cons of "at-large" versus single-member district elections.

Both nonpartisan elections and at-large elections were designed by Progressive-era reforms to reduce the power of special interests and to minimize the influence of clientelistic machine-based political parties. Given the dearth of research on both institutional choices in the context of the developing world, I draw heavily on the urban politics literature in the United States. My goal is not to summarize the state of academic knowledge, but mostly to point to the significance of these institutions in order to steer new directions for future research.[7]

Partisanship and Local Elections

Should local elections be partisan or nonpartisan? Progressive-era reformers assumed that partisan elections helped to increase the power of party elites. As a result, they promoted the creation of nonpartisan elections for municipal office (Trounstine, 2010). In nonpartisan elections, parties do not officially nominate candidates for office, and candidates' party affiliations generally do not appear on the ballot. The intent of the change to a nonpartisan format was to remove party cues from voters' decision, thereby causing voters to seek out other information about the merits and qualifications of candidates (Schaffner, Streb, and Wright, 2001).

In partisan elections, the party label provides a low-cost policy guide for voting, at least where parties are somewhat programmatic. In nonpartisan elections, by contrast, voters are deprived of the party cue and thus must draw on whatever information they have or can infer from the ballot. In these types of contests, researchers have found that voters rely on a wide variety of

---

[7] For a recent summary of the state of the academic knowledge of Progressive-era city reforms, see Trounstine (2010).

cues that are not necessarily welfare-enhancing; these include race, ethnicity, familiarity, and religion (Wright, 2008).

Though the US-based urban politics literature is still debating the effect of partisanship election on local government responsiveness, some clear findings emerge. First, nonpartisan elections depress turnout, most likely because without party cues a significant fraction of the electorate finds no basis for a decision. Second, nonpartisan elections increase incumbency advantage as compared to partisan local elections (Schaffner, Streb, and Wright, 2001). This is mostly because nonpartisan elections increase the importance of candidates' name recognition. Finally, recent studies have found significant differences in the types of people elected when the nonpartisan ballot is adopted. Specifically, nonpartisan local elections seem to hurt minority and working-class representation since they crowd out less-informed voters with lower socioeconomic status (Wright, 2008).

The extent to which these findings apply to the developing world – characterized by non-programmatic parties as well as by dominant ruling parties – is an open question that should be explored by future work.

"At-Large" versus Single-Member District Elections

Progressive-era reformers in the United States also promoted citywide (at-large) elections to prevent narrow interests from influencing local government. When local politicians are elected by "district," the political unit (e.g., city, town) is divided into geographic areas of roughly equal population size, each of which elects a single member to the local government or city council. An "at-large" system, by contrast, is one in which all local government councilors are selected by the entire city/town electorate.

What key trade-offs are associated with this choice? One is between government responsiveness and descriptive representation of ethnic and racial minorities (Ferree, Powell, and Scheiner, 2013). At-large systems are expected to increase local government responsiveness since they shift electoral power away from geographically concentrated interests toward a single median voter (Trounstine, 2010). On the other hand, at-large systems reduce representation of minority groups. Indeed, one of the most persistent findings by scholars of urban politics in the United States is that compared to single-member district elections, at-large systems reduce representation of underrepresented racial and ethnic groups on local government councils. This finding has support from quantitative studies as well as from extensive case study and historical research. Single-member districts are especially conducive for minority representation when voting is polarized along racial lines and when racial and ethnic minorities live in segregated communities (Trounstine and Valdini, 2008). Similarly, Crowder-Meyer, Gadarian, and Trounstine (2013) find that women are significantly advantaged in districted elections. They argue that this is a result of competitiveness: single-member district elections are generally viewed as easier and less expensive to win.

The choice of district magnitude at the local level entails a second trade-off: between voting for candidates with policy positions closest to one's own and candidates who are more competent, i.e., more capable of designing effective policies (Beath et al., 2016). The main idea is that anticipation of bargaining over policy causes voters in elections with multiple single-member districts to prefer candidates with polarized policy positions over more competent candidates. This theoretical expectation has found support in the context of a community-driven development field experiment in Afghanistan, where the authors randomized the electoral rule for selecting local leaders.

CONCLUSION

In this chapter, I examine the relevance of leader selection rules to the effectiveness of decentralized governments. The chapter seeks to advance two key arguments. First, the choice of leader selection rules is highly consequential for efficiency, responsiveness, and representation, and hence should receive greater attention from students of decentralization than has been the case to date. Indeed, understanding the conditions that impact the effectiveness of leader selection rules should be viewed as an integral part of the study of the effectiveness of decentralized programs and reform policies.

Second, the choice of one leader selection over another – e.g., elections versus appointments – entails trade-offs. In other words, each selection rule has pros and cons and the choice between them crucially depends on the objective function of the implementer. In the case of leader selection rules, not all good things come together.

REFERENCES

Alatas, Vivi, Abhijit Banerjee, Rema Hanna, Benjamin A. Olken, Ririn Purnamasari, and Matthew Wai-Poi. 2013. Does Elite Capture Matter? Local Elites and Targeted Welfare Programs in Indonesia. National Bureau of Economic Research.

Alderman, Harold. 2002. "Do Local Officials Know Something We Don't? Decentralization of Targeted Transfers in Albania." *Journal of Public Economics* 83 (3): 375–404.

Alesina, Alberto and Roberto Perotti. 1996. "Income Distribution, Political Instability, and Investment." *European Economic Review* 40(6): 1203–1228.

Amsden, Alice Hoffenberg. 1992. *Asia's Next Giant: South Korea and Late Industrialization.* Oxford, UK: Oxford University Press.

Baird, Sarah, Craig McIntosh, and Berk Özler. 2013. "The Regressive Demands of Demand-Driven Development." *Journal of Public Economics* 106: 27–41.

Baldassarri, Delia and Guy Grossman. 2013. "The Effect of Group Attachment and Social Position on Prosocial Behavior: Evidence from Lab-in-the-Field Experiments." *PloS One* 8(3): e58750.

Bardhan, Pranab. 2002. "Decentralization of Governance and Development." *Journal of Economic Perspectives* 16(4): 185–205.

Bardhan, Pranab and Dilip Mookherjee. 2000. "Capture Governance at Local and National Levels." *American Economic Review* 90(2): 135–139.

Bardhan, Pranab and Dilip Mookherjee. 2006. "Pro-Poor Targeting and Accountability of Local Governments in West Bengal." *Journal of Development Economics* 79(2): 303–327.

Beath, Andrew, Fotini Christia, Georgy Egorov, and Ruben Enikolopov. 2016. Electoral Rules and Political Selection: Theory and Evidence from a Field Experiment in Afghanistan. *The Review of Economic Studies*, 83(3): 932–968.

Beazer, Quintin H. 2015. "Political Centralization and Economic Performance: Evidence from Russia." *Journal of Politics* 77(1): 128–145.

Besley, Timothy and Robin Burgess. 2002. "The Political Economy of Government Responsiveness: Theory and Evidence from India." *Quarterly Journal of Economics* 117(4): 1415–1451.

Besley, Timothy and Anne Case. 1995. "Does Electoral Accountability Affect Economic Policy Choices? Evidence from Gubernatorial Term Limits." *Quarterly Journal of Economics* 110(3): 769–798.

Besley, Timothy and Stephen Coate. 2003. "Elected versus Appointed Regulators: Theory and Evidence." *Journal of the European Economic Association* 1(5): 1176–1206.

Besley, Timothy, Rohini Pande, and Vijayendra Rao. 2012. "Just Rewards? Local Politics and Public Resource Allocation in South India." *World Bank Economic Review* 26(2): 191–216.

Birney, Mayling. 2014. "Decentralization and Veiled Corruption under China's Rule of Mandates." *World Development* 53: 55–67.

Blanchard, Olivier and Andrei Shleifer. 2002. "Federalism with and without Political Centralization: China versus Russia." IMF Staff Papers: Volume 48: Special Issue: Transition Economies: How Much Progress? 48: 171.

Bueno de Mesquita, Bruce and Alastair Smith. 2005. *The Logic of Political Survival.* MIT Press.

Careaga, Maite and Barry Weingast. 2003. "Fiscal Federalism, Good Governance, and Economic Growth in Mexico." In *In Search of Prosperity: Analytical Narratives on Economic Growth*, pp. 399–435.

Casey, Katherine. 2015. "Crossing Party Lines: The Effects of Information on Redistributive Politics." *American Economic Review* 105(8): 2410–2448.

Coady, David, Margaret Grosh, and John Hoddinott. 2004. "Targeting Outcomes Redux." *World Bank Research Observer* 19(1): 61–85.

Crowder-Meyer, Melody, Shana Kushner Gadarian, and Jessica Trounstine. 2015. Electoral institutions, gender stereotypes, and women's local representation. Politics, Groups, and Identities, 3(2): 318–334.

Dal Bó, Pedro, Andrew Foster, and Louis Putterman. 2010. "Institutions and Behavior: Experimental Evidence on the Effects of Democracy." *American Economic Review* 100(5): 2205–2229.

Dasgupta, Aniruddha and Victoria A. Beard. 2007. "Community Driven Development, Collective Action and Elite Capture in Indonesia." *Development and Change* 38(2): 229–249.

Enikolopov, Ruben and Ekaterina Zhuravskaya. 2007. "Decentralization and Political Institutions." *Journal of Public Economics* 91(11): 2261–2290.

Fafchamps, Marcel. 1992. "Solidarity Networks in Preindustrial Societies: Rational Peasants with a Moral Economy." *Economic Development and Cultural Change* 41 (1): 147–174.

Falleti, Tulia G. 2005. "A Sequential Theory of Decentralization: Latin American Cases in Comparative Perspective." *American Political Science Review* 99(3): 327–346.

Ferraz, Claudio and Frederico Finan. 2011. "Electoral Accountability and Corruption: Evidence from the Audits of Local Governments." *American Economic Review* 101 (4): 1274–1311.

Ferree, Karen E., G. Bingham Powell, and Ethan Scheiner. 2013. "How Context Shapes the Effects of Electoral Rules." In Political Science, Electoral Rules, and Democratic Governance, pp. 14–30.

Foster, Andrew D. and Mark R. Rosenzweig. 2001. "Democratization, Decentralization and the Distribution of Local Public Goods in a Poor Rural Economy." PIER Working Paper 01–056.

Fritzen, Scott A. 2007. "Can the Design of Community-Driven Development Reduce the Risk of Elite Capture? Evidence from Indonesia." *World Development* 35(8): 1359–1375.

Fujiwara, Thomas. 2015. "Voting Technology, Political Responsiveness, and Infant Health: Evidence from Brazil." *Econometrica* 83(2): 423–464.

Galasso, Emanuela and Martin Ravallion. 2005. "Decentralized Targeting of an Antipoverty Program." *Journal of Public Economics* 89(4): 705–727.

Gélineau, François and Karen L. Remmer. 2006. "Political Decentralization and Electoral Accountability: The Argentine Experience, 1983–2001." *British Journal of Political Science* 36(1): 133–157.

Grossman, Guy. 2014. "Do Selection Rules Affect Leader Responsiveness? Evidence from Rural Uganda." *Quarterly Journal of Political Science* 9: 1–44.

Grossman, Guy and Delia Baldassarri. 2012. "The Impact of Elections on Cooperation: Evidence from a Lab-in-the-Field Experiment in Uganda." *American Journal of Political Science* 56(4): 964–985.

Guo, Gang. 2007. "Retrospective Economic Accountability under Authoritarianism." *Political Research Quarterly* 60(3): 378–390.

Hayek, Friedrich A. 1948. *Individualism and Economic Order*. Chicago, IL: University of Chicago Press.

Huber, Gregory A. and Sanford C. Gordon. 2004. "Accountability and Coercion: Is Justice Blind When It Runs for Office?" *American Journal of Political Science* 48(2): 247–263.

Inman, Robert P. and Daniel L. Rubinfeld. 1997. "Rethinking Federalism." *Journal of Economic Perspectives* 11(4): 43–64.

Jia, Ruixue. 2017. *Pollution for Promotion*. Unpublished manuscript.

Keefer, Philip. 2007. "Clientelism, Credibility, and the Policy Choices of Young Democracies." *American Journal of Political Science* 51(4): 804–821.

Labonne, Julien and Robert S. Chase. 2009. "Who Is at the Wheel When Communities Drive Development? Evidence from the Philippines." *World Development* 37(1): 219–231.

Li, Hongbin and Li-An Zhou. 2005. "Political Turnover and Economic Performance: The Incentive Role of Personnel Control in China." *Journal of Public Economics* 89 (9): 1743–1762.

Lierl, Malte. 2018. *Corruption and Accountability at the Grassroots Level: An Experiment on the Preferences and Incentives of Village Leaders.* Unpublished manuscript.

Luo, Renfu, Linxiu Zhang, Jikun Huang, and Scott Rozelle. 2010. "Village Elections, Public Goods Investments and Pork Barrel Politics, Chinese-Style." *Journal of Development Studies* 46(4): 662–684.

Martinez-Bravo, Monica, Gerard Padró i Miquel, Nancy Qian, and Yang Yao. 2017. *Making Democracy Work: Formal Institutions and Culture in Rural China.* Unpublished manuscript.

Nooruddin, Irfan. 2010. *Coalition Politics and Economic Development: Credibility and the Strength of Weak Governments.* New York, NY: Cambridge University Press.

Nye, John V. C. and Olga Vasilyeva. 2015. "When Does Local Political Competition Lead to More Public Goods? Evidence from Russian Regions." *Journal of Comparative Economics* 43(3): 650–676.

Oates, Wallace E. 1972. *Fiscal Federalism.* New York, NY: Harcourt Brace Jovanovich.

Oates, Wallace E. 2005. "Toward a Second-Generation Theory of Fiscal Federalism." *International Tax and Public Finance* 12(4): 349–373.

Persson, Torsten and Guido Tabellini. 2000. *Political Economics.* Cambridge, MA: MIT Press.

Persson, Torsten and Guido Tabellini. 2005. *The Economic Effects of Constitutions.* Cambridge, MA: MIT Press.

Platteau, Jean-Philippe and Anita Abraham. 2002. "Participatory Development in the Presence of Endogenous Community Imperfections." *Journal of Development Studies* 39(2): 104–136.

Platteau, Jean-Philippe and Frédéric Gaspart. 2004. "The Risk of Resource Misappropriation in Community-Driven Development." *World Development* 31 (10): 1687–1703.

Reinikka, Ritva and Jakob Svensson. 2004. "Local Capture: Evidence from a Central Government Transfer Program in Uganda." *Quarterly Journal of Economics* 119(2): 679–705.

Riker, William H. 1964. *Federalism: Origin, Operation, Significance.* Boston, MA: Little, Brown and Co.

Rodden, Jonathan. 2002. "The Dilemma of Fiscal Federalism: Grants and Fiscal Performance around the World." *American Journal of Political Science* 46(3): 670–687.

Rodden, Jonathan and Erik Wibbels. 2002. "Beyond the Fiction of Federalism: Macroeconomic Management in Multitiered Systems." *World Politics* 54(4): 494–531.

Rodden, Jonathan, Gunner S. Eskeland, and Jennie I. Litvack, eds. 2003. *Fiscal Decentralization and the Challenge of Hard Budget Constraints.* Cambridge, MA: MIT Press.

Schaffner, Brian F., Matthew Streb, and Gerald Wright. 2001. "Teams without Uniforms: The Nonpartisan Ballot in State and Local Elections." *Political Research Quarterly* 54(1): 7–30.

Schneider, Mark and Neelanjan Sircar. 2018. *Does Local Democracy Serve the Poor? Identifying the Distributive Preferences of Village Politicians in India.* Unpublished manuscript.

Scott, James C. 1977. *The Moral Economy of the Peasant: Rebellion and Subsistence in Southeast Asia*. New Haven, CT: Yale University Press.

Seabright, Paul. 1996. "Accountability and Decentralisation in Government: An Incomplete Contracts Model." *European Economic Review* 40(1): 61–89.

Sharp, Elaine B. 1997. "A Comparative Anatomy of Urban Social Conflict." *Political Research Quarterly* 50(2): 261–280.

Shen, Yan and Yang Yao. 2008. "Does Grassroots Democracy Reduce Income Inequality in China?" *Journal of Public Economics* 92(10–11): 2182–2198.

Stein, Robert M. 1990. *Urban Alternatives: Public and Private Markets in the Provision of Local Services*. Pittsburgh, PA: University of Pittsburgh Press.

Tiebout, Charles M. 1956. "A Pure Theory of Local Expenditures." *Journal of Political Economy* 64(5): 416–424.

Trounstine, Jessica. 2010. "Representation and Accountability in Cities." *Annual Review of Political Science* 13: 407–423.

Trounstine, Jessica and Melody E. Valdini. 2008. "The Context Matters: The Effects of Single-Member versus At-Large Districts on City Council Diversity." *American Journal of Political Science* 52(3): 554–569.

Tsai, Lily L. 2007. "Solidary Groups, Informal Accountability, and Local Public Goods Provision in Rural China." *American Political Science Review* 101(2): 355–372.

Wang, Shuna and Yao Yang. 2010. "Grassroots Democracy and Local Governance: Evidence from Rural China." Procedia – Social and Behavioral Sciences 2(5): 7164–7180. The Harmony of Civilization and Prosperity for All: Selected Papers of Beijing Forum (2004–2008).

Wibbels, Erik. 2006. "Madison in Baghdad? Decentralization and Federalism in Comparative Politics." *Annual Review of Political Science* 9: 165–188.

Wright, Gerald C. 2008. "Charles Adrian and the Study of Nonpartisan Elections." *Political Research Quarterly* 61(1): 13–16.

Xu, Chenggang. 2011. "The Fundamental Institutions of China's Reforms and Development." *Journal of Economic Literature* 49(4): 1076–1151.

Zhang, Xiaobo, Shenggen Fan, Linxiu Zhang, and Jikun Huang. 2004. "Local Governance and Public Goods Provision in Rural China." *Journal of Public Economics* 88(12): 2857–2871.

4

Traditional Leaders, Service Delivery, and Electoral Accountability

Kate Baldwin and Pia Raffler

INTRODUCTION

Traditional leaders and customary governance institutions remain important, especially at the local level, in many low-income countries. Indeed, many observers have noted a recent resurgence in the importance of traditional institutions (Englebert, 2002; Holzinger, Kern, and Kromrey, 2013; Logan, 2009), contrary to the expectations and goals of modernists (Mamdani, 1996). The persistence and revival of these institutions is particularly obvious in Africa (Baldwin, 2016b; Logan, 2013), but has also been noted in Latin America (Díaz-Cayeros, Magaloni, and Ruiz-Euler, 2014; Van Cott, 2008) and Asia (Henley and Davidson, 2008; Murtazashvili, 2016).

As a result, aid agencies are constantly making choices about how best to interact with traditional leaders. In programming areas as diverse as justice, the environment, security sector reform, public health, and community empowerment, donors need to decide how to treat traditional chiefs, whether it be by adopting conscious strategies of engagement, choosing deliberate policies of avoidance, or taking ad hoc decisions based on the logistical needs in specific settings.[1] In light of this, the goal of this chapter is to review recent evidence on the effects of traditional leaders on locally organized public goods provision, government performance, and electoral accountability, with an eye to informing future choices by policymakers and program coordinators. This topic is relevant to aid agencies working in diverse geographic areas, although as an empirical matter, most academic research on this topic has been conducted in sub-Saharan Africa.

We start by defining traditional leaders, adopting a deliberately broad definition of these leaders as "rulers who have power by virtue of their association with the

---

[1] For examples of each of these types of choices, see Sheely (2013b), Denney (2013), and Vajja and White (2018), respectively.

customary mode of governing a place-based community" (Baldwin, 2016b, p. 21).[2] This definition includes a wide range of leaders, from *caciques* in Latin America to *maliks* in the Middle East and Central Asia to tribal chiefs in sub-Saharan Africa. It encompasses leaders who rule communities as small as villages and as large as countries. However, the definition excludes leaders unless they play a role in the governance of a geographic community; thus, *marabouts* in Senegal and village *mullahs* in rural Afghanistan are included (Cruise O'Brien, 1971; Murtazashvili, 2016), but many religious leaders are not. Communities are often governed by traditional institutions that include multiple leaders, such as customary courts and councils. When referring collectively to the diverse group of leaders who fall under this definition, we use the terms *traditional leaders* and *traditional chiefs* interchangeably throughout this review.

A distinguishing feature of these leaders is their ability to associate themselves with custom. As a result, their status in their communities is legitimized by something *beyond* appointment by the state.[3] By emphasizing only that these leaders are associated with custom, the definition allows for the fact that custom is not static but often changing, contested, and even sometimes "invented" (Ranger, 1983).

The power of traditional leaders in the contemporary world differs dramatically from place to place. Some countries have successfully displaced traditional forms of governance, replacing customary leaders with elected politicians or appointed bureaucrats; others have not. In addition, the power of chiefs often varies dramatically within countries. The status of chiefs in contemporary communities is a result of complex historical processes. It is partly a function of governments' bureaucratic capacity to project power into territories (Herbst, 2000). Empirical studies have found that chiefs have greater status in rural and ethnically diverse countries (Holzinger et al., 2018) and in more remote, less densely populated regions of these countries (Baldwin, 2014). In addition, postcolonial governments have often made shrewd economic and political calculations when deciding whether to try to displace or to bolster these leaders (Boone, 2003). Empirically, they have been more likely to support chiefs who are valuable economic or political partners as a result of their control of cash crops or voters (Baldwin, 2014).

Because the question of how best to engage with traditional leaders is only relevant in places where they still have significant status, we begin our chapter by providing some comparative data on the power and function of chiefs. Unfortunately, it is no simple matter to assess how much power traditional

---

[2] See Holzinger, Kern, and Kromrey (2018, p. 3) for a similar definition.
[3] The definition is encompassing enough to include chiefs whose authority is propped up by the state insofar as there is still some appeal to tradition in legitimizing them. Only in instances in which authors adopt the extreme view that traditional chiefs' authority derives entirely and only from the state (for the closest example to this extreme, see Ntsebeza [2005]) does the definition become nonsensical.

leaders maintain in particular communities, especially because the de facto power of traditional leaders often does not correspond closely with their de jure powers under official laws. The best comparative data on traditional leaders have been collected via the Afrobarometer's surveys of citizens in sub-Saharan Africa, and we use it to examine cross-national variation in the power of chiefs on this continent in Table 4.1. Column 1 of the table measures variation in traditional leaders' influence, broadly conceived; it reports the percentage of citizens (across urban and rural areas) who say that traditional leaders have some or a lot of influence over the governance of their local community. Traditional leaders have almost no power in countries like Madagascar and Tanzania, while remaining very powerful in countries like Botswana, Ghana, Lesotho, Malawi, and Zimbabwe.

Although there is a great deal of variation in the overall influence of traditional leaders, there is somewhat less divergence in their main responsibilities in communities where they remain powerful. Drawing again on data from the Afrobarometer survey, columns 2 to 7 in Table 4.1 report the percentage of citizens who say traditional leaders have primary responsibility for different tasks. The data show that traditional leaders in sub-Saharan Africa often play leading roles in resolving disputes and managing land, but citizens do not expect them to take primary responsibility for social services, environmental management, security, or tax collection. Indeed, the importance of traditional institutions in managing disputes, especially over property rights and land, is widely noted beyond Africa too (Murtazashvili, 2016). Yet, even in areas where the government, rather than traditional leaders, is expected to take the lead, traditional leaders often act as facilitators; for example, they may encourage members of the community to volunteer labor for infrastructure projects, or they may report security risks to the police.

The mode of appointing traditional leaders also varies between communities, depending on how local custom is conceived; as a result, the method of appointment is not explicitly incorporated into our definition of a traditional leader. However, as an empirical fact, it is unusual for communities to have historically selected leaders via periodic election.[4] In the contemporary period, traditional leaders typically have indefinite tenure and often rule for life (Baldwin, 2016b).

The fact that most traditional leaders are not regularly elected is important for two reasons. It means both citizens and higher-level leaders have difficulty motivating these leaders to act on behalf of their interests through threat of removal from office; this important mechanism for generating accountable leadership is not typically available in the case of traditional leaders. But the fact that traditional leaders have indefinite tenure also means that these leaders have long time horizons. Insofar as they expect to rule their communities for

---

[4] For data on the rarity of elections as a procedure for selecting village-level leaders, see Giuliano and Nunn (2013).

TABLE 4.1 *Perceptions of Traditional Leaders (TLs) in Select African Countries*

Country	TLs have some or a great deal of influence in governing local community	Traditional leaders primarily responsible for:					
		Local dispute resolution	Land allocation	Managing schools or health care centers	Keeping community clean	Law and order	Tax collection
	(1)	(2)	(3)	(4)	(5)	(6)	(7)
Zimbabwe	79%	54%	46%	2%	32%	12%	4%
Malawi	75%	56%	63%	10%	27%	17%	4%
Botswana	73%	76%	25%	2%	9%	13%	3%
Ghana	69%	60%	70%	4%	30%	12%	5%
Lesotho	65%	76%	42%	4%	38%	29%	3%
Liberia	62%	29%	15%	3%	10%	3%	2%
Burkina Faso	59%	26%	30%	3%	7%	3%	3%
Mali	59%	46%	37%	5%	16%	9%	12%
Zambia	58%	40%	42%	2%	24%	9%	4%
Nigeria	56%	29%	21%	5%	11%	3%	4%
Senegal	53%	34%	16%	2%	4%	3%	9%
Kenya	51%	53%	20%	5%	10%	3%	3%
Namibia	49%	23%	24%	6%	15%	10%	6%
Uganda	47%	29%	32%	4%	10%	5%	5%
Benin	42%	13%	17%	1%	4%	1%	1%
South Africa	40%	14%	19%	8%	12%	7%	4%
Tanzania	24%	4%	1%	0%	1%	1%	0%
Madagascar	22%	7%	2%	0%	2%	0%	0%

Notes: Survey questions for column 1: "How much influence do traditional leaders currently have in governing your local community?" Note that this question was not asked in urban Zimbabwe. Columns 2–7: "Who do you think actually has primary responsibility for managing each of the following tasks. Is it the central government, the local government, traditional leaders, or members of your community?" Measures for (a) managing health care centers and schools and (b) keeping the community clean and protecting rivers and forests were combined. The full description of the tasks referred to in Column 5 is "Keeping community clean or protecting rivers and forests."

Source: Round 4 of the Afrobarometer survey.

life, they have an incentive to invest in building local institutions with long-term benefits in a way that elected leaders do not (Baldwin, 2016b). A critical challenge, then, is ensuring traditional leaders are motivated to build institutions that will provide public rather than private benefits.

Although historically it has proved difficult to motivate good leadership at the national level without the threat of electoral sanctions (Lake and Baum, 2001; Stasavage, 2005), traditional leaders may have non-electoral motivations for governing well. In particular, scholars have emphasized two reasons that traditional leaders may be motivated to govern well – the effectiveness of the process by which they are selected in choosing "good types" (Acemoglu, Reed, and Robinson, 2014), and the social and economic incentives they have to govern in the interest of the broader community (Baldwin, 2016b; Gottlieb, 2017; Tsai, 2007a).

First, some processes of selecting traditional leaders may be fairly effective in selecting good leaders. In particular, some scholars emphasize how competitive the processes for selecting chiefs are (Acemoglu, Reed, and Robinson, 2014). There is great variation here; in some instances, multiple candidates compete to be elected chief-for-life, and in other instances, one individual is appointed by virtue of his or her position in the family tree of the ruling family or by the stated preferences of the previous traditional leader. Competition should increase the breadth of candidates considered and therefore the quality of the leader selected.[5] However, the amount of competition in the selection of traditional chiefs may be a double-edged sword; in particular, it may foster divides in communities that make chiefs less representative of community interests and less effective community mobilizers (Baldwin, 2016a; Baldwin and Mvukiyehe, 2015).

Second, traditional leaders may have social and economic incentives to govern in the interest of their broader community. Specifically, some scholars argue that traditional leaders who are economically and socially embedded in their communities may govern well; economic links to the local economy or social pressure may provide incentives to deliver public goods, even absent electoral incentives (Baldwin, 2016b; Tsai, 2007a). Indeed, the strength of customary leaders' ties to local communities often distinguish them from other political leaders. However, there is also great variation among traditional leaders in the extent of local embeddedness. At one extreme, some leaders earn all their income from local businesses or contributions from community members for services they provide; at the other extreme, some chiefs receive large monthly stipends from the government or royalties from

---

[5] In addition, competition among ruling families could create incentives for individual leaders to act in the interest of their community while in office. Acemoglu, Reed, and Robinson (2014) argue that traditional leaders have an interest not only in perpetuating their own rule but also in perpetuating the rule of their direct descendants. In this case, citizens may be able to use the threat of removing the family from office to enforce accountable leadership even without the possibility of removing individual leaders from office.

multinational companies. Similarly, some chiefs live full time in their communities and have broad social ties, while others make their primary residence in distant cities or towns or are connected to only a subset of the population. We argue that the social and economic embeddedness of leaders is critical in determining whether chiefs have incentives to govern well; for example, Zambian chiefs who are more socially and economically embedded in their communities are less likely to prioritize private goods over public goods, and communities make fewer complaints about their rule (Baldwin, 2016a). Historically, the threat of social and economic sanctions was essential in encouraging good governance by traditional leaders (Ayittey, 1991).

In what settings do socially and economically embedded traditional leaders exist? Very few data exist that allow us to compare the economic and social position of traditional leaders, and so we can provide only tentative answers. The best data available to us are from Zambia; these data, collected through a survey of 110 traditional leaders, measure how often chiefs travel to the capital city for nonmedical reasons (a proxy for lack of "social embeddedness") and whether they run local businesses in their chiefdoms (a proxy for "economic embeddedness"). In the Zambian context, chiefs are more likely to be socially embedded in more remote communities, and they are more likely to be economically embedded if they live in less economically developed communities and are from more centralized ethnic groups.[6] Indeed, research in China and Senegal also suggests traditional leaders are more likely to have incentives that align with their communities in more remote and economically underdeveloped communities (Gottlieb, 2017; Mattingly, 2016). However, more analysis and data collection on this topic is necessary so we can understand when traditional leaders have strong ties to their local communities and when they do not.

Indeed, one of the more general takeaways of this chapter is the importance of local context in determining the best strategies with regards to engaging traditional leaders and traditional institutions. In reviewing the academic literature on the effects of traditional leaders on local public goods provision, government performance and electoral accountability, we return to the importance of the competitiveness of the selection of leaders and their embeddedness in their communities numerous times to explain divergent outcomes. Our review shows that traditional leaders in weak states often play constructive roles in providing public goods and improving governance; in these settings, development programs that exclude traditional leaders ignore a critical resource and are unlikely to achieve their maximum potential. But we also note a quandary for aid agencies: locally embedded traditional leaders make the best partners in terms of implementing effective development programming, but without careful program design, the act of partnering with these leaders may reduce their embeddedness in their communities, thus having potentially adverse effects in the longer run.

---

[6] See Table 4.2.

WHAT WE KNOW FROM ACADEMIC STUDIES

This section summarizes what we know about traditional leaders, service delivery, and democracy from the academic literature. We first discuss the direct role of traditional leaders in the provision of local public goods, before turning to their effects on government performance, especially service provision by the state. We conclude this section by discussing the literature on the role of traditional chiefs in elections.

Our review focuses primarily on two types of research: studies that make critical theoretical contributions to these topics, and studies based on quantitative empirical analysis from the contemporary period. Important, we exclude from our review much of the growing literature on the legacies of precolonial institutions; this is because, in most of this literature, it remains ambiguous whether the legacies of precolonial institutions operate through strong traditional institutions in the contemporary period.[7] We geographically limit the scope of our study to developing and emerging countries; in fact, the majority of the studies we review are from Africa due to the greater academic attention given to traditional institutions by scholarship on this region. Traditional leadership is by its nature an interdisciplinary topic, and – though we engage with arguments made by scholars from a wide variety of disciplines – our review of empirical studies focuses mainly on research conducted by political scientists and economists. The advantage of this is that we can be comprehensive in reviewing empirical studies that address the topics of interest within these parameters.[8]

Chiefs and Locally Organized Public Goods and Services

We begin by examining the effectiveness of traditional leaders in organizing locally provided public goods and services. The focus here is on goods and services that are financed and organized by communities rather than by a higher-level government. The range of examples in the studies we review includes boreholes, waste collection, and public order. We first consider studies that compare whether traditional leaders and/or customary institutions are more effective than alternative leaders and institutions in organizing local public goods and services, and then we review the smaller set of studies examining how the characteristics of traditional leaders influence their effectiveness in organizing local public goods.

---

[7] For a review of the literature on precolonial institutions, see Michalopoulos and Papaioannou (2015).

[8] For readers interested in interdisciplinary reviews of the literature on traditional leaders, see Nuesiri (2014) and Holzinger, Kern, and Kromrey (2016).

TABLE 4.2 *Covariates of Embeddedness*

| | Social embeddedness | | | | | Economic embeddedness | | | | |
| | Embedded | | Not embedded | | | Embedded | | Not embedded | | |
Variable	n	mean	n	mean	p-value	n	mean	n	mean	p-value
Distance to Lusaka (km)	47	466	61	375	0.009	44	449	66	384	0.069
% of chiefdom pop. working in agriculture	47	76%	61	76%	0.996	44	83%	66	71%	0.005
% of chiefdom pop. with formal FT work	47	3%	61	3%	0.577	44	2%	66	3%	0.142
Chief from centralized ethnicity	47	38%	61	52%	0.146	44	70%	66	29%	0.000
Chief is senior chief	47	11%	61	11%	0.892	44	7%	66	14%	0.265
ELF	47	0.42	61	0.37	0.251	44	0.37	66	0.42	0.227
% of chiefdom pop. of chief's ethnicity	47	65%	61	68%	0.479	44	63%	66	68%	0.281
Population of chiefdom	47	16,856	61	19,081	0.444	44	18,264	66	17,940	0.911

Notes: Data are from a survey with 110 traditional leaders in Zambia. Social embeddedness is proxied by not traveling to the national capital for any but medical reasons. Economic embeddedness is proxied by owning a local business.

Public Goods Organization: Traditional Leaders versus Alternative Institutions

From a theoretical perspective, it is uncertain whether traditional leaders or officials subject to electoral accountability should be more effective in organizing contributions to local public goods. Elected leaders should have incentives to provide local public goods and services, which are valued by citizens, and may have the legitimacy to increase voter contributions toward their provision (Dal Bó, Foster, and Putterman, 2010; Grossman and Baldassarri, 2012). But traditional leaders who are embedded in communities may also have incentives to provide local public goods; they also typically have longer time horizons and thereby often have stronger local institutions for coordinating and sanctioning (Baldwin, 2016b). As a result, theoretically, traditional leaders could be more or less effective than alternative leaders in directly organizing local public goods.

Several recent studies assess the quality of local public goods provision by traditional leaders, as compared to public goods provision by formal governments. For example, in the Mexican state of Oaxaca, Díaz-Cayeros, Magaloni, and Ruiz-Euler (2014) find that municipalities ruled by traditional *usos y costumbres* are better than party-led municipalities at providing electricity. In 1995, indigenous communities had the opportunity to opt into the *usos* system, a traditional governance system characterized by high levels of participation, the nonpartisan election of leaders according to customary law and a parallel justice system. Using a matching strategy, these municipalities are compared to communities with similar characteristics and long-term settlement patterns that instead chose to be governed by political parties. Communities with the *usos* system are found to be more likely to have higher levels of political participation and higher provision of electricity. However, there was no or only an inconsistent impact on sewage, water, and literacy rates.

Similarly, Baldwin (2016b) finds that traditional chiefs play a unique role in organizing local public goods that depend on community contributions in rural Zambia. This analysis takes advantage of the fact that the leadership of Zambian chiefdoms lapses for a period following the death of the chief, and that the death of chiefs in any given time period is typically exogenous to local political and socioeconomic factors. She finds that lapses in traditional leadership result in significant decreases in the provision of coproduced local public goods, in particular schools and boreholes, suggesting chiefs play a critical role in mobilizing communities to contribute to these goods. In contrast, lapses in political leadership following the death of elected Members of Parliament do not result in the same reduction in local public goods provision.[9]

Two related studies in Afghanistan focus on the effect of customary councils (*shuras*) on dispute resolution. Using data from two nationwide surveys,

---

[9] The latter result is presented in Baldwin (2018).

Murtazashvili (2016) finds that, across a variety of measures of dispute levels, communities with access to customary institutions fare better than communities with access to community-development committees (CDCs), World Bank–sponsored councils that are supposed to be elected. Consistent with this finding, Jochem, Murtazashvili, and Murtazashvili (2016) find that customary councils are *expected* by voters to perform better than elected CDC councils with regard to reducing social divisions and furthering reconciliation with the Taliban. The analysis is based on a nationally representative survey experiment with 8,000 Afghan households. Note that the survey experiment presented voters with hypothetical vignettes about different forms of local governance.

In a related field experiment in Sierra Leone, Turley et al. (2017) ask a more basic question: whether traditional leaders are better than *average* villagers at managing small-scale community-level projects. They find that the traditional leaders perform better, since traditional leaders have greater management capacity and better mobilization skills than average citizens. While comparing traditional leaders to randomly selected citizens is a relatively low bar, the findings assuage fears of traditional chiefs being *worse* leaders than the citizens they represent.

On the other hand, two recent field experiments do not find any evidence for a difference between traditional leaders and their alternatives. Sheely (2013a) finds no difference in the effectiveness of official state bureaucrats and traditional elders in ensuring continued compliance with a clean-up campaign in Kenya. Similarly, Beath, Christia, and Enikolopov (2013a) find no difference in either embezzlement or community mobilization in villages in Afghanistan where newly formed, elected CDCs were explicitly tasked with food aid distribution and villages without these institutions, where traditional leaders were asked to perform the task. Instead, the villages where traditional councils distributed wheat were worse at targeting objectively vulnerable households compared to elected councils.

We conclude from these studies that traditional leaders are often – albeit not always – very effective in organizing local public goods that require high levels of community contributions and/or compliance, rendering them potentially effective brokers between their citizens and the state. Two aspects are noteworthy. First, when it comes to community mobilization in particular, traditional leaders are never found to be worse than the alternative leaders and institutions to which they are compared, and they are often significantly better. Second, the cases where studies found no difference between traditional and formal leaders, or found that traditional leaders performed worse with regard to targeting, are in the context of randomized control trials; in these settings, the tasks assigned to leaders by the intervention may have a certain degree of novelty, and traditional leaders may not be able to apply their organizational capacity to these new tasks. An important caveat is that the existing literature has focused on the effects of traditional governance in contexts where the state has fairly weak bureaucratic capacity and low accountability. These are settings where the involvement of traditional leaders is likely to result in greater improvements in public goods provision, compared to more developed states.

Collective Action and Traditional Leaders' Characteristics

Are there studies that explicitly examine how variation in traditional institutions affect the ability of traditional leaders to coordinate their communities and provide local public goods? More research is recommended on this topic, but a handful of studies have empirically examined how the selection method of chiefs affects their mobilizational capacity. Here again we have uncertain theoretical priors. On one hand, we may expect competitively selected leaders to enjoy greater legitimacy and thus to have greater capacity to mobilize voluntary contributions. On the other hand, leaders who face fewer constraints may wield greater social control.

Taking advantage of plausibly exogenous variation in the number of ruling families, and thus political competition, across chiefdoms in Sierra Leone, Acemoglu, Reed, and Robinson (2014) find that although competitively selected chiefs appear more accountable, as discussed further later in this chapter, they wield lower levels of social control, which in turn renders them worse at coordinating community contributions to local public goods such as road brushing. Social control is a double-edged sword: while it may be used to increase contributions to local public goods, it can also be misused. For example, Acemoglu, Reed, and Robinson (2014) find that noncompetitively selected chiefs are less likely to allow their citizens to resell their land. They interpret their findings as suggesting that noncompetitively selected chiefs exercise social control through the capture of civil society.

Similarly, Baldwin and Mvukiyehe (2015) find that competitively selected chiefs are worse at organizing compliance with public order and contributions to local public goods in Liberia. Taking advantage of a break in the way village leaders are selected after the civil war, they find that when traditional leaders are selected by elections, this has little to no effect on political participation in their communities but negative effects on public order. Outcome measures consist of self-reported participation in community and national governance, participation in protests, and contributions in public goods games. While participation in noncontentious politics does not increase when chiefs are elected, participation in protests becomes more likely and contributions to public goods decrease.

The takeaway from these two studies is that competitively selected chiefs tend to be worse at coordinating their communities to comply with public order and to contribute to local public goods compared to chiefs who face fewer constraints. These chiefs appear to wield lower levels of social control; however, their incentives may be more aligned with those of their communities, as is discussed in greater detail in the following sections.

Chiefs and Government Performance

Next we review the literature on the effects of traditional leaders on government performance in the area of service provision. While the previous section focused on whether the direct involvement of traditional leaders in organizing local public goods and services was more effective than available alternatives, this section examines how the existence of traditional leaders and customary institutions impacts the government's performance. In theory, there are two models by which traditional leaders could positively or negatively impact the government's performance in delivering services: by acting in parallel to the state's activities (*parallel systems*), or by establishing relationships with state actors that influence their incentives and capacity (*integrated systems*).[10]

However, competition between traditional leaders and the state to provide specific services turns out to be relatively rare in the contemporary period. There are few documented instances of traditional leaders competing with the state to provide local public goods or services; for example, traditional leaders do not typically engage in running schools or providing health care in parallel to the government's efforts. The result is that traditional leaders do not provide citizens a viable alternative option to the state in these sectors. The exception is the justice sector, where traditional courts often do run in parallel to the formal justice system. This creates situations where some citizens are in a position to choose whether to pursue justice in the customary or formal justice system. Corstange (2008) draws on public opinion data from Yemen to show that some groups view tribal judicial institutions as a favorable substitute for state courts in settings where state capacity to enforce the rule of law is weak. Sandefur and Siddiqi (2013) also draw on survey data to show that citizens in rural Liberia rationally weigh the favorability of the treatment they can expect in each court system against the cost of accessing it when deciding where to take disputes.

In theory, competition between state courts and traditional courts could improve the state's administration of justice. However, Hartman's (2015) dissertation on conflict resolution in Liberia argues that they can also harm it, because disputants must be able to coordinate on a dispute resolution mechanism if disputes are to be resolved quickly and peacefully. Drawing on evidence from an original database of 958 conflicts, she shows that in areas where the formal Liberian justice system faces competition from traditional institutions, conflicts that emerge are more prolonged and violent. However, her analysis does not distinguish between disputes first taken to traditional courts and disputes first taken to official state courts, so it is not clear whether state courts are less effective in the presence of traditional courts or whether traditional courts are simply less effective than state courts.

---

[10] For a similar distinction between "parallel" and "interactive" approaches to the study of traditional governance, see Holzinger, Kern, and Kromrey (2016).

Another instance of the parallel operation of traditional and nontraditional institutions was created as the result of a donor-funded intervention in Afghanistan. Specifically, elected village councils were created in parallel to the existing traditional governance institutions as part of a randomized control trial. Here, Beath, Christia, and Enikolopov (2013a) find that in villages where the two parallel leadership institutions were tasked with the distribution of food aid, embezzlement and mismanagement increased, compared to villages where either the traditional or the new elected leaders were explicitly tasked. This suggests that the introduction of parallel systems of governance without a clear allocation of responsibilities can have adverse effects on the quality of local public goods provision.

The Effects of Mediated Citizen-State Relationships

More often than they compete with the state, traditional leaders mediate relationships between citizens and elected leaders. This mediation has varying effects on the quality of service delivery. As we have discussed earlier in this chapter, traditional leaders tend to have mobilization and coordination capacity among their communities, rendering them potentially effective brokers for development and service delivery, especially in settings where local state institutions are weak (Baldwin, 2013, 2016b). In addition, they may act as checks and balances to state institutions by coordinating collective action and by holding government officials accountable through informal channels and shared norms (Tsai, 2007a, 2007b). However, in settings where traditional leaders are not accountable to their communities, they may take advantage of their role as intermediaries between the citizens and the state and use it to amass personal rents.

Two sets of studies are relevant to this section of our review, the first comparing the effects of strong versus weak chiefs on government performance, and the second comparing the effects of traditional leaders' integration into the formal political system on government service provision. In the first category of studies, Schultz, Wibbels, and Huntington (2015) argue that strong chiefs in Ghana use their influence to mediate the relationship between voters and formal government institutions, resulting in lower levels of clientelism and better service provision. Ironically, this also results in a better perception of government institutions among voters. Strong chiefs, so the argument goes, have a greater capacity to mobilize votes than weak ones. Their capacity to mobilize votes renders them important assets for politicians who seek to maximize their vote share. Since Ghanaian chiefs tend to be embedded in their communities, they have an incentive to ensure that the government provides goods and services. They therefore use their bargaining position vis-à-vis politicians to negotiate for better service delivery in return for votes. In areas where there are no strong chiefs, on the other hand, politicians have to rely on clientelism and vote-buying to garner votes. Hence, strong chiefs serve as a substitute for clientelistic vote brokers, with better development outcomes. One can think of them as bundling votes, thus helping their constituents to overcome collective action problems and negotiating a better deal: service delivery instead of vote-buying. Results from surveys and survey experimental data collected from voters, administrators, and elected leaders in 150 rural districts of Ghana support the argument.

In addition, strong traditional leaders can serve as important checks and balances to the state. In Senegal, Honig (2015) finds that having traditional leaders mediate the relationship with the state can help protect communities from expropriation of communal land. The first part of the empirical analysis compares areas formerly colonized by the French or the British within the Senegal River Valley. British colonizers are argued to have led through indirect rule, thereby allowing traditional governance institutions to survive. This contrasts with the approach taken by French colonizers, who installed their own administrators, hence replacing existing governance institutions and power structures. Honig presents case study evidence that traditional leaders in the areas formerly ruled by the British now help protect communities from the cessation of communal land by the state by coordinating collective action. The second part of the empirical analysis combines data on all new land titles in Senegal between 2007 and 2013 with data on precolonial governance structures and finds that higher levels of centralization of precolonial governance institutions are associated with fewer land cessations by the state today, suggesting that traditional governance institutions persist and continue to play a role in facilitating collective action and shaping property rights.

Similarly, in Afghanistan, Murtazashvili (2016) finds that traditional councils (*shuras*) provide an important counterbalance to the power of the central state. Drawing on public opinion data, she finds that citizens have better views of the performance of the central government in communities where *shuras* have a greater presence. She argues that most Afghan citizens are wary of the power of the central government and so powerful village-level customary institutions provide an important check.

Other relevant studies focus not on variation in the strength of traditional institutions but on variation in how integrated they are with other government actors. Baldwin (2013, 2016b) argues that the state's performance in delivering basic services is improved when political representatives have stronger relationships with local traditional leaders. Drawing on observational evidence from Zambia, she shows that the government is more effective in building schools and rehabilitating roads in rural areas when elected Members of Parliament have longer relationships with the local chief. Strong relationships between chiefs and politicians are beneficial in part because they allow chiefs to better lobby for public goods for their communities, as Schultz, Wibbels and Huntington (2015) also find in Ghana. However, they are also important because the delivery of services typically requires the mobilization of local resources to complement state funding, and traditional chiefs with stronger relationships to elected politicians are more likely to collaborate effectively with them to "coproduce" services.

In contrast, Clayton, Noveck, and Levi (2015) find that traditional leaders only serve as effective checks and balances if they do *not* have a close relationship with elected local councilors. Using data from two national surveys conducted in Sierra Leone, they find that areas in which elected councilors have frequent contact with and/or share a large number of familiar ties with the paramount chief, citizens exhibit lower satisfaction with the quality of local public goods and lower utilization rates of public health care facilities and schools. In contrast, areas in which councilors reported frequent conflicts with the paramount chief experienced improvements in local development outcomes. The authors conclude that in Sierra Leone, inter-elite competition – rather than collaboration – between local councilors and paramount chiefs is conducive to the quality of local service delivery.

Finally, in China, Xu and Yao (2015) find that public goods provision is higher when the elected village head is a member of one of the two largest lineage groups in the village, suggesting greater integration of traditional institutions and formal state institutions. Using panel data on 220 Chinese villages between 1986 and 2005, they find that village members' contributions to village-level public investments are higher when the elected village head is a member of one of the two largest lineage groups in the village. In contrast, Mattingly (2016) suggests that integration into the state may weaken the downward accountability of traditional lineage leaders in China in a way that harms their ability to protect citizens from government predation. Autonomous lineage leaders may play an important role in protecting communities from land cessations, but when lineage leaders are elected to official village leadership positions and become part of the Chinese state apparatus, he argues, they use their traditional legitimacy to confiscate land on behalf of the central government.[11] Mattingly uses a national survey to show that villages in which the clan chief becomes a village official are 14–20% more likely to experience land confiscations, resulting in measurable negative welfare effects. A survey experiment and case studies corroborate that an endorsement by the clan chief increases compliance with confiscation plans.

Thus, the effects of traditional leaders on government performance are not straightforward. Stronger traditional leaders improve government performance in Ghana, Senegal, and Afghanistan by lobbying and checking the state. Traditional leaders with stronger ties to formal politics improve governance in the case of local public goods provision in both Zambia and China, but harm it in the case of service delivery in Sierra Leone and land reform in China. How are we to make sense of these different findings? Part, but not all, of the answer

---

[11] Note, however, that it is impossible to disentangle election to formal office and the appreciation of land value here, as the two are highly correlated.

is the different downward accountability of leaders in these different settings, which we discuss in the next subsection, before turning to a discussion of additional factors.

Government Performance by Traditional Leaders' Characteristics

One important type of variation to consider is differences in the incentives and downward accountability of traditional leaders and customary institutions. In Sierra Leone, Acemoglu, Reed, and Robinson (2014) find that competitively selected leaders are less likely to collude with the state, resulting in higher levels of local development. Competitively selected chiefs are defined as those coming from chiefdoms with a greater number of ruling families, a plausibly exogenous characteristic. Therefore, they face greater political competition and see a greater need to negotiate constraints with the other ruling families in order to ensure the future of their lineage.[12] Competitively selected chiefs are more likely to allocate resources to education and to let constituents resell their land, resulting in higher local economic development.

In the Chinese context, Tsai (2007a) compares the efficacy of a variety of village-level informal institutions in improving governance based on the extent to which they embed leaders in their networks and the extent to which they encompass all citizens. She finds that temple groups are effective in mobilizing pressure on local leaders to provide local public goods, as are lineage groups in homogeneous villages, but church groups and lineage groups in heterogeneous villages are not. She argues that only in the first two sets of cases are informal institutions both embedding and encompassing, thereby explaining the difference. This argument, which focuses on the proportion of citizens included in the traditional institution in which official leaders are integrated, has important parallels to our emphasis on traditional leaders being embedded in their broader communities if they are to play a positive role. It also emphasizes the importance of geographic overlap between traditional and formal spheres of influence, a point we return to later. Thus, variation in the characteristics of traditional institutions, and especially their downward accountability, is critical in understanding why traditional leaders sometimes improve and sometimes harm government performance.

Explaining Variation in Traditional Leaders' Effects on Government Performance

Our divergent findings can largely be explained by two factors, where the first factor is whether the incentives of the traditional leaders are aligned with those of their constituents, or, in other words, whether they are downwardly accountable. As argued earlier in this chapter, downward accountability is shaped by the competitiveness of the selection process and by the degree of social and economic embeddedness. The second factor is whether the

---

[12] And/or communities are able to select a better traditional leader when picking from a larger pool.

government's interests are aligned with those of its citizens. Note that this may vary from context to context – a given state may act in the interest of citizens in some instances or at some levels of decentralization, but not in others.

In cases where traditional leaders are downwardly accountable and the state seeks to deliver services, traditional leaders can play an important role in coproducing public goods and services, as described in the cases of Ghana (Schultz, Wibbels, and Huntington, 2015), Zambia (Baldwin, 2016b), and local officials in China (Xu and Yao, 2015). In instances where traditional leaders are downwardly accountable and the state's development goals directly conflict with those of its citizens, strong traditional leaders can serve as checks and balances, as was observed in the case of land reforms in Senegal (Honig, 2015). If, however, traditional leaders are not downwardly accountable and the state is predatory, traditional leaders are likely to collude with the state, as Mattingly (2016) found in China. Finally, if traditional leaders are not downwardly accountable and a state is seeking to deliver goods and services, traditional leaders may at best be irrelevant to governance but at worst harm it, as appears to be the case of paramount chiefs in Sierra Leone (Clayton, Noveck, and Levi, 2015), who are able to impede service delivery by the local government.

Effects of Traditional Chiefs on Democratic Norms and Electoral Accountability

What is the role of traditional chiefs in elections and democratic development in general? One area of contention is whether the existence of traditional chiefs, and customary institutions more broadly, furthers or harms democratic *attitudes, norms, and rights*. Some scholars maintain that because traditional leaders are not elected, their existence fosters undemocratic norms. (Beall, Mkhize, and Vawda, 2005; Mamdani, 1996).

Recent empirical work questions this assessment. In Afghanistan, Murtazashvili (2016) finds that customary institutions are associated with more *positive* views of democratic governance. Using data from two nationwide surveys, she finds that in communities where customary councils (*shuras*) are stronger, citizens are more likely to think that their vote is influential, to tolerate opposing parties, to believe that opposition is good for Afghanistan, and to support women's rights. Similarly, analyzing nationally representative data[13] from nineteen African countries, Logan (2009, 2013) finds that respondents who view traditional leaders positively tend to have a more positive attitude toward their elected leaders as well. The perception index includes measures of trustworthiness, interest, and involvement in corruption. She concludes that African citizens view traditional and elected leaders as part of an integrated system. Logan (2013) does not find any

---

[13] Rounds 1, 2, and 4 of the Afrobarometer.

relationship between support for traditional leaders and commitment to democracy.

A particular area of concern for many donor agencies is the influence of traditional leaders on attitudes toward women. Most traditional leaders are male, and they are often accused of bias against women in their decision making. However, the empirical evidence on the effect of traditional leaders on women's rights is also ambiguous. Clayton (2014) uses randomized quotas for female councilors in Lesotho to show that the political influence of traditional leaders may be at odds with the political influence of women; in places with quota-mandated female councilors, respondents perceive traditional leaders as having reduced influence. Similarly, Beath, Christia, and Enikolopov (2013b) find that the displacement of traditional governance structures with gender-inclusive village development committees in randomly selected villages in Afghanistan results in improved attitudes toward women's political participation. Yet it is not clear that weaker traditional institutions would by themselves advance women's rights, or, conversely, that stronger traditional institutions necessarily harm them; in fact, Murtazashvili (2016) finds that in Afghani villages where traditional *shuras* are strong, citizens are more likely to express support for women's rights.

A second area of contention is whether the existence of strong chiefs hampers or helps communities in holding their elected leaders to account. Two different narratives have been presented in the academic literature. One casts chiefs as clientelistic vote brokers, who deliver votes to the candidate who gives them the highest personal benefits, with negative implications for development. The other casts them as representatives of their constituents' interests who mobilize votes in return for future service delivery, or "development brokers," with positive consequences for development (Baldwin, 2016b). Gottlieb (2017) makes a similar distinction when she argues that brokers might lead to coordination on leader-preferred outcomes (negative) or voter-preferred outcomes (positive).

Baldwin (2013, 2016b) provides evidence that chiefs in Africa have limited ability to deliver votes to candidates that citizens do not genuinely prefer. Instead, she argues that – to the extent that chiefs are able to mobilize votes for candidates that the chiefs prefer – it is a function of their recognized role as "development brokers." Communities on average receive more public goods in cases where their chiefs have stronger relationships to elected officials. When voters recognize this, they have incentives to vote with their chiefs to ensure they elect the candidate who will perform best in providing access to public goods once in office. She provides evidence from a survey experiment in Zambia that shows the types of respondents who are most influenced by finding out their chiefs' true opinions of candidates are respondents who recognize the role of chiefs as "development brokers," not respondents who are motivated by concerns about punishment or other mechanisms that could underlie clientelistic brokering. Similarly, Schultz, Wibbels, and Huntington (2015) find that in Ghana, stronger chiefs are associated with better service delivery and less vote-buying and clientelism, as discussed in greater detail in the previous section.

Koter (2013) examines the role of traditional leaders in building cross-ethnic allegiances during elections in Senegal and Benin. She argues that the relatively strong traditional leaders in Senegal facilitate voting across ethnic lines, while the absence of strong traditional leaders in Benin leads to the predominance of ethnic bloc voting. Relying on strong local leaders to mobilize votes enables politicians to make appeals across ethnic lines instead of making ethnic appeals, thus reducing ethnic bloc voting and ultimately increasing political competition. Traditional leaders exchange vote mobilization against service delivery for their communities and (at times) personal benefits. Both sides to the bargain – politicians and traditional leaders – seek the best potential partner to close a deal in the market of votes against services and/or material benefits. Drawing on case studies in Benin and Senegal, Koter argues that the collaboration between politicians and traditional leaders is not constrained by ethnicity, since both sides have an incentive to grow their pool of potential partners.

On the other hand, De Kadt and Larreguy (2017) find that some South African traditional chiefs act as clientelistic vote brokers for co-ethnic politicians, with adverse effects on electoral accountability. Using two sources of arguably exogenous variation, the borders of the Bantustan homelands where traditional chiefs wield a lot of influence and a one-time switch in the ethnicity of the ANC president from Xhosa to Zulu, the authors argue the chiefs will engage in a quid pro quo with elected leaders if they are ethnically aligned. The legal status of these chiefs is fragile and their income is largely dependent on the state. In return for continued tenure and personal rents, they deliver votes. De Kadt and Larreguy find that the support of chiefs increases the ANC vote share in the Bantustans by 8.2 percentage points and significantly influences the distribution of seats in the national parliament. The authors provide suggestive evidence that the underlying mechanism is vote-buying and intimidation, rather than service delivery.

A related question, but with a different outcome variable, is whether the involvement of different types of traditional leaders results in more or less alignment on elite-preferred (versus voter-preferred) outcomes. Taking advantage of variation with regard to the degree of (i) competitive selection and (ii) autonomy of traditional leaders from the community across societies in Senegal, Gottlieb (2017) designed and conducted behavioral games to assess how these factors affect strategic interactions between voters and traditional leaders. She finds that voters are more likely to follow their traditional leaders if they are relatively independent from the community even when it implies personal sacrifices. A manipulation in the confidentiality of the games suggests that this finding is explained by a fear of sanctions, rather than greater legitimacy.

Taken together, these studies suggest that the degree of dependency on the formal government is important in determining the role chiefs play in elections. The legal status and rents of the traditional chiefs in Bantustans are dependent on the state, while Zambian chiefs are more dependent on their communities. Senegalese chiefs vary from group to group, a fact that's exploited in Gottlieb's (2017) subnational study. If politicians prefer clientelism to service delivery, chiefs who are dependent on the state have little leverage, regardless of their preferences. What is more, if chiefs do not depend on the community for survival, they have little incentive to bargain for service delivery instead of personal rents.

TRADITIONAL LEADERS AND DEVELOPMENT POLICY

Development practitioners working in a wide variety of sectors confront the question of how best to work with traditional leaders. Practitioners working in fields like governance, security reform, and justice have to decide at a strategic level whether engagement with traditional institutions is a programming goal (Denney, 2013). However, even practitioners working in fields that appear at first glance to have little to do with local governance – such as health care and basic infrastructure – must often make tactical decisions about how best to engage with traditional leaders (Sheely, 2013b; Vajja and White, 2018). In this section, we describe with very broad brush strokes the two most typical donor strategies toward traditional leaders – strategies of exclusion and disempowerment versus strategies of recognition and reform. We try to synthesize the lessons learned from policy evaluations of both types of strategies with the findings from our review of the academic literature.

Strategy 1: Exclusion and Disempowerment

Historically, donors have typically chosen to exclude or ignore traditional institutions when designing development programming strategies. As Denney (2013) explains in a recent review, traditional institutions are a tricky target of engagement for aid agencies, which are bureaucratic organizations who take their own legitimacy from modern legal-rational processes and who must ultimately justify their actions to voters in liberal democracies who are uncomfortable with traditional forms of governance. The results of donors' discomfort with customary institutions were policies such as the 1975 World Bank land reform policy that recommended an abandonment of communal tenure systems (Deininger and Binswanger, 1999) and good governance programs that focused exclusively on reforms to institutions like the civil service, the formal judiciary, and the central bank (Grindle, 2004, 2007; Kelsall, 2008). Although donors have generally become more accommodating toward engaging customary institutions in recent years, in some programming areas, such as community-driven development projects, aid agencies still adopt rules that exclude traditional leaders from participating.[14]

However, policies that seek to disempower customary institutions or to exclude traditional leaders as a general rule are rarely optimal. In a best-case scenario, their blanket approach fails to take advantage of the unique mobilizational capacities of these actors in many communities. In a worst-case scenario, they may undermine the only institutions capable of providing critical public goods in a particular setting. As the evidence presented earlier in this chapter showed, traditional leaders are often very effective in organizing communities to provide public goods. The studies reviewed in this section all focused on cases where formal state institutions were weak, but in these settings, traditional institutions often performed better than other available partners in providing local public goods. Aid programs that fail to include traditional leaders as development partners in settings where traditional leaders are socially and economically embedded in communities and alternative partners are weak are unlikely to have the maximum possible impact.

Strategy 2: Recognition and Reform

In reaction to past strategies of excluding and disempowering traditional institutions, a small but growing group within the aid community has begun to grapple with alternative modes of engaging with customary institutions. In the past decade, some development practitioners have embraced notions of "good enough governance" (Grindle, 2004, 2007) and "going with the grain" in development (Kelsall, 2008), concepts that emphasize the need to work with the de facto structures of power on the ground. In this vein, the UK's Department for International Development (DFID) sponsored its "Drivers of Change" research program in 2004, which aimed to uncover the informal and formal institutions influencing development initiatives in twenty countries. DFID followed it up with the Africa Power and Politics Programme in 2007, which was intended to study the nature of power on the African subcontinent specifically. Inevitably, these approaches pointed toward the importance of traditional leaders and customary institutions in many communities.

In tandem with this shift in perspective, some aid agencies have become more willing to sponsor governance programs intended to recognize or reform traditional institutions. Particularly in post-conflict settings, some donors have embraced the idea of supporting traditional leaders and their courts as a means of reestablishing order. An early example of a donor-sponsored program in this vein is the USAID-sponsored Decentralization/Traditional

---

[14] Personal communications with Eric Mvukiyehe, World Bank, January 4, 2016, and Sheree Bennett, IRC, December 24, 2015.

Authority (DTA) Program in Mozambique, which organized district-level workshops to gauge support for traditional authorities immediately after the end of the civil war in that country and then distributed brochures on the topic of traditional authority to government officials and made recommendations to the government regarding policy toward them (Fry, 1997). DFID supported the similar Chiefdom Governance Reform Program (CGRP) in Sierra Leone between 1999 and 2002, sponsoring public workshops in seventy-five chiefdoms to gauge support for the reestablishment of paramount chiefs, supporting elections in cases where the position of paramount chief was vacant, and facilitating the repatriation of chiefs and the construction of houses for them (Fanthorpe, 2004). Another ambitious effort has been the pilot project run by the United States Institute of Peace (USIP) in six districts in Afghanistan since 2009; this project has involved both researching the landscape of informal justice providers that exists in each district and then making proposals regarding the best way to make reforms (Dempsey and Coburn, 2010). Other aid agencies and NGOs have organized smaller-scale efforts to engage with and reform traditional institutions, especially in the judicial sector.

Both USAID's DTA program in Mozambique and DFID's CGRP in Sierra Leone were evaluated at length by consultants, and these reports indicate the minefields involved when donors engage with traditional leaders (Fanthorpe, 2004; Fry, 1997). For example, the DTA program in Mozambique was ostensibly mainly a research program; however, even just the organization of district-level consultations on the topic of traditional leaders gave many people the impression that traditional leadership – which had been formally abolished by the Mozambican government in 1978 – had been sanctioned by donors and the government. As an academic involved in the mid-term evaluation of the program wrote, some traditional authorities took the workshops themselves "as a mandate to tell their communities that they once again had authority to govern."[15] This impression was particularly unfortunate because, although the project ultimately did prepare policy documents recommending official recognition of these leaders for the Mozambican government, these recommendations were not adopted. Instead, the most lasting impact of the program appears to have been the socialization of government officials so that they accepted the idea of working with traditional authorities (Fry, 1997; West and Kloeck-Jenson, 1999). The government ultimately adopted a more flexible law that called for official recognition of traditional authorities at the discretion of the local community (Buur and Kyed, 2006).

The CGRP sponsored by DFID in Sierra Leone also illustrates the problems posed by donor recognition of specific traditional authorities. The CGRP had the goal of building houses for each of the future paramount chiefs, but, because different ruling families often lived in different towns, the

---

[15] Cited in Fry (1997, p. 6).

decision about where to build the house implicitly favored some ruling families over others (Denney, 2013). In addition, DFID was accused of political bias because, for security reasons, the program operated only in areas of the country that also happened to be historic government strongholds. Ultimately, this program was deemed a failure and was aborted in 2002 after review (Denney, 2013).

One of the main lessons that DFID appears to have taken from the failure of the CGRP in Sierra Leone is the difficulty of engaging with traditional authorities without simultaneously reforming them (Denney, 2013; Fanthorpe, 2006). But, in fact, both the evidence from the DTA and CGRP evaluations and the academic literature suggest the challenge of ensuring that donors constructively engage with traditional authorities cannot be solved by reforms from above. One critical takeaway from our review of the academic literature is that the extent to which traditional chiefs facilitate rather than hamper economic and political development is a function of their dependence on and embeddedness in their communities. Donor engagement with traditional leaders may reduce their local dependence, especially when this engagement involves the transfer of substantial resources, like the houses built with DFID's support in Sierra Leone. However, even in cases when this engagement involves little transfer of material resources, as in the case of the USAID-sponsored program in Mozambique, donor engagement may give the impression that these leaders have mandates from above and thereby reduce their local embeddedness. Thus, traditional leaders' degree of embeddedness is both an important criterion to consider when deciding whether to design programming to involve traditional leaders and a caution to donors: insofar as formal recognition of and material support to traditional governance institutions makes traditional leaders less dependent on their communities, such initiatives may very well backfire.

A Way Forward for Engaging Traditional Leaders?

Is there a way for aid practitioners to simultaneously make sure they design programs that are maximally effective by engaging with traditional leaders when they are powerful and locally embedded without undermining the linkages that exist between these leaders and their communities? In our view, this is the critical challenge for aid agencies. It requires creative and flexible program designs, but it is not an impossible needle to thread.

In one promising example, the International Rescue Committee (IRC) tested an innovative approach to reforming village-level traditional institutions in eastern Zimbabwe. Its goal was to make the village head's court more adherent to process, less biased, and therefore more effective in resolving conflict. The IRC was also concerned with determining the best way to make reforms without undermining the authority of village-level customary leaders. As a result, it tested two variants of its program in a randomized control trial.

In the first variant of the program, the village heads were engaged in classic "capacity-building" workshops run by the donor in conjunction with local NGOs and the government; donors frequently use this approach when engaging with traditional leaders, but – in a worst-case scenario – it could be not just ineffective but detrimental to the perceived local embeddedness of these leaders. In the second variant of the program, both the village head and a second community leader were included in the workshop, with the hope that the second leader would help mediate the effect of the workshop on the village head's behavior. In this way, it was hoped that any change in behavior would be locally enforced and the village head would become more, not less, beholden to community pressures. Indeed, the results of the program evaluation suggest that only the second variant was effective in changing the behavior of the village head, and this variant also resulted in village heads who were viewed as more locally legitimate (Baldwin, Muyengwa, and Mvukiyehe, 2016).

Thus, constructive engagement with traditional leaders is possible. Development practitioners deciding on the degree to which to integrate and engage with traditional leaders should therefore ask themselves two series of questions: First, to what degree are the traditional leaders accountable to their communities? And are they likely more or less accountable than the alternative partners who would be engaged in the program? Second, will the involvement of traditional leaders in the program make them less embedded in, and thus less accountable to, their communities? If this is a concern, are there ways to design the program so that it increases rather than decreases the embeddedness of traditional leaders?

AREAS FOR FURTHER RESEARCH

The study of the effects of traditional leaders on service delivery and political accountability is still a developing field, as evidenced by the fact that more than one third of the citations in the references to this chapter are from the past five years. As a result, there is room for more research in a wide variety of areas. In this section, we highlight two avenues for further research that we view as particularly relevant for the aid community.

As a first priority, we recommend data collection efforts that would allow researchers and aid practitioners to better distinguish within the broad set of leaders that fall under the definition of traditional chiefs. At the moment, three large-scale data sets are available on traditional leadership, each of which has limitations. First, there are data on the types of institutions that governed regions in the precolonial era (Murdock, 1967), which is interesting in its own right but does not necessarily correspond in a predictable fashion with the types of traditional institutions that exist in these regions in the contemporary period. Second, there has been a recent effort by a team of researchers at the University Konstanz to collect data on the legal integration of traditional institutions into states' political systems in sub-Saharan Africa (Holzinger,

Kern, and Kromrey, 2013). This is also valuable information, but does not provide us with information on the de facto power of chiefs or within-country variation in the status of these leaders. Finally, the Afrobarometer survey, especially the fourth round of the survey, collected data on citizens' perceptions of traditional leaders in many countries in sub-Saharan Africa (Logan, 2009, 2013). These data begin to permit the examination of regional differences in the status of traditional leaders. However, besides existing for only nineteen African countries, they do not easily allow us to distinguish between how citizens feel about different traditional leaders; the survey questions do not distinguish between leaders at different levels of the traditional hierarchy, making it impossible to distinguish between how people feel about paramount chiefs versus village headmen, and, in most countries, we do not know how the survey lines up with the geographic boundaries of different traditional chiefdoms and territories.

We recommend additional data collection in order to better understand the lay of the land in this area. Unfortunately, for this data collection process to be valuable, it will likely be time-intensive and costly. Due to the fact that there is great variation in the extent to which traditional institutions are incorporated into the state, we see inherent limitations in working only with official data provided by the state to try to map out these institutions. Instead, both surveys of traditional leaders themselves and surveys of citizens are likely to be necessary in order to understand the variety of traditional leaders that exist in different communities, their de facto power, and the extent to which they are downwardly accountable. In particular, in order to distinguish between leaders who can act as development partners and those who cannot, we recommend including suites of questions on the methods by which these leaders are selected and internal governance structures (to get at competitiveness), but also their social ties and their sources of economic revenue (to get at embeddedness). In addition, we recommend collecting detailed data on the geographic spheres of different traditional leaders in order to be able to better map out overlap with administrative boundaries.

As a second priority, we recommend additional research on the effect of donor engagement and government intervention on how embedded traditional leaders are in their communities. As we noted in the previous section, a critical challenge for aid agencies is to figure out how to harness the potential benefits of partnering with locally embedded traditional leaders without undermining the ties that bind these leaders to their communities. Even in circumstances where it appears that governance may be better when strong traditional institutions have organically developed ties to elected political leaders and state institutions, as in Zambia and Ghana, it does not necessarily hold that donor-led or state-led efforts to increase the integration of these two sets of leaders would improve governance (Baldwin, 2016b; Schultz, Wibbels, and Huntington, 2015). Furthermore, the mere act of donor acknowledgment of traditional institutions can be enough to change the relationships of these institutions to their communities, as the cautionary example of the DTA program in Mozambique suggests (Fry, 1997).

In fact, research on whether the effects of aid agencies' efforts to engage with traditional institutions has unintended consequences for the legitimacy of traditional institutions should be relatively easy to accomplish. Although donors may naturally be primarily interested in the immediate effects of involving traditional leaders on the main outcomes of interest in their targeted sectors, whether this is infrastructure delivery, justice, security, or overall governance, in cases where the effects of incorporating traditional leaders on these outcomes are being systematically evaluated, it should be relatively cheap to also consider whether the programming influences the operation of traditional institutions. Evaluations of programs incorporating traditional leaders should measure whether the programs affect the operation of the traditional institutions with which they engage, even when this is not the explicit goal of the program.

CONCLUSION

The empirical literature on the interaction between traditional leaders and formal state institutions is a relatively recent and diverse body of work. While traditional governance institutions are a broad group, consistent data on them are still wanting, and many of the findings are context-specific, we see several consistent patterns emerge from the existing evidence.

We conclude from the studies on traditional leaders' role in the provision of decentralized public goods that traditional chiefs are often very effective in organizing local public goods that require high levels of community contributions and/or compliance. In weak states, traditional leaders play critical roles in facilitating local public goods, although they appear more effective in sectors where they have a tradition of involvement and less effective when they are asked to take on new tasks.

Our findings are more complicated regarding the effects of traditional leaders on governments' performance in providing services. The dynamics of the interaction between traditional leaders and governments vary depending on the downward accountability of the traditional leaders and the incentives of the government. The extent to which traditional leaders are locally embedded appears especially important in determining whether their role as intermediaries between citizens and the state has beneficial or harmful effects on government performance.

Finally, we reviewed the evidence on the role of traditional leaders with regard to democratic norms and electoral accountability. None of the reviewed studies finds that either the presence of or support for traditional leaders is associated with lower levels of support for democratic norms. Here again we conclude that the degree of dependency on the formal government is important in determining the role chiefs play in elections. When the legal status and livelihood of traditional chiefs depend on the state, they are likely to use their position to deliver votes in return for personal benefits. On the other hand, when chiefs are both strong and embedded into their communities, then they are likely to use their leverage as potential vote bundlers in order to negotiate for improved service delivery.

Based both on the academic literature and on a review of a number of recent policy programs, we conclude that a constructive engagement with traditional leaders is possible. Development practitioners deciding on the degree to which to engage with and integrate traditional leaders should therefore ask themselves two broad sets of questions: First, to what degree are the traditional leaders accountable to their communities (especially compared to alternative partners)? Second, will the involvement of traditional leaders in the program make them less embedded in, and thus less accountable to, their communities? By carefully considering these two factors, aid agencies can design programs that harness the benefits of partnering with traditional leaders without undermining their local legitimacy.

REFERENCES

Acemoglu, Daron, Tristan Reed, and James A. Robinson. 2014. "Chiefs: Economic Development and Elite Control of Civil Society in Sierra Leone." *Journal of Political Economy* 122(2): 319–368.

Ayittey, George. 1991. *Indigenous African Institutions*. New York, NY: Transnational Publishers.

Baldwin, Kate. 2013. "Why Vote with the Chief? Political Connections and Public Goods Provision in Zambia." *American Journal of Political Science* 57(4): 794–809.

Baldwin, Kate. 2014. "When Politicians Cede Control of Resources: Land, Chiefs, and Coalition-Building in Africa." *Comparative Politics* 46(3): 253–271.

Baldwin, Kate. 2016a. "Hereditary Rule in Democratic Africa: Reconciling Citizens and Chiefs." In *Growing Democracy in Africa: Elections, Accountable Governance and Political Economy*, ed. Muna Ndulo and Mamoudou Gazibo. New Castle upon Tyne: Cambridge Scholars Publishing.

Baldwin, Kate. 2016b. *The Paradox of Traditional Chiefs in Democratic Africa*. Cambridge University Press.

Baldwin, Kate. 2018. "Elected MPs, Traditional Chiefs, and Local Public Goods: Evidence on the Role of Leaders in Co-Production from Rural Zambia." *Comparative Political Studies*.

Baldwin, Kate, Shylock Muyengwa, and Eric Mvukiyehe. 2016. "Reforming Village-Level Governance via Horizontal Pressure? Evidence from an Experiment in Zimbabwe." Working Paper.

Baldwin, Kate and Eric Mvukiyehe. 2015. "Elections and Collective Action: Evidence from Changes in Traditional Institutions in Liberia." *World Politics* 67(4): 690–725.

Beall, Jo, Sibongiseni Mkhize, and Shahid Vawda. 2005. "Emergent Democracy and 'Resurgent' Tradition: Institutions, Chieftaincy and Transition in KwaZulu-Natal." *Journal of Southern African Studies* 31(4): 755–771.

Beath, Andrew, Fotini Christia, and Ruben Enikolopov. 2013a. "Do Elected Councils Improve Governance? Experimental Evidence on Local Institutions in Afghanistan." MIT Political Science Department Research Paper.

Beath, Andrew, Fotini Christia, and Ruben Enikolopov. 2013b. "Empowering Women through Development Aid: Evidence from a Field Experiment in Afghanistan." *American Political Science Review* 107(3): 540–557.

Boone, Catherine. 2003. *Political Topographies of the African State: Territorial Authority and Institutional Choice*. Cambridge: Cambridge University Press.

Buur, Lars and Helene Maria Kyed. 2006. "Contested Sources of Authority: Re-Claiming State Sovereignty by Formalizing Traditional Authority in Mozambique." *Development and Change* 37(4): 847–869.

Clayton, Amanda. 2014. "Electoral Gender Quotas and Attitudes toward Traditional Leaders: A Policy Experiment in Lesotho." *Journal of Policy Analysis and Management* 33(4): 1007–1026.

Clayton, Amanda, Jennifer Noveck, and Margaret Levi. 2015. "When Elites Meet: Decentralization, Power-Sharing, and Public Goods Provision in Post-Conflict Sierra Leone." Policy Research Working Paper; no. WPS 7335.

Corstange, Daniel. 2008. "Tribes and the Rule of Law in Yemen." *Al-Masar* 10 (1): 3–54.

Cruise O'Brien, Donal Brian. 1971. *The Mourides of Senegal: The Political and Economic Organization of an Islamic Brotherhood*. Oxford: Oxford University Press.

Dal Bó, Pedro, Andrew Foster, and Louis Putterman. 2010. "Institutions and Behavior: Experimental Evidence on the Effects of Democracy." *American Economic Review* 100(5): 2205–2229.

De Kadt, Daniel and Horacio Arbesu Larreguy. 2018. Agents of the regime? Traditional leaders and electoral politics in South Africa. *The Journal of Politics*, 80(2), pp.382–399.

Deininger, Klaus and Hans Binswanger. 1999. "The Evolution of the World Bank's Land Policy: Principles, Experience, and Future Challenges." *World Bank Research Observer* 14(2): 247–276.

Dempsey, John and Noah Coburn. 2010. "Traditional Dispute Resolution and Stability in Afghanistan." Peace Brief. Washington, DC: United States Institute of Peace.

Denney, Lisa. 2013. "Liberal Chiefs or Illiberal Development? The Challenge of Engaging Chiefs in DFID's Security Sector Reform Programme in Sierra Leone." *Development Policy Review* 31(1): 5–25.

Díaz-Cayeros, Alberto, Beatriz Magaloni, and Alexander Ruiz-Euler. 2014. "Traditional Governance, Citizen Engagement, and Local Public Goods: Evidence from Mexico." *World Development* 53: 80–93.

Englebert, Pierre. 2002. "Born-Again Buganda or the Limits of Traditional Resurgence in Africa." *Journal of Modern African Studies* 40(3): 345–368.

Fanthorpe, Richard. 2004. "Post-War Reconstruction in Rural Sierra Leone: What Political Structures May Prove Viable." Final Report for DFID Security Sector Reform Project. London: Department for International Development.

Fanthorpe, Richard. 2006. "On the Limits of Liberal Peace: Chiefs and Democratic Decentralization in Post-War Sierra Leone." *African Affairs* 105(418): 27–49.

Fry, Peter. 1997. "Final Evaluation of the Decentralization/Traditional Authority Component of the Africa-America Institute's Project 'Democratic Development in Mozambique'" (Cooperative Agreement# 656-A-00-4029-00). Maputo, Mozambique: USAID.

Giuliano, Paola and Nathan Nunn. 2013. "The Transmission of Democracy: From the Village to the Nation-State." *American Economic Review* 103(3): 86–92.

Gottlieb, Jessica. 2017. "Explaining Variation in Broker Strategies: A Lab-in-the-Field Experiment in Senegal." *Comparative Politics Studies* 50(11): 1556–1592.

Grindle, Merilee S. 2004. "Good Enough Governance: Poverty Reduction and Reform in Developing Countries." *Governance* 17(4): 525–548.

Grindle, Merilee S. 2007. "Good Enough Governance Revisited." *Development Policy Review* 25(5): 533–574.

Grossman, Guy and Delia Baldassarri. 2012. "The Impact of Elections on Cooperation: Evidence from a Lab-in-the-Field Experiment in Uganda." *American Journal of Political Science* 56(4): 964–985.

Hartman, Alexandra. 2015. "This Land Is My Land: Access to Justice and the Sacred Stakes of Land Disputes in Liberia." PhD Dissertation, Yale University.

Henley, David and Jamie S. Davidson. 2008. "In the Name of Adat: Regional Perspectives on Reform, Tradition, and Democracy in Indonesia." *Modern Asian Studies* 42(4): 815–852.

Herbst, Jeffrey. 2000. *States and Power in Africa: Comparative Lessons in Authority and Control*. Princeton, NJ: Princeton University Press.

Holzinger, Katharina, Florian Kern, and Daniela Kromrey. 2013. "Database of the Constitutions of Sub-Saharan Africa." Universitat Konstanz.

Holzinger, Katharina, Florian G. Kern, and Daniela Kromrey. 2016. "The Dualism of Contemporary Traditional Governance and the State: Institutional Setups and Political Consequences." *Political Research Quarterly* 69(3): 469–481.

Holzinger, Katharina, Roos van der Haer, Axel Bayer, Daniela Behr, and Clara Neupert-Wentz. 2018. "The Constitutionalization of Ethnic Group Rights, Customary Law, and Traditional Political Institutions." *Comparative Political Studies*.

Honig, Lauren. 2015. "Land, State-Building, and Political Authority in Senegal." Working Paper.

Jochem, Torsten, Ilia Murtazashvili, and Jennifer Murtazashvili. 2016. "Establishing Local Government in Fragile States: Experimental Evidence from Afghanistan." *World Development* 77: 293–310.

Kelsall, Tim. 2008. "Going with the Grain in African Development?" *Development Policy Review* 26(6): 627–655.

Koter, Dominika. 2013. "King Makers: Local Leaders and Ethnic Politics in Africa." *World Politics* 65(2): 187–232.

Lake, David A. and Matthew A. Baum. 2001. "The Invisible Hand of Democracy Political Control and the Provision of Public Services." *Comparative Political Studies* 34(6): 587–621.

Logan, Carolyn. 2009. "Selected Chiefs, Elected Councillors and Hybrid Democrats: Popular Perspectives on the Co-Existence of Democracy and Traditional Authority." *Journal of Modern African Studies* 47(1): 101–128.

Logan, Carolyn. 2013. "The Roots of Resilience: Exploring Popular Support for African Traditional Authorities." *African Affairs* 112(448): 353–376.

Mamdani, Mahmood. 1996. *Citizen and Subject: Contemporary Africa and the Legacy of Late Colonialism*. Princeton, NJ: Princeton University Press.

Mattingly, Daniel. 2016. Elite capture: How decentralization and informal institutions weaken property rights in China. *World Politics*, 68(3), pp.383–412.

Michalopoulos, Stelios and Elias Papaioannou. 2015. "On the Ethnic Origins of African Development: Chiefs and Precolonial Political Centralization." *Academy of Management Perspectives* 29(1): 32–71.

Murdock, George Peter. 1967. *Ethnographic Atlas*. Pittsburgh, PA: University of Pittsburgh Press.

Murtazashvili, Jennifer Brick. 2016. *Informal Order and the State in Afghanistan*. Cambridge: Cambridge University Press.

Ntsebeza, Lungisile. 2005. *Democracy Compromised: Chiefs and the Politics of the Land in South Africa*. Leiden: Brill.

Nuesiri, Emmanuel O. 2014. "The Re-Emergence of Customary Authority and Its Relation with Local Democratic Government." RFGI Working Paper.

Ranger, Terence O. 1983. "The Invention of Tradition in Colonial Africa." In *The Invention of Tradition*, ed. Terence O. Ranger and Eric J. Hobsbawm. Pp. 597–612. Cambridge: Cambridge University Press.

Sandefur, Justin and Bilal Siddiqi. 2013. "Delivering Justice to the Poor: Theory and Experimental Evidence from Liberia." Working Paper.

Schultz, Anna, Erik Wibbels, and Heather Huntington. 2015. "Clientelism, Tribes and Governance: Evidence from Ghana." Working Paper.

Sheely, Ryan. 2013a. "Maintaining Local Public Goods: Evidence from Rural Kenya." Working Paper.

Sheely, Ryan. 2013b. "Skipping the State: Ethnographic and Experimental Evidence on the Dynamics of Non-State Social Welfare Provision in Sierra Leone." Working Paper.

Stasavage, David. 2005. "Democracy and Education Spending in Africa." *American Journal of Political Science* 49(2): 343–358.

Tsai, Lily L. 2007a. *Accountability without Democracy: Solidary Groups and Public Goods Provision in Rural China*. New York, NY: Cambridge University Press.

Tsai, Lily L. 2007b. "Solidary Groups, Informal Accountability, and Local Public Goods Provision in Rural China." *American Political Science Review* 101(2): 355–372.

Turley, Ty, Maarten Voors, Erwin Bulte, Andreas Kontoleon, and John A. List. 2017. "Chief for a Day. Elite Capture and Management Performance: Evidence from a Field Experiment in Sierra Leone." Management Science.

Vajja, Anu and Howard White. 2008. Can the World Bank build social capital? The experience of social funds in Malawi and Zambia. *The Journal of Development Studies*, 44(8), pp.1145–1168.

Van Cott, Donna Lee. 2008. *Radical Democracy in the Andes*. Cambridge: Cambridge University Press.

West, Harry G. and Scott Kloeck-Jenson. 1999. "Betwixt and Between: 'Traditional Authority' and Democratic Decentralization in Post-War Mozambique." *African Affairs* 98(393): 455–484.

Xu, Yiqing and Yang Yao. 2015. "Informal Institutions, Collective Action, and Public Investment in Rural China." *American Political Science Review* 109(2): 371–391.

5

Decentralized Rule and Revenue

Jonathan A. Rodden

INTRODUCTION

The stylized advantages of fiscal decentralization have always seemed intuitive. The devolution of authority from the capital city to local public officials should create stronger performance incentives for those officials, who will be monitored by a more active, engaged, and informed population. Stronger accountability should beget more efficient service provision that better matches the preferences of local citizens.

When these advantages failed to show up after decentralization reforms were promulgated in developing countries around the world in the 1980s and 1990s, the academic literature landed on a consensus about the main culprit: the structure of revenue. The wave of fiscal decentralization at the end of the twentieth century was funded overwhelmingly by intergovernmental grants rather than increased local taxation. A central theme of what Barry Weingast (2014) has called the "second generation" of fiscal federalism research is the danger of so-called partial decentralization (Devarajan et al. 2007; Brueckner 2009). Expenditure decentralization often takes place without corresponding revenue decentralization, which can create new forms of inefficiency and rent-seeking (i.e., stealing from public funds) that are potentially no better than the prior centralized status quo. The key problem identified in this literature is that under partial decentralization, citizens are unable to hold local government officials accountable for budgetary allocations and policy outcomes (Devarajan et al. 2007).

The disadvantages of partial decentralization are perhaps as intuitive as the advantages of "pure" decentralization, and draw upon classic themes in political economy that link rule and revenue (Levi 1988). In short, the

The author wishes to thank Erik Wibbels, Eddy Malesky, Arthur Drampian, Tony Levitas, and an anonymous reviewer for helpful comments.

argument is that strong accountability and monitoring require taxation. In their classic account, North and Weingast (1989) argue that the very foundation of limited government and accountability can be traced to the need of the sovereign to raise revenues. Citizens demand accountability when they provide government with tax payments in exchange for specific collective goods. In contrast, when the government is able to fund its activities through rents from natural resources (Ross 2004; Van der Ploeg 2011), foreign aid (Moore 1998; Morrison 2009), tariffs, or other forms of "taxless finance" like bank charters or land sales (Wallis 2004), citizens face weak incentives to demand good government or to closely monitor government behavior.

This same logic clearly applies to local taxation vis-à-vis intergovernmental grants in decentralized countries. A large literature in public economics focuses on intergovernmental grants as contributors to a so-called fiscal illusion that occurs when government revenues are at least in part unobserved by voters, who develop an inaccurate perception of the true cost of providing collective goods (Buchanan and Wagner 1977). This results in the so-called flypaper effect of money sticking where it lands, whereby lump-sum grants received by local governments are used differently than revenues generated through own-source taxation (Hines and Thaler 1995; Mueller 2003). Voters are more likely to care about government inefficiency when there is "fiscal equivalence" (Olson 1969) – a clear connection between those who consume and those who pay for a service. Voters face strong incentives to monitor service provision when they understand their role in paying the bill, and may be willing to tolerate much higher levels of inefficiency and rent-seeking if intergovernmental transfers foster the perception that other people's money is being wasted (Bahl and Lin 1992; Ambrosanio and Bordignon 2006; Bird 2010).

This logic was recently formalized by Brollo et al. (2013). In their model, increased transfers allow the incumbent "more room to grab political rents without disappointing rational but imperfectly informed voters" (p. 1760). As the flow of grants increases, the electoral punishment of corruption decreases, which induces incumbents to misbehave more often. This creates a second-order effect whereby the pool of individuals entering local politics becomes increasingly dominated by those who value political payoffs. These individuals tend to be of lower quality, which in turn allows corrupt politicians to grab riches but nevertheless gain reelection.

These are compelling and intuitive theoretical claims with important policy implications around the world. The task of this chapter is to review the state of the empirical literature they have inspired. What are the facts from observational studies, and what causal claims can be supported by experimental and quasi-experimental studies?

I argue that we have learned far more about the causal impact of increased grants to local governments than about the impact of increased local taxation. I review a growing number of studies demonstrating that increases in intergovernmental grants indeed appear to be associated with a variety of disappointing outcomes. However, policymakers should address this literature with caution. In the search for causal identification, researchers have focused on discontinuities in grant formulae and exogenous increases akin to windfalls, such that the counterfactual is a smaller grant or no grant at all rather than some form of direct central government provision or local taxation. Moreover, the literature has not yet built up a firm body of knowledge about the different incentive effects of different types of grants and shared taxes, or about many potential ways of monitoring the use of grants by local governments, punishing abuse, and rewarding good performance.

Unfortunately, we know even less about the causal impact of increased local taxation on such outcomes as efficiency, accountability, monitoring, and participation. I argue that this can be explained by the simple fact that increased local taxation is often politically expedient neither for central nor for local officials. Direct and visible forms of local taxation are often extremely unpopular. As a result, controlled experiments involving variation in local taxation are rare. However, I argue that in spite of these challenges, various efforts of international lending and aid agencies to facilitate enhanced local revenue collection offer excellent learning opportunities, and these should not be wasted.

I also draw attention to a fascinating set of purely local "informal" forms of taxation that have been curiously absent from the academic literature. Experiences in countries like Kenya and Indonesia reveal that fiscal equivalence already exists without any intervention from governments or aid agencies in the form of pure local benefit taxes organized by village leaders and associations around specific projects. Much basic research remains to be done about whether and how such traditional forms of local taxation can be scaled up or implemented more broadly as solutions to the political challenges of local revenue mobilization.

In the next section, I begin by reviewing an empirical literature that has generated a number of important stylized facts about grants versus local taxation while leaving basic questions about causality unanswered. I then review a nascent literature that attempts to solve these causal inference problems by focusing on exogenous variation in intergovernmental grants. Next, I discuss the challenge of causal identification in the study of local taxation. I conclude by describing the types of partnerships between governments, aid agencies, and academics that might generate a solid base of policy-relevant knowledge about the impact of revenue structure on governance.

THE PERILS OF PARTIAL DECENTRALIZATION: OBSERVATIONAL STUDIES

Intergovernmental grants are commonly viewed as unearned "windfalls" that weaken the incentives and ability of local citizens to monitor local officials.

Insofar as the central government is constrained in its capacity to monitor hundreds or thousands of lower-level governments, uninformed or indifferent citizens allow for considerable "agency slack" (Perrson and Tabellini 2000): local officials not only exert little effort but, even worse, also exploit opportunities for theft and other forms of corruption. Thus transfer-dependent local governments are viewed through the same lens as central governments that rely on natural resource rents or foreign aid rather than local taxation (Brollo et al. 2013). As in the literature on natural resources and foreign aid, this logic informs a number of observational empirical studies in which reliance on external finance appears to correlate with a number of undesirable outcomes.

Perhaps the starting point for this literature was a series of empirical studies in the United States in the early 1970s (Inman 1971; Gramlich 1977; Fisher 1982). State and local governments in the United States have financed a range of government activities through autonomous local taxation since the seventeenth century, and a central government with substantial tax power to rival the states and municipalities only emerged in the middle of the twentieth century, after the Great Depression and two world wars. When the central government started layering intergovernmental grants on top of existing local taxation late in the twentieth century, state and local governments were already spending around five cents of every dollar of locally generated income on government goods and services. Economists noticed that for every dollar of intergovernmental grants received, state and local governments were spending far more than five cents – in fact, more than fifty cents, and, in many studies, the entire dollar – in the public sector rather than distributing the external "windfall" income to citizens via lower taxes.

A variety of explanations have been offered, including econometric misspecification (more on this later in this chapter), stories about the costs of distortionary taxation (Hamilton 1986; Vegh and Vuletin 2010; Aragon 2013; Dahlby and Ferede 2016), and a story where citizens engage in a kind of "mental accounting" in which grants are not viewed as fungible (Hines and Thaler 1995). A popular interpretation emerged in the late 1970s and early 1980s from the nascent "Leviathan" view of government. While local tax revenues in the context of mobile capital and mobile voters represent a hard-earned social contract between voters and local governments and hence reflect voters' willingness to pay for public goods, grants represent something altogether different: a free pass for potentially rapacious local bureaucrats and elected officials to pursue their own ends absent careful scrutiny from voters (Brennan and Buchanan 1980; Filimon, Romer, and Rosenthal 1982).

Whether it was accurate or not, this interpretation of intergovernmental grants emerged in the United States – the country that, along with Switzerland and Canada, had the most fiscally autonomous local governments in the world at the end of the twentieth century (Rodden 2006). This view of intergovernmental grants soon had far more resonance, however, in countries like Argentina,

Mexico, India, and Russia, where local tax autonomy had long ago given way to centralized tax systems, and in many of the newly decentralizing African countries, where strong systems of local tax collection were destroyed in the twentieth century or were never built. In these contexts, the problem was not that an increase in intergovernmental grants as part of a decentralization program started to fray preexisting local links between taxes and benefits, but that they obviated any incentives to build such links in the first place. Regional and local officials presided over opaque funds that arrived through complex and nontransparent transfer systems, providing citizens with neither the information nor the incentives to monitor and punish abuse.

Even when local officials had the legal authority and capacity to raise additional revenues to produce potentially valuable public goods, transfer-dependent governments faced weak incentives to pay the political costs of extracting revenue from their citizens. Zhuravskaya (2000) demonstrates this problem using panel data from Russian city budgets. Singh and Srinivasan (2006) provide a related analysis of Indian states. The role of transfers in undermining incentives for local tax collection in Mexico is examined by Díaz-Cayeros (1997), Careaga and Weingast (2003), and Raich (2004).

The overarching theme in this literature is that compliance with visible and direct local taxes is always voluntary to some extent, and local governments must earn it by providing goods and services that are valued by local citizens. Unpopular taxes can lead to tax revolts, noncompliance, capital mobility, or electoral punishment. All of these unpleasant possibilities can be avoided by intergovernmental transfers.

Some studies go further and argue that by weakening incentives to raise revenues and breaking the tax-benefit link, intergovernmental grants subvert local officials' incentive to provide useful public goods and foster a good business environment, thus undermining economic development. Shleifer and Vishny (1998) compare the incentives of local officials in Poland and Russia, arguing that Polish local officials are more responsive to the needs of businesses than their Russian counterparts because of the need to raise revenue through local taxes. Freinkman and Plekhanov (2005) argue that transfer-dependent Russian regions impose inefficiently centralized fiscal systems on their lower-tier governments, undermining fiscal incentives for job creation and growth in the urban centers of the various regions. Desai, Freinkman, and Goldberg (2005) argue further that transfer-dependent Russian regions are more likely to shelter loss-making enterprises from market forces.

These arguments return to Ronald McKinnon's (1997) claim that transfer-dependence among the Canadian Maritime Provinces and the southern Italian Mezzogiorno has provided disincentives to innovation and adaptation by allowing regional governments to subsidize failing industries. In contrast, he argues, without similar subsidies, state and local officials in the US South were forced to develop a strategy to attract new industrial investment.

Consistent with the logic of Brollo et al. (2013), several studies demonstrate a cross-sectional correlation between transfer dependence and corruption across states and provinces within federations. For instance, Fisman and Gatti (2002) demonstrate a positive correlation between the transfer dependence of US states and the number of convictions of public employees for abuse of public office. Gervasoni (2010, 2011) analyzes Argentine provinces, showing that transfer-dependent provinces demonstrate not only higher levels of corruption but also lower levels of civic engagement, higher levels of patronage, and evidence of what he calls "subnational authoritarianism."

A related literature in (mostly) European public finance seeks to understand the sources of technical inefficiency, or "X-inefficiency" (Leibenstein 1966) among local governments. Silkman and Young (1982) examine the efficiency of the provision of school bus transportation and public libraries using cross-sectional data from the United States, and find that higher degrees of transfer dependence are associated with lower levels of technical efficiency. Related studies were undertaken by Athanassopoulos and Triantis (1998) in Greece, Balaguer-Coll et al. (2002) in Spain, De Borger and Kerstens (1996) in Belgium, Loikkanen and Susiluoto (2005) in Finland, and Kalb (2010) in Germany. In each of these studies, transfer dependence was correlated with a measure of technical inefficiency in the provision of local government services. In a study of tightly managed grants to Flemish municipalities, Geys and Moesen (2009) find a positive relationship, however.

In a recent paper using German municipalities, Geys et al. (2010) find a correlation between a broad set of indicators of voter involvement and government efficiency. This relationship appears to be strongest in the most tax-dependent municipalities, and weakest in the most transfer-dependent municipalities.

Finally, Rodden and Wibbels (2002) and Rodden (2006) argue that transfer dependence can create expectations among voters and creditors that higher-level governments will be forced to provide bailouts in the event of a subnational debt-servicing crisis. This in turn creates weak incentives for such governments to adjust to negative shocks and pursue prudent fiscal policies, leading to larger deficits and higher inflation.

GRANTS AND GOVERNANCE: IS THERE A CAUSAL RELATIONSHIP?

The facts are not attractive. In various studies, transfer dependence appears to be correlated with weak revenue mobilization, lack of effort, underdevelopment, inefficiency, corruption, patronage, and poor fiscal management. However, most of these studies are not designed to enable strong causal claims. Countries with robust and long-standing systems of local taxation might have a variety of features – e.g., the interregional distribution of income or political factors that forestalled revenue centralization – that distinguish them from countries in which local governments are largely dependent on transfers.

Likewise, transfer-dependent states, provinces, or localities inevitably have underlying qualities that differentiate them more from successful subnational entities that have built up a robust system of local taxation. For example, transfer dependence is likely to emerge in agricultural regions with a history of poverty, inequality, and dominance by prominent political families. In some cases, the subnational units themselves may have been created as part of a constitutional bargain that overrepresented sparsely populated areas dominated by elites who were expected to provide legislative votes in exchange for fiscal transfers going forward (Dragu and Rodden 2011). In some countries, existing low-income subnational entities with poor governance face incentives to subdivide in order to receive more federal grants (Grossman, Pierskalla and Dean 2017). Corrupt politicians may have a comparative advantage in attracting grants, and poor regions might choose corrupt or low-quality politicians and benefit disproportionately from a progressive interregional transfer system (Brollo et al. 2013).

In short, intergovernmental grants are not randomly assigned, and it is entirely plausible that many of the pathologies that correlate with transfer dependence predated the intergovernmental fiscal system and would still be present under a counterfactual system of pure centralization or pure revenue decentralization. That is, transfer dependence and poor governance may both be symptoms of some other underlying illness. Haber and Menaldo (2011) have made the same point about the correlation between natural resource dependence, poor governance, and low growth. Moreover, it goes without saying that foreign aid is not randomly assigned, and aid-dependent countries may experience bad governance outcomes for reasons unrelated to the corrupting influence of aid.

In order to deal with this problem, studies of intergovernmental grants have recently attempted to adopt stronger causal identification strategies by instrumenting for grants, exploiting discontinuities in grant formulas, or analyzing situations in which grants can plausibly be seen as unexpected windfalls.

Again, it is useful to start with the US literature on the flypaper effect. Bryan Knight (2002) argues that the entire empirical literature on the flypaper effect suffers from a severe endogeneity problem, since intergovernmental grants are inherent to a political process in which bargains are struck among politically motivated representatives of localities whose voters have vastly different preferences over various taxes and expenditures. As a result of this bargaining process, grants may flow to jurisdictions whose voters place great value on expenditures in a particular policy area, such that they are willing to pay high local taxes and spend all the federal funds they receive. Knight provides the example of highway spending and Boston voters during the era of the "Big

Dig." If this is common, we should not be surprised to see very large coefficients in models that regress expenditures on federal grant receipts.

Knight then tries to account for the endogeneity of intergovernmental grants by instrumenting for grants with a variable capturing the membership of a state's representative on the relevant transportation committees in Congress. This estimation strategy leads to a coefficient at odds with the typical flypaper literature, suggesting that increased grants are associated with lower state-funded highway expenditures, which Knight interprets as grants "crowding out" local taxation.

This study highlights some of the difficulties of finding instruments for grants. The instruments Knight studied appear to be weak and sometimes have the wrong sign, and subsequent work suggests that committee membership may not be a valid instrument, since representatives of places with infrastructure demands find their way onto powerful spending committees (Berry and Fowler 2016).

Rather than searching for better instruments, the literature has moved toward seeking causal inference through discontinuities in the flow of grants. Gordon (2004) exploits sharp per-pupil changes in the size of education grants associated with the release of the decennial census in the United States, and like Knight (2002), finds evidence that grants almost completely crowd out local taxation after three years. Lutz (2010) exploits a school finance reform in New Hampshire and also finds evidence that windfalls in external resources to school districts are almost completely allocated to tax reduction. Discontinuities in grant formulae have also been exploited in studies of the flypaper effect in Sweden (Dahlberg et al. 2006) and Canada (Dahlby and Ferede 2016).

The implications for citizen welfare of grants that "crowd in" or "crowd out" expenditures in decentralized fiscal systems are ambiguous. But this literature demonstrates the importance of moving beyond simple ordinary least squares (OLS) models that correlate grants with outcomes. The exploitation of discontinuities in the flow of grants is now the dominant strategy in studies that focus more directly on governance. Beginning with Litschig (2008), a series of papers exploit a population-based discontinuity in the formula for distributing grants to Brazilian municipalities that dates to the era of the military regime. This step-function in the distribution of grants allows researchers to examine municipalities just below and just above the population threshold for increased grants in a regression-discontinuity framework. Litschig and Morrison (2009) find that increased co-participation grants are associated with a higher probability that the party of the incumbent mayor is reelected. Brollo et al. (2013) find that increased co-participation transfers are associated with greater levels of corruption – as measured through random municipal audits – as well as a less-educated candidate pool and incumbents who are more likely to be reelected. Mattos, Rocha, and Arvate (2011) also exploit the discontinuity in Brazilian co-participation transfers, finding that increased transfers are associated with reduced efficiency in municipal tax collection.

Litschig and Morrison (2013) exploit the same discontinuity to ask a different set of questions about Brazilian municipalities in the late 1980s: how did additional transfers received by municipalities just over the population threshold shape spending, taxation, schooling outcomes, literacy, income, and poverty a few years later? Their results suggest that these municipalities ended up with more years of schooling per capita, higher literacy, and lower poverty rates. They do not find evidence that the additional transfers led to tax reductions. Neither do they find evidence that grants affected the efficiency of local service provision in either a positive or negative direction. Their claim is simply that more money was spent in these communities, and even accounting for potential leakage and corruption, "more financing to local governments at the margin improved education outcomes at a reasonable cost" (p. 4). They raise the interesting possibility that higher reelection rates among incumbents might be explained not by the mechanism posited by Brollo et al. (2013), but rather by citizen satisfaction with increased expenditures.

Gadenne (2015) replicates the Litschig and Morrison (2013) result and extends the analysis past the 1980s and into a larger group of municipalities. She finds that the result did not extend past the initial period: transfer increases in more recent years and in a larger group of municipalities did not have any measurable impact on education outcomes.

A related Brazilian literature focuses on a different exogenous source of variation in windfall external resources available to Brazilian subnational governments: natural resource royalties. Caselli and Michaels (2013) contrast coastal Brazilian municipalities that received windfalls from offshore oil and natural gas royalties with those that did not. They find that reported expenditures increased dramatically in all policy areas. As in the initial American "flypaper" studies and in the Brazilian grant discontinuity papers discussed earlier in this chapter, the windfall resources appear not to have been used to fund tax cuts. However, in spite of massive increases in reported expenditures, Caselli and Michaels (2013) found extremely limited or no improvements in the supply or quality of housing, educational and health inputs, road quality, or welfare receipts. They imply that a massive quantity of money has gone missing, likely into the pockets of public officials.

Monteiro and Ferraz (2010) study the same royalty payments in Brazil. Consistent with Casseli and Michaels (2013), they report dramatic increases in public employment associated with the resource boom, without significant impacts on education or health. They focus in particular on the issue of electoral accountability. In the short term, they find that the increase in funds and public employment is associated with an increase in the probability of reelecting incumbents, as in the regression discontinuity papers cited earlier in this chapter. However, they also discover that this effect is short-lived, and as public employment continues to increase without noticeable improvements in citizen welfare, incumbents actually fare worse than those in municipalities that did not receive windfalls. This "punishment" effect was especially pronounced in municipalities with strong local newspapers, radio stations, and television stations that might reveal information about misuse of resource royalties.

The "missing money" discovered in these Brazilian studies is a serious problem, and it calls for a different research approach that goes beyond reliance on official statistics. Published statistics might tell us that grants were received and that every *peso* or *real* was spent, when even a rudimentary effort to check up on the expenditures reveals that the money never reached its intended target. Recent efforts to carefully track intergovernmental grants in developing countries have led to alarming findings. In a classic paper, Reinikka and Svensson (2004) use a survey of primary schools in Uganda to show that only a tiny fraction of education grants reached the schools for which they were earmarked, and the majority of schools received nothing at all. The resources were simply captured by local elected and appointed officials. Moreover, they discover that the actual final allocation of grants is highly regressive, since only the parents in relatively wealthy communities are able to claw back some resources from rapacious officials. Very large estimates of theft were also obtained in studies of an antipoverty program (Olken 2006) and road construction (Olken 2007) in Indonesia.

In sum, recent improvements in causal identification and measurement have done little to improve the picture that emerged from earlier observational studies. This literature is still in its infancy and has been dominated by studies of Brazil – a middle-income country with an unusually decentralized public sector and a reputation for corruption. However, thus far it appears that exogenous increases in grants are associated with inefficiency and corruption, while the implications for electoral accountability are less clear.

There are several reasons to be careful, however, about drawing policy implications from the current literature. We are simply learning that in some developing-country contexts, exogenous windfalls appear to be misused or transformed into private income in the pockets of elites. In some other contexts with vigilant taxpayers and strong accountability mechanisms – like US school districts – such windfalls might simply be transformed into more equitable private income through tax cuts.

Unfortunately, by focusing on exogenous windfalls, we may have sacrificed some of our ability to answer the questions that are most important to policymakers. The current approach is to examine the effect of an additional dollar of grant money that falls from the sky into the hands of a municipal official who is responsible for the provision of a public good like education. We learn, essentially, that more money leads to more governance problems, but perhaps also some improvements in education. The implicit alternative in these studies is a world in which that money did not fall from the sky.

However, the relevant scenario of interest to USAID, the World Bank, or a government contemplating a decentralization reform might be one in which that same dollar never went to a municipal official at all, but was spent instead by the central government's education bureaucracy. In this scenario, some education would be purchased at the cost of some theft and corruption. We would like to be able to compare the educational results and theft under these two alternative scenarios. Existing studies put us in a very poor position to estimate those quantities.

Moreover, before making blanket determinations about the dangers of intergovernmental grants, we need to invest in learning far more about the incentives and capabilities of central governments to plug holes in the leaking pipes that lead to local expenditures via intergovernmental grants. Perhaps Brazilian natural resource payoffs are a very different scenario than grants raised by the central government through politically costly taxation. When central governments have the will and the administrative capacity to implement serious audits of local recipients of intergovernmental grants, backed by a high-functioning and apolitical judiciary, evidence from Brazil (Ferraz and Finan 2008) and Indonesia (Olken 2007) suggests they can have a large impact on the behavior of local governments.

As I discuss in greater detail in what follows, in much of the developing world, it is impractical to expect that grants and shared taxes will somehow be replaced by local revenue in the near future. Indeed, the same can be said about most developed countries, where wide-ranging subnational tax authority of the US variety is quite rare (see Rodden 2004; Bloechlinger and King 2006). Shared taxes and various types of transfer schemes – some involving equalization and some based on the origin principle, some lump-sum and some involving matching, some specific-purpose and some general-purpose – will continue to be the mainstay of local government finance in developing countries. A large literature in public economics has addressed some of the incentive effects of different types of intergovernmental transfers, but largely from a welfare economics perspective in which central and local governments are assumed to be benevolent and the governance problems emphasized earlier in this chapter are swept under the rug (see, e.g., Boadway and Shah 2007).

As discussed further later in this chapter, an important goal for future collaborations between development professionals and academics is to facilitate learning – in part through experimentation – about ways of structuring transfer systems, oversight and monitoring mechanisms, and rules-based systems of punishments and rewards so as to reduce the incentive problems associated with intergovernmental transfers. Many developing countries have been moving in the direction of stabilized, rule-based transfer systems. These reforms often involve conditionality and mechanisms that, in theory, facilitate monitoring by higher-level governments. An important goal for future collaborative studies is to explore the conditions under which such mechanisms generate greater hierarchical accountability. Under what conditions do higher-level governments abide by the rules for the distribution of transfers? To what extent do lower-level governments abide by the conditions established by higher-level governments? When and where do higher-level governments make credible promises to punish noncompliance among lower-level governments?

DOES LOCAL TAXATION IMPROVE GOVERNANCE?

Given the theoretical literature emphasizing the governance advantages of local taxation, perhaps the most interesting policy question is not whether a dollar of tax revenue raised by the central government is spent more efficiently by a district-level official than by a central bureaucrat, but whether that same dollar would be better spent if raised directly by the district-level official in the first place. Unfortunately, the world has not been kind to researchers who would like to answer this question: plausibly exogenous increases in local taxation are rare.

In large part, this is the case because direct and visible local taxes are extremely unpopular. While the strong tax-benefit link fostered by American tax decentralization is much admired from afar, voters in US state and municipal elections are famous for their periodic tax revolts and the binding constitutional and statutory constraints they place on their elected officials. According to Cabral and Hoxby (2015), "people report disliking the property tax more than any other tax even though they simultaneously report that property tax revenue is better spent than any other tax revenue" (p. 1). Americans are not alone. Direct, visible local taxes are even less popular in much of the rest of the world, where there is no semblance of Levi's (1988) negotiated fiscal contract between the local government and local citizens.

Even when they have the statutory right or responsibility to collect property taxes or head taxes, local government officials in many poor and middle-income countries are reluctant to do so because they fear political reprisal. Everyone may come to believe that no one else is paying, and noncompliance becomes the norm. It can be extremely difficult for local officials to "provide reassurance that they will deliver promised goods and services" (Levi 1988, p. 60) when the logic of transfer dependence described by Brollo et al. (2013) has already become common knowledge to all. If local citizens already view local officials as rent-seeking thieves, new attempts to collect local taxes will be viewed as efforts to expand the pool of payoffs on the backs of local citizens and met with hostility.

Even when such taxes have considerable revenue potential and help fund valuable local public goods, local officials may face incentives not to collect them, and politically motivated higher-level officials face incentives to undermine local tax collection by denouncing local officials for collecting taxes, arbitrarily announcing tax holidays, or unilaterally abolishing the taxes. For example, President Museveni did all three with the controversial Ugandan graduated tax, ultimately abolishing the main source of local revenue – and the only direct and broad-based tax in the country – during a heated presidential election campaign in 2005. More generally, a number of developing countries had rather well-developed local revenue mobilization capacity during the colonial era, but it has slipped away after independence.

Local tax collection is quite difficult, and poor revenue mobilization has many causes other than local administrative capacity. The ubiquity of hostility to local taxation indicates that researchers must be very careful when making causal claims about the benefits of local taxation using cross-sectional or time-series data. It is likely that successful revenue mobilization is an effect rather than a cause of a high level of trust, local accountability, and efficient public goods provision. Local quasi-voluntary tax compliance is more likely to emerge in settings where local officials can credibly commit to provide desirable services.

Thus causal inference about the benefits of local taxation requires opportunities to exploit exogenous variation in taxation. Returning once again to the Brazilian municipalities, Gadenne (2017) has seized one of the best opportunities in the literature thus far. She examines the impact of participating in a program that provided subsidized loans to Brazilian municipalities to increase their tax capacity by investing in updated registers, improving skills and software, streamlining audit processes, and upgrading the means of communicating between taxpayers and governments. Causal inference is made difficult by the fact that municipalities self-select into the program, but she is able to gain leverage due to the fact that the timing of loan disbursements was out of their control. She finds that the program indeed led to impressive increases in tax collection such that the investment in capacity was well worth it.

More important, she finds that the additional tax revenues were used to increase the number of classrooms in use per capita and to raise an index of municipal school quality. Using the population-discontinuity design described earlier in this chapter, she examines the impact of additional co-participation transfers during the same period on the same variables, and finds no impact. This leads her to conclude that increased taxes stimulated greater educational improvements than did increased grants. Although her research design does not allow a direct comparison of the same sample of municipalities in which Brollo et al. (2013) found that increased grants led to substantial increases in corruption, she finds no evidence that increased taxes had an impact on any of several corruption measures. Although she does not have direct evidence of improved citizen participation or oversight, her results are consistent with the notion that taxes are used in ways that translate more directly into citizen welfare than grants due to greater citizen information or oversight.

Martinez (2016) reaches similar conclusions in a study of the effects of exogenous updates to the property tax register used by local governments in Colombia. He finds that exogenous increases in property taxation had a large positive impact on the provision of health care, water, and education services. He also examines the impact of exogenous changes in local revenue from oil royalties by relying on fluctuations in global oil prices. Like Gadenne (2017), Martinez finds that the impact of taxes on public services was far more positive than the impact of windfall revenue from royalties. Moreover, he uncovers a relationship between an increase in oil royalties and an elevated probability that local officials are found guilty of corruption.

To my knowledge, the Gadenne and Martinez papers are the only attempts to examine the impact of plausibly exogenous variation in taxation in a context that facilitates comparison with similar exogenous increases in nontax revenues. Yet these papers only hint at the possible causal mechanisms involving the information and incentives of voters. Paler (2013) uses a survey experiment in Indonesia to shed light on the mechanisms that might lie behind their findings. She primed some participants to think about local taxation by conducting an exercise in which participants paid a simulated tax and were encouraged to think about the share of locally generated taxes in the district's budget. Participants in an alternative group were primed to think of the district's resources as flowing from natural resources and intergovernmental transfers. The participants in the first group reported a greater willingness to monitor the budget, and were more likely to send postcards aimed at pressuring the district government to improve its budgetary management.

Lucy Martin (2014) has conducted a related behavioral game in Uganda. She simulates an interaction between a "citizen" and a "leader" focusing on how the latter allocates a group fund, which is explained to the respondent either as a windfall accruing to the leader or as having been derived from a tax on the endowment of the respondent. She finds that respondents are more willing to punish the leader for low allocations when the group fund was framed as a tax rather than funds from an external source.

In another paper, Dynes and Martin (2016) shed further light on possible causal mechanisms connecting taxation and accountability using surveys of public officials. They find evidence suggesting that officials believe that citizens pay more attention and demand greater accountability for local taxes than grants, and anticipate larger electoral consequences for misusing taxes, and hence take greater care to focus on citizen priorities when spending money raised through local taxation.

Jonathan Weigel (2017) focuses on the link between taxation and political engagement. He examines a randomized door-to-door tax collection campaign in the Democratic Republic of Congo, and finds that households in the treatment group were more likely to attend town hall meetings and submit suggestion cards to the government. He argues that the causal mechanism has to do with perceptions of state capacity: citizens who realize that the local government has the capacity to engage in extensive tax collection efforts update their beliefs about its capacity to affect local outcomes, which in turn alters the perceived benefits of political participation at the local level.

A RESEARCH AGENDA ON RULE AND REVENUE

While it is possible to gain insights from surveys, behavioral games, and lab-in-the-field exercises, there is no replacement for data from real-world experiences with decentralized finance. Researchers will undoubtedly find more opportunities for quasi-experiments akin to the discontinuities in transfer formulae or programs aimed at technical improvements in local revenue mobilization in the years ahead.

Even the best of these opportunities, however, leave something to be desired. First, there are often vexing challenges to causal inference, such as self-selection into local revenue mobilization programs and endogenous differential effort levels among participating governments. Second, these scenarios often do not afford researchers the opportunity to examine accountability or monitoring behavior on the part of local citizens. Third, these studies only allow us to compare a condition of more grants or more taxation with a counterfactual of less. Missing is the study in which we can directly compare a process of grant-led decentralization with one of tax-driven decentralization, or in which either of these can be compared with some form of centralization.

Further progress in the learning agenda related to decentralized public finance will involve greater experimental control borne of careful planning and productive collaboration between researchers, governments, and aid agencies. Those in a position to orchestrate such collaborations must be vigilant about identifying opportunities and bringing them to fruition. In the ideal scenario, a government has a relatively clear idea about what it hopes to achieve with a decentralization reform, and it receives external support to build an experiment into its rollout, as has been the case with some of the conditional cash transfer programs in Latin America.

Enhanced efforts at local revenue mobilization will provide especially attractive opportunities of this kind in the years ahead. Based in part on lessons like those learned from the Brazilian and Colombian programs of local tax modernization described earlier in this chapter, central governments and aid agencies are learning that even without changing laws or regulations, there is potentially great value in providing local governments with simple administrative support for things like training workers, updating and computerizing registries, and conducting outreach to taxpayers in order to enhance the mobilization of revenue from existing local sources. Since it can be difficult to introduce such programs in all municipalities at once, phased rollouts are often necessary as a practical matter.

Such programs provide ideal opportunities for researchers to help design stratified randomized rollouts in ways that maximize learning potential. Research can collect data not only on how much revenue is collected in treatment and control communities but also on how additional taxation affects the quality and quantity of local expenditures, theft, indicators of rent-seeking and corruption, and, above all, citizen efforts at oversight, monitoring, and political participation. In addition to technical enhancements to the mobilization of existing revenue sources, one can also imagine opportunities to pursue phased rollouts of new or revived local taxes. For example, there is frequent discussion in Uganda about bringing back the graduated tax. When such reforms are contemplated in countries where strong partnerships exist with aid agencies and lending institutions, advocates of the learning agenda must work hard to make the case for a careful rollout that enables a path-breaking study.

If this agenda takes off, its designers will need to give careful consideration to the context and incentive system created by each type of tax being enhanced or introduced. First, the benefits of local revenue mobilization are not entirely clear in settings, like Uganda, where the central government is expanding its efforts to directly control local government planning, budgeting, and hiring, and attempting to use local governments as agents – or perhaps even bystanders – in a process of policy implementation that is dominated by central government ministries.

Second, the causal mechanisms suggesting that taxes create incentives for greater oversight and monitoring probably only apply to those actually paying the taxes. In fact, Cabral and Hoxby (2015) suggest that the mechanism only affects those who are made aware of the fact that they are paying the taxes. However, many local taxes in the developing world have very narrow bases. For instance, local governments collect market taxes, butchering taxes, fishing landing fees, and taxes on kiosks and shop owners. Thus researchers will want to pay special attention to the effects of such taxes on the relevant local business community. One possibility is that enhanced collection of such taxes generates greater political participation and monitoring only among the relevant business owners.

When taxes have a narrow base, it might be useful to experiment with ways of enhancing the tax-benefit link by creating treatment arms in which market stall sellers, for example, are convinced that they will receive valuable public goods like regular cleaning, trash collection, or physical upgrades in exchange for some share of their tax payments.

Other types of taxes – like head taxes, hut taxes, sales taxes, or property taxes – have a broader base. As mentioned earlier in this chapter, such taxes can be unpopular, making it difficult for local tax collectors to achieve compliance. Again, it may be possible to create better compliance in treatment conditions where the tax-benefit link is clarified by a campaign that advertises the public goods that will be produced with the additional resources. Perhaps there are ways to facilitate more directly the contractual quasi-compliance scenario described by Levi (1988) in treatment conditions where some type of deliberative or participatory budget process seeks input from taxpayers on the best use for the proceeds even before the revenue mobilization drive begins. Perhaps compliance and citizen satisfaction with taxation depend upon making citizens feel like stakeholders.

In fact, exactly this type of local revenue mobilization surrounding specific, agreed-upon public goods is already quite commonplace in many rural settings outside the formal realm of taxation (Ostrom 1991). Perhaps the best-known examples are the Kenyan tradition of *harambee* and the Indonesian practice of *gotong royong*. Through these and other related practices, village-level elites mobilize contribution schemes in order to facilitate the provision of valuable local public goods. Contributions are often indexed to income, and low-income households are often expected to contribute labor rather than money. Sometimes these projects involve contributions – e.g., road repair materials or building supplies – from the local or central government that are combined with resources and labor raised through quasi-voluntary local efforts. Compliance is achieved largely through forms of local social pressure such as shaming, posting lists of names, or otherwise ostracizing non-compliers.

In many respects, these efforts quite closely resemble the ideal scenario of tax equivalence favored in the traditional public finance literature, and involve the kind of strong tax-benefit link that would seem to facilitate active monitoring and citizen engagement. Thus it is surprising that the academic literature has done so little to understand these revenue tools and how they relate to more formal types of taxation. There have been a smattering of descriptive studies of specific practices (e.g., Barkan and Holmquist 1989; Wilson 1992), and recently, an initial effort at systematic data gathering by Olken and Singhal (2011).

The research agenda on enhanced local revenue mobilization has much to learn about these efforts. Relative to grants or formal taxation, do these informal taxation mechanisms facilitate better citizen monitoring and oversight? Are *harambee* funds less likely to be stolen than grants or formal local taxes? Are these mechanisms better ways of mobilizing revenues for needed local public goods than formal local taxes, or are they second-best alternatives that only emerge in societies like Kenya where government officials are held in extremely low regard? Under what conditions are such institutions coopted by local politicians for their own interests in reelection (or theft)? Can the best features of these programs be improved or expanded? How might governments and aid agencies help make them fairer and more efficient? Can Kenyan or Indonesian practices be transplanted to other settings where more formal taxation is precluded due to lack of capacity or lack of trust? In such settings, should aid agencies consider working to facilitate informal taxation mechanisms rather than investing in building up the formal tax administration? In places where such mechanisms are already in place, what are the dangers that enhancements of formal tax administration might crowd out well-functioning existing forms of informal taxation? Is it the case that efforts to help expand informal taxation would stunt or crowd out the growth of a modern, formal tax structure? These are pressing questions in need of further observational and experimental research.

While there is much to like about a romanticized notion of local taxation and a strong tax-benefit link involving active and engaged taxpayers, it is quite plausible that the absence of local revenue mobilization in many impoverished settings reflects the fact that there is simply no tax base, or that the marginal cost of raising funds is too high. In such settings, it may very well be the case that in spite of the incentive problems and well-known instances of theft and corruption described in the many studies reviewed in this chapter, progressive intergovernmental grants or even centralized provision are still the only way to bring much-needed public goods to poor communities.

Thus an additional part of the research agenda on decentralized public finance must focus on ways to limit the corruption and theft associated with transfers. As demonstrated in Olken's (2007) research in Indonesia, there are likely many situations where independent and professional auditors are better monitors of local governments than are busy, information-constrained local citizens. In many decentralizing countries, it may be the case that enthusiasm for local revenue mobilization is misplaced, and the most important task for improved local governance is the rationalization of the intergovernmental transfer system (Levitas 2011).

The notion of enhancing local revenue mobilization is appealing, but researchers should seek to understand a complex set of trade-offs. In addition to looking out for learning opportunities related to local revenue mobilization, aid agencies and development lenders should look for opportunities to contrast such efforts with various forms of grants and direct central provision. Whenever a government is considering a change in the mechanism of intergovernmental finance in a sector like health care or education, aid partners should be poised to assist in the design of a phased rollout containing experiments. In the ideal scenario, the same public good might be funded in some randomly selected communities through centralized provision, in others by grants, and in others by some form of taxation.

In most cases, decentralization will continue to be carried out through grants and revenue-sharing schemes. A growing policy literature describes, largely through case studies, the recent efforts of central governments to replace ad hoc with rule-based transfer mechanisms, and to implement conditional transfers and monitoring mechanisms. However, we have much to learn about the conditions under which these schemes are credible and enforceable. Thus one of the most important items on the learning agenda in the years ahead will be to work with governments to assess these reforms.

This is an area in which experiments might be especially useful. New matching provisions or formulae governing the transfer of resources from the center to local governments might be carried out in different ways, or the rollout might be staggered, from one province or region to another.

CONCLUSIONS

In conclusion, the literature on local rule and revenue is still in its infancy, and is only beginning to grapple with vexing questions of causal inference. As these efforts continue, it will be important not to confuse clear causal inference with policy relevance. While the theoretical and empirical literatures provide many reasons for optimism about the benefits of enhanced local revenue mobilization, we still have much to learn about trade-offs and the necessary conditions for success. In most cases, locally generated revenues that are tightly linked to local public goods are unlikely to replace shared taxes and transfers. Thus an important goal for the research agenda is to go beyond the simple distinction between taxes and transfers, and to explore the details of different types of transfer and tax-sharing systems from a political-economy perspective that focuses on governance. Innovation and experimentation related to monitoring and auditing are especially important. Continued progress will require experiments that can only be carried out via close collaboration between researchers, aid agencies, and governments.

Unfortunately, this learning agenda presents some rather daunting challenges. The projects with the best learning potential will require a large commitment of effort and resources over a long period of time, and strong buy-in from governments. Such projects are often incompatible with short-term political incentives, not to mention the programming modalities and staffing cycles of most donor agencies. However, as governments continue to propose and implement various decentralization reforms, and donor agencies continue to provide support, it is worthwhile for academics and practitioners to keep a keen eye out for learning opportunities. Precisely because many reforms are large and expensive, it often makes sense to roll them out in a limited or staggered way, with a variety of learning opportunities built in.

Even if the vast majority of potentially illuminating academic collaborations are destined to fail for practical or political reasons, it is worthwhile to continue searching for the small share that can get off the ground. It can be frustrating for all involved to invest substantial time and resources into project evaluations that do not move forward. Only by continuing to communicate, vet projects, and explore possibilities in a collaborative fashion, however, will we locate the right mix of donors, academics, and governments to achieve success.

REFERENCES

Ambrosanio, Maria Flavia, and Massimo Bordignon, 2006. "Normative versus Positive Theories of Revenue Assignments in Federations." In Ehtisham Ahmad and Giorgio Brosio (eds.), *Handbook of Fiscal Federalism*. Cheltham: Edward Elgar, 306–338.

Aragon, Fernando. 2013. "Local Spending, Transfers, and Costly Tax Collection." *National Tax Journal* 66(2): 343–370.

Athanassopoulos, Antreas, and Konstantino Triantis. 1998. "Assessing Aggregate Cost Efficiency and the Related Policy Implications for Greek Local Municipalities." *INFOR* 36(3): 66–83.

Bahl, Roy W., and Johannes F. Linn. 1992. *Urban Public Finance in Developing Countries*. Oxford: Oxford University Press.

Balaguer-Coll, Maria, Diego Prior-Jimenez, and Jose Vela-Bargues. 2002. Efficiency and Quality in Local Government Management. The Case of Spanish Local Authorities, Universitat Autònoma de Barcelona, WP 2002/2.

Barkan, Joel, and Rank Holmquist. 1989. "Peasant-State Relations and the Social Base of Self-Help in Kenya." *World Politics* 41(3): 359–380.

Berry, Christopher, and James Fowler. 2016. "Cardinals or Clerics? Congressional Committees and the Distribution of Pork." *American Journal of Political Science* 60 (3): 692–708.

Bird, Richard. 2010. "Subnational Taxation in Developing Countries: A Review of the Literature." *Journal of International Commerce, Economics and Policy* 2(1): 139–161.

Bloechlinger, Hansjoerg, and David King. 2006. "Less Than You Thought: The Fiscal Autonomy of Sub-Central Governments." *OECD Economic Studies* 43(2): 155–188.

Boadway, Robin, and Anwar Shah. 2007. *Intergovernmental Fiscal Transfers: Principles and Practice*. Washington, DC: World Bank Publications.

Brennan, Geoffrey, and James Buchanan. 1980. *The Power to Tax: Analytic Foundations of a Fiscal Constitution*. Cambridge: Cambridge University Press.

Brollo, Fernanda, Tommaso Nannicini, Roberto Perotti, and Guido Tabellini. 2013. "The Political Resource Curse." *American Economic Review*, 103(5): 1759–1796.

Brueckner, Jan. 2009. "Partial Fiscal Decentralization." *Regional Science and Urban Economics* 39(1): 23–32.

Buchanan, James, and Richard Wagner. 1977. *Democracy in Deficit: The Political Legacy of Lord Keynes*. Indianapolis, IN: Liberty Fund.

Cabral, Marika, and Caroline Hoxby. 2015. "The Hated Property Tax: Salience, Tax Rates, and Tax Revolts." NBER Working Paper no. 18514.

Careaga, Maite, and Barry R. Weingast. 2003. "Fiscal Federalism, Good Governance, and Economic Growth in Mexico," in Dani Rodrik (ed.), *In Search of Prosperity: Analytic Narratives on Economic Growth*. Princeton, NJ: Princeton University Press.

Caselli, Francesco, and Guy Michaels. 2013. "Do Oil Windfalls Improve Living Standards? Evidence from Brazil." *American Economic Journal: Applied Economics* 5(1): 208–238.

Dahlberg, Matz, Eva Mörk, Jørn Rattsø, and Hanna Ågren. 2006. "Using a Discontinuous Grant Rule to Identify the Effect of Grants on Local Taxes and Spending." *Journal of Public Economics* 92(12): 2320–2335.

Dahlby, Bev, and Ergete Ferede. 2016. "The Stimulative Effects of Intergovernmental Grants and the Marginal Cost of Public Funds." *International Tax and Public Finance* 23(1): 114–139.

De Borger, Bruno, and Kristiaan Kerstens. 1996. "Cost Efficiency of Belgian Local Governments: A Comparative Analysis of FDH, DEA, and Econometric Approaches." *Regional Science and Urban Economics* 26(2): 145–170.

Desai, Raj, Lev Freinkman, and Itzhak Goldberg. 2005. "Fiscal Federalism in Rentier Regions: Evidence from Russia." *Journal of Comparative Economics* 33(4): 814–834.

Devarajan, Shantayanan, Stuti Khemani, and Shekhar Shah. 2007. "The Politics of Partial Decentralization." Unpublished paper, World Bank.

Díaz-Cayeros, Alberto. 1997. "Asignación política de recursos en el federalismo mexicano incentivos y limitaciones." *Perfiles Latinoamericanos* 6(10).

Dragu, Tiberiu, and Jonathan Rodden. 2011. "Representation and Redistribution in Federations." *Proceedings of the National Academy of Science* 108(21): 8601–8604.

Dynes, Adam, and Lucy Martin. 2016. "Revenue Sources and Electoral Accountability: Experimental Evidence from Local U.S. Policymakers." Unpublished paper, University of North Carolina, Chapel Hill.

Ferraz, Claudio, and Frederico Finan. 2008. "Exposing Corrupt Politicians: The Effects of Brazil's Publicly Released Audits on Electoral Outcomes." *Quarterly Journal of Economics* 12(2): 703–745.

Filimon, Radu, Thomas Romer, and Howard Rosenthal. 1982. "Asymmetric Information and Agenda Control." *Journal of Public Economics* 17(1): 51–70.

Fisher, Ronald. 1982. "Income and Grant Effects on Local Expenditure: The Flypaper Effect and Other Difficulties." *Journal of Urban Economics* 12: 324–345.

Fisman, Raymond, and Roberta Gatti. 2002. "Decentralization and Corruption: Evidence from U.S. Federal Transfer Programs." *Public Choice* 113(1–2): 25–35.

Freinkman, Lev, and Alexander Plekhanov. 2005. "What Determines the Extent of Fiscal Decentralization? The Russian Paradox." World Bank Policy Research Working Paper No. 3710.

Gadenne, Lucie. 2017. "Tax Me, But Spend Wisely? Sources of Public Finance and Government Accountability." *American Economic Journal: Applied Economics* 9(1): 274–314.

Gervasoni, Carlos. 2010. "Measuring Variance in Subnational Regimes: Results from an Expert-Based Operationalization of Democracy in the Argentine Provinces." *Journal of Politics in Latin America* 2(2): 13–52.

Gervasoni, Carlos. 2011. "A Rentier Theory of Subnational Regimes: Fiscal Federalism, Democracy, and Authoritarianism in the Argentine Provinces." *World Politics* 65: 302–340.

Geys, Benny, Friedrich Heinemann, and Alexander Kalb. 2010. "Voter Involvement, Fiscal Autonomy and Public Sector Efficiency: Evidence from German Municipalities." *European Journal of Political Economy* 26: 265–278.

Geys, Benny, and Wim Moesen. 2009. "Exploring Sources of Local Government Technical Inefficiency: Evidence from Flemish Municipalities." *Public Finance and Management* 9(1): 1–29.

Gordon, Nora. 2004. "Do Federal Grants Boost School Spending? Evidence from Title I." *Journal of Public Economics* 88(9–10): 1771–1792.

Gramlich, Edward. 1977. "Intergovernmental Grants: A Review of the Empirical Literature." In Wallace Oates (ed.), *The Political Economy of Fiscal Federalism.* Lexington, MA: D.C. Heath, 219–240.

Grossman, Guy, Jan Pierskalla, and Emma Boswell Dean. 2017. "Government Fragmentation and Public Goods Provision." *Journal of Politics* 79(3): 823–840.

Haber, Stephen, and Victor Menaldo. 2011. "Do Natural Resources Fuel Authoritarianism? A Reappraisal of the Resource Curse." *American Political Science Review* 105(1): 1–26.

Hamilton, Jonathan. 1986. "The Flypaper Effect and the Deadweight Loss from Taxation." *Journal of Urban Economics* 19(2): 148–155.

Hines, James R., and Richard H. Thaler. 1995. "Anomalies: The Flypaper Effect." *Journal of Economic Perspectives* 9(4): 217–226.

Inman, Robert. 1971. "Towards an Econometric Model of Local Budgeting." In *Proceedings of the 64th Annual Conference on Taxation.* Lexington, KY: National Tax Association, 699–719.

Kalb, Alexander. 2010. "The Impact of Intergovernmental Grants on Cost Efficiency: Theory and Evidence from German Municipalities." *Economic Analysis and Policy* 40 (1): 23–48.

Knight, Brian. 2002. "Endogenous Federal Grants and Crowd-Out of State Government Spending: Theory and Evidence from the Federal Highway Aid Program." *American Economic Review* 92(1): 71–92.

Leibenstein, Harvey. 1966. "Allocative Efficiency vs. 'X-Efficiency.'" *American Economic Review* 56(3): 392–415.

Levi, Margaret. 1988. *Of Rule and Revenue*. Berkeley, CA: University of California Press.

Levitas, Anthony. 2011. "Too Much of a Good Thing? Own Revenues and the Political Economy of Intergovernmental Finance Reform: The Albanian Case." Urban Institute Center on International Development and Governance Working Paper 2011-04.

Litschig, Stephan. 2008. "Three Essays on Intergovernmental Transfers and Local Public Services in Brazil." PhD dissertation. New York, NY: Columbia University.

Litschig, Stephan, and Kevin Morrison. 2013. "The Impact of Intergovernmental Transfers on Education Outcomes and Poverty Reduction." *American Economic Journal: Applied Economics* 5(4): 206–240.

Loikkanen, Heikki, and Ilkka Susiluoto. 2005. "Cost Efficiency of Finnish Municipalities in Basic Service Provision 1994–2002." Paper presented at the 45th Congress of the European Regional Science Association, Amsterdam, the Netherlands.

Lutz, Byron. 2010. "Taxation with Representation: Intergovernmental Grants in a Plebiscite Democracy." *Review of Economics and Statistics* 92(2): 316–332.

Martin, Lucy. 2014. "Taxation, Loss Aversion, and Accountability: Theory and Experimental Evidence for Taxation's Effect on Citizen Behavior." Unpublished paper, Innovations for Poverty Action.

Martinez, Luis. 2016. "Sources of Revenue and Government Performance: Evidence from Colombia." Unpublished paper, London School of Economics and Political Science.

Mattos, Enlinson, Rabiana Rocha, and Paulo Arvate. 2011. "Flypaper Effect Revisited: Evidence for Tax Collection Efficiency in Brazilian Municipalities." *Estudos Económicos* 41(2).

McKinnon, Ronald I. 1997. "Market-Preserving Fiscal Federalism in the American Monetary Union." In Mario I. Blejer and Teresa Ter-Minassian (eds.), *Macroeconomic Dimensions of Public Finance*. New York, NY: Routledge, 73–93.

Monteiro, Joana and Claudio Ferraz. 2010. "Does Oil Make Leaders Unaccountable? Evidence from Brazil's Offshore Oil Boom." Unpublished paper, PUC-Rio.

Moore, Mick. 1998. "Death without Taxes: Democracy, State Capacity, and Aid Dependence in the Fourth World." In Mark Robinson and Gordon White (eds.), *The Democratic Developmental State*. New York, NY: Oxford University Press, 50–67.

Morrison, Kevin. 2009. "Oil, Nontax Revenue, and the Redistributional Foundations of Regime Stability." *International Organization* 63: 107–138.

Mueller, Dennis. 2003. *Public Choice III*. Cambridge: Cambridge University Press.

North, Douglas, and Barry Weingast. 1989. "Constitutions and Commitment: The Evolution of Institutions Governing Public Choice in 17th Century England." *Journal of Economic History* 49(4): 803–832.

Olken, Benjamin. 2006. "Corruption and the Costs of Redistribution: Micro Evidence from Indonesia." *Journal of Public Economics* 90(4–5): 853–870.

Olken, Benjamin. 2007. "Monitoring Corruption: Evidence from a Field Experiment in Indonesia." *Journal of Political Economy* 115(2): 200–249.

Olken, Benjamin, and Monica Singhal. 2011. "Informal Taxation." *American Economic Journal: Applied Economics* 3: 128.

Olson, Mancur. 1969. "The Principle of Fiscal Equivalence: The Distribution of Responsibilities among Different Levels of Government." *American Economic Review* 59(10): 479–487.

Ostrom, Elinor. 1991. *Governing the Commons: The Evolution of Institutions for Collective Action*. Cambridge: Cambridge University Press.

Paler, Laura. 2013. "Keeping the Public Purse: An Experiment in Windfalls, Taxes, and the Incentives to Restrain Government." *American Political Science Review* 107(4): 706–725.

Persson, Torsten, and Guido Tabellini. 2000. *Political Economics: Explaining Economic Policy*. Cambridge, MA: MIT Press.

Pöschl, Caroline, and Barry Weingast. "The Fiscal Interest Approach: The Design of Tax and Transfer Systems," In Jean-Paul Faguet and Caroline Pöschle, eds. *Is Decentralization Good for Development? Perspectives from Academics and Policy Makers*. Oxford: Oxford University Press.

Raich Portman, Uri. 2004. "Impacto de la descentralización del gasto en los municipios mexicanos." CIDE, División de Economía, Documento de trabajo No. 281.

Reinikka, Ritva, and Jakob Svensson. 2004. "Local Capture: Evidence from a Central Government Transfer Program in Uganda." *Quarterly Journal of Economics* 119(2): 679–705.

Rodden, Jonathan. 2004. "Comparative Federalism and Decentralization: On Meaning and Measurement." *Comparative Politics* 36(4): 481–500.

Rodden, Jonathan. 2006. *Hamilton's Paradox: The Promise and Peril of Fiscal Federalism*. Cambridge: Cambridge University Press.

Rodden, Jonathan, and Erik Wibbels. 2002. "Beyond the Fiction of Federalism: Macroeconomic Management in Multi-Tiered Systems." *World Politics* 54(4): 494–531.

Ross, Michael. 2004. "Does Taxation Lead to Representation?" *British Journal of Political Science* 34: 229–249.

Shleifer, Andrei, and Robert W. Vishny. 1998. *The Grabbing Hand: Government Pathologies and Their Cures*. Cambridge, MA: Harvard University Press.

Silkman, Richard, and Dennis Young. 1982. "X-Efficiency and State Formula Grants." *National Tax Journal* 35(3): 383–397.

Singh, Nirvikar, and T. N. Srinivasan. 2006. "Federalism and Economic Development in India: An Assessment." SSRN: http://ssrn.com/abstract=950309.

Van der Ploeg, Frederick. 2011. "Nature Resources: Curse or Blessing?" *Journal of Economic Literature* 49(2): 366–420.

Végh, Carlos, and Guillermo Vuletin. 2016. "Unsticking the Flypaper Effect Using Distortionary Taxation." NBER Working Paper No. 22304.

Wallis, John Joseph. 2004. "Constitutions, Corporations, and Corruption: American States and Constitutional Change, 1842–1852." NBER Working Paper 10451.

Weigel, Jonathan. 2017. "Building State and Citizen: How Tax Collection in Congo Engenders Citizen Engagement with the State." Unpublished paper, London School of Economics.

Weingast, Barry. 2014. "Second Generation Fiscal Federalism: Political Aspects of Decentralization and Economic Development." *World Development* 53: 14–25.

Wilson, L. S. 1992. "The Harambee Movement and Efficient Public Good Provision in Kenya." *Journal of Public Economics* 48: 1–19.

Zhuravskaya, Ekaterina. 2000. "Incentives to Provide Local Public Goods: Fiscal Federalism, Russian Style." *Journal of Public Economics* 76(3): 337–368.

6

The Proliferation of Decentralized Governing Units

Jan H. Pierskalla

INTRODUCTION

Decentralization reforms have swept through the developing world over the past three decades (Bardhan 2002). While much academic and policy attention has been paid to the determinants and consequences of decentralization reforms – i.e., the allocation of rights and responsibilities across vertical tiers of government – another, related process has unfolded in relative obscurity: the proliferation of regional and local government units. Many developing countries, particularly in sub-Saharan Africa, have experienced substantial changes in the number and shape of provincial, regional, or local government units. This phenomenon of "administrative unit proliferation" (Grossman and Lewis 2014) or "government fragmentation" (Grossman et al. 2017) has, in some cases, dramatically reorganized the territorial structure of government (and, as a consequence, reshaped political processes and outcomes), yet has largely been neglected by academic researchers and policymakers. While administrative unit proliferation is often intimately tied to decentralization reforms, it poses distinct and important questions about the organization of government. In fact, understanding the determinants and consequences of government unit proliferation is merely an indirect way of asking a deeper question: what explains the territorial organization of states?

This chapter reviews emerging research that investigates how subnational government tiers are partitioned geographically, and how this affects political and economic outcomes, with a particular focus on the developing world. It spans and connects to a number of related substantive research areas,

This chapter has benefited tremendously from the valuable feedback of Alison Post, Erik Wibbels, Jonathan Rodden, Guy Grossman, Mike Keshishian, Pablo Beramendi, and other participants at the workshop "Geospatial Data, Governance and the Future of Development" at Duke University, February 4–5, 2016.

ranging from representation and electoral accountability, identity politics, regime stability, the quality of service delivery, growth, and corruption to political violence. The review identifies the commonalities and differences with existing research on political and fiscal decentralization, while summarizing the state of current theoretical and empirical research on government unit proliferation and the territorial organization of states.

The next section provides descriptive information and conceptual guidance about government unit proliferation and states' territorial organization. The following sections chart current theoretical and empirical knowledge about the determinants of the number and size of government units, and their potential consequences for outcomes like service delivery, the quality of democracy, and social conflict.

GOVERNMENT UNIT PROLIFERATION AND THE TERRITORIAL ORGANIZATION OF GOVERNMENT

Government unit proliferation[1] is the process of redrawing jurisdictional boundaries to create new government units. It almost always requires splitting up current units, and produces a larger number of smaller entities within the same vertical tier of government.

Territorial government structures allow for several tiers of government, typically including the national/central level, regional governments (e.g., states or provinces), and local and municipal governments (e.g., districts or counties). A government tier is said to exist if the executive is funded from the public budget, has the authority to administer public services, and has a territorial jurisdiction (Treisman 2002). Treisman (2002) reports that for a cross-section of 154 countries in the mid-1990s, the number of government tiers ranged from one (Singapore) to six (Cameroon, Uganda, Gabon), with an average of 3.6. Note that territorial government structures exist in highly centralized systems, where units have little to no independent authority, but also in highly decentralized or federal systems in which subnational territorial units can have substantial decision making and fiscal authority.

Traditional decentralization reforms address how political, fiscal, and other government rights and responsibilities are distributed across these vertical tiers of government. Yet this narrow interpretation neglects the larger question of the territorial organization of states. Within each tier below the top one, a specific set of self-contained, nonoverlapping territorial government units partitions the physical geography of the highest tier. The specifics of this partition are distinct from the allocation of rights and responsibilities across vertical tiers of government. Nonetheless, changes in territorial unit boundaries are intimately

---

[1] Throughout the chapter I use the terms *government unit proliferation, administrative unit proliferation*, and *government fragmentation* interchangeably, unless noted otherwise.

linked to the vertical allocation of rights and responsibilities because this structures the political process that governs potential partitions.

For example, Uganda has a multitier government structure below the national level that ranges from districts to counties, subcounties, parishes, and villages. A far-reaching decentralization reform delegated new fiscal and political authority to the district level in the 1990s (Francis and James 2003); the number of district governments increased from 39 in 1995 to 112 in 2011 (Grossman and Lewis 2014). Decentralization affected the vertical, i.e., hierarchical, allocation of rights and responsibilities, and changed the size and shape of territorial units endowed with these rights.[2] Likewise, the number of districts in Kenya increased from 47 in 1990 to 70 in 2010, only to subsequently be consolidated back to a single tier of 47 counties, while Ghana went from 65 districts in 1988 to 216 in 2012 (Ayee 2013). Since independence in 1960, Nigeria has increased the number of states from 3 to 37.[3]

This trend continues in Asia. Vietnam created a number of new provinces, raising its total from 40 in 1996 to 64 in 2003 (Malesky 2009). Likewise, in 2014, Indonesia increased the number of provinces from 26 to 34, and the number of districts from 302 to 514 (Fitrani et al. 2005; Bazzi and Gudgeon 2017).

The proliferation of government units also goes beyond the provincial or district levels. For example, Indonesia has experienced the large-scale proliferation of subdistrict units and village governments – the latter increased from roughly 68,000 in 2002 to more than 80,000 in 2013. Kenya's locations and sub-locations (administrative units below the district level) roughly doubled between 1992 and 2001 (Hassan and Sheely 2015).

Grossman et al. (2017) provide original data on the number of top-tier regional government units below the central government level from 1960 to 2012 for all developing countries. Figure 6.1 illustrates regional trends in the absolute number of government units. The top two panels illustrate the broader significance of administrative unit proliferation. Sub-Saharan Africa and the Middle East and Northern Africa have experienced an increase in the average number of regional government units, especially after 1980 and 1990. The panel showing the trend for countries in Eastern Europe and Central Asia depicts a substantial decline in the average number of regional government units, but this change is completely driven by the entry of independent nations into the data set at the end of the 1980s. After 1989, Eastern Europe and Central Asia also experienced a slight increase in the fragmentation of regional governments. In contrast, Latin America, East Asia, and South Asia have

---

[2] Noteworthy is that the extensive proliferation of districts has subsequently allowed the central government to factually reclaim control over some nominally local service provision and, furthermore, to strengthen control over district governments via the increased use of conditional fiscal transfers.

[3] Counting the federal capital territory of Abuja as a separate unit.

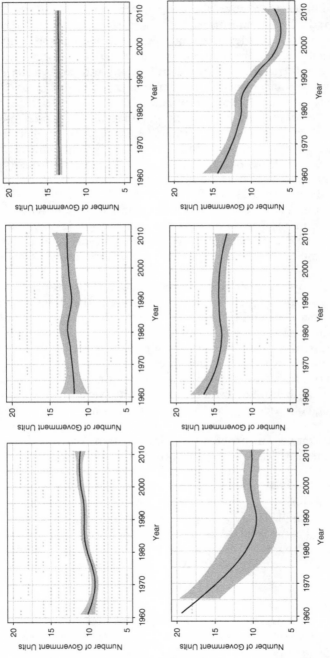

FIGURE 6.1 LOESS Fit for the Number of Government Units from 1960 to 2012

remained either fairly stable or have experienced a downward trend in the number of government units.

This countervailing trend toward fewer regional government units in some developing countries resembles patterns observed in advanced industrialized democracies. For example, the United States reduced the number of municipalities by about 90% during the twentieth century (Alesina et al. 2004). Similar reforms in Denmark, Japan, Finland, Canada, Germany, Sweden, and Switzerland have consolidated local jurisdictions (Sancton 2000; Dafflon 2012; Hansen et al. 2014). Similar to mergers and amalgamations, processes of municipal annexations around major cities have also reshaped the territorial structure of local governments both in advanced industrialized democracies and across the developing world (Austin 1999; Edwards 2008). In China, substantial urban growth around industrial centers triggered municipal annexations (Zhang and Wu 2006).

More complicated cases combine elements of government unit proliferation with a simultaneous – and at times asymmetric – reallocation of rights and responsibilities. A prominent example in the United States is the growth of special-purpose governments; this type of government proliferation mixes jurisdictional boundary changes and the functional fractionalization of government (Berry 2009). Similarly, Hooghe and Marks (2003) discuss the rise of flexible, overlapping jurisdictions in multilevel governance structures. In contrast, this chapter focuses more narrowly on the process of redrawing jurisdictional boundaries for a set of nonoverlapping territorial government units with equal rights and responsibilities.

In general, the broad descriptive patterns in the data underlying Figure 6.1 illustrate several points. First, countries differ enormously in the number of territorial units they create at each vertical tier of government. Why does Mexico, with a population of more than 120 million citizens, opt for 32 states, while Thailand (which has 67 million people) has 77 provinces? Second, changes in the number of government units over time follow a variety of patterns. Many countries enjoy strong institutional persistence: the number of territorial units hardly changes, or only changes slowly in proportion to population growth. Other countries, such as Uganda, experience administrative unit proliferation: the number of government units increases significantly in a short period of time. Then there are cases like Rwanda, which has had periods of consolidation, mirroring amalgamation processes found in many Organisation for Economic Co-operation and Development (OECD) countries. There are also plentiful cases of creeping municipal expansion and annexation around major urban centers that reshape the local territorial organization of governing units. Last, there are cases like, e.g., Libya, which exhibit patterns of instability, frequently changing the number of government tiers and the number of units within each tier.

While the drawing and redrawing of government unit boundaries is particularly relevant in the context of decentralization reforms or during periods of dramatic change, as in the case of unit proliferation, it fundamentally applies to all types of regimes. For example, even in heavily centralized regimes, where all political and fiscal authority is formally concentrated in one top tier of government and policy applies uniformly across the state, governments still often adopt bureaucratic structures that implement policies within assigned territorial jurisdictions. All types of regimes need to make decisions about the number and size of territorial administrative units. Democracies and autocracies alike structure their state apparatus into territorial jurisdictions, and we ought to develop an understanding of their underlying rationale. Here, we explore the determinants of jurisdictional size across different types of regimes.

THE DETERMINANTS OF JURISDICTIONAL SIZE

What determines the size and shape of government administrative units, and which factors can explain movements toward administrative unit proliferation?

The first question has been explicitly and implicitly debated for a long time by political philosophers and political economists. While philosophers like Aristotle, Plato, Montesquieu, or Rousseau advocated fairly small polities[4] to allow personal contact between citizens while simultaneously enabling economic self-sufficiency, more modern approaches rely heavily on the insights of the "optimal federalism" literature to provide a framework for evaluating the trade-off related to the size of subnational units or even whole nation-states (Oates 1972; Alesina and Spolaore 1997). This line of thinking produces a number of functional arguments about which factors determine the size of local political jurisdictions. More recent political science work has taken administrative unit proliferation as its starting point and introduced a number of explicitly political arguments about changes in jurisdictional size. Broadly, one can distinguish between top-down (or supply-side) and bottom-up (or demand-side) factors that generate political pressures for changes in the number of local government units. Supply-side arguments emphasize the political payoffs from reforming jurisdictional boundaries for national-level elites and leaders. Top-down reforms are driven by national leaders' desire for political survival, which makes boundary reform a tool for patronage, electoral control, or weakening local or regional opposition. Demand-side arguments stress the importance of grassroots activism of ethnic minorities in the process of administrative unit proliferation. Each approach illustrates important facets of the larger puzzle.

---

[4] Plato puts the optimal size for a polity at 5,040 (Plato 1992), whereas Robert Dahl famously suggested that the optimum size for a city was between 50,000 and 200,000 citizens (Dahl 1967).

Functional Determinants

Functional arguments are rooted in the notion that territorial government structures have important welfare implications via their effects on public goods provision, taxation, and local accountability relationships. To understand the empirical variation in the number and size of local government units, one has to understand the theoretical trade-offs inherent to potential choices about jurisdictional size. The optimal federalism literature is the most important reference point for such an analysis (Oates 1972). Although it is largely focused on understanding the welfare implications of decentralizing political and fiscal authority vertically across levels of government, a smaller subset of this scholarship also speaks to the debate about jurisdictional size (Alesina and Spolaore 1997).[5] This literature generally starts with the assumption of a welfare-maximizing benevolent ruler and tries to understand the consequences of varying the territorial size and makeup of local government units.

The core insight of this prescriptive and heavily theoretical approach contends that a trade-off between efficiency in public goods provision and preference heterogeneity governs optimal jurisdictional size (Alesina and Spolaore 1997). When evaluating the size of local governments, one has to consider the fixed costs associated with delivering public goods. Fixed costs generate scale economies, which implies that larger jurisdictions can reap greater efficiency gains than smaller ones. Larger jurisdictions can also take advantage of scale economies in procurement, leverage administrative capacity to efficiently provide services for the whole jurisdiction, and internalize externalities associated with local public goods provision. Smaller government units might lack the administrative capacity or human capital to deliver high-quality public goods and services or to adapt to economic and social shocks. Larger government units are also less likely to be captured by local elites for their own enrichment (Bardhan and Mookherjee 2006).

At the same time, increasing the size of a local jurisdiction also increases the likelihood of preference heterogeneity (thought to be driven by ethnic diversity or income differences, see Alesina et al. 2004) among the population. Providing a particular set of public goods to a more heterogeneous population can offset efficiency gains by lowering the welfare gains of individual citizens. More ethnically homogenous populations are likely to be associated with higher-quality public goods provision due to a shared preference for specific types of public goods (Alesina et al. 1999; Banerjee et al. 2005). Moreover, there seems to be a clear empirical preference for more homogenous local jurisdictions (Nelson 1992; Brasington 2003; Alesina et al. 2004; Gordon and Knight 2009). While this line of argument assumes that preference heterogeneity – e.g., in the

---

[5] Hooghe and Marks (2009) review how efficiency concerns affect the structure of multilevel government.

form of ethnic identities – is fixed, historical experiences with state and nation building suggest that identities can change or be supplanted by other identity categories.

A second advantage of smaller jurisdictions derives from informational benefits. Smaller local governments imply that locally elected leaders and local bureaucrats are better known to citizens (Hooghe and Marks 2009), which increases citizens' ability to monitor and sanction them (Tommasi and Weinschelbaum 2007). These factors may encourage the selection of better candidates for political office (Casey 2015) and more effective local accountability relationships (Grossman 2014). Administrators of smaller government units also have better knowledge of local needs and preferences, so they can tailor public goods and services more accurately.

A recent theoretical investigation by Boffa et al. (2016) combines issues of preference heterogeneity, information, and agency problems. Boffa and colleagues suggest that political centralization yields an important informational advantage: combining regions with diverse numbers of informed voters increases the average level of information, which limits rent-seeking, i.e., leaders' search for their own profits. Their analysis suggests that optimal jurisdictional boundaries should balance the desire for shared local tastes, while ensuring a diversity of information at the local level. In other words, conditional on shared tastes, when redrawing jurisdictional boundaries, planners should try to merge localities with many informed citizens with those with less-informed citizens in order to generate informational efficiency gains when redrawing jurisdictional boundaries.

Increasing the number of local jurisdictions can also generate important spillover effects. A large number of small local governments increases competition for citizens and enterprises (Oates 1972; Besley and Case 1995), ideally engendering Tiebout sorting and competition (Tiebout 1956). It also increases the chances that local experimentation with policy reform will produce policy innovations (Oates 1972). Work by Myerson (2006) suggests that increasing the number of jurisdictions also increases the talent pool for national leadership and improves the chances of selecting capable administrators. In electoral regimes, increasing the number of local governments multiplies the entry points for new political talent, which will encourage incumbent leaders at the national level to enhance their performance due to heightened competition from emerging regional leaders. In non-electoral regimes, increasing the number of local governments can be equally beneficial. If autocratic regimes depend (at least partially) on the provision of goods and services, they have an incentive to screen for talented administrators. Creating yardstick competition between self-contained political units allows them to identify highly skilled individuals and encourage them to perform well to enhance their careers (Maskin et al. 2000; Guo 2007).

Many of these mechanisms are often associated with the decentralization literature, since reassigning responsibility for public service delivery to subnational units in effect repartitions local territorial government units. Conceptual clarity is needed. Several important theoretical mechanisms – like scale economies, preference heterogeneity, local informational advantages, and competition – have more to do with the size and number of units than the specifics of the vertical allocation of political or fiscal responsibilities.

Although they do not explicitly seek to explain or predict the variation in the number and size of local jurisdictions, functional arguments have some observable implications. Most important, the trade-off between public goods efficiency and preference heterogeneity implies that countries with higher levels of ethnic homogeneity should have fewer (and larger) local jurisdictions. Similarly, countries with strong ethnic clustering and geographic segregation will have incentives to create smaller units. Regions like sub-Saharan Africa, which are heavily affected by borders drawn arbitrarily during colonial times (Alesina et al. 2011), might be particularly receptive to the promise of changes in states' territorial organization. Informational arguments about the benefits of smaller jurisdictions suggest that variables that improve information transmission ought to make small jurisdictions less advantageous. Hence, countries with a strong and vibrant media and widely available modern communication technology have to rely less on physical proximity to learn about the behavior of local administrators or the preferences of the local population, and can reap the benefits by amalgamating existing jurisdictions. To date, there have been few credible investigations of most of these implied observable implications. For example, a cross-sectional, correlational analysis of the number of jurisdictions by Gómez-Reino and Martinez-Vazquez (2013) tests a selection of these hypotheses. They find, unsurprisingly, that more populous countries have more jurisdictions, but also that democracy correlates with government fragmentation. Surprisingly, they find that higher GDP per capita and ethnic heterogeneity are associated with fewer local jurisdictions.

The clear drawback of functional arguments about jurisdictional size is the assumption that political actors in charge of decision making and institutional reform are actually concerned with citizens' welfare or overall efficiency. Similar to the literature on decentralization (Treisman 2007), more recent work by political scientists has instead focused on the explicitly political considerations driving changes in the territorial organization of states.

Supply-Side Determinants

Careful examination of the phenomenon of administrative unit proliferation has produced a number of useful theoretical arguments that take political incentives seriously. In particular, several supply-side and top-down mechanisms have been identified as important drivers in changing states' territorial organization. At their core, such arguments posit that national leaders might be interested in administrative unit proliferation as a political survival strategy. Especially in systems with a nondemocratic (or particularly powerful) executive that has the power to change administrative boundaries, creating new units might have a number of useful benefits. For one, clientelism and patronage seem to be core concerns. For example, Green (2010) argues that economic decentralization reforms in Uganda – which moved substantial fiscal resources to the district level – deprived President Museveni of traditional payoffs for the central government and forced him to generate new sources of patronage.[6]

More generally, creating new government units generates new opportunities for patronage that can be used to reward core supporters or attract the support of swing voters (Kasara 2006). Local government officers, if appointed by the national executive, can serve as powerful intermediaries who control and manage national elections at the local level. This logic of patronage suggests that increasing the number of administrative units might be correlated with electoral schedules, and may be particularly common in areas with stronger opposition parties (Hassan 2016; Grossman and Lewis 2014).

Evidence from Western Europe also suggests that local politicians are keenly aware of the political implications of jurisdictional boundary changes. Hyytinen et al. (2014) use anticipated changes in municipal boundaries to evaluate the behavior of local politicians in Finland. Municipal mergers are expected to change the electoral landscape in which local councilors operate: increasing the size of the local electoral district while limiting the number of available seats increases competition and makes local politicians vote against municipal mergers. The study reveals that the desire to avoid increased electoral competitiveness provides clear incentives to create suboptimally small jurisdictions. Apart from purely individual incentives, political congruence at the party level between merging units is another important predictor of successful amalgamations in Finland (Saarimaa and Tukiainen 2014), a finding that is replicated in the context of municipal mergers in the German state of Brandenburg (Bruns et al. 2015).

In an autocratic setting, creating new government units for patronage can be equally important for rewarding members of the ruling coalition or shoring up support (Suberu 2001). Controlling a local government unit is a valuable patronage opportunity both because it provides control over substantial fiscal resources and regulatory influence and because it represents an institutionalized form of patronage. In other words, unlike direct monetary transfers, appointing a member of the ruling coalition to a local government office gives the individual a limited form of autonomy. Similar to creating a partially autonomous legislature or a powerful ruling party, using administrative units as a patronage tool increases the credibility of the autocrat's promises.

---

[6] Ugandan members of parliament also play a role in the creation of new administrative units because the number of counties is linked to the number of electoral constituencies and hence the overall number of MPs.

Increasing the number of regional government offices also allows an autocrat to reassign and shuffle skilled and powerful administrators who could threaten his or her power (Debs 2007). In a similar vein, work on Kenya suggests that autocrats can use the proliferation of lower-level administrative units to generate legislative compliance by members of parliament (Hassan and Sheely 2015) and thus help manage ruling coalitions.

Rulers also use administrative unit proliferation as a divide-and-rule strategy. There are at least two important contexts in which pursuing such a strategy by splitting government units is useful. The first pertains to a recentralization scenario. Grossman and Lewis (2014) and Lewis (2014b) point out that Uganda's substantial increase in the number of government units should be partly interpreted as a central government effort to reclaim some of the influence it lost in the vertical decentralization of the 1990s. By increasing the number of government units, each individual unit has less bargaining power vis-à-vis the central government, and coordination across units becomes more difficult.

Indonesia's unusual decentralization reforms, which leapfrogged the provinces and endowed district governments with the most important new rights and responsibilities for service delivery, can be interpreted similarly. By avoiding direct confrontations with powerful and large provincial governments and enabling the massive proliferation of district governments, the Indonesian central government has been able to retain considerable influence and control over many aspects of the decentralization program (e.g., tax transfers) (Crouch 2010).

"Divide and rule" becomes a motivation for the proliferation of local governments in a second scenario: a credible separatist threat or regional opposition to central government rule. Walter (2009) argues that central governments often respond to separatist threats with violence because they fear the reputational effects of cascading demands for increased autonomy or independence. If a peripheral region of the country harbors deep-seated grievances (or wants to retain control over local natural resources), splitting existing government units can be a powerful strategy and an alternative to the use of violence (Griffiths 2015). The central government can, in effect, weaken the institutional coherence of a separatist movement and encourage the emergence of splinter ethnic identities by creating new and smaller government units. Hale (2004) points out that federations that feature one core ethnic region, as opposed to a dominant group divided across multiple provinces, are much less stable. The use of a divide-and-rule strategy to limit threats of separatist violence seems to have been important in Indonesia (Chauvel 2004) and Nigeria (Suberu 2001).[7]

---

[7] Similarly, Kraxberger (2004) details of Nigerian dictator Sani Abachi's strategy of using state creation to splinter opposition movements against his rule.

Finally, officials may be motivated to change administrative boundaries in order to upset the status quo (Hellman 1998). Malesky (2009) details the case of Vietnam, in which a coalition of reform-minded national legislators was able to use a form of gerrymandering to split the provinces of reform opponents into new units to disturb the existing political equilibrium.

Demand-Side Determinants

In the case of Indonesian district proliferation, there is a clear bottom-up component that is driven by local ethnic minorities' desire to attain institutional representation by creating new local governments (Fitrani et al. 2005; Pierskalla 2016). In fact, contrary to the desire of the central government executive, local elites in Indonesia forged multilevel territorial coalitions with national lawmakers and lobbyists to push proposals to create districts (and provinces) through the legislature (Kimura 2013).[8] This process was facilitated by a combination of a local desire for new government units and the political capacity to facilitate national-level coalition building (Pierskalla 2016). Locally marginalized ethnic groups' ability to create their own districts in the initial stages of this process has also helped revive local ethnic identities in other regions (Mietzner 2014).

Similarly, there has been a long-standing debate about the desire of local ethnic groups in Nigeria to redraw state boundaries to match ethno-territorial groups' settlement patterns (Akinyele 1996). The British colonial policy of creating three large administrative regions for the territory of modern-day Nigeria resulted in a particularly egregious mismatch between regional jurisdictions and local identity groups. Local groups' demands for a better match between government structures and ethnic groups, paired with a real threat of separatism, has fueled the creation of new state governments, which has not stabilized the country (Alapiki 2005).

The demand for local representation seems to be fairly ubiquitous, and is supported by additional evidence from Western Europe. For example, work by Saarimaa and Tukiainen (2016) on voting before and after municipal mergers in Finland shows that voters exhibit clear and strong preferences for local representation. Voters strategically concentrate their votes on local candidates who have a chance of winning instead of taking advantage of the larger pool of candidates available after a municipal merger.

In Uganda, supply- and demand-side mechanisms combined to create powerful incentives for government unit proliferation. Grossman and Lewis (2014) argue that President Museveni had clear political incentives to create new districts in order to increase political support for himself, but the demands of marginalized or peripheral ethnic groups were an essential component of this

---

[8] Parts of the Indonesian central government oppose excessive district proliferation, due to the considerable fiscal implications and the limited electoral gains for the office of the president.

process. Without the desire of such groups, which lacked access to public resources within existing district government structures, no advantageous bargain for Museveni would have been possible. Mawdsley (2002) offers a similar account for the creation of the states of Uttaranchal, Jharkhand, and Chhattisgarh in India. There, regional demands for better and more accountable local government combined with national-level political parties' desire to curry favor with local political elites in order to win votes in national-level elections.

Local actors may also champion administrative unit proliferation for more mundane reasons, such as fiscal incentives, personal gain, or local electoral dominance. Fiscal transfer systems might generate strong incentives for splitting or merging local jurisdictions, depending on the specifics of the fiscal transfer formula (Fitrani et al. 2005; Weese 2015). Local elites also have very strong incentives to support the splitting of government units in order to gain access to government resources (Fitrani et al. 2005). By mobilizing local ethnic identities, local elites can gain control over local or regional governments, institutionalizing access to substantial rents (Ekekwe 1986; Suberu 1991). Similarly, districts in which two equally sized ethnic groups are vying for electoral control (or where a dominant ethnic or political group is expecting future electoral decline) might be inclined to create two new, electorally safe, government units.

Summary

Functional arguments and supply- and demand-side theories offer a number of plausible mechanisms that link factors such as ethnic heterogeneity or electoral incentives to changes in states' territorial organization. While single-country studies of Uganda, Nigeria, Kenya, or Indonesia offer suggestive empirical evidence that local and national political incentives are core determinants of jurisdictional boundary changes in the developing world, there are no cross-country comparative qualitative or quantitative studies of government unit proliferation. Therefore no general comparative theory of administrative unit proliferation has yet been developed.

THE EFFECTS OF UNIT PROLIFERATION

While a small, but growing literature helps us understand the determinants of administrative unit proliferation, much less is known about its consequences. Redrawing jurisdictional boundaries is likely to dramatically affect the quality of public goods provision, local elections, and accountability relationships, as well as organized violence and local social conflict. To date, very few observational studies have explicitly addressed any of these issues.

There are two challenges to estimating the effects of jurisdictional changes. First, jurisdictional changes are not randomly assigned; they are determined via a highly political process. Hence, the splitting government units are likely to be substantially different along a number of observable and unobservable characteristics that also correlate with the outcome of interest. The second challenge pertains to the construction of useful counterfactual comparisons. Changing jurisdictional boundaries affects the structure of the original units of analysis. For example, when comparing units before and after a split, one has to decide whether to compare the originating unit to the new mother or daughter units post-split. Moreover, it is unclear whether such a comparison is particularly meaningful, since a split changes the composition of a unit. We might misattribute any observed effects to the splitting process, when they were in fact caused by a change in the demographic composition or economic structure. This illustrates that in such a research design, district splitting is a very complex compound treatment.

To avoid these challenges, researchers have at least three options. First, they can change the level of analysis to the level of government above the splitting units. For example, when evaluating the macro effects of administrative unit proliferation on, for example, growth or the quality of services provision, country-level comparisons avoid the issue of fundamental changes in the unit of analysis. Second, researchers can analyze the level of government below the one experiencing boundary changes. By analyzing subregions or individuals nested in changing jurisdictions, they can construct theoretical comparisons between micro-level units that are subject to a boundary change and comparable units in non-splitting regions. Third, they can keep the original units of analysis in their pre-split configuration and reconstruct artificial comparison units after the split by combining outcomes from the new units (see, for example, Bazzi and Gudgeon 2017).

A small set of studies has begun to unpack the effects of unit proliferation on the quality of public goods and services provision. Lewis (2017) assesses Indonesian district governments and finds that newly created governments do worse, on average, than non-splitting governments at providing basic services. This echoes earlier findings from an official government report (Decentralization Support Facility 2007), but contrasts with findings of modest improvements in the provision of some health care and education services in newly created districts (Qibthiyyah 2008; Imansyah and Martinez-Vazquez 2009). Mensah et al. (2015) document weak human resources, low fiscal capacity, and poor management in a newly created district in Ghana. In a similar vein, qualitative work on Uganda (Lewis 2014b) finds evidence that extreme administrative unit proliferation severely hampers local governments' administrative capacity. All these findings are limited by the difficulty of constructing meaningful comparisons across splitting and non-splitting units. Moreover, it is unlikely that newly created districts are immediately able to sustain or improve public services provision during the first few years.

In contrast, Grossman et al. (2017) provide the first large-scale, cross-country comparative study of the effects of administrative unit proliferation on the quality of public services. They argue that increasing the number of jurisdictions should have an inverted U-shaped effect on the quality of services provision. First, increasing the number of local or regional governments – i.e., reducing their average size – should increase the efficiency of public services provision via two mechanisms. The first is by multiplying the entry points for capable leaders and increasing the competition between local government units. Second, by splitting existing jurisdictions, new fiscal and administrative resources are allocated to peripheral regions. Given that a large share of government resources is often inefficiently concentrated in or around local administrative capitals, adding a second administrative center to serve as a new district capital reallocates government resources in a way that is likely to improve public goods provision. Yet increasing the number of government units too drastically diminishes scale economies in the provision of public goods and increases the chance that revenue will be captured by local rent-seekers. Grossman et al. (2017) test this argument using cross-national and subnational data from sub-Saharan Africa. Drawing on original data on the number of top-tier regional governments in all sub-Saharan countries from 1960 to 2012, they implement a fixed-effects panel estimation that shows clear evidence of an inverted U-shaped effect. These findings are complemented by an instrumental variable strategy that exploits changes in the number of administrative units in neighboring countries and the topographic fractionalization of the territory. They also use geo-referenced Demographic and Health Survey data from Nigeria, Malawi, and Uganda in a difference-in-differences design to show that reductions in infant mortality and maternal health occur predominantly in splinter regions as opposed to comparable non-splinter areas of the country.

A related study by Asher and Novosad (2015) uses a border regression discontinuity design to test the effects of boundary changes on economic outcomes in three new states in India. By comparing similar localities across newly drawn state lines, they are able to attribute any changes in outcomes to only the boundary change and no other observable or unobservable characteristics. They find evidence that overall economic activity, as measured by nighttime light intensity, sharply increases in the border regions of new states after the change. Using additional individual-level data, they also show that children's educational attainment dramatically increases in villages close to the border in the new states, whereas villages across the border in the old state experience no meaningful change.

While these findings point toward potential benefits associated with administrative unit proliferation, research on corruption shows more mixed findings. Nelson (2013), using cross-sectional data on the size of local governments in 94 countries, finds evidence that smaller units are associated with higher levels of perceived corruption. Mazaheri and Barber (2015) study the consequences of the division of the Indian state of Bihar. The two new states created by the split are dramatically more economically specialized than before. This exogenous shock to economic specialization is associated with a sizable reduction in education expenditures and an increase in sector subsidies. In contrast, work by Arikan (2004) on dishonest behavior in municipalities finds that smaller municipalities perform better. Fiorino et al. (2013) also find that increased government fragmentation, paired with fiscal decentralization, is associated with a reduction in perceived corruption.

Increased ethnic homogeneity may also affect the quality of public provision. From unrelated work on ethnic heterogeneity, there is ample evidence that more homogenous jurisdictions are better at providing public goods and services (e.g., Alesina et al. 1999). If administrative unit proliferation, on average, increases the homogeneity of local government jurisdictions, we might observe commensurate gains in public goods delivery. While empirical studies have demonstrated that unit proliferation does push local governments toward more homogeneity (Grossman and Lewis 2014; Pierskalla 2016), it remains unclear whether this affects the provision of public goods.

Studies on the effects of local government unit amalgamation in Western Europe have largely found that larger jurisdictions are more efficient. Blom-Hansen et al. (2014) study a Danish local government reform that merged 239 municipalities into 66 and left 32 municipalities unaffected. They find robust evidence that the reform substantially reduced the per capita administrative costs of running local governments. Hansen et al. (2014) find that this merger also improved fiscal outcomes. Similarly, Reingewertz (2012) finds that municipal mergers in Israel from 1999 to 2007 reduced average local expenditures by 9% while maintaining levels of service provision, and mergers in the German state of Brandenburg also produced substantial reductions in administrative expenditures, particularly in municipalities that were forced to merge (Blesse and Baskaran 2013). By contrast, Fritz (201.. finds that amalgamations in the German state of Baden-Württemberg red... administrative expenditures, but increased debt and general expenditu... Breuillé and Zanaj (2013) theoretically explore the effects of mergers interjurisdictional capital tax competition, and find that mergers increa... regional tax rates but decrease local tax rates.

While administrative mergers might create efficiency gains downstream, some empirical research also suggests there are substantial problems with *ex ante* free riding if jurisdictional reforms are expected. Tyrefors Hinnerich (2009) examines the effects of compulsory municipal mergers in Sweden on fiscal policy choices before their implementation.[9] He finds that local governments subject to compulsory merging have an incentive to accumulate extra debt in the anticipation of cost sharing in the future (larger) jurisdiction.

The literature on country size has theoretically and empirically investigated how the size of a polity affects the democratic process. Dahl and Tufte (1973) discuss the trade-off between citizen effectiveness and community capacity inherent to jurisdiction size. Smaller jurisdictions may improve the quality of

---

[9] Between 1969 and 1974, Sweden reduced the number of local governments from 848 to 278.

democracy by facilitating the participation of ordinary citizens, increasing trust in government and their fellow citizens, and fostering civic-mindedness, while limiting the emergence of conflicts and divisions (Dahl and Tufte 1973). As citizen effectiveness increases, though, local governments' capacity to address local demands for services declines. Also, from a rational voting perspective, smaller government units increase the chance that a given voter will be the pivotal voter, and hence should be associated with higher turnout. By making government more accessible, smaller jurisdictions might benefit from more meaningful interactions between politicians and voters (Lewis 2011). Citizens might also be empowered by their ability to "vote with their feet" (Tiebout 1956; Warren 2011), putting pressure on local politicians to serve their constituents' interests (Rogowski 1998). Less driven by increased civic-mindedness in the population, smaller government units in developing countries might also affect political participation by fostering clientelism. Clientelistic exchanges, namely vote and turnout monitoring (Kitschelt and Wilkinson 2007), are easier in smaller jurisdictions, due to the nature of face-to-face interactions between vote-brokers and clients (Remmer 2010).

Yet larger jurisdictions might also bring about substantial benefits for the democratic process (Newton 1982). Larger jurisdictions are more likely to have effective media reporting and to promote the entry of new political talent and ideas (Gerring et al. 2015). Moreover, the professionalization and regularization of the political process is more likely in larger government units. Denters et al. (2014) use survey data from Switzerland, Norway, Denmark, and the Netherlands to examine contrasting views of the effect of municipality size on local democracy, which they term the *Lilliput* versus *Brobdingnag* argument – inspired by Jonathan Swift's *Gulliver's Travels*. They find some, albeit weak, evidence that citizens in smaller municipalities report higher levels of satisfaction and contact with local government, stronger feelings of political competence, and higher local party activity. Charron et al. (2013), also using survey data from European regions across 40 countries, find no clear relationship between the size of a polity and perceptions of political representation, but they do find higher polarization in citizens' assessments in larger political units.

Other empirical work on the link between the population size of countries or local jurisdictions and political participation has generally found an inverse relationship between size and various forms of citizen participation (Oliver 2000; Weldon 2006; Remmer 2010).[10] Remmer (2010), for example, using aggregate and individual-level data from Costa Rica, finds clear evidence that political participation declines with community size. Related to size and, implicitly, the creation of smaller administrative units, more homogenous localities feature higher rates of participation (Alesina and La Ferrara 2000; Costa and Kahn 2003).

---

[10] Anckar (2008) instead finds little explanatory power of size for democracy.

In contrast, Gerring et al. (2015) analyze the competitiveness of elections across 134 countries – a total of more than 400,000 individual contests – and document a robust relationship between the size of electoral constituencies and competitiveness. This suggests that district-splitting might satisfy the demands of locally marginalized populations for more accountable government and increase local participation, but might also have the unintended side effect of generating noncompetitive local politics by reducing the number of viable contestants for political office.

Yet none of these studies explicitly examines the consequences of administrative unit proliferation. Instead, they typically compare cross-sectional differences in participation between countries or jurisdictions of different sizes. Naturally, concerns about unobserved confounding factors make it difficult to put too much stock in existing findings. Few studies assess the effects of government unit splitting or merging or exploit more credible research designs. Hansen (2015), using public opinion data on citizen satisfaction with local government, estimates the effect of municipal government amalgamation in Denmark. He finds that, on average, merging local governments has a negative (albeit moderately sized) effect on satisfaction with government. In a separate study, Hansen (2013) finds that municipal amalgamation in Denmark reduced local political trust. Size might also affect the subjective perception of political efficacy: Lassen and Serritzlew (2011) document that citizens affected by the Danish reform reported a substantial increase in feelings of political efficacy after the reform.

Jurisdictional boundary changes can also have national-level electoral consequences that upend existing political equilibria (Malesky 2009). In addition, local government reforms can affect the ability of national politicians to use lower-level administrative structures to influence elections. According to Horiuchi et al. (2015), municipal mergers in Japan severely hampered the ability of national politicians from the ruling Liberal Democratic Party to mobilize the vote and win elections. This extends prior work by Shimizu (2012), which found that municipal mergers in Japan worsened the electoral success of the ruling party in local elections. Similarly, work on Kenya by Hassan and Sheely (2015) highlights the role of local administrative units in elections.

Last, a handful of studies have investigated the links between unit proliferation and different forms of violence and separatism. Administrative unit proliferation might affect local forms of violence via various channels. Creating new, accountable local government units might address preexisting grievances and appease marginalized ethnic minorities, reducing incentives for separatist violence against the state or communal violence against neighboring ethnic groups. Similarly, by splitting regional governments into smaller units, central governments might be able to effectively divide separatist movements and increase coordination costs for those separatist groups. In effect, it may allow central governments to effectively manage separatist demands without the risk of eliciting new demands for increased autonomy (Griffiths 2015). Yet multiplying the number of local or regional governments might offer more opportunities for local elites to use government resources to mobilize separatist sentiment (Brancati 2006). It could also incite violent competition for the control of local government resources and patronage opportunities (Bazzi and Gudgeon 2017). Local groups might also use violence to signal the desire for new government units. Reports on the Indonesian province of Papua have suggested that some local violence was motivated by the desire of local groups to attain access to government resources via the process of district splitting (Nolan et al. 2014).

Few studies, qualitative or quantitative, have empirically analyzed any links between district-splitting and violence. Pierskalla and Sacks (2017) study the effects of Indonesia's decentralization reform on different forms of social conflict, including separatist violence, communal violence, and violent crime. Using high-quality district-level violent-event data from 2001 to 2012, and looking at different dimensions of the decentralization reform, they find that newly created districts report far fewer incidents of violence. This finding is limited in that it compares average levels of violence in newly created districts to the average levels of violence in all other districts. An ingenious study by Bazzi and Gudgeon (2017) provides a much better comparison by using the pre-reform set of districts to test the effects of later splits on the average number of violent events in artificially reconstructed districts. They find more mixed evidence. While on average, district-splitting does not seem to have affected levels of violence, Bazzi and Gudgeon find clear evidence that localities with the greatest increases in ethnic or religious homogeneity (as a consequence of district splitting) experience a reduction in conflict. They also find evidence of an increase in violence – especially around election time – in new government units that experience ethnic polarization. These findings suggest that district creation can have powerful effects on social conflict, but that these effects are mediated by local ethnic configurations and how ethnic groups interact with each other and the state. In contrast, Alapiki (2005) argues that state creation in Nigeria has only exacerbated interethnic and intergroup conflicts. Failed movements for state creation, motivated by earlier examples of successful campaigns, have led to substantial violence and local conflict. Similarly, conflicts over specific boundary decisions have accompanied the creation of new states.

Summary

It is surprisingly difficult to condense and synthesize the current state of knowledge about the effects of government unit proliferation. Given the disparate and small set of empirical studies, the dearth of strong research designs, and the challenges of comparing and generalizing findings from single-country studies, it is difficult to clearly identify the effects of administrative unit proliferation. While findings from the developed world, especially with regard to political participation and the efficiency of local government, are more homogenous, they are also likely to be largely irrelevant for developing countries. Evidence from Western Europe suggests that smaller local governments increase participation and citizen satisfaction with local government, yet limit the effectiveness of public goods provision. Neither finding is likely to have direct implications for the quality of government and politics in low- and middle-income countries. While smaller jurisdictions might also increase participation in developing democracies, clientelism and corruption might dramatically alter the implications for representation in small government units compared to Western Europe. Evidence from developing countries also suggests that administrative unit proliferation has the potential to both improve and deteriorate the provision of public goods and services, but we do not yet have sufficient information on the boundary conditions for each type of outcome.

THE KNOWLEDGE FRONTIER

Studying the determinants and consequences of changes in territorial government units represents an important area for future research and policy dialog. It offers the opportunity to shine new light on fundamental questions in political science, economics, and public administration research dealing with decentralization, the organization of states, local political accountability, identity politics, and the provision of public goods and services. Innovative theoretical and empirical work on the proliferation of governing units also has the potential to inform policymakers in the developing world to a substantial degree.

Successful research will have to address a number of important challenges that thus far have limited the ability of existing research to generate a coherent set of theoretical frameworks and empirical findings. These challenges relate to insufficient dialog between academic research and practitioners, the variation in institutional rules and context that generates fairly different versions of government unit proliferation, and methodological challenges that range from lack of suitable data to difficulty in identifying meaningful causal-effects estimates in the absence of experimental research designs.

First, academic researchers have produced the vast majority of the (admittedly limited) research dealing with administrative unit proliferation. The small amount of policy-focused work (e.g., Decentralization Support Facility 2007) has been limited in scope. This lack of engagement means there is no active dialog between policymakers and the research community on the territorial organization of states. The policy discourse is largely dominated by traditional questions of the vertical allocation of rights and responsibilities, and often treats decisions on administrative unit proliferation as technical issues to be solved with little conceptualization. Likewise, academic work on unit proliferation has not sufficiently tried to engage the needs of policymakers, especially in developing and middle-income settings. While academic and policy work on municipal amalgamations in Western Europe seems to have emerged from healthy dialog between practical concerns and public administration research (see, for example, Schaap and Karsten 2015), the same cannot be said about, for example, discussions of district creation in Uganda or Indonesia.

A second challenge that limits our general knowledge of administrative unit proliferation is the importance of the specific institutional rules and contexts governing changes in jurisdictional boundaries. For example, while the large increases in district governments in Uganda and Indonesia seem similar at first glance, the different institutional rules governing the creation of new units are fundamentally different, and therefore generate distinct political processes. The detailed institutional context (e.g., the identity of formal decision makers), the relationship between administrative units and national electoral districts, and the formal rights and responsibilities of the units in question are crucial for understanding the determinants and consequences of jurisdictional changes. This problem is also compounded by interactions between multiple layers of government. Given that formal rights and responsibilities as well as socioeconomic and political conditions vary across levels of government, unique dynamics can emerge that pit local, regional, and national actors against each other or lead to the emergence of unusual alliances that cross traditional political, social, or ethno-religious cleavages. This often makes empirical cases *sui generis*, and poses a challenge for generating a cross-case debate that could inform policymaking more generally. It also requires researchers to be familiar with the details of each case, and hinders their ability to easily engage in cross-country comparisons.

Most striking, there is a real paucity of work that sufficiently engages the challenges of causal inference when assessing the determinants or effects of unit proliferation. Even though governments, international donors, and researchers are paying increased attention to the challenges inherent to unit proliferation – often in response to the impact of recent reforms – there is a real challenge in producing relevant research. This is due in part to the high-level and political nature of changes in jurisdictional boundaries. It is often difficult to find suitable research designs that can exploit random variation in decisions over territorial boundaries. Moreover, high-quality work on the consequences of administrative unit proliferation requires data that are not always available. For example, few governments or agencies provide accurate and up-to-date geographic information system maps ("shapefiles") of lower-level administrative units (especially on a yearly basis), or regular, relevant, geo-referenced surveys that track outcomes at the subnational or individual level, which are needed to construct meaningful hypotheses. To date there have been no randomized controlled trials on administrative unit proliferation or jurisdictional size, partially due to the extraordinary costs and constraints associated with designing studies on jurisdictional size. This also reflects important ethical concerns about the targeted reorganization of political and administrative government units.

Despite the challenges, a number of strategies could allow future research to make meaningful contributions. On the methodological side, researchers will have to more creatively address threats to causal inference. In order to improve empirical designs, researchers should start exploiting local variations in institutional rules that govern changes in jurisdictional boundaries. For example, territorial reforms and the creation of new governing units are often not taking place at the same time, but are phased in. As in Indonesia, national moratoria might induce exogenous variation in the ability to implement institutional changes, which might permit useful comparisons of units at different stages of institutional reform. Similarly, the creation of new governing units often requires the fulfillment of certain technical requirements or approval processes. For example, creating or merging new district governments might require a certain population size, the existence of a necessary number of subdistrict administrative structures, minimum economic viability, or citizens' explicit political approval. Exploiting variation in such thresholds could make possible regression-discontinuity designs that can compare units right above vs. right below minimum population thresholds, or units whose merger was barely approved vs. barely failed in a local vote. There may also be subnational variation in the procedures governing changes to governing units that can be exploited for useful empirical analysis. Especially for the lowest-level units (e.g., villages), there may be variation in the location (urban or rural) or role of indigenous groups and practices in modifying village-level institutions.

While few surveys have been constructed explicitly to trace the determinants or effects of territorial boundary changes, several existing data sources promise to shed light on such processes. For example, geo-referenced survey data, e.g., Demographic and Health Surveys or Afrobarometer, are inherently suitable for studies dealing with administrative unit proliferation. Similarly, the rise of geo-referenced violent event data (e.g., UCDP-GED [Sundberg et al. 2011] or ACLED [Raleigh et al. 2010]) can be used to study local conflict in relation to changes in territorial boundaries. Likewise, ongoing advances in satellite imaging and image extraction will allow future researchers to track cross-sectional and temporal variation in relevant outcomes in much more detail. For example, satellite and drone imaging technology make it theoretically possible to use nighttime light-intensity data to track economic development and/or electrification (Asher and Novosad 2015), changes in vegetation and ground cover to measure agricultural activity, and changes in road infrastructure or the quality of roofs in urban dwellings (Marx et al. 2018) to discern targeted public and private goods provision.

Conceptually, the literature will have to work harder to distinguish between processes of territorial boundary changes in the developing versus the developed world. Given the contradictory trends and findings from these two contexts, it will be important to clarify and question the conditions under which one set of outcomes is more likely to materialize. Moreover, it will be important to distinguish more clearly between changes to jurisdictional boundaries across different tiers of government. What determines the creation of new village government units is likely to be different from what leads to the splitting of states.

A number of important substantive research topics deserve attention, particularly within the body of work on decentralization. While past work has heavily concentrated on the vertical allocation of rights and responsibilities across levels of government, future work ought to analyze the interaction between decentralization reforms and territorial boundary changes. Since some of the mechanisms purportedly underlying the benefits of decentralization are inherently related to the size of governing units, it remains to be seen whether the contradictory findings in the literature (Treisman 2007) can be resolved by empirically accounting for simultaneous changes in the vertical allocation of rights and the horizontal reform of jurisdictional boundaries.

A second area of research that is intimately intertwined with the size of governing units is the structure of political accountability and representation. Future work on citizen involvement, political participation, and social capital has to engage the effects of governing size on political processes. This applies equally to the fast-growing body of work on clientelism and alternative modes of citizen–politician linkages. How does the size of governing units condition and structure the nature of linkages between voters and their representatives? These questions also relate to the role of ethnic homogeneity in local politics. For example, if administrative unit proliferation increases homogeneity within a unit, what does this imply for local electoral competitiveness? Does the creation of new administrative units create a series of local ethnic fiefdoms, or do other divisions supplant former ethnic splits? How do jurisdictional boundary changes affect the fortunes of local incumbents?

Work on unit proliferation also has to engage the established literature on political parties and party systems. Similar to decentralization reforms, the structure of national party systems is likely to play an important role in mediating the political process of unit proliferation, and in turn transform representational patterns in developing democracies.

Territorial reorganization also has a lot to contribute to the study of separatism and local violence. Future studies will have to determine the extent to which divide-and-rule strategies truly diminish the risks of separatist violence. Also, even if unit proliferation can address local grievances and satisfy a desire for local representation, does this affect larger projects of nation building and the formation of a national identity? Related to political violence and conflict, unit proliferation as a tool of patronage and opposition management in autocracies offers plenty of opportunities to enrich our understanding of autocratic regime stability. When does unit proliferation increase the stability and longevity of a leader's tenure? When does it empower subnational leaders and equip them with the necessary resources to challenge incumbents? A more thorough understanding of states' territorial organization will be an important complement to the existing literature on autocratic parties and legislatures.

Last, we are only beginning to understand the trade-offs related to public goods and services provision inherent to jurisdictional boundary changes. While some attention has been paid to the effects of amalgamation and the creation of new government units, we know little about how dramatic changes in the territorial organization of states affect the horizontal and vertical interactions between government units. Challenges of multilevel governance – e.g., dealing with externalities, spillovers, and coordination – are directly affected by the number, size, and type of government units.

REFERENCES

Akinyele, R. T. 1996. "States Creation in Nigeria: The Willink Report in Retrospect." *African Studies Review* 39(2): 71–94.

Alapiki, Henry E. 2005. "State Creation in Nigeria: Failed Approaches to National Integration and Local Autonomy." *African Studies Review* 48(3): 49–65.

Alesina, Alberto, Reza Baqir, and William Easterly. 1999. "Public Goods and Ethnic Divisions." *Quarterly Journal of Economics* 114(4): 1243–1284.

Alesina, Alberto, Reza Baqir, and Caroline Hoxby. 2004. "Political Jurisdictions in Heterogeneous Communities." *Journal of Political Economy* 112(2): 348–396.

Alesina, Alberto, William Easterly, and Janina Matuszeski. 2011. "Artificial States." *Journal of the European Economic Association* 9(2): 246–277.

Alesina, Alberto, and Eliana La Ferrara. 2000. "Participation in Heterogeneous Communities." *Quarterly Journal of Economics* 115(3): 847–904.

Alesina, Alberto, and Enrico Spolaore. 1997. "On the Number and Size of Nations." *Quarterly Journal of Economics* 112 (4): 1027–1056.

Anckar, Carsten. 2008. "Size, Islandness, and Democracy: A Global Comparison." *International Political Science Review* 29(4): 433–459.

Arikan, G. Gulsun. 2004. "Fiscal Decentralization: A Remedy for Corruption." *International Tax and Public Finance* 11: 175–195.

Asher, Sam, and Paul Novosad. 2015. "The Impacts of Local Control over Political Institutions: Evidence from State Splitting in India." Working paper, University of Oxford.

Austin, D. Andrew. 1999. "Politics vs Economics: Evidence from Municipal Annexation." *Journal of Urban Economics* 45(3): 501–532.

Ayee, Joseph R. A. 2013. "The Political Economy of the Creation of Districts in Ghana." *Journal of Asian and African Studies* 48(5): 623–645.

Banerjee, Abhijit, Lakshmi Iyer, and Somanathan Rohini. 2005. "History, Social Divisions, and Public Goods in Rural India." *Journal of the European Economic Association* 3(2–3): 639–647.

Bardhan, Pranab. 2002. "Decentralization of Governance and Development." *Journal of Economic Perspectives* 16(4): 185–205.

Bardhan, Pranab, and Dilip Mookherjee. 2006. "Decentralisation and Accountability in Infrastructure Delivery in Developing Countries." *Economic Journal* 116(508): 101–127.

Bazzi, Samuel, and Matthew Gudgeon. 2017. "The Political Boundaries of Ethnic Divisions." NBER Working Paper No. 24625.

Berry, Christopher R. 2009. *Imperfect Union: Representation and Taxation in Multilevel Governments*. Cambridge University Press.

Besley, Timothy, and Anna Case. 1995. "Does Electoral Accountability Affect Economic Policy Choices? Evidence from Gubernatorial Term Limits." *Quarterly Journal of Economics* 110(3): 769–798.

Blesse, Sebastian, and Thushyanthan Baskaran. 2013. "Do Municipal Mergers Result in Scale Economies? Evidence from a German Federal State." Center for European, Governance and Economic Development Research Discussion Paper 176. University of Göttingen, Department of Economics.

Blom-Hansen, Jens, Kurt Houlberg, and Søren Serritzlew. 2014. "Size, Democracy, and the Economic Costs of Running the Political System." *American Journal of Political Science* 58(4): 790–803.

Boffa, Federico, Amedeo Piolatto, and Giacomo A. M. Ponzetto. 2016. "Political Centralization and Government Accountability." *Quarterly Journal of Economics* 131(1): 381–422.

Brancati, Dawn. 2006. "Decentralization: Fueling the Fire or Dampening the Flames of Ethnic Conflict and Secessionism?" *International Organization* 60(3): 651–685.

Brasington, David M. 2003. "Snobbery, Racism, or Mutual Distaste: What Promotes and Hinders Cooperation in Local Public-Good Provision?" *Review of Economics and Statistics* 85(4): 874–883.

Breuillé, Marie-Laure, and Skerdilajda Zanaj. 2013. "Mergers in Fiscal Federalism." *Journal of Public Economics* 105: 11–22.

Bruns, Benjamin, Ronny Freier, and Abel Schumann. 2015. "Finding Your Right (or Left) Partner to Merge." Working paper, Humboldt University.

Casey, Katherine. 2015. "Crossing Party Lines: The Effects of Information on Redistributive Politics." *American Economic Review* 105 (8): 2410–2448

Charron, Nicholas, José Fernández-Albertos, and Victor Lapuente. 2013. "Small Is Different: Size, Political Representation and Governance." In The Challenge of Local Government Size: Theoretical Perspectives, International Experience and Policy Reform. Ed. Santiago Lago-Penas and Jorge Martinez-Vazques. Pp. 55–82. Cheltenham, UK: Edward Elgar.

Chauvel, Richard. 2004. "Divide and Who Rules?" *Inside Indonesia* 78(April–June).

Costa, Dora L., and Matthew E. Kahn. 2003. "Civic Engagement and Community Heterogeneity: An Economist's Perspective." *Perspectives on Politics* 1(1): 103–111.

Crouch, Harold. 2010. *Political Reform in Indonesia after Soeharto*. Singapore: Institute of Southeast Asian Studies.

Dafflon, Bernard. 2012. "Voluntary Amalgamation of Local Governments: The Swiss Debate in the European Context." International Center for Public Policy Working Paper Series.

Dahl, Robert A. 1967. "The City in the Future of Democracy." *American Political Science Review* 61(4): 953–970.

Dahl, Robert A., and Edward R. Tufte. 1973. *Size and Democracy*. Palo Alto, CA: Stanford University Press.

Debs, Alexandre. 2007. "The Wheel of Fortune: Agency Problems in Dictatorships." Working Paper.

Decentralization Support Facility. 2007. *Costs and Benefits of New Region Creation in Indonesia.* Published: Final Report.

Denters, Bas, Michael Goldsmith, Andreas Ladner, Poul Erik Mouritzen, and Lawrence E. Rose. 2014. *Size and Local Democracy.* Cheltenham, UK: Edward Elgar.

Edwards, Mary M. 2008. "Understanding the Complexities of Annexation." *Journal of Planning Literature* 23(2): 119–135.

Ekekwe, Eme. 1986. *Class and State in Nigeria.* London: Longman.

Fiorino, Nadia, Emma Galli, and Fabio Padovano. 2013. "Do Fiscal Decentralization and Government Fragmentation Affect Corruption in Different Ways? Evidence from Panel Data Analysis." In *The Challenge of Local Government Size: Theoretical Perspectives, International Experience and Policy Reform.* Ed. Santiago Lago-Penas and Jorge Martinez-Vazques. Pp. 121–147. Cheltenham, UK: Edward Elgar.

Fitrani, Fitria, Bert Hofman, and Kai Kaiser. 2005. "Unity in Diversity? The Creation of New Local Governments in a Decentralising Indonesia." *Bulletin of Indonesian Economic Studies* 41(1): 57–79.

Francis, Paul, and Robert James. 2003. "Balancing Rural Poverty Reduction and Citizen Participation: The Contradictions of Uganda's Decentralization Program." *World Development* 31(2): 325–337.

Fritz, Benedikt. 2011. "Fiscal Effects of Municipal Amalgamation." Working paper, Walter Eucken Institute.

Gerring, John, Maxwell Palmer, Jan Teorell, and Dominic Zarecki. 2015. "Demography and Democracy: A Global, District-Level Analysis of Electoral Contestation." *American Political Science Review* 109(3): 574–591.

Gómez-Reino, Juan Luis, and Jorge Martinez-Vazquez. 2013. "An International Perspective on the Determinants of Local Government Fragmentation." In *The Challenge of Local Government Size: Theoretical Perspectives, International Experience and Policy Reform.* Ed. Santiago Lago-Penas and Jorge Martinez-Vazques. Pp. 8–54. Cheltenham, UK: Edward Elgar.

Gordon, Nora, and Brian Knight. 2009. "A Spatial Merger Estimator with an Application to School District Consolidation." *Journal of Public Economics* 93(5–6): 752–765.

Green, Elliott. 2010. "Patronage, District Creation, and Reform in Uganda." *Studies in Comparative International Development* 45(1): 83–103.

Griffiths, Ryan D. 2015. "Between Dissolution and Blood: How Administrative Lines and Categories Shape Secessionist Outcomes." *International Organization* 69(3): 731–751.

Grossman, Guy. 2014. "Do Selection Rules Affect Leader Responsiveness? Evidence from Rural Uganda." *Quarterly Journal of Political Science* 9(1): 1–44.

Grossman, Guy, and Janet I. Lewis. 2014. "Administrative Unit Proliferation." *American Political Science Review* 108(1): 196–217.

Grossman, Guy, Jan H. Pierskalla, and Emma Boswell Dean. 2017. "Government Fragmentation and Public Goods Provision." *Journal of Politics* 79(3): 823–840.

Guo, Gang. 2007. "Retrospective Economic Accountability under Authoritarianism Evidence from China." *Political Research Quarterly* 60(3): 378–390.

Hale, Henry E. 2004. "Divided We Stand: Institutional Sources of Ethnofederal State Survival and Collapse." *World Politics* 56(2): 165–193.

Hansen, Sune Welling. 2013. "Polity Size and Local Political Trust: A Quasi-Experiment Using Municipal Mergers in Denmark." *Scandinavian Political Studies* 36(1): 43–66.

Hansen, Sune Welling. 2015. "The Democratic Costs of Size: How Increasing Size Affects Citizen Satisfaction with Local Government." *Political Studies* 63(2): 373–389.

Hansen, Sune Welling, Kurt Houlberg, and Lene Holm Pedersen. 2014. "Do Municipal Mergers Improve Fiscal Outcomes?" *Scandinavian Political Studies* 37(2): 196–214.

Hassan, Mai. 2016. "A State of Change: District Creation in Kenya after the Beginning of Multi-party Elections." *Political Research Quarterly* 69(3): 510–521.

Hassan, Mai, and Ryan Sheely. 2015. "Executive–Legislative Relations, Party Defections, and Lower-Level Administrative Unit Proliferation: Evidence from Kenya." Working paper, University of Michigan.

Hellman, Joel S. 1998. "Winners Take All: The Politics of Partial Reform in Post Transitions." *World Politics* 50(2): 203–234.

Hooghe, Liesbet, and Gary Marks. 2003. "Unraveling the Central State, but How? Types of Multi-Level Governance." *American Political Science Review* 97(2): 233–243.

Hooghe, Liesbet, and Gary Marks. 2009. "Does Efficiency Shape the Territorial Structure of Government?" *Annual Review of Political Science* 12: 225–241.

Horiuchi, Yusaku, Jun Saito, and Kyohei Yamada. 2015. "Removing Boundaries, Losing Connections: Electoral Consequences of Local Government Reform in Japan." *Journal of East Asian Studies* 15(1): 99–125.

Hyytinen, Ari, Tuukka Saarimaa, and Janne Tukiainen. 2014. "Electoral Vulnerability and Size of Local Governments: Evidence from Voting on Municipal Mergers." *Journal of Public Economics* 120(December): 193–204.

Imansyah, M. H., and J. Martinez-Vazquez. 2009. "Understanding Subnational Government Fragmentation in Indonesia and Options for Reform: Background for a 'Grand Strategy' for Pemekaran." Technical Report. Asian Development Bank.

Kasara, Kimuli. 2006. "Ethnic Beachheads and Vote Buying: The Creation of New Administrative Districts in Kenya, 1963–2001." Working Paper.

Kimura, Ehito. 2013. *Political Change and Territoriality in Indonesia: Provincial Proliferation*. Abingdon, UK: Routledge.

Kitschelt, Herbert, and Steven I. Wilkinson (eds.). 2007. *Patrons, Clients, and Policies: Patterns of Democratic Accountability and Political Competition*. Cambridge: Cambridge University Press.

Kraxberger, Brennan. 2004. "The Geography of Regime Survival: Abacha's Nigeria." *African Affairs* 103(412): 413–430.

Lassen, David Dreyer, and Søren Serritzlew. 2011. "Jurisdiction Size and Local Democracy: Evidence on Internal Political Efficacy from Large-Scale Municipal Reform." *American Political Science Review* 105(2): 238–258.

Lewis, Blane D. 2017. "Local Government Proliferation and Public Service Delivery: Causes and Consequences." *Journal of Urban Affairs* 39 (8): 1047–1065.

Lewis, Janet I. 2014b. "When Decentralization Leads to Recentralization: Subnational State Transformation in Uganda." *Regional and Federal Studies* 24(5): 571–588.

Lewis, Paul G. 2011. "Size and Local Democracy: Scale Effects in City Politics." *PS: Political Science and Politics* 44(1): 107–109.

Malesky, Edmund. 2009. "Gerrymandering Vietnam Style: Escaping Partial Reform Equilibrium in a Non-Democratic Regime." *Journal of Politics* 71(1): 132–159.

Marx, Benjamin, Thomas M. Stoker, and Tavneet Suri. 2018. "There Is No Free House: Ethnic Patronage in a Kenyan Slum." *American Economic Journal Applied Economics*, Forthcoming.

Maskin, Eric, Yingyi Qian, and Chenggang Xu. 2000. "Incentives, Information, and Organizational Form." *Review of Economic Studies* 67(2): 359–378.

Mawdsley, Emma. 2002. "Redrawing the Body Politic: Federalism, Regionalism and the Creation of New States in India." *Commonwealth and Comparative Politics* 40(3): 34–54.

Mazaheri, Nimah, and Benjamin Barber. 2015. "The Specialization Curse: Economic Specialization and Its Effect on Public Goods Provision." Working paper, Tufts University.

Mensah, John Victor, Ronald Adamtey, and Abdul-Wadudu Adam Mohammed. 2015. "Challenges of Newly Created Districts in Ghana: A Case Study of the Asante Akim North District." *Advances in Social Sciences Research Journal* 2(10): 224–239.

Mietzner, Marcus. 2014. "Indonesia's Decentralization: The Rise of Local Identities and the Survival of the Nation-State." In *Regional Dynamics in a Decentralized Indonesia*. Ed. Hal Hill. Pp. 45–67. Singapore: Institute of Southeast Asian Studies.

Myerson, Roger B. 2006. "Federalism and Incentives for Success of Democracy." *Quarterly Journal of Political Science* 1(1): 3–23.

Nelson, Michael A. 1992. "Municipal Amalgamation and the Growth of the Local Public Sector in Sweden." *Journal of Regional Science* 32(1): 39–53.

Nelson, Michael A. 2013. "Corruption and the Size of Local Governments: Are They Related?" In *The Challenge of Local Government Size: Theoretical Perspectives, International Experience and Policy Reform*. Eds. Santiago Lago-Penas and Jorge Martinez-Vazques. Pp. 83–120. Cheltenham, UK: Edward Elgar.

Newton, K. 1982. "Is Small Really so Beautiful? Is Big Really so Ugly? Size, Effectiveness, and Democracy in Local Government." *Political Studies* 30(2): 190–206.

Nolan, Cillian, Sidney Jones, and Solahudin. 2014. "The Political Impact of Carving up Papua." In *Regional Dynamics in a Decentralized Indonesia*. Ed. Hal Hill. Pp. 409–432. Institute of Southeast Asian Studies.

Oates, Wallace E. 1972. *Fiscal Federalism*. New York, NY: Harcourt.

Oliver, J. Eric. 2000. "City Size and Civic Involvement in Metropolitan America." *American Political Science Review* 94(2): 361–373.

Pierskalla, Jan H. 2016. "Splitting the Difference? The Politics of District Creation in Indonesia." *Comparative Politics* 48(2): 249–268.

Pierskalla, Jan H., and Audrey Sacks. 2017. "Unpacking the Effect of Decentralized Governance on Routine Violence: Lessons from Indonesia" *World Development* 90: 213–228.

Plato. 1992. *The Republic*. Indianapolis, IN: Hackett Publishing Company.

Qibthiyyah, Riatu. 2008. Essays on Political and Fiscal Decentralization. Dissertation, Georgia State University, Atlanta, Georgia.

Raleigh, Clionadh, Andrew Linke, Håvard Hegre, and Joakim Karlsen. 2010. "Introducing ACLED-Armed Conflict Location and Event Data." *Journal of Peace Research* 47(5): 1–10.

Reingewertz, Yaniv. 2012. "Do Municipal Amalgamations Work? Evidence from Municipalities in Israel." *Journal of Urban Economics* 72(2–3): 240–251.

Remmer, Karen L. 2010. "Political Scale and Electoral Turnout: Evidence from the Less Industrialized World." *Comparative Political Studies* 43(3): 275–303.

Rogowski, Ronald. 1998. "Democracy, Capital, Skill, and Country Size: Effects of Asset Mobility and Regime Monopoly on the Odds of Democratic Rule." In *The Origins of Modern Freedom in the West*. Ed. R. W. Davis. Pp. 48–69. Palo Alto, CA: Stanford University Press.

Saarimaa, Tuukka, and Janne Tukiainen. 2014. "I Don't Care to Belong to Any Club That Will Have Me as a Member: Empirical Analysis of Municipal Mergers." *Political Science Research and Methods* 2(1): 97–117.

Saarimaa, Tuukka, and Janne Tukiainen. 2016. "Local Representation and Strategic Voting: Evidence from Electoral Boundary Reforms." *European Journal of Political Economy* 41(Jan.): 31–45.

Sancton, Andrew. 2000. *Merger Mania: The Assault on Local Government*. Montreal: McGill-Queen's University Press.

Schaap, Linze, and Niels Karsten. 2015. "Evaluating Municipal Mergers' Effects: A Review of Amalgamation Studies in the Netherlands." Working paper, Tilburg University.

Shimizu, Kay. 2012. "Electoral Consequences of Municipal Mergers." *Journal of East Asian Studies* 12(3): 381–408.

Suberu, Rotimi T. 1991. "The Struggle for New States in Nigeria, 1976–1990." *African Affairs* 90(361): 499–522.

Suberu, Rotimi T. 2001. *Federalism and Ethnic Conflict in Nigeria*. Washington, DC: US Institute of Peace Press.

Sundberg, Ralph, Mathilda Lindgren, and Ausra Padskocimaite. 2011. UCDP GED Codebook Version 1.0–2011. Codebook. Department of Peace and Conflict Research, Uppsala University. http://ucdp.uu.se/ged/data/ucdp ged v.1.0-codebook .pdf (accessed January 20, 2012).

Tiebout, Charles M. 1956. "A Pure Theory of Local Expenditures." *Journal of Political Economy* 64(5): 416–424.

Tommasi, Mariano, and Federico Weinschelbaum. 2007. "Centralization vs. Decentralization: A Principal-Agent Analysis." *Journal of Public Economic Theory* 9(2): 369–389.

Treisman, Daniel. 2002. "Defining and Measuring Decentralization: A Global Perspective." Working Paper, UCLA.

Treisman, Daniel. 2007. *The Architecture of Government*. Cambridge: Cambridge University Press.

Tyrefors Hinnerich, Björn. 2009. "Do Merging Local Governments Free Ride on Their Counterparts When Facing Boundary Reform?" *Journal of Public Economics* 93(5–6): 721–728.

Walter, Barbara F. 2009. *Reputation and Civil War: Why Separatist Conflicts Are So Violent*. Cambridge: Cambridge University Press.

Warren, Mark E. 2011. "Voting with Your Feet: Exit-Based Empowerment in Democratic Theory." *American Political Science Review* 105(4): 683–701.

Weese, Eric. 2015. "Political Mergers As Coalition Formation: An Analysis of the Heisei Municipal Amalgamations." *Quantitative Economics* 6(2): 257–307.

Weldon, Steven. 2006. "Downsize My Polity? The Impact of Size on Party Membership and Member Activism." *Party Politics* 12(4): 467–481.

Zhang, Jingxiang, and Fulong Wu. 2006. "China's Changing Economic Governance: Administrative Annexation and the Reorganization of Local Governments in the Yangtze River Delta." *Regional Studies* 40(1): 3–21.

7

Decentralization and Business Performance

Edmund Malesky

INTRODUCTION

The perceptions and actions of businesses play critical roles in the three core theoretical arguments linking decentralization to economic growth. Scholars who argue that political, administrative, and fiscal decentralization allows for better tailoring of public services to local needs and therefore more efficient allocations of public spending (Oates 1972, 1999) believe that decentralization will allow services to be better targeted to the location and therefore will enhance business productivity. Scholars who argue that decentralization stimulates competition assume that labor and businesses will move to capitalize on differences between regions, sparking innovation and efficiency in public services delivery, institutions, and policy (Tiebout 1956; Brennan and Buchanan 1980; Besley and Case 1995; Weingast 1995; Qian and Roland 1998). Scholars who argue that political decentralization facilitates responsiveness to local voters believe that businesses in a locality will be able to organize themselves to advocate for changes that will enhance their performance (Cremer et al. 1995; Seabright 1996). In short, if decentralization is working effectively, we should see evidence of it in innovation, expansion, and productivity of existing firms in a given locality. Furthermore, we should see more mobile businesses (large domestic or foreign investors) exploiting differences between regions in their location decisions.

Despite the clear theoretical role for business performance in the literature, the empirical evidence linking decentralization to business outcomes is surprisingly thin. Most of the existing literature operates at the macroeconomic level, studying economic growth or levels of per capita GDP (Davoodi and Zou 1998; Thiessen 2000; Martinez et al. 2003; Enikolopov and Zhuravskaya 2007; Rodríguez-Pose Ezcurra 2011). The most recent contribution to the literature is by Asatrayan and Feld (2014), who after addressing critical methodological shortcomings of previous work, find that there is no robust relationship, either positive or negative, between decentralization and growth.

Only a few studies actually use measures of business performance and productivity as their outcome variables. More confusing, the studies that do look directly at business performance come to widely divergent conclusions about the effects of decentralization. Akai and Sakata (2002) find a positive effect on business performance, Sobel et al. (2013) and Abdullatif et al. (2013) find a negative one, and Kessing et al. (2007) identify differential effects of decentralization depending on the way decentralization is measured.

In sharp contrast, there is an active and comprehensive literature looking at differences in the conditions for business performance at the subnational level. Different scholars use different names to describe this concept, including business climate, business environment, business friendliness, investment climate, investment environment, and subnational competitiveness (Plaut and Pluta 1983; Steinnes 1984; Holmes 1998; Begg 1999; Budd 2004; Iarossi 2013). Scholars working on foreign direct investment (FDI) flows tend to describe the same concepts as investment attractiveness or locational determinants (Dunning 2001; Meyer and Nguyen 2005; Chan et al. 2010; McCann and Acs 2011; Dai, Eden, and Beamish 2013; Goerzen, Asmussen, and Nielsen 2013; Ma, Tong, and Fitza 2013). The concept has also been embraced by aid practitioners in the form of subnational economic governance indices, which rank subnational units based on their business environment (Campos and Hellman 2005; Malesky and Merchant-Vega 2011). In general, these terms are used to describe a constellation of subnational factors that are associated with business performance, ranging from endowments, to infrastructure, to institutions, to economic governance. Scholars working in these literatures have found dramatic variations in business outcomes within a country due to differences in these factors.

The connection of the subnational business environment to the decentralization literature is limited for two reasons. First, scholars studying business environment are not always concerned with the level of authority of the local decision makers. In some cases, this is because the key differences are due to endowments or long-term factors that leaders are unable to alter during their tenure. In other cases, the differences are driven by variation in the implementation of central *diktats*, so formal decentralization policies are less relevant and useful at staving off central demands than informal powers gained by central leaders due to sociocultural, historical, or structural factors.

Second, the two literatures are operating at different levels of analysis. Because it is very difficult to observe variation in decentralization within a country, most scholars studying decentralization and economic outcomes abstract up to the country level. They decide to simplify in order to compare decentralization metrics across states and study the impact on aggregate levels of economic performance. By contrast, the subnational business environment literature predominantly focuses on within-country analyses, exploiting variation in determinants across districts or provinces within a specific country. Studying decentralization is difficult in these environments because, with rare exceptions, decentralization occurred as a uniform policy, affecting every unit of government at a particular level at the same time. Thus there is no control group and therefore no way to see the trajectory a unit would have followed in the absence of the decentralization policy. Some scholars have tried to overcome this by operationalizing decentralization as variation in subnational expenditures or revenue collection (Lin and Liu 2000; Zhang 2006; Nguyen 2011; Vu 2014), but this is clearly endogenous to underlying business performance.

The gap between decentralization theory and the subnational business environment literature is unfortunate, because so many of the theoretical arguments in favor of decentralization hinge on how subnational leaders might change institutions or policies that should enhance business activity. In this chapter, I try to connect these two disparate literatures. I begin by clarifying some key terms. Second, I lay out the major factors that affect business performance, organizing them by when they can be altered by subnational leaders and experienced by businesses. Third, I work through the three key arguments for decentralization (tailoring, monitoring and accountability, competition), pointing out the assumptions regarding business activity that underpin them. In lieu of a conclusion, in the final section, I tie the two streams of literature together to draw out the policy implications for developmental interventions. Once we understand the factors that influence business performance, it is easier to show where decentralization may prove fruitful and where it may have perverse effects.

I have participated in these debates as both an academic and a practitioner. As a practitioner, for eleven years, I have been the primary author of the USAID-funded Vietnamese Provincial Competitiveness Index (PCI), an annual ranking of the economic governance of Vietnam's sixty-three provinces based on a survey of 10,000 private businesses. The goal of the PCI has been to stimulate competition on governance innovation and implementation between provincial leaders to ultimately generate greater private sector performance and economic growth. Because of the PCI's enduring success, I have also been invited to help develop similar economic governance indices (EGIs) in Bangladesh, El Salvador, Kosovo, Indonesia, Laos, Malaysia, Myanmar, Serbia, and Sri Lanka.

Working on EGIs has provided me with a unique perspective on decentralization as it relates to the private business sector, because generating a precise measure means intimately understanding how private businesses interact with government in a variety of settings. The first few months of every EGI require mapping out all of the necessary registration documents, regulatory hurdles, government interventions in business activities, and government programs to promote investment. These activities are housed in dozens of different institutions across multiple levels of government, giving me insight into how different modes of decentralization can result in fascinating interactions and roadblocks often unanticipated by the architects of decentralization. I hope to convey some of these complexities in this chapter.

EMPIRICAL DIFFICULTIES IN CONNECTING DECENTRALIZATION TO BUSINESS PERFORMANCE

Before diving too deeply into the analysis, a little brush-clearing is in order. A key reason for the mixed results and confusion about the relationship between decentralization and performance is authors' different conceptual definitions on both sides of the business-decentralization equation.

Conceptualizing and Measuring Decentralization

Other sections of this book pay careful attention to particular forms of decentralization, using a three-category classification advocated by Rodden (2004): fiscal, administrative, and political decentralization.

Generally, the distinction made is that fiscal decentralization provides local governments with the power to tax citizens and businesses, raise money through borrowing either domestically or overseas, and decide how to spend that money through the preparation and implementation of local budgets. Fiscal decentralization, which is explained well by Rodden's contribution to this volume (Chapter 5), has been measured as the subnational share of government revenue and expenditures and vertical imbalances (the ratio of grants to revenue). Administrative decentralization involves recruitment and retention of staff, allocation of civil service according to local needs, and the ability to hold staff accountable for performance (Green 2005). It has been measured by the number of government tiers and the surface area of the lowest-level political unit. Finally, political decentralization, analyzed by Grossman's piece in this volume (Chapter 3), provides the local election of subnational legislatures or executives and downward accountability to the local citizenry, who can sanction or reward local policymakers through elections. Political decentralization has been measured by the presence of local elections, the number of powers specifically granted to local authorities, and the presence of constitutional provisions granting autonomy.

When trying to apply the distinctions and measurements to business performance, the clear theoretical distinctions can be muddied (Martinez-Vasquez et al. 2017). Political decentralization is irrelevant if local authorities do not have control over some fiscal and administrative decisions. Administrative decentralization requires some control over budget expenditures, as human resource allocations require decisions about which government services will be prioritized. Taking these overlaps into account, Hooghe, Marks, and Schakel propose the Regional Authority Index (RAI), which is a composite measure of taxing and expenditure authority, autonomy in decision making, and independent local elections of legislatures and executives. Following Hooghe et al. (2008) in my theoretical discussion of decentralization later in this chapter, I pay less attention to the specific type of decentralization and more attention to the theoretical mechanisms proposed by the authors, which often draw on multiple types of decentralization at the same time. As I detail in what follows, these include arguments for tailoring and efficiency, competition, and responsiveness and accountability.

Even when the type of decentralization is clear, the metric used to operationalize the concept can lead to very different findings. The two most cited papers in the debate over decentralization and perceptions of corruption reported by businesses, for instance, measure decentralization in two very different ways. Fisman and Gatti (2002) use the subnational share of government spending and find that greater shares are associated with less corruption. Fan et al. (2009) find that the number of government tiers is positively associated with corruption. The two papers reach very different conclusions about the presence of decentralization and corruption, but the lack of uniformity in measurement implies different theoretical mechanisms at work and extremely different policy conclusions. Indeed, Kessing et al. (2007) recast the two measurements, calling subnational expenditures horizontal decentralization and number of tiers vertical decentralization. Consistent with the work on corruption, they find that vertical decentralization attracts foreign investment while horizontal decentralization repels it.

Conceptualizing and Measuring Business Performance

The discussion of foreign investment attraction leads to the next problem in assessing the relationship. The measurement of business performance is uniform in either the decentralization or business environment literatures. According to economists, subnational economic development is mostly likely to occur in educated regions that concentrate entrepreneurs, who run productive firms (Banerjee and Duflo 2005; La Porta and Shleifer 2008). While this seems straightforward, multiple outcome variables are used in the literature to assess whether these conditions are met.

First, scholars have emphasized different types of firms in their theoretical and empirical treatments: 1) nonmobile domestic firms that, due to cultural or structural conditions, are unable to leave their subnational jurisdiction; 2) mobile domestic firms (often larger than their nonmobile peers) that have the ability to uproot and take advantage of differences in the subnational business environment; and 3) foreign firms that are coming to the country and have full control over their subnational location decision. In Bai et al. (2017), the distinction between firm types 1 and 2 is critical for understanding how subnational competition influences corruption. Mobile firms are much less susceptible to bribe requests because it is far easier for them to uproot and shift production to a competing location. In the management literature on the "liability of foreignness" in subnational investment decisions, the distinction between firm types 2 and 3 matters; both firms are mobile, but foreigners are more influenced by problematic governance because they have less understanding of the business environment and benefit less from local relationships (Monaghan et al. 2014). An additional distinction can be made regarding the market orientation of the business. Is it operating in a sector that depends primarily on sales to the subnational market or is it using the locality to produce goods for other subnational entities or exports overseas? As we see later in this chapter, the factors that determine business performance differ based on the answer to this question.

Second, different measurements of business performance have been analyzed. The most common approach for scholars assessing decentralization is to stop short of business performance and use an index of business environment, usually prepared by a survey firm or rating agency as the key dependent variable (Akai et al. 2002; Dreher 2006). Scholars trying to connect business environment to business decisions have emphasized measures of business entry, such as new firm formation, business formalization, and attraction of investment (both foreign and domestic). Economists have tended to focus on investment expansion, employment growth, or changes in firm-level productivity (usually operationalized by total factor productivity). Management scholars have looked at return on investment (ROI) and profitability. They have also focused on entry decisions, studying how business environment affected whether foreign companies form joint ventures or enter as 100% foreign owned, and have emphasized innovation decisions, usually measured by patents. Finally, a small group of scholars has studied spillover: how the business environment is related to whether foreign investment enhances the productivity of domestic firms (Yi et al. 2015).

Again, different arguments about decentralization imply different dependent variables for analysis, and the choices have substantial implications. For instance, low regulatory barriers to business entry will encourage business entry and formalization (i.e., moving out of the gray or black market), but the fiercer competition will lower average survival rates and drive down individual firm profitability. From an economics perspective, this is beneficial; consumers will benefit from lower-cost and higher-quality products and services, but scholars measuring business performance by firm-level ROI will find negative results as competition lowers profits.

WHAT DO BUSINESSES WANT?

In 1973, John H. Dunning advanced what would come to be called the "eclectic paradigm" or "OLI-Framework" in the foreign investment literature, arguing that firms made decisions to expand abroad based on three factors: O) *ownership* advantages that are intrinsic to the enterprise (i.e., trademarks, production techniques); L) unique advantages of the host country or *location* to which the firm might move; and I) advantages of *internationalizing* production by moving to the host country, rather than simply partnering with an entity already there. The "L" component, originally criticized as a "laundry list" of variables ranging from market size to investment incentives, (Stopford and Strange 1991), proved useful and enduring in that it articulated the range of factors that businesses considered important in making investment decisions. Later, scholars explaining differential investment growth rates within countries returned to Dunning's list to help guide their analyses.

As a result of having its origins in a long list of potential factors, the literature on subnational investment climates/business environments is complex and fragmented. Scholars agree that multiple factors are important, but highlight particular factors in their analysis. This makes sense from a research perspective, as the goal is to isolate and identify the specific effects of a treatment variable. For practitioners, however, it can be frustrating because it is not clear how to fit the partial effects of that particular variable (e.g., infrastructure, agglomeration, governance, human capital) into the larger milieu of effects that are operating at the same time.

The situation is further complicated when we try to think through the causal effects of decentralization on business performance, because the factors we care about have different gestation periods even when all political actors in the locality agree and there are zero barriers to policy change and implementation. By gestation periods, we can consider two distinct waiting periods. First is the length of time needed to alter the investment criterion, so that the location becomes attractive to business. This first period includes long-term structural and historical changes, political decisions, legislation, and policy implementation. The second period is the length of time between altering the criterion and when the alteration is experienced by business executives. From a program-evaluation perspective, the first period is the time necessary to produce an output (change in the factor), and the second period is the time needed for outputs to lead to measurable outcomes (business performance resulting from the factor).

For example, regulatory change has a very short gestation period. If the key impediment to business growth is a regulatory obstacle, it requires only a straightforward policy change to remove that additional license, stamp, or service fee. The return on the policy change will also be immediate. Businesses that were impeded from entering the market or expanding investment by that regulation will be able to respond quite quickly.

By contrast, the benefits of infrastructure improvements will appear much more slowly. The infrastructure changes will have to be planned and implemented, which in the case of roads or bridges can sometimes take years. Eventually, companies will also have to learn to adapt their business models to these changes. Better infrastructure might connect a manufacturing firm to potential customers, but that firm will still need to develop sales contacts and a distribution system to reach them. With telecommunications and Internet infrastructure, these business model adaptations can even take longer.

And obviously, if the key obstacle to business performance is a missing endowment, forget it. No amount of decentralization is going to bring in missing natural resources, make the soil more fertile, increase market size, or bring a landlocked place any closer to a deepwater port. These changes occur over decades and centuries, and only later generations will experience their payoff.

This is not rocket science, of course. All scholars, practitioners, and government leaders implicitly understand the distinction between endowments and short-, medium-, and long-term policy change. They also understand that economic development has multiple causes and cannot be reduced to a monocausal explanation. The style of an academic paper, however, can obscure this fact by focusing on the causal variable the authors care about in order to demonstrate the net effect of their theoretical innovation, without accounting for the influence of other factors. The business environment literature includes very little general work on the multiplicity of causes. Even the best work isolates the partial effects of a particular determinant that the authors' theory has highlighted. Other factors are rendered to control variables in a regression table or confounders in a balance table for a randomized experiment. Rarely do scholars try to present a general model of economic development that assesses the marginal effects of every determinant.

Moreover, there is somewhat of a bias toward new thinking in academic presentation, so traditional measures that we know to be important receive less attention then the next big idea. Demographic pyramids and infrastructure are kind of boring when placed alongside sexier topics like institutions, economic governance, and e-governance.

When analyzing the economic effects of decentralization and subnational investment environments, however, it is worth thinking systematically about what can and cannot be changed within the timeframe of a particular leader or regime. What policy levers do they have available? And what sets of determinants should be thought of as fixed parameters that constrain the set of options available to them? I set these out in the next few pages.

Factor Endowments

We generally think of factor endowments as the amount of land, labor, and capital that a locality possesses and can exploit to further economic development. Some scholars have added sociocultural determinants, such as entrepreneurship, to this list as well (Alesina and Giuliano 2015), although the stability of underlying cultural factors is controversial. Endowments are features of the investment environment that cannot be changed in the short, medium, or long term. Consequently, endowments are glacial in their rates of change. They are inherited by leadership and later determine the sets of choices available for future policy decisions (Gallup et al. 1999). In particular, three sets of endowments are critically important for both foreign and domestic business decisions.

First, businesses benefit from proximity to natural resources (Dunning 2000; Ghemawat 2001; Asiedu and Lien 2011). These include access to oil, minerals, or wood for businesses focused on natural resources production. For businesses in agriculture, access to plentiful and fertile land is important. For manufacturing, resources include inputs into the production process, such as cotton and silk for textiles and lumber for wood furnishings. These inputs can be imported, of course, but it will raise costs for the producer and can pose a barrier to domestic firms.

Second, some businesses require access to land and space. Manufacturing and agriculture, in particular, can require large enough plots of land to achieve economies of scale and enhance productivity. Subnational entities that are burdened by low-quality soil or limited space due to natural terrain or urbanization will find it difficult to attract businesses that need sizable business premises to start up or grow existing operations. Certainly, policy options exist. Land can be rezoned from agriculture to commercial use to make space for manufacturing. Localities can invest in land clearance and create industrial zones that offer large tracts of land to businesses, as was done in Singapore in the 1970s, China in the 1980s, and Vietnam in the 1990s. Yet even these decisions are constrained by the availability of land. Industrial zones obviously cannot be created in mountain ranges or in the middle of a city.

Third, businesses benefit from proximity to large markets. Large population centers, which are the result of historical migration patterns, allow for both service and manufacturing businesses to grow rapidly. Yu and Shen (2013), for instance, demonstrate that market proximity has a dramatic effect on the location decisions of Taiwanese firms in China. By the same token, proximity to export markets also has enormous advantages for businesses. Localities near border gates or deepwater ports have enormous advantages for both growing their domestic businesses and attracting foreign inputs (Ekholm et al. 2007).

Population size and density affect the supply side of business production as well. Variation in fertility rates and historical population growth rates affect business development by providing a suitable workforce. Demographers often refer to the "demographic bonus" or "golden period" when the proportion of the population age that is working age reaches its peak (Lee 2003; Lee and Mason 2006). With healthy young people entering the labor market each year, productivity increases (Lorentzen et al. 2008).

These endowments are critical for economic development. As Nobel Laureate economist William D. Nordhaus (2006) wrote, "The linkage between economic activity and geography is obvious as populations cluster mainly on coasts and rarely on ice-sheets." However, there is very little that subnational leaders can do to effect geography or demography within the time horizon of today's businesses. These are the product of fortune and the very long-term effects of historical decisions. Demographic factors may have been influenced by conflict or economic crises in previous eras. Resource endowments might have been depleted or damaged by previous leaders' decisions. Consequently, they simply must be treated as the cards current leaders have been dealt.

Long-Term Factors

Local governments can alter a second set of determinants of business performance, but the benefits may take several years or even decades to come to fruition. These include institutions and public services, such as infrastructure, human capital, and public health.

Institutions: In recent years, the economics literature on subnational economic and business development has focused on institutions. Following North (1981), two key institutions have received pride of place in the economics literature (Acemoglu and Johnson 2005). First, scholars have emphasized property-rights institutions that protect businesses from state expropriation of land, capital, or intellectual property (Johnson et al. 2002). Property rights cannot simply be promised by fiat; they must be ensured by cross-cutting institutions that check the power of the state (Keefer and Knack 1997; Hensiz 2000), provide representation of the business community in decision making, and allow businesses to appeal state actors' decisions in independent courts. A great deal of work has shown that within states, subnational governments that protect property rights experience greater business entry and investment growth, as businesses feel more confident taking long-term risks (Agrawal and Ostrom 2001; Banerjee and Iyer 2005; Malesky and Taussig 2009a; Michalopulous and Papaioannu 2013).

Second, scholars have studied contracting institutions, which assist in settling business disputes with other non-state entities. An independent legal system that allows small businesses and minority shareholders to defend their rights is essential for business growth (Djankov et al. 2008). Without the ability to uphold contracts, businesses will be forced to depend on social enforcement, relying on family, friends, and local notables to shame vendors who refuse to deliver or customers who fail to pay (McMillan and Woodruff 1999). This will limit the scope of potential business partners to those in a firms' immediate social network. Only with external enforcement possibilities will firms be willing to do business outside of their social network, allowing for greater expansion and growth (Malesky and Taussig 2009b). The law-and-finance-nexus literature has further shown that credit markets function best in locations with regions with better legal protections (Levine 1999). Because contracting institutions require independent courts, which are rarely decentralized, subnational differences in this factor are actually quite rare in the developing world.

Changing institutions requires changing the fundamental architecture of the political entity. As a result, it is extremely difficult to accomplish quickly. New institutions must be devised, debated, and implemented. More often than not, existing elites who benefit from previous institutional configurations do not want to lose their powerful positions and will work to undermine or weaken change (Geddes 1995). As a result, constitutional changes of this nature are quite rare and usually involve external shocks. Indeed, the bulk of literature on subnational institutions and economic performance focuses on historical shocks' enduring effects on institutions. These papers demonstrate how institutions inherited during imperial expansions, colonization, or wars shaped the institutions in place in subnational governments today (Banerjee and Iyer 2005; Acemoglu et al. 2009; Dell 2010; Pepinsky 2016).

Reading these historical pieces is fascinating but depressing from a developmental perspective. When so much of a region's current success is an artifact of historical fortune, it presents a legacy of despair for subnational territories on the wrong side of a historical roll of the dice. In a recent paper, Maloney and Caciedo (2016) show that subnational differences in economic performance across developing nations in North and South America have persisted for a half millennium and even predate the enormous shock of European colonization and dramatic reductions in the native population.

Given these persistent effects at the subnational level, what can be done to enhance property rights or contracting institutions short of constitutional change? One particularly fruitful line of study has been on the allocation of land titles to ensure property rights to individuals and small businesses (de Soto 2000). While this literature has demonstrated impressive returns in inspiring individuals to invest in their personal property and family (Field 2005; Galiani and Schargrodsky 2010), it has shown less robust effects on business decisions and credit allocation to entrepreneurs. For contracting institutions, development practitioners have explored the use of arbitration centers in areas where systematic legal reform seems impossible (Mattli 2001; Dixit 2007). Currently, there is little strong empirical evidence for the effects of arbitration on business investment decisions.

Public Services: The vital public services necessary to enhance subnational business performance are transportation infrastructure, communications infrastructure, education, and public health.

Transportation infrastructure includes traditional measures, such as roads, bridges, airports, and deepwater ports. High-quality infrastructure improves business productivity by reducing shipping and transaction costs, limiting space needs for warehousing if rapid delivery of inputs can be assured (known as just-in-time management), and lessening the risk of damaged and spoiled products (Estache and Sinha 1999; Demurger 2001; Fedderke et al. 2006). In a study of subnational business performance in Latin America, Acemoglu and Dell (2010) find that increasing a municipality's average distance from paved roads by 1% reduces labor income of prime-aged males by 0.06% in Brazil, 0.09% in Mexico, and 0.14% in Panama. In an era of multinational production with components manufactured in multiple locations, bottlenecks in a supply chain can be incredibly costly. Improving infrastructure also creates new markets for existing firms by introducing their products and services to new customers and reducing the time necessary for final delivery. Global supply chains and the containerization of shipping has also brought greater attention to the need for local governments to assure connectivity between modes of transportation infrastructure. Modern firms want to be assured that their products and vital inputs can move seamlessly from truck to train to ship to airplane (Notteboom and Rodrigue 2009).

Telecommunication infrastructure, including adequate phone coverage and Internet bandwidth, continues to gain importance, helping businesses connect with suppliers and customers, expand potential markets, engage new partners, and acquire new skills and technology (Roller and Waverman 2001). Commodity producers in emerging markets now regularly use technology to stay abreast of rapid changes in pricing and weather that affect the bottom line.

As for human capital, beyond the demographic trends discussed in the endowment section, leaders can invest by improving education and training. High-quality human capital increases productivity and reduces the costs of in-house training for businesses, which can be expensive and risky for small operations.

In their paper on Latin America, Acemoglu and Dell (2010) further find that about half of the within-country variation in levels of GDP per capita is accounted for by education. They tie these income benefits to Total Factor Productivity (TFP) growth among businesses. Raising education levels of one subnational unit above the sample mean of 6.58 years is associated with a TFP increase of 6.7%, which is comparable to estimates calculated by Rauch (1993) and Acemoglu and Angrist (1999), who look at variation across US states. They also find that one year of college education enhances output per capita by 7.9%, which leads to an average 6% growth rate in TFP.

Improving human capital requires enhancing curriculum and teacher quality in elementary, secondary, and tertiary education, as well as vocational training programs. While vocational training changes can be implemented relatively quickly and the productivity effects observed immediately in the workplace, it can take years or decades to observe the ultimate benefits of general education improvements. This is particularly true for Iranzo et al. (2009), who claim that the benefits of spillover from education to the subnational economy are greatest for college education. High-quality tertiary education can only be rarely developed within a local leader's political time horizon. In addition to training, localities can seek to attract human capital through targeted migration and guest labor programs. Human capital improvements should also lead to gains in bureaucratic capacity when high-quality employees are available for local bureaucratic agencies (Gennailoi et al. 2011).

Other long-term public service factors include ensuring public health through adequate access to electricity, potable water, and health care services through local hospitals and clinics (Banerjee and Duflo 2005). By ensuring a healthy and efficient workforce, these services enhance the quality of life in a locality. And numerous studies have shown how small improvements in public health have long-term effects on the population's productivity.

Long-term factors in business performance require vision and intelligent planning by leaders, who must look beyond short-term political calculations to put in place structures that have dividends long after they are out of office, potentially even allowing rivals to take credit for the improvements they make.

Short-Term Factors

Short-term factors are those that can be altered within the timeframe of an existing administration and immediately affect the performance of businesses. Theoretically, they should be most influenced by decentralization of authority. Such short-term policy levers include tax policy, economic governance, and bureaucratic capacity.

Tax Policy

The first short-term factor is local tax policy, which has received the greatest attention from scholars studying subnational competition (Epple and Zelenitz 1981a, 1981b). Businesses prefer low and predictable tax rates that do not unnecessarily cut into the bottom line. On the other hand, as discussed earlier in this chapter, businesses have demands for high-quality public services, particularly infrastructure and human capital, that require local revenue. Low taxes or tax giveaways that undermine vital public services can be counterproductive (Wilson and Wildasin 2004).

Subnational governments can compete to attract or grow business by lowering business taxes[1] for the entire community or by offering policies targeted at specific businesses or sectors called tax incentives. Tax incentives include tax abatements, tax holidays for limited periods of time, and reductions on individual tax items. In investment climate surveys, businesses often cite tax policy among the most important factors in location selections. Jensen et al. (2015) argue that tax incentives have proliferated because they are particularly attractive to subnational leaders with short-term outlooks. While it is difficult for politicians to claim credit for endowments or infrastructure and educational reforms put in place years before they took office, tax incentives allow politicians to associate

---

[1] Business taxes include corporate income taxes (CIT), capital taxes, nonresidential property taxes, and various forms of an "industry and commerce" tax that are found in many developing countries.

themselves directly with incentives targeted at particular firms. This allows them to sell their development bona fides to voters (Jensen et al. 2014) or central benefactors in authoritarian systems (Jensen and Malesky 2018, Ch. 8).

The early fiscal federalism literature did not attribute an important role to subnational entities in taxation. As Bahl and Bird (2008) detail, the only good local taxes were those that could be easily administered at the local level, were paid solely (or predominantly) by local residents, could be harmonized with central or other taxes, and did not generate dangerous competition between subnational, local, or regional governments or between subnational and national governments. According to Bahl and Bird, for the early fiscal federalists, the only tax that fit this bill was the property tax.

As the literature has developed, scholars have identified various forms of tax-sharing arrangements that can be beneficial for subnational governments. These are profiled by Rodden in this volume. Economic geographers and tax specialists, however, remain skeptical of subnational business tax competition (McClure 1994). As Bird (1999) writes, "experts have looked at the distortions and problems arising from local business taxes, shuddered, and said, more or less, 'just don't do it.'" While there is clear evidence of the distortionary effects of subnational business taxes, which I profile later in this chapter, Bird argues that these taxes are attractive to both politicians and individual business and will be a component of the subnational business environment far into the future. Consequently, he argues that the most appropriate form of tax for this purpose would seem to be a "value-added income tax" or a VAT levied on the basis of income (production, origin) rather than consumption (destination).

Economic Governance Policy

In Avanish Dixit's lecture as president of the American Economics Association, he defined economic governance as "the processes that support economic activity and economic transactions by protecting property rights, enforcing contracts, and taking collective action to provide appropriate organizational infrastructure" (Dixit 2009, p. 5). While this definition is extremely useful, it merges the long-term economic institutions of property rights and contracting institutions discussed earlier with policies that can be altered in the short and medium term by current leaders.

Three sets of policies have received widespread attention from economists and political scientists interested in subnational business performance: regulation, corruption, and transparency. Not coincidentally, these sets form the core of the US-AID Provincial Competitiveness Index in Vietnam and other subnational economic governance indices around the world. These three sets interact and overlap in important ways. For instance, the endogenous regulation literature has shown how regulatory barriers are put in place specifically to generate rents and opportunities for bribery (Henderson and Kuncoro 2004). Further, lack of transparency creates opportunities and hides corruption. Ferraz and Finan (2011) demonstrate significant reductions in corruption after the release of local audit reports in Brazil, while Francken (2009) shows less capture of public funds in Madagascar after a public education treatment. Nevertheless, it is important to consider the three sets as analytically distinct.

Regulation: Due to the prominence of the World Bank's Doing Business Index and its more recent subnational versions, regulatory burden has become a focal point of economic development policy. Theoretically, regulations are meant to protect the public by ensuring labor safety, safe products, and sanitary food quality, and to limit environmental damage. In practice, however, regulation can tie up businesses in red tape, thereby reducing productivity and limiting their expansion. Regulations have been shown to raise entry costs, limit entrepreneurship, and protect inefficient monopolies. Djankov et al. (2002) identified a strong correlation between the costs and time of starting a business and the size of the informal economy. Subsequent micro-level studies have shown that registrations of new companies and of new corporate entities are higher when entry and other more general regulatory obstacles to business are lower (Desai et al. 2003; Klapper et al. 2006). This is especially true in industries with higher nonregulatory obstacles to entry – for example, more expensive equipment or other inputs (Fisman and Sarria-Allende 2010) – and where technology or global demand shifts have occurred (Ciccone and Papaioannou 2007). Ardagna and Lusardi (2009) also find that the higher entry costs lower the share of entrepreneurs with a growth orientation. In perhaps the best causally identified work in this area, Bruhn (2011) takes advantage of a business-entry reform that was implemented at different times in Mexico. Taking advantage of the reform rollout, she finds that reducing entry regulations increased the number of registered businesses by 5%. The entire increase was due to former wage owners starting new businesses. The regulation had no impact on registration of existing informal businesses.

Corruption: Corruption, often pithily defined as the "use of public office for private gain," is among the most pervasive and well-studied problems in the social sciences. In the academic literature analyzing political corruption, scholars distinguish between two general basic forms: petty and macro-corruption. Petty corruption consists primarily of the small bribes and informal fees incurred by individual citizens as they go about their normal activities. It also occurs when businesses must pay informal fees, above and beyond legally stipulated service fees, to facilitate regulatory compliance or receive public services. Petty corruption is the most commonly analyzed form of corruption, as it can be plausibly identified using survey data of individuals, businesses, and nongovernmental organizations. By contrast, macro-corruption takes place at the highest levels of national and local governments, and consists of activities that are not directly observed by average citizens, although they certainly have an impact on general welfare. Macro-corruption commonly includes such activities as (1) accepting kickbacks on the issuance of government procurement contracts (e.g., for construction, equipment, or technical services), (2) taking bribes for policies that favor particular economic actors, and (3) allocating limited resources (including natural resources, telecommunications spectrums, export or production quotas, and high-ranking positions) on a nonmarket basis that benefits family, friends, or those with close relationships to the policymakers.

Corruption affects business performance in multiple ways. It raises the costs of doing business, leads to worse public services when less efficient providers are improperly selected in procurement contracts, and creates costly policy uncertainty (Olken and Pander 2012). In a review of the literature, Gurgur and Shah (2005) demonstrate the important role that corruption has in subnational business entry, expansion, and performance. From a management perspective, Chan et al. (2010) demonstrate statistically the effects of corruption on foreign affiliate performance across subregions. In a two-country study, they find little evidence for a relationship between corruption and performance in the United States, but find corruption has a strong negative effect on performance in China.

Corruption is one of the few areas where there is a significant overlap between scholars studying subnational business performance and those studying decentralization. The key debate has to do with which outcomes of decentralization are better at reducing corruption. Scholars focused on the competition between subunits have argued that increased corruption can reduce the bribe price paid by firms (Fisman and Gatti 2002; Bai et al. 2017). Indeed, Menes (2003) found in a qualitative study of US cities that firms' ability to relocate to other jurisdictions was one possible reason why urban corruption in the pre-Progressive era was not more severe. Scholars who worry about capture of the decision-making process and the role of government unit proliferation in increasing the number of places where businesses must pay bribes have warned that decentralization might increase corruption (Ackerman 1978; Shleifer and Vishny 1993; Fan et al. 2009).

Transparency and Access to Information: Businesses need access to local budgets, land and infrastructure plans, and legal documents necessary to run their businesses. Transparency has enormous benefits in its ability to reduce the risk and uncertainty for investors, allowing them to engage in long-term planning, predict legal and macroeconomic changes that may affect their business, and reduce adjustment costs (Broz 2002; Stasavage 2003) and the need for self-insurance (Aizenmen and Marion 1993). Transparency has important direct and indirect effects on investors' decisions to expand their operations (Drabek and Payne 2002; Gelos and Wei 2005). Information on land and provincial planning may be legally available to all, but accessing that information can often be problematic. This can have a detrimental effect on the growth of the private sector, because firms cannot take advantage of provincial initiatives. When changes in the legal regime are not readily accessible, a firm may operate successfully for several years, only to find itself on the wrong side of the law simply out of ignorance. In most cases, such ignorance will cost the firm little, but there is always the potential for an unscrupulous official to exploit asymmetric information about the legal code to his/her advantage. Conversely, a firm may be eligible for savings, investment opportunities, or tax refunds, but never takes advantage of them because it is unaware of these benefits (Malesky et al. 2015).

Lack of transparency can also affect investment through its impact on predictability, or the notion that provincial laws and regulations are implemented in a manner that would allow firms to forecast and thus build new developments into their business plans (Hollyer et al. 2011). With transparency, firms can understand the decisions that are made and how they will be implemented, so that they have a better chance at predicting the direction and risk of long-term strategies and increase their ability to make informed investment decisions (Gelos and Wei 2005).

Transparency can also affect investment indirectly through its impact on the equitable use of provincial resources. Indeed, a lack of transparency can lead to severe inefficiencies in such resources – inefficiencies that represent more than a simple transfer of resources from one party to another. Take, for instance, the issue of subnational planning. The impact of infrastructure and land-conversion plans is limited if the details are available to only a select few insiders. One of the reasons this impact may be limited is because of the limited transparency of the real estate market. Only a few knowledgeable insiders know the location of future infrastructure projects and industrial zones. These insiders can then profit by buying up the land ahead of time. Other investors in real estate must make large conjectures based on small bits of information.

In a panel model of transparency in Vietnam using the PCI data, Malesky et al. (2015) find that transparency proves the most robust governance determinant of investment in Vietnam, outperforming more widely studied measures such as property rights, contracting institutions, regulatory costs, and corruption. They find that one standard deviation in the ten-point transparency index is associated with a 10% increase in firm investment. This effect is most pronounced for foreign firms and small, private operations. Large domestic firms already enjoy a unique information advantage and do not benefit from additional increases in transparency. Digging deeper, the authors find that the single most influential aspect of transparency is simply making subnational planning documents available to a wider swathe of investors.

Bureaucratic Capacity

A final factor in subnational business performance is the skill and efficiency of the local bureaucracy (Acemoglu et al. 2015). Do local subunits have the resources to attract high-quality employees who can provide bureaucratic services and efficient regulatory monitoring? Francis Fukuyama (2013) has been arguing that this factor is critically important for economic outcomes, but has been understudied by the discipline. Indeed, there is very little work specifically looking at subnational differences in bureaucratic capacity. One notable exception is Brown et al. (2009), who find that privatization leads to greater firm productivity in Russian regions with bigger state bureaucracies as measured by the number of employees. They argue that higher levels of staffing allow for greater policy implementation and support services. Libman (2013) further finds that bureaucratic capacity is associated with the growth benefits of energy resources across Russian regions. Finally, Ma et al. (2013) show how the performance of Fortune 500 corporations is influenced by bureaucratic capacity across China's provinces.

Endogenous Subnational Determinants

A final set of business determinants are endogenous in the sense that they result from the preexisting presence of a business community. Other factors, such as geography or infrastructure, may have lured the first movers in, but once a certain tipping point is reached, clusters of businesses can reduce transaction costs and create opportunities for new entrants.

The most well-known example is economies of agglomeration, first made famous by Krugman (1991), and later developed into a developmental strategy of creating business clusters by Porter (1998) and Fairbanks and Lindsay (1997). The basic argument for agglomeration centers on the upstream and downstream productivity benefits of colocation. Upstream, businesses benefit from greater access to and declining costs of inputs and business support services, such as specialized mechanics, accountants, financing, and marketing. The larger the cluster, the greater the opportunities for competing vendors, but also the greater the likelihood of specialization and division of labor, leading to more nuanced and sophisticated inputs. Places without large populations of businesses cannot support large populations of vendors. Second, colocation also leads to greater attraction of customers than businesses could achieve alone (Chung and Song 2004). Famous subnational business clusters include Silicon Valley, Hollywood, Vancouver's computer animation industries, and financial capitals in Frankfurt, London, and New York. Others have pointed to the semiconductor industry in Singapore and manufacturing in Guadalajara, Mexico, as examples of successful clusters in developing countries.

For foreign investors, an additional advantage of clustering is what has been called "soft infrastructure." A large presence of foreign firms generates markets for support services targeted specifically at foreign business executives, including international schools, hospitals, and entertainment opportunities. These factors can play significant roles in business attraction when foreign producers know they will have to locate expatriates in a developing country in the early years of operations.

The evidence is not clear that clusters can be created by policy. Geographic factors often play a role in the first set of movements; efforts to circumvent the long, organic process of clustering through tax incentives or targeted infrastructure spending sprees have not proved universally successful. Further, some scholars have argued that there can be diseconomies to clustering as well. Most obviously, price competition limits monopoly rents, but high degrees of business density can also generate traffic snarls and environmental damage that raise transaction costs and decrease livability (Newlands 2003).

Endogenous determinants of business performance are important, but by definition they require stimulating a large density of businesses in the first place. Policy and institutional change can play some role in driving these choices, but these strategies have proven risky and there are widespread examples of costly failures. Subnational governments give away thousands of dollars in costly tax incentives to companies that would have come anyway in order to jump-start development, but see little evidence of spillover from those companies into their economies (*The Economist* 2007; Jensen et al. 2018).

THEORETICAL BENEFITS OF DECENTRALIZATION FOR BUSINESS

The literature on the mechanisms connecting decentralization and economic growth is vast, but it can be simplified by focusing on the three mechanisms that appear repeatedly in theoretical discussions: 1) better tailoring of services to local needs and consequently more efficient public spending; 2) increased responsiveness of local leaders to citizens and local firms; 3) competition for investment, labor, and career advancement.

These mechanisms are discussed in detail in other chapters of this volume. Rather than simply repeating those arguments, I want to connect them more directly to the business performance determinants outlined earlier. To do this, I briefly summarize the argument and then highlight the key assumptions necessary for the mechanism to operate, paying careful attention to whether these assumptions are met in practice.

Tailoring

Going back to the Oates (1972) decentralization theorem, a critical argument of the fiscal federalism literature is that increased efficiency and welfare benefits accrue when decisions are made by those closest to the local situation who understand the needs of the community best. Sometimes the literature will refer to differences in language, ethnicity, or culture, but for our purposes the key differences are likely to be in the economic base of the region and the sectoral distribution of firms. Firms in different industries will have different needs, and a uniform central policy may prove inadequate, accidentally favoring some firms over others. The uniform policy may also be wasteful, as services are over-provided in locations that don't have the needs or capacity to exploit them. Advocates of the tailoring mechanism emphasize the innovation benefits of giving local leaders policy leeway to respond creatively to firms' needs (Bird 1999). Supreme Court Justice Louis Brandeis famously coined the term "laboratories of democracy" to highlight this effect across US states. It has also been observed in China. Coase and Wang (2012) emphasize how the secret ingredient to Chinese development was the willingness to "seek truth from fact," using regional pilots as the way to identify successful policies that were then implemented on a broad scale. Chengang Xu (2011) has described the system that generates these local experiments in China, regional decentralized authoritarianism (RDA).

It is also important to note that factor mobility is not a necessary assumption for this mechanism (Oates 1999). We do not need households and businesses voting with their feet as in the Tiebout (1956) model.

Four theoretical assumptions, however, do undergird the tailoring mechanism for business performance. First, preferences must differ substantially across groups of businesses. Second, these preference differences must be concentrated within subnational administrative jurisdictions and not across them. Third, local governments must listen better to local firms' needs than central authorities do. Fourth, the central government must have difficulty providing specialized service provision to subnational units. If these assumptions are not met in the country, it is unlikely that services will be better tailored than under centralized systems (Treisman 2007). In cases where the second and third assumptions are not met, centralized service provision is preferable.

Monitoring and Accountability

The discussion of local political decentralization leads to the second mechanism, namely monitoring. According to scholars, political decentralization provides accountability by enabling firms to demand services and policies from their local leaders and to sanction them if they fail to respond to those demands (Bardhan and Mookherjee 2005). As a consequence, rational politicians should adapt their behavior to local needs and concerns. The argument found particular resonance for advocates and development practitioners in overcentralized or authoritarian systems (Grindle 2007), as it provided opportunities to improve participation and avoid direct confrontation with central authorities (Cheem and Rondinelli 2007; Wunsch 1998).

Beyond more efficient service delivery, the improved accountability brought by decentralization is also linked to better governance. In particular, scholars argue that decentralization could ward off predation. When government administration is brought closer to the individuals who actually use these services, locals should have a greater stake in monitoring because they have a greater stake in the outcome. At the same time, corruption should be more visible because the guardians would be on site rather than in a distant national capital. Moreover, in a decentralized system, citizens should be better able to monitor quality, and, if necessary, to demand and achieve change from officials near them. Consequently, local officials should be more responsive because of the greater possibility of public sanction and disruption (Cheema and Rondinelli 2007; Falleti 2005).

Monitoring and accountability mechanisms depend on three assumptions. First, local officials must have the incentive to promote general economic growth, rather than try to benefit a particular local monopoly or line their own pockets (Schragger 2010). Second, local businesses must be sufficiently informed about local policy and alternatives to press for change. Third, local firms must be able to mobilize and organize effectively to vote the bums out. Again, these assumptions are critical. In locations where local officials are not motivated to reform, transparency is limited, and there is no electoral sanctioning capacity, decentralization can lead to corruption or capture of the local policy-making process (Bardhan and Mookherjee 2005).

Competition for Capital and Labor

In the third mechanism, decentralization creates competition for capital and labor that leads to improved governance outcomes, as subnational governments compete for business with better services, institutions, and governance policies (Tiebout 1956; Inman and Rubinfeld 1997). In the literature on China, the notion of competition has been expanded beyond capital and labor to include local officials' career incentives (Xu 2011; Bell 2015). Officials have incentives to cater to businesses and innovate on governance because they will be rewarded for improving on cadre evaluation criteria (Li and Zhu 2005; Landry 2008).

The key assumption for the competition theory is the free movement of capital and labor (Tiebout 1956). In sharp contrast to the responsiveness theory, the competition argument is primarily aimed at mobile domestic and foreign firms. Indeed, Weingast (1995) argues in the fourth component of his Market-Preserving Federalism framework that central authorities must police and guarantee a common market to ensure competition. Second, there must be hard budget constraints. Local authorities must raise and spend their own budgets, and they cannot print money or receive bailouts from higher authorities (Schragger 2010). Third, workers and businesses must have sufficient information about alternative jurisdictions so that they know where to go in order to take advantage of differences in institutions and policy. When these conditions are not met, sufficient competition will not take place, which can exacerbate initial inequality among subnational governments.

POLICY LESSONS FOR DEVELOPMENT

In this final section, I seek to unite the business performance and decentralization literatures by connecting the concrete lessons we learned about the determinants of business success with the assumptions of the decentralization literature. Although decentralization can successfully promote economic growth, when key assumptions of the theoretical models for decentralization are not met, devolving authority to local levels could prove ineffective or even harmful. In lieu of a conclusion, I outline six policy lessons for development practitioners considering a decentralization intervention, which cover the areas where decentralization is likely to be more or less effective. I also provide supplemental interventions that are likely to enhance the effectiveness of decentralization policy.

There Is No Clear Evidence That Decentralization Enhances Business Performance

While there is a clear relationship between subnational environments and business performance, it is not obvious that decentralization improves either the determinants or business performance. Although the theoretical arguments are strong, scholars have been unable to pin down clear causal evidence of a relationship. There are three reasons for this. First, the key assumptions for each of the decentralization arguments are rarely met in practice. Businesses are not fully informed of subnational differences (Rodden and Rose-Ackerman 1997); even if they are, they are unable to move to take advantage of differences in policy due to cultural or geographical reasons (Pepinsky and Wihardja 2011), or they are unable to mobilize politically to alter policies at the subnational level (Olken 2007; Yadav and Mukherjee 2015). Treisman (2007) and Schragger (2010) have further challenged the notion that local authorities have citizens' best intentions at heart and understand local preferences better than national counterparts (or the central government's local agents). Whether local governments are better listeners depends on other institutions in the locality. In local governments characterized by insufficient electoral competition, patronage-based voting, or local capture of legislative and executive institutions, local leaders might not have the appropriate incentives to listen to the broader business community (Hankla 2009). Second, decentralization unleashes multiple forces, some of which can have sharply countervailing and even negative effects. Third, in locations where endowments or long-term factors are most important for business performance, the timeframe for observing benefits may be too short.

Determinants with Short Gestation Periods Are Likely to See the Greatest Change under Decentralization

Delineating the assumptions of arguments for decentralization makes clear that the three mechanisms listed earlier are most likely to influence the determinants with short gestation periods. Tax, governance, and management of bureaucracy are the attributes that can be most effectively managed by local government officials within a promotion or management cycle. Infrastructure and education are subject to change, but their gestation periods may be longer than an official's time horizon. Leaders would need to be far-sighted to engage in these types of reforms.

The mobility of businesses also plays a role. For mobile firms, the short-term features can be most easily capitalized on by changing jurisdiction, thereby triggering the competition mechanism. For less mobile domestic firms, which cannot move but are active in the local government and may be able to influence the process, short-term factors are also the most likely to be influenced by political decentralization. In these conditions, however, local businesses will need to mobilize and demand change within the term of an incumbent politician.

Regulatory policy is the most likely short-term factor to require customized local handling if business sectors are highly concentrated in administrative jurisdictions. Certainly, natural resources–based economies need very specific policies for licensing resource exploitation rights. Similarly, labor safety rules are likely to be more relevant in more dangerous manufacturing sectors. It is harder, however, to make an argument for the benefits of tailoring for the other governance measures. Beliefs about transparency, corruption, and bureaucratic capacity are unlikely to differ dramatically across administrative units.

Tax policy may be the riskiest short-term determinant to expose to decentralization (Bahl and Bird 2008). Decentralizing tax policy can be quite distortionary, with secondary effects that are hard to control and isolate. For instance, "tax exporting" can occur when government units with firms selling products outside their jurisdiction (cigarette manufacturers, gas distributors, breweries) impose heavy taxes on firms in their location in the expectation that the taxes will be passed along and paid elsewhere.

A Nuanced Understanding of Endowments

Where endowments play the crucial role in investment decisions, we should not expect decentralization to directly influence business performance. In these settings, decentralization might impact investment choices by influencing the choices between two locations with similar endowments but differing qualities of public services or governance. Theoretically, decentralization might also have a mediating effect by influencing the productive use of endowments.

Endowments, however, are likely to shape preferences that businesses have in particular jurisdictions over long-term and short-term determinants. Thus the tailoring mechanism may come into play. Urban centers are likely to need different services than rural areas. Resource-based economies will require different infrastructure and regulatory policies than manufacturing-based economies. The key question raised by Treisman (2007) and Beramendi (2007), though, is whether it is clear that subnational governments know and understand these different preferences better than central bureaucrats.

Decentralization Can Exacerbate Inequality in Subnational Units

A potential negative side of decentralization in business environments where endowments or long-term determinants play key roles in business decisions is the potential for vicious and virtuous feedback loops. Particularly in the case of fiscal decentralization, where local expenditures are funded predominantly through own-source revenue, wide differences in endowments at the onset of decentralization can send subnational entities onto very different development tracks. Well-endowed places will attract greater business investment, which leads to greater growth and revenue accumulation, which in turn can be allocated to better public services and government capacity, leading to future investment. By contrast, poorly endowed locations will find themselves squeezed for revenue and unable to fund improvements in public services or expenditures. Even worse, these locations may have an incentive to increase local taxes and service fees in order to generate revenue, which can squeeze the nascent business community.

Tax experts also warn of destructive "tax competition" in such settings where richer locations with large tax bases at the onset of decentralization lower their rates below other regions to further expand the size of their base by attracting firms from other locations (Bird 1999). At the extreme, this can generate opportunities for firms to move their tax headquarters to a low-tax jurisdiction without moving their production facilities in a high-tax jurisdiction, allowing them to use transfer pricing to declare losses in the high-tax location and profits in the low-tax location and thereby shift profits out of the jurisdiction where external factors are most likely to have an impact.

In every subnational index I have worked on, we have noted the strong correlation between pre-decentralization endowments and post-intervention governance quality. On average, localities that had closer proximity to markets, resources, better infrastructure, and human capital prior to decentralization tended to have better governance of the private sector today. Certainly, there were always a few underdeveloped regions that managed to provide excellent governance and later became dynamic economic centers (Binh Duong and Da Nang in Vietnam, Solo in Indonesia, Kampong Cham in Cambodia). The more common phenomenon, however, has been that rich regions developed greater governance and entered a positive cycle of business attraction, greater revenue, greater public service outlays, better governance, and greater business attraction. Poorly endowed provinces tended to enter vicious cycles of poor business attraction and declining governance.

The Benefits of Long-Term Decentralization Depend on the Concentration of Business Preferences

For infrastructure and public services, the appropriate decision-making level depends on the assumption that preferences are homogenous across business units (Schragger 2010). On issues where preferences are concentrated in administrative jurisdictions, tailoring may lead to efficiency benefits. On issues where preferences are not concentrated, however, decentralization and local tailoring may not be the most appropriate strategy.

The design of infrastructure networks and educational curriculum may benefit from a broader perspective. Duplication in infrastructure arrangements can be damaging. It makes little sense for every subnational district to have a deepwater port, international airport, or multilane highway. While these projects can generate prestige or pecuniary benefits for local leaders, most countries do not have the shipping or tourist traffic to take advantage of such outlays. In these situations, it makes greater sense for central decision makers to design these projects with an eye to creating regional or national synergies. The same case could be made for educational reforms. Ensuring labor mobility across regions might require a national curriculum, granting businesses confidence that they can rely on a basic set of foundational skills when hiring workers from outside the region.

Access to Information Is Critical for Decentralization to Work

Among the most important theoretical flaws in the decentralization literature is the assumption of perfect information that facilitates capital and labor movements, responsive governments, and activist constituencies. Entrepreneurs and workers often cannot relocate because they are not fully informed about which level of government provides a particular service (Rodden and Rose-Ackerman 1997). Newly empowered local authorities do not have full information on local preferences (Cai and Treisman 2004; Treisman 2007). Nonmobile local businesses do not have enough knowledge of local policy or the relative performance of their locality to advocate for change.

In particular, researchers have shown that local elites can capture grassroots monitoring, taking advantage of their concentrated and political resources to manipulate public decisions in their favor (Campos and Hellman 2005; Reinikka and Svensson 2005; Bardhan and Mookherjee 2006). More benignly, monitoring may simply pose a collective-action problem for locals, as the time costs of ferreting out malfeasance in every public service quickly outweigh the individual benefits (Olken 2007). Even when corruption and poor performance can be identified, local businesses may attribute the activities to the wrong level of government in elections. In sum, the businesses lack full information (Wibbels 2006).

A potential policy solution for the knowledge gap is available. Advocates of subnational economic governance indices (EGIs) have proposed them as a solution to many of these informational problems. By carefully researching, documenting, and operationalizing the services provided by a particular level of government, these indices erase the confusion about which level is responsible for the measured outcomes, and provide detailed and actionable metrics on issues citizens and local businesses understand (Malesky and Merchant 2011; World Bank 2013; Bland and Vaz 2017). By publishing these rankings, subnational indices inform businesses and citizens about which locations have the highest-quality services, facilitating competition for capital and labor movements and more effective advocacy. By identifying the best subnational governments in a particular country, EGIs facilitate innovation on the part of local leaders, providing them with incentives to change and role models to seek out within their own national context (The Asia Foundation 2011). Better access to information seems to force local politicians to respond more appropriately to business demands, in both developed and developing countries.

***

The many studies I have reviewed here show that decentralization is not a panacea for economic performance. Devolving authority to subnational units may generate greater economic activity, but success depends on: 1) making sure the context meets the strict assumptions of the underlying theoretical models; 2) understanding the needs of the business sector and determining that the obstacles to performance can be reduced within a reasonable political timeline; and 3) ensuring that local institutions offer appropriate levels of accountability, so that local politicians have incentives to make the best decisions for locations where they work.

REFERENCES

Abdullatif, L., J. Martinez-Vasquez, and C. Musharraf (2013). "Is Fiscal Decentralization Harmful to Business Climate?" International Center for Public Policy, Andrew Young School of Public Policy, Georgia State University.

Acemoglu, D. and J. Angrist (1999). "How Large Are the Social Returns to Education? Evidence from Compulsory Schooling Laws." NBER Working Paper 7444.

Acemoglu, D., D. Cantoni, S. Johnson, and J. A. Robinson (2009). "The Consequences of Radical Reform: The French Revolution." NBER Working Paper 14831.

Acemoglu, D., and M. Dell (2010). "Productivity Differences between and within Countries." *American Economic Journal: Macroeconomics* 2(1): 169–188.

Acemoglu, D., C. García-Jimeno, and J. A. Robinson (2015). "State Capacity and Economic Development: A Network Approach." *American Economic Review* 105 (8): 2364–2409.

Acemoglu, D., and S. Johnson (2005). "Unbundling Institutions." *Journal of Political Economy* 113(5): 949–995.

Ackerman, S. R. (1978). *Corruption: A Study in Political Economy*. New York, NY: Academic Press.

Agrawal, A., and E. Ostrom (2001). "Collective Action, Property Rights, and Decentralization in Resource Use in India and Nepal." *Politics & Society* 29(4): 485–514.

Aizenman, J., and N. P. Marion (1993). "Policy Uncertainty, Persistence and Growth." *Review of International Economics* 1(2): 145–163.

Akai, N., and M. Sakata (2002). "Fiscal Decentralization Contributes to Economic Growth: Evidence from State-Level Cross-Section Data for the United States." *Journal of Urban Economics* 52(1): 93–108.

Alesina, A., and P. Giuliano (2015). "Culture and Institutions." *Journal of Economic Literature* 53(4): 898–944.

Ardagna, S., and A. Lusardi (2009). "Where Does Regulation Hurt? Evidence from New Businesses across Countries." NBER Working Paper 14747.

Asatryan, Z., and L. P. Feld (2015). "Revisiting the Link between Growth and Federalism: A Bayesian Model Averaging Approach." *Journal of Comparative Economics* 43(3): 772–781.

The Asia Foundation (2011). "Innovations and Strengthening Local Economic Governance in Asia." Technical Report. San Francisco, CA: The Asia Foundation.

Asiedu, E., and D. Lien (2011). "Democracy, Foreign Direct Investment and Natural Resources." *Journal of International Economics* 84(1): 99–111.

Bahl, R., and R. Bird (2008). "Subnational Taxes in Developing Countries: The Way Forward." *Public Budgeting and Finance* 28(4): 1–25.

Bai, J., S. Jayachandran, E. J. Malesky, and B. A. Olken (2017). "Firm Growth and Corruption: Empirical Evidence from Vietnam." *Economic Journal* https://doi.org/10.1111/ecoj.12560.

Banerjee, A. V., and E. Duflo (2005). "Growth Theory through the Lens of Development Economics." *Handbook of Economic Growth* 1 (Part A): 473–552.

Banerjee, A., and L. Iyer (2005). "History, Institutions, and Economic Performance: The Legacy of Colonial Land Tenure Systems in India." *American Economic Review* 95(4): 1190–1213.

Bardhan, P., and D. Mookherjee (2005). "Decentralizing Antipoverty Program Delivery in Developing Countries." *Journal of Public Economics* 89(4): 675–704.

Bardhan, P., and D. Mookherjee (2006). "Decentralization, Corruption, and Government Accountability." *International Handbook on the Economics of Corruption* 6: 161–188.

Begg, I. (1999). "Cities and Competitiveness." *Urban Studies* 36(5/6): 795.

Bell, D. A. (2015). *The China Model: Political Meritocracy and the Limits of Democracy*. Princeton, NJ: Princeton University Press.

Beramendi, P. (2007). "Federalism." In C. Boix and S. C. Stokes (eds.), *The Oxford Handbook of Comparative Politics* (pp. 752–781). New York, NY: Oxford University Press.

Besley, T., and A. Case (1992). "Incumbent Behavior: Vote Seeking, Tax Setting and Yardstick Competition." *American Economic Review* 85(1): 25–45.

Bird, M. R. M. (1999). "Rethinking Subnational Taxes: A New Look at Tax Assignment." IMF Working Paper 99–165.

Bland, G., and P. Vaz (2017). "An Effective Tool for Promoting Growth and Effectiveness? The Sustainability of the Subnational Business Environment Index." RTI Press. 10.3768/rtipress.2017.op.0038.1704.

Brennan, G., and J. M. Buchanan (1980). *The Power to Tax: Analytic Foundations of a Fiscal Constitution*. Cambridge, UK: Cambridge University Press.

Brown, J. D., J. Earle, and S. Gehlbach (2009). "Helping Hand or Grabbing Hand? State Bureaucracy and Privatization Effectiveness." *American Political Science Review* 103 (2): 264–283.

Broz, J. L. (2002). "Political System Transparency and Monetary Commitment Regimes." *International Organization* 56(4): 861–887.

Bruhn, M. (2011). "License to Sell: The Effect of Business Registration Reform on Entrepreneurial Activity in Mexico." *Review of Economics and Statistics* 93(1): 382–386.

Budd, L., and A. Hirmis (2004). "Conceptual Framework for Regional Competitiveness." *Regional Studies* 38(9): 1015–1028.

Cai, H., and D. Treisman (2004). "Does Competition for Capital Discipline Governments? Decentralization, Globalization, and Public Policy." *American Economic Review* 95(3): 817–830.

Campos, J. E., and J. S. Hellman (2005). "Governance Gone Local: Does Decentralization Improve Accountability?" In R. White and P. Smoke (eds.), *East Asia Decentralizes: Making Local Government Work* (pp. 237–252). Washington, DC: World Bank Publications.

Chan, C. M., S. Makino, and T. Isobe (2010). "Does Subnational Region Matter? Foreign Affiliate Performance in the United States and China." *Strategic Management Journal* 31(11): 1226–1243.

Cheema, G. S., and D. A. Rondinelli (eds.) (2007). *Decentralizing Governance: Emerging Concepts and Practices*. Washington, DC: Brookings Institution Press.

Chung, W., and J. Song (2004). "Sequential Investment, Firm Motives, and Agglomeration of Japanese Electronics Firms in the United States." *Journal of Economics and Management Strategy* 13(3): 539–560.

Ciccone, A., and E. Papaioannou (2007). "Red Tape and Delayed Entry." *Journal of the European Economic Association* 5(2–3): 444–458.

Coase, R., and N. Wang (2012). *How China Became Capitalist*. New York, NY: Palgrave Macmillan.

Crémer, J. (1995). "Arm's Length Relationships." *Quarterly Journal of Economics* 110 (2): 275–295.

Dai, L., L. Eden, and P. W. Beamish (2013). "Place, Space, and Geographical Exposure: Foreign Subsidiary Survival in Conflict Zones." *Journal of International Business Studies* 44(6): 554–578.

Davoodi, H., and H. F. Zou (1998). "Fiscal Decentralization and Economic Growth: A Cross-Country Study." *Journal of Urban Economics* 43(2): 244–257.

De Soto, H. (2000). *The Mystery of Capital: Why Capitalism Triumphs in the West and Fails Everywhere Else*. London: Basic Books.

Dell, M. (2010). "The Persistent Effects of Peru's Mining Mita." *Econometrica* 78(6): 1863–1903.

Demurger, S. (2001). "Infrastructure Development and Economic Growth: An Explanation for Regional Disparities in China?" *Journal of Comparative Economics* 29(1): 95–117.

Desai, M., P. Gompers, and J. Lerner (2003). "Institutions, Capital Constraints and Entrepreneurial Firm Dynamics: Evidence from Europe." NBER Working Paper 10165.

Dixit, A. K. (2007). *Lawlessness and Economics: Alternative Modes of Governance*. Princeton, NJ: Princeton University Press.

Dixit, A. (2009). "Governance Institutions and Economic Activity." *American Economic Review* 99(1): 3–24.

Djankov, S., R. La Porta, F. Lopez-de-Silanes, and A. Shleifer (2002). "The Regulation of Entry." *Quarterly Journal of Economics* 117(1): 1–37.

Djankov, S., R. La Porta, F. Lopez-de-Silanes, and A. Shleifer (2008). "The Law and Economics of Self-Dealing." *Journal of Financial Economics* 88(3): 430–465.

Drabek, Z., and W. Payne (2002). "The Impact of Transparency on Foreign Direct Investment." *Journal of Economic Integration* 17(4): 777–810.

Dreher, A. (2006). "Power to the People? The Impact of Decentralization on Governance." Swiss Institute for Business Cycle Research (KOF) Working Paper 121.

Dunning, J. H. (2000). "The Eclectic Paradigm As an Envelope for Economic and Business Theories of MNE Activity." *International Business Review* 9(2): 163–190.

Dunning, J. H. (2001). "The Eclectic (OLI) Paradigm of International Production: Past, Present and Future." *International Journal of the Economics of Business* 8(2): 173–190.

The Economist (2007). "The Fading Lustre of Clusters." October 11. www.economist .com/node/9928211. Accessed Sept. 15, 2016.

Ekholm, K., R. Forslid, and J. R. Markusen (2007). "Export-Platform Foreign Direct Investment." *Journal of the European Economic Association* 5(4): 776–795.

Enikolopov, R. and E. Zhuravskaya (2007). "Decentralization and Political Institutions." *Journal of Public Economics* 91(11–12): 2261–2290.

Epple, D., and A. Zelenitz (1981a). "The Implications of Competition among Jurisdictions: Does Tiebout Need Politics?" *Journal of Political Economy* 89(6): 1197–1217.

Epple, D., and A. Zelenitz (1981b). "The Roles of Jurisdictional Competition and of Collective Choice Institutions in the Market for Local Public Goods." *American Economic Review* 71(2): 87–92.

Estache, A., and S. Sinha (1999). *Does Decentralization Increase Spending on Public Infrastructure?* Washington, DC: World Bank Publications.

Fairbanks, M., and S. Lindsay (1997). *Plowing the Sea: Nurturing the Hidden Sources of Growth in the Developing World.* Cambridge, MA: Harvard Business Press.

Falleti, T. G. (2005). "A Sequential Theory of Decentralization: Latin American Cases in Comparative Perspective." *American Political Science Review* 99(3): 327–346.

Fan, C. S., C. Lin, and D. Treisman (2009). "Political Decentralization and Corruption: Evidence from Around the World." *Journal of Public Economics* 93(1): 14–34.

Fedderke, J. W., P. Perkins, and J. M. Luiz (2006). "Infrastructural Investment in Long-Run Economic Growth: South Africa 1875–2001." *World Development* 34(6): 1037–1059.

Ferraz, C., and F. Finan (2011). "Electoral Accountability and Corruption: Evidence from the Audits of Local Governments." *American Economic Review* 101(4): 1274–1311.

Field, E. (2005). "Property Rights and Investment in Urban Slums." *Journal of the European Economic Association Papers and Proceedings.* May 2005, 3(2–3): 279–290.

Fisman, R., and V. S. Allende (2010). "Regulation of Entry and the Distortion of Industrial Organization." *Journal of Applied Economics* 13(1): 91–111.

Fisman, R., and R. Gatti (2002). "Decentralization and Corruption: Evidence across Countries." *Journal of Public Economics* 83(3): 325–345.

Francken, N., B. Minten, and J. F. Swinnen (2009). "Media, Monitoring, and Capture of Public Funds: Evidence from Madagascar." *World Development* 37(1): 242–255.

Fukuyama, F. (2013). "What Is Governance?" *Governance* 26(3): 347–368.

Galiani, S., and E. Schargrodsky (2010). "Property Rights for the Poor: Effects of Land Titling." *Journal of Public Economics* 94(9): 700–729.

Gallup, J. L., J. D. Sachs, and A. D. Mellinger (1999). "Geography and Economic Development." *International Regional Science Review* 22(2): 179–232.

Geddes, B. (1995). "A Comparative Perspective on the Leninist Legacy in Eastern Europe." *Comparative Political Studies* 28(2): 239–274.

Gelos, R. G., and S. J. Wei (2005). "Transparency and International Portfolio Holdings." *Journal of Finance* 60(6): 2987–3020.

Ghemawat, P. (2001). "Distance Still Matters." *Harvard Business Review* 79(8): 137–147.

Gennaioli, N., R. L. Porta, F. Lopez-de-Silanes, and A. Shleifer (2011). "Human Capital and Regional Development." NBER Working Paper 17158.

Goerzen, A., C. G. Asmussen, and B. B. Nielsen (2013). "Global Cities and Multinational Enterprise Location Strategy." *Journal of International Business Studies* 44(5): 427–450.

Green, A. (2005). "Managing Human Resources in a Decentralized Context." In R. White and P. Smoke (eds.), *East Asia Decentralizes: Making Local Government Work in Asia* (pp. 129–155). Washington, DC: World Bank Publications.

Grindle, M. S. (2007). *Going Local: Decentralization, Democratization, and the Promise of Good Governance.* Princeton, NJ: Princeton University Press.

Gurgur, T., and A. Shah (2005). *Localization and Corruption: Panacea or Pandora's Box?* (Vol. 3486). Washington, DC: World Bank Publications.

Hankla, C. R. (2009). "When Is Fiscal Decentralization Good for Governance?" *Publius: Journal of Federalism* 39(4): 632–650.

Henderson, J. V., and A. Kuncoro (2004). "Corruption in Indonesia." NBER Working Paper 10674.

Henisz, W. J. (2000). "The Institutional Environment for Economic Growth." *Economics and Politics* 12(1): 1–31.

Hollyer, J. R., B. P. Rosendorff, and J. R. Vreeland (2011). "Democracy and Transparency." *Journal of Politics* 73(4): 1191–1205.

Holmes, T. J. (1998). "The Effect of State Policies on the Location of Manufacturing: Evidence from State Borders." *Journal of Political Economy* 106(4): 667–705.

Iarossi, G. (2013). "Measuring Competitiveness at the Subnational Level: The Case of 37 Nigerian States." *Journal of CENTRUM Cathedra: The Business and Economics Research Journal* 6(2): 193–218.

Inman, R. P., and D. L. Rubinfeld (1997). "Rethinking Federalism." *Journal of Economic Perspectives* 11(4): 43–64.

Iranzo, S., and G. Peri (2009). "Schooling Externalities, Technology, and Productivity: Theory and Evidence from US States." *Review of Economics and Statistics* 91(2): 420–431.

Jensen, N. M., E. Malesky, M. Medina, and U. Ozdemir (2014). "Pass the Bucks: Credit, Blame, and the Global Competition for Investment." *International Studies Quarterly* 58(3): 433–447.

Jensen, N. M., E. J. Malesky, and M. Walsh (2015). "Competing for Global Capital or Local Voters? The Politics of Business Location Incentives." *Public Choice* 164(3–4): 331–356.

Jensen, N. M. and E. J. Malesky (2018). *Incentives to Pander: How Politicians Use Corporate Welfare for Political Gain.* New York: Cambridge University Press.

Johnson, S., J. McMillan, and C. Woodruff (2002). "Property Rights and Finance." *American Economic Review* 92(5): 1335–1356.

Keefer, P., and S. Knack (1997). "Why Don't Poor Countries Catch Up? A Cross-National Test of an Institutional Explanation." *Economic Inquiry* 35(3): 590–602.

Kessing, S. G., K. A. Konrad, and C. Kotsogiannis (2007). "Foreign Direct Investment and the Dark Side of Decentralization." *Economic Policy* 22(49): 6–70.

Klapper, L., L. Laeven, and R. Rajan (2006). "Entry Regulation As a Barrier to Entrepreneurship." *Journal of Financial Economics* 82(3): 591–629.

Krugman, P. (1991). "Increasing Returns and Economic Geography." *Journal of Political Economy* 99(3): 483–499.

La Porta, R., and A. Shleifer (2008). "The Unofficial Economy and Economic Development." In *Brookings Papers on Economic Activity* (pp. 275–364). Washington, DC: Brookings Institution Press.

Landry, P. F. (2008). *Decentralized Authoritarianism in China*. New York, NY: Cambridge University Press.

Lee, R. (2003). "The Demographic Transition: Three Centuries of Fundamental Change." *Journal of Economic Perspectives* 17(4): 167–190.

Lee, R., and A. Mason (2006). "What Is the Demographic Dividend?" *Finance and Development* 43(3): 16.

Levine, R. (1999). "Law, Finance, and Economic Growth." *Journal of Financial Intermediation* 8(1): 8–35.

Li, H., and L. A. Zhou (2005). "Political Turnover and Economic Performance: The Incentive Role of Personnel Control in China." *Journal of Public Economics* 89(9): 1743–1762.

Libman, A. (2013). "Natural Resources and Sub-National Economic Performance: Does Sub-National Democracy Matter?" *Energy Economics* 37: 82–99.

Lin, J. Y., and Z. Liu (2000). "Fiscal Decentralization and Economic Growth in China." *Economic Development and Cultural Change* 49(1): 1–21.

Lorentzen, P., J. McMillan, and R. Wacziarg (2008). "Death and Development." *Journal of Economic Growth* 13(2): 81–124.

Ma, X., T. W. Tong, and M. Fitza (2013). "How Much Does Subnational Region Matter to Foreign Subsidiary Performance? Evidence from Fortune Global 500 Corporations' Investment in China." *Journal of International Business Studies* 44(1): 66–87.

Malesky, E., N. McCulloch, and N. D. Nhat (2015). "The Impact of Governance and Transparency on Firm Investment in Vietnam." *Economics of Transition* 23(4): 677–715.

Malesky, E. J., and N. Merchant-Vega (2011). "A Peek under the Engine Hood: The Methodology of Subnational Economic Governance Indices." *Hague Journal on the Rule of Law* 3(2): 186–219.

Malesky, E. J., and M. D. Taussig (2009a). "Out of the Gray: The Impact of Provincial Institutions on Business Formalization in Vietnam." *Journal of East Asian Studies* 9(2): 249–290.

Malesky, E. J., and M. D. Taussig (2009b). "Where Is Credit Due? Legal Institutions, Connections, and the Efficiency of Bank Lending in Vietnam." *Journal of Law, Economics, and Organization* 25(2): 535–578.

Maloney, W. F., and F. Valencia Caicedo (2016). "The Persistence of (Subnational) Fortune." The Economic Journal (Jan.). 10.1111/ecoj.12276.

Marks, G., L. Hooghe, and A. H. Schakel (2008). "Measuring Regional Authority." *Regional and Federal Studies* 18(2–3): 111–121.

Martinez-Vazquez, J., S. Lago-Peñas, and A. Sacchi (2017). "The Impact of Fiscal Decentralization: A Survey." *Journal of Economic Surveys* 31(4): 1095–1129.

Martinez-Vazquez, J., and R. M. McNab (2003). "Fiscal Decentralization and Economic Growth." *World Development* 31(9): 1597–1616.

Mattli, W. (2001). "Private Justice in a Global Economy: From Litigation to Arbitration." *International Organization* 55(4): 919–947.

McCann, P., and Z. J. Acs (2011). "Globalization: Countries, Cities and Multinationals." *Regional Studies* 45(1): 17–32.

McLure Jr., C. E. (1994). "The Tax Assignment Problem: Ends, Means, and Constraints." *Australian Tax Forum*.

McMillan, J., and C. Woodruff (1999). "Interfirm Relationships and Informal Credit in Vietnam." *Quarterly Journal of Economics* 114(4): 1285–1320.

Menes, R. (2003). "Corruption in Cities: Graft and Politics in American Cities at the Turn of the Twentieth Century." NBER Research Paper No. 9990.

Meyer, K. E., and H. V. Nguyen (2005). "Foreign Investment Strategies and Sub-National Institutions in Emerging Markets: Evidence from Vietnam." *Journal of Management Studies* 42(1): 63–93.

Michalopoulos, S., and E. Papaioannou (2013). "Pre-Colonial Ethnic Institutions and Contemporary African Development." *Econometrica* 81(1): 113–152.

Monaghan, S., P. Gunnigle, and J. Lavelle (2014). "Courting the Multinational: Subnational Institutional Capacity and Foreign Market Insidership." *Journal of International Business Studies* 45(2): 131–150.

Newlands, D. (2003). "Competition and Cooperation in Industrial Clusters: The Implications for Public Policy." *European Planning Studies* 11(5): 521–532.

Nguyen, L. P., and S. Anwar (2011). "Fiscal Decentralisation and Economic Growth in Vietnam." *Journal of the Asia Pacific Economy* 16(1): 3–14.

Nordhaus, W. D. (2006). "Geography and Macroeconomics: New Data and New Findings." *Proceedings of the National Academy of Sciences of the United States of America* 103(10): 3510–3517.

North, D. C. (1981). *Structure and Change in Economic History*. New York, NY: W. W. Norton & Company.

Notteboom, T., and J. P. Rodrigue (2009). "The Future of Containerization: Perspectives from Maritime and Inland Freight Distribution." *Geojournal* 74 (1): 7–22.

Oates, W. (1972). *Fiscal Decentralization*. New York, NJ: Harcourt Brace Jovanovich.

Oates, W. E. (1999). "An Essay on Fiscal Federalism." *Journal of Economic Literature* 37(3): 1120–1149.

Olken, B. A. (2007). "Monitoring Corruption: Evidence from a Field Experiment in Indonesia." *Journal of Political Economy* 115(2): 200–249.

Olken, B. A. and R. Pande (2012). "Corruption in Developing Countries." *Annual Review of Economics* 4(1): 479–509.

Pepinsky, T. B. (2016). "Colonial Migration and the Origins of Governance Theory and Evidence from Java." Comparative Political Studies. doi:10.1177/0010414015626442

Pepinsky, T. B., and M. M. Wihardja (2011). "Decentralization and Economic Performance in Indonesia." *Journal of East Asian Studies* 11(3): 3.

Plaut, T. R., and J. E. Pluta (1983). "Business Climate, Taxes and Expenditures, and State Industrial Growth in the United States." *Southern Economic Journal* 50(1): 99–119.

Porter, M. (1998). "Clusters and the New Economics of Competition." *Harvard Business Review* 76(6): 77–90.

Qian, Y., and G. Roland (1998). "Federalism and the Soft Budget Constraint." *American Economic Review* 88(5):1146–1162.

Rauch, J. E. (1993). "Productivity Gains from Geographic Concentration of Human Capital: Evidence from the Cities." *Journal of Urban Economics* 34(3): 380–400.

Reinikka, R., and J. Svensson (2005). "Fighting Corruption to Improve Schooling: Evidence from a Newspaper Campaign in Uganda." *Journal of the European Economic Association* 3(2–3): 259–267.

Rodden, J. (2004). "Comparative Federalism and Decentralization: On Meaning and Measurement." *Comparative Politics* 36(4): 481–500.

Rodden, J., and S. Rose-Ackerman (1997). "Does Federalism Preserve Markets?" *Virginia Law Review* 83(7): 1521–1572.

Rodríguez-Pose, A., and R. Ezcurra (2011). "Is Fiscal Decentralization Harmful for Economic Growth? Evidence from the OECD Countries." *Journal of Economic Geography* 11(4): 619–643.

Röller, L. H., and L. Waverman (2001). "Telecommunications Infrastructure and Economic Development: A Simultaneous Approach." *American Economic Review* 91(4): 909–923.

Schragger, R. C. (2010). "Decentralization and Development." *Virginia Law Review* 96 (8): 1837–1910.

Seabright, P. (1996). "Accountability and Decentralisation in Government: An Incomplete Contracts Model." *European Economic Review* 40(1): 61–89.

Shleifer, A., and R. W. Vishny (1993). "Corruption." *Quarterly Journal of Economics* 108(3): 599–617.

Sobel, R. S., N. Dutta, and S. Roy (2013). "Does Fiscal Decentralization Result in a Better Business Climate?" *Applied Economics Letters* 20(1): 84–91.

Stasavage, D. (2003). "Transparency, Democratic Accountability, and the Economic Consequences of Monetary Institutions." *American Journal of Political Science* 47(3): 389–402.

Steinnes, D. N. (1984). "Business Climate, Tax Incentives, and Regional Economic Development." *Growth and Change* 15(2): 38–47.

Stopford, J. M., S. Strange, and J. S. Henley (1991). *Rival States, Rival Firms: Competition for World Market Shares* (Vol. 18). Cambridge, UK: Cambridge University Press.

Thiessen, U. (2000). *Fiscal Federalism in Western European and Selected Other Countries: Centralization or Decentralization? What Is Better for Economic Growth?* Berlin: Deutsches Institut für Wirtschaftsforschung.

Tiebout, C. M. (1956). "A Pure Theory of Local Expenditures." *Journal of Political Economy* 64(5): 416–424.

Treisman, D. (2007). *The Architecture of Government: Rethinking Political Decentralization.* New York, NY: Cambridge University Press.

Vu, T. T., M. Zouikri, and B. Deffains (2014). "The Interrelationship between Formal and Informal Decentralization and Its Impact on Subcentral Governance Performance: the Case of Vietnam." *CESifo Economic Studies* 60(3): 613–652.

Weingast, B. R. (1995). "The Economic Role of Political Institutions: Market-Preserving Federalism and Economic Development." *Journal of Law, Economics, and Organization* 11(1): 1–31.

Wibbels, E. (2006). "Madison in Baghdad? Decentralization and Federalism in Comparative Politics." *Annual Review of Political Science* 9: 165–188.

Wilson, J. D. and D. E. Wildasin (2004). "Capital Tax Competition: Bane or Boon." *Journal of Public Economics* 88(6): 1065–1091.

World Bank Group (ed.). (2013). *Doing Business 2014: Understanding Regulations for Small and Medium-Size Enterprises* (Vol. 11). Washington, DC: World Bank Publications.

Wunsch, J. S. (1998). "Decentralization, Local Governance and the Democratic Transition in Southern Africa: A Comparative Analysis." *African Studies Quarterly* 2(1): 19–45.

Xu, C. (2011). "The Fundamental Institutions of China's Reforms and Development." *Journal of Economic Literature* 49(4): 1076–1151.

Yadav, V., and B. Mukherjee (2015). *The Politics of Corruption in Dictatorships*. New York, NY: Cambridge University Press.

Yi, J., Y. Chen, C. Wang, and M. Kafouros (2015). "Spillover Effects of Foreign Direct Investment: How Do Region-Specific Institutions Matter?" *Management International Review* 55(4): 539–561.

Yu, S. H., and C. F. Shen (2013). "Geographic Proximity and Location Choice of Foreign Direct Investment in China." *Asian Business and Management* 12(3): 351–380.

Zhang, X. (2006). "Fiscal Decentralization and Political Centralization in China: Implications for Growth and Inequality." *Journal of Comparative Economics* 34(4): 713–726.

8

Decentralization and Urban Governance in the Developing World

Experiences to Date and Avenues for Future Research

Christopher L. Carter and Alison E. Post

Over the past thirty-five years, governments throughout the developing world have engaged in political, fiscal, and administrative decentralization. In response to domestic and international pressures, numerous countries have passed legal reforms increasing the formal autonomy of municipal governments and providing for local elections. By 2008, 57 of 114 developing nations had held municipal-level elections.[1] Municipal and state governments also have more funds at their disposal with local expenditures accounting for almost 20% of total public spending in Latin America and nearly 80% of total public spending in China (United Cities and Local Governments 2008; World Bank 2008). During this same period, many national governments have also transferred administrative responsibilities for "urban" services such as land use planning and property market regulation, water and sanitation, and mass transit to municipal governments. While shifts in administrative and fiscal responsibilities have not been uniform – with African, Eurasian, and Middle Eastern municipalities, for example, receiving far less revenue to meet new service responsibilities than their counterparts in Latin America – they have nonetheless been significant.[2]

As increasingly large shares of the developing world's population come to live in cities, it is important to examine the effects of political, fiscal, and administrative decentralization on urban governance and service delivery. As of 2014, nearly half of all residents of the developing world lived in urban areas (United Nations 2014), typically defined as settlements of at least 5,000–10,000 inhabitants.[3] By 2050, nearly two-thirds of the developing world's population

---

[1] Using data from United Cities' 2008 report and the World Bank's classification of developing countries with populations greater than 1 million.

[2] In Africa, local expenditures as a percentage of national GDP are typically lower than 4%, and in many cases lower than 1% (Paulais 2012, p. 120; World Bank 2008, p. 40).

[3] While population thresholds used to classify settlements as urban or rural vary, they typically range between 2,000 and 20,000. However, the criteria used to determine whether an area is urban or rural can vary greatly from country to country. In China, for example, urban areas are "settlements with more than 3,000 residents" (UN-HABITAT, 2010a, p. 13). In India, the

will reside in cities (United Nations 2015). Urban services traditionally provided by or newly transferred to city governments, such as land regulation and piped water and sanitation, are crucial for the health and livelihood of these burgeoning urban populations. Infant mortality rates, for example, vary dramatically depending on access to clean water and levels of fecal exposure in the local environment.[4] Land use regulation, or a lack thereof, also influences livelihoods: when governments do not restrict toxic industries to areas segregated from residential neighborhoods or fail to enforce building codes intended to prevent mudslides, they put lives at risk (Hardoy, Mitlin, and Satterthwaite 2013). Meanwhile, rural-to-urban migration and *in situ* growth are putting pressure on aging infrastructure and service delivery systems in cities of the developing world. It is therefore important to examine what sorts of institutional arrangements are best suited to meet the needs of increasingly urban populations in the Global South.

This chapter reviews what we know regarding the effects of political, fiscal, and administrative decentralization on urban governance and services. Studies that speak directly to the question of the effects of decentralization on urban governance in particular are few and far between.[5] Research is hampered by a lack of baseline data, and decentralization is rarely randomly assigned. There are also fewer comparable urban than rural cases with which to conduct controlled comparisons. As a result, much of the academic work on decentralization focuses on villages.

We therefore also review studies examining urban governance in politically decentralized settings. This work on local governance suggests that clientelism, populism, and local leaders' theft of public resources (i.e., "capture") often persist following the establishment of municipal elections; conditions such as political competition, independent fiscal resources, and strong civil societies facilitate more democratic outcomes following decentralization. However, our analysis of decentralization's impact on two quintessentially "urban"[6] services – land market regulation and urban water and sanitation – shows that decentralization also involves important trade-offs. On one hand, decentralization can help citizens to lobby more effectively for inclusion and access, particularly in the presence of political competition and a robust civil society. On the other hand, it can make it more difficult for policymakers to address metropolitan-level or long-run concerns regarding investments in basic infrastructure that are often not at

---

definition of an urban area is more demanding, including not only population but also density and nonagricultural economic activity (World Bank 2013, p. 25).

[4] See Hardoy et al. (2001, pp. 43–69) on the importance of adequate water and sanitation infrastructure for public health.

[5] Faguet (2014) notes the lack of research on the impact of decentralization on governance more generally.

[6] Other services, like education and policing, are also often managed by local governments, but water provision and land use regulation are particularly salient concerns for local governments in urban areas.

the forefront of voters' minds. When decentralization involves such trade-offs, it may be advisable to provide services at intermediate or metropolitan tiers of government.

This chapter proceeds as follows. We begin by reviewing the academic and policy literatures on urban governance. We then review the literatures on urban land market regulation and urban water and sanitation. We conclude by highlighting gaps in the literature and outlining promising areas for future research. We discuss data collection efforts that would facilitate more rigorous research, and suggest methodological strategies for obtaining greater confidence regarding the impact of decentralization on urban governance. We also note that important aspects of urban governance in the developing world have received little attention by scholars or policy analysts, including urban institutional design, and services such as small business regulation, transportation regulation, and solid waste management.

DECENTRALIZATION AND URBAN GOVERNANCE

The academic literature relevant for understanding the impact of decentralization on urban governance falls into two groups. A small set of studies explicitly examines the impact of decentralization, focusing on the importance of pairing political and fiscal decentralization. A broader literature studies variation in local governance in the many countries that have undergone political decentralization, which has swept through Latin America, as well as parts of Africa and Asia (Table 8.1). This has provided scholars with a substantial amount of empirical terrain to examine the circumstances under which local elections improve political accountability.[7]

Overall, the literature suggests that political decentralization alone has done little to increase political participation by the poor or non-clientelistic forms of citizen political engagement in cities. A potential exception to this is Latin America, where the urban poor appear to exert more influence now than prior to democratization and decentralization. There, a combination of strong civil society and political competition appears to have helped many citizens reap the full benefits of decentralization. Meanwhile, municipal term limits may worsen, rather than improve, governance outcomes.

A first body of work argues that political decentralization only offers meaningful local decision making where local governments are granted independent revenue-raising powers or automatic transfers (i.e., transfers that cannot be withdrawn based on political criteria). For example, local autonomy was severely limited in Senegal and South Africa because local governments could

---

[7] The Wibbels (Chapter 2) and Grossman (Chapter 3) chapters in this volume also treat this theme, focusing on social accountability mechanisms and leadership selection mechanisms respectively, but do not restrict their focus to urban areas.

TABLE 8.1 *Countries with Municipal Elections in the Developing World in 2008*

Africa	Asia	Eurasia
Benin	Bangladesh	Armenia
Cameroon	China	Azerbaijan
Côte d'Ivoire	India	Belarus
Gabon	Indonesia	Georgia
Ghana	Pakistan	Moldova
Guinea	Philippines	Russia
Madagascar	Thailand	Ukraine
Mali	Vietnam	Uzbekistan
Morocco		
Mozambique		
Niger		
Nigeria		
Senegal		
South Africa		
Tunisia		
Uganda		
Zambia		

Latin America	Middle East
Argentina	Iran
Bolivia	Iraq
Brazil	Kuwait
Chile	Jordan
Colombia	Lebanon
Costa Rica	Palestine
Dominican Republic	Qatar
Ecuador	Saudi Arabia
El Salvador	Turkey
Guatemala	Yemen
Honduras	
Mexico	

(*continued*)

TABLE 8.1 *(continued)*

Latin America
Nicaragua
Panama
Paraguay
Peru
Venezuela

Note: We define elections as contests in which citizens vote directly for mayor or council members. While elections may be held in these cases, they are not necessarily "free and fair."
Source: United Cities and Local Governments (2008, pp. 43, 79, 81, 114–117, 190–194, 221–225, 229).

not control their own revenue (Dickovick 2005). The ability of the public to hold public officials to account is particularly difficult in the context of an unfunded mandate. In such cases, central government officials can withdraw resources from lower-level officials who pose threats to them. Limited access to financial resources makes it difficult for politicians to deliver on their promises to voters, as Resnick (2014) observes for the case of Dakar, Senegal. Unfunded mandates also allow entrenched political parties to maintain power by steering resources to co-partisans at the local level. For example, the performance of Mexico's municipal leaders depends crucially on their ability to competently negotiate access to resources with higher tiers of government (Grindle 2007). The most important determinant of such intergovernmental linkages in Brazil is co-partisanship (Novaes 2015) and also in Dhaka, Bangladesh (Islam et al. 2003).

While the aforementioned scholarship focuses directly on political decentralization, most scholarly work of relevance instead explains variation in the quality of municipal democracy after the establishment of autonomous local governments and local elections. Important outcomes in this literature include political competition, responsiveness, trust in government, capture by local elites, and levels of clientelism. The bulk of this work examines municipal-level variation in Latin America, where local elections are widespread and three-quarters of the population is urban.

A first strand of the literature examines how electoral institutions affect municipal government responsiveness and performance. One analysis of Brazilian data shows that mayors in their last term of office are more likely to engage in corrupt acts than those who can stand for reelection (Ferraz and Finan 2011); term limits shorten time horizons, thereby increasing the likelihood that officials will engage in corruption. Research on Mexico shows that not only the prohibition of mayoral reelection but also, short, three-year terms increases the difficulty of generating enduring, successful municipal-level programs (Cleary 2007; Grindle 2007).[8]

Scholarship on municipal-level variation in the quality of local democracy has also examined the type of citizen-politician linkages that predominate following the establishment of local elections. Numerous studies point to the survival – and even flowering – of clientelism following decentralization in Latin America (Auyero 2000; Gay 1994; Grindle 2007; Levitsky 2003; Szwarcberg 2015; Weitz-Shapiro 2014).[9] Recent studies of clientelism in other regions show how the availability of local resources after decentralization can help perpetuate clientelistic relationships.[10] One reason for this continuation of clientelistic relationships is that decentralization alone does not ensure that politicians are able to make credible policy commitments; when politicians operate in a context of low resources and weak institutions, offering handouts is a better electoral strategy than making programmatic appeals that are not credible.[11] The literature on Latin America has also shown that decentralization is not sufficient for eliminating clientelistic ties. Research from Argentina has suggested that clientelism can be overcome only where both a middle class has emerged and political competition is robust (Weitz-Shapiro 2014), or where a strong labor movement can provide an alternative means of mobilizing low-income voters (Levitsky 2003).

A limited number of studies have analyzed changes in the *type* of clientelism that emerges once decentralization reforms have been implemented. In a case study of clientelism in Caracas (García-Guadilla and Pérez 2002), resources were increasingly directed away from the poor following decentralization. Examining security politics in Colombia following its major decentralization program, another scholar (Eaton 2006) argues that the establishment of local elections and the transfer of greater resources to municipalities allowed militant groups to continue financing their operations by diverting funds from urban projects.

Another body of work examines who governs following political decentralization. Within this area, some studies consider the extent to which the urban poor interact with or influence elected city authorities. A classic study of slum politics in Lima (Stokes 1995) finds that exposure to schools, unions, and neighborhood organizations leads slum residents to be more assertive in making demands of politicians. Another Lima study concludes that the urban

---

[8] Other electoral rules such as quotas have also been shown to increase representation of underserved groups (e.g., gender quotas in Mumbai [Bhavnani 2009]).

[9] In a countervailing account, Pasotti (2010, pp. 74–89) argues that direct elections allowed the mayors of Bogotá to liberate themselves from clientelistic parties.

[10] See Berenschot (2010) on Gujarat, India; Nathan (2016) on Accra, Ghana; and Meagher (2011) on Ilorin and Aba, Nigeria.

[11] See Keefer (2007) on the prevalence of clientelism where politicians cannot make credible promises. See also León and Wantchekon in this volume (Chapter 10).

poor only contact local government officials when the state is actually capable of providing services; when faced with low state capacity, the poor find their own solutions to problems (Dietz 1998). Evidence from South Asia suggests that it is not just structural characteristics or civil society organizations but also slum governance that determines how slum residents engage the government. In a study of eighty slums in northern India, for instance, slums with dense party networks – where only one party is competitive – are more likely to secure public services from the state (Auerbach 2016). On average, however, slum residents often have only limited access to government assistance.[12] For example, a study found that only 2% of Bangalore slum residents have connections with government officials (Krishna 2013).

Related work examines whether participatory institutions guard against elite "capture" of local governments following political decentralization and suggests elite dominance is common and only mitigated under certain circumstances.[13] One strand of this literature examines "community-driven development" (CDD) projects in urban Indonesia. It suggests that, surprisingly, elite participation can help ensure effective pro-poor targeting (Dasgupta and Beard 2007; Fritzen 2007), and that increasing the participation of the poor in CDD projects has no effect on welfare outcomes (Pradhan et al. 2009). This stands in contrast to broader theoretical work and empirical studies on CDDs in rural contexts, which suggests that elite interference may lead to capture of resources or corruption and thus offset the otherwise positive benefits associated with community-led development (Conning and Kevane 2002; Olken 2010). Evaluations of other social programs involving provisions for "community" participation also find that elite influence over decision making remains common. A 2002 analysis of "social funds," or World Bank–administered social assistance programs that solicit input from program recipients, in both urban and rural areas in Jamaica, Malawi, Nicaragua, and Zambia, finds that while the majority of beneficiaries were satisfied with projects that had been financed, elites or "prime movers" tended to dominate decision-making processes (Carvalho et al. 2002).[14] A mixed-method analysis of social fund implementation in Jamaica reports similar results, also aggregated across rural and urban jurisdictions (Rao and Ibáñez 2003).

The literature on participatory budgeting in Latin American cities, meanwhile, has found that participatory budgeting only curbs elite domination of politics in cities with an already strong civil society and weakly institutionalized parties

---

[12] Jha et al. (2007, p. 244) earlier found that a "remarkably high" percentage of Delhi slum residents contacted their local officials. However, many fewer actually came into contact with bureaucrats.

[13] Political decentralization may therefore improve or detract from the democratic quality of a system depending on the context (Bardhan and Mookherjee 2006, p. 9).

[14] They base their conclusions on analyses of surveys with country and sector directors and beneficiaries, as well as analyses of internal World Bank reports.

(Avritzer 2006; Baiocchi et al. 2008; Goldfrank 2007; Wampler 2008). This scholarship offers an important counterpoint to early work that solely focused on successful outcomes in Porto Alegre (e.g., Abers 1998). Recent work on India suggests that participatory institutions can fail to increase the political influence of the poor. Examining participatory institutions in Delhi, one study concluded that they grant the middle class a privileged position in local government, replacing the informal ties with the urban poor that once characterized local-level politics (Ghertner 2011). However, the participatory institutions examined in these studies influence just a small segment of local politics.

In summary, the existing literature suggests that where national governments have established local elections but failed to provide local governments with independent revenue sources, local democracy is highly constrained by the political prerogatives of higher authorities. Additionally, a few studies suggest term limits may actually worsen local governance. Decentralization also may augment, rather than decrease clientelism; clientelism only appears to recede when municipalities possess a significant middle class and reasonable levels of political competition, or when civil society provides alternative formats for political incorporation of the poor, such as labor unions. Finally, participatory institutions designed to limit elite capture are more effective where civil society is strong.

DECENTRALIZATION AND URBAN SERVICES

How does decentralization affect the provision of urban services? To answer this question, we focus in this section on two quintessentially "urban" services: land market regulation and networked water and sanitation. We can think of these as urban services because they become more necessary as population density increases and settlements grow. In the countryside or villages, governments tend to regulate land use less actively, at least in part because lower density means industrial facilities create fewer negative impacts on neighboring residential areas. Water and sanitation infrastructure, meanwhile, looks very different for low- and high-density settings: simple systems relying on wells and on-site sewerage disposal become unviable at high population densities, making it necessary to turn to more complex networked systems. These two service areas also vary in capital intensity, and whether users are typically charged regular fees for service delivery. While governments conduct urban planning and maintain land registries without charging residents regular fees,[15] they typically charge households and businesses for water and sewerage service in order to finance the significant infrastructure operations and maintenance costs.

For these two service areas, the literature suggests, decentralization involves an important trade-off. Decentralization to the local level can empower poor

---

[15] Governments may charge one-time fees related to land transactions, and in some cases levy property taxes. This is distinct from a fee for simply receiving a public service.

TABLE 8.2 *Administrative Responsibilities for Key Urban Services in Developing Countries*

Country/Region	Urban Planning	Water and Sanitation
Africa		
Algeria	Municipal	Municipal
Benin	Municipal	Municipal
Cameroon	Municipal	Municipal
Côte d'Ivoire	Municipal	Municipal
Egypt	Municipal	Municipal
Gabon	Municipal	Municipal
Ghana	Municipal	Municipal
Guinea	Municipal	Municipal
Kenya	Municipal	Municipal
Madagascar	Provincial	Municipal
Mali	Municipal	Municipal
Morocco	Municipal	Municipal
Mozambique	Municipal	Municipal
Niger	Municipal	Municipal
Nigeria	Municipal	Municipal
Senegal	Municipal	Municipal
South Africa	Municipal	Municipal
Togo	Municipal	Municipal
Tunisia	Municipal	National government
Uganda	Municipal	Municipal
Zambia	Municipal	Municipal
Latin America		
Argentina	Municipal	Shared with higher tier
Bolivia	Municipal	Municipal
Brazil	Municipal	Municipal
Chile	Municipal	Privatized
Colombia	Municipal	Municipal
Costa Rica	Municipal	National government
Dominican Republic	Varies	Municipal
Ecuador	Municipal	Municipal
El Salvador	Municipal	Situation varies

(*continued*)

TABLE 8.2 (*continued*)

Country/Region	Urban Planning	Water and Sanitation
Guatemala	Municipal	Municipal
Honduras	Municipal	Municipal
Mexico	Municipal	Municipal
Nicaragua	Municipal	Shared with higher tier
Panama	Central government	National government
Paraguay	Municipal	Shared with higher tier
Peru	Municipal	Municipal
Uruguay	Municipal	Municipal
Venezuela	Municipal	Municipal
Asia		
China	Municipal	Municipal
India	Municipal	Municipal
Indonesia	Municipal	Municipal
Japan	Municipal	Municipal
Malaysia	Municipal	Municipal
Pakistan	Municipal	Municipal
Philippines	Municipal	Municipal
South Korea	Municipal	Municipal
Thailand	Municipal	Municipal
Vietnam	Municipal	Municipal

Source: United Cities and Local Governments (2008, pp. 35, 68, 186–187). Asian data refers to water supply only.

citizens to pressure more effectively for inclusion, provided local politics is competitive and civil society is robust. These pressures, however, can complicate efforts to address metropolitan-level or long-run concerns that may not be at the forefront of voters' minds. In the case of water and sanitation, political pressure on local officials to keep fees low is often so strong – even in nondemocratic settings – that it can undermine efforts to maintain basic infrastructure and enable network extensions to new populations.

LAND MARKET REGULATION

One of the greatest challenges facing cities of the developing world is regulating land markets. Throughout the developing world, municipal governments are charged with urban planning (i.e., zoning, building regulation, building project approval, and inspection) and maintaining property registries, or cadastral systems (Table 8.2). Creating cadastral registries involves deciding whether or not to formalize illegally constructed dwellings by granting inhabitants land title.[16] Ideally, governments should maintain simple land registration systems, which resolve conflicting claims and reconcile different land tenure regimes (Childress 2004; Napier 2009; Paulais 2012).[17]

Undertaking these tasks is not easy during periods of rural-to-urban migration, when new migrants (or politicians) organize illegal "land invasions" that establish new settlements on state-owned or private land belonging to others. Private firms also engage in "pirate development," building new homes without respecting regulations and in areas without infrastructure (UN-HABITAT 2005). Development occurring outside the regulatory framework in much of the developing world leads to sprawl (Childress 2004 on East Asia; UN-HABITAT 2010b on Central Africa; UN-HABITAT 2012 on Latin America; UN-HABITAT 2014 on East Africa). The expansion of cities beyond the urban core at low densities has increased the difficulty of providing important public services like water, sanitation, and transportation (Libertun de Duren and Guerrero Compeán 2016; United Cities and Local Governments 2016; UN-HABITAT 2016).

The rapid rise of slums – defined as the "most deprived and excluded form of informal settlements" – also attests to an inability or unwillingness of governments to respond to rapid urbanization (UN-HABITAT 2015). More than half of African urban residents, a third of Asian urban residents, and a quarter of Latin American urban residents reside in slums (UN-HABITAT 2015). Much of this regulatory evasion is driven not just by housing demand but also by strict building regulations, which impose prohibitive costs on the time and limited financial resources of poor urban residents (Adam 2014; De Soto 2000; Gough and Yankson 2000; Interamerican Development Bank 2012; Kironde 2006).

How has political decentralization affected land market regulation? Here, it is helpful to consider how decentralization affects the interests and ability of different parties to affect policy: developers, local political officials, and poor households in informal settlements. On one hand, existing scholarship suggests that political decentralization works against coordinated decision making and cross-subsidization within urban regions comprised of multiple municipalities. One study argues that municipal fragmentation in large urban areas of Latin America tends to undermine coordinated service provision, especially with respect to land use and transportation planning, as well as the delivery of urban services (Nickson 1995). Case studies from major South American capital cities support this assertion (Mitchell 2000; Rodriguez-Acosta and

---

[16] In some countries, state and/or national tiers of government may also influence decisions.
[17] In much of Africa, "formal" land tenure regimes inherited from colonial times coexist with "customary" regimes.

Rosenbaum 2008). According to a World Bank study, 350 urban areas in East Asia are multijurisdictional, and 135 of these have no dominant local authority (World Bank 2015). In such areas, coordination among municipalities to address issues with land and housing markets is next to impossible (World Bank 2015). Turning to South Asia, in the fragmented institutional environment in Ahmedabad, India, 163 villages, towns, and municipal councils comprise the urban periphery outside the city (Devas 2005). When administrative units are under-resourced, as is the case in Ahmedabad, service provision is less efficient than it would be if all units were to combine their financial resources, skills, and information (Devas 2005). Political fragmentation can also contribute to inequality, as resources are not redistributed from wealthier to poorer municipalities. In other words, while political decentralization may ensure that municipalities within a larger metropolitan area become more accountable to the narrow concerns of their residents, this accountability comes at important costs in the form of urban sprawl, poor coordination between land use and transportation infrastructure, major traffic jams, and regional inequality.

A second body of work, largely academic, examines the circumstances under which residents of informal settlements avoid eviction or obtain formal title in countries that have undergone political decentralization, and where local governments now influence land markets. This primarily qualitative literature suggests that decentralization may – in politically competitive contexts, and where the poor possess connections to other societal actors – help the poor obtain title, and thereby access to a broader range of urban services and improved livelihoods. Latin Americanist scholarship on the post-decentralization period (Holland 2016; Holston 2009; Holston and Caldeira 2008) highlights the political power of slum residents in democratic contexts: politicians have incentives to refrain from evicting residents, and even court them by providing them with land titles, especially as elections become increasingly competitive.[18] In contrast, the gradual incorporation of peri-urban land (city outskirts) – traditionally regulated through customary regimes – into modern urban land markets in Africa has often privileged the interests of local elites such as chiefs and politicians rather than the urban poor or longtime residents (Benjaminsen et al. 2009; Joireman 2011; Marx, Stoker, and Suri 2013; Ubink 2007).[19] Shanghai's urban poor also appear to be less powerful than the Latin American poor, not surprising given the authoritarian

---

[18] Donaghy's (2015) work on the eviction of slum residents in Rio de Janeiro in advance of the World Cup is a notable exception.

[19] In some countries, country, state or national governments influence these processes alongside local governments, especially when they control cadastral registries as in North and West Africa (UN Habitat 2010b, pp. 78, 120). Note that formal rules and responsibilities do not always provide an accurate indication of which political actors actually control land markets. Customary authorities such as chiefs may also exercise influence and operate at cross-purposes with local governments (e.g., local chiefs in peri-urban Ghana [Ubink 2007]). Alternatively, local

context (Weinstein and Ren 2009). Evidence from India has yielded slightly less uniform findings on the political power of slum residents. One group of scholars has argued that despite some municipal recognition of slum dwellers' rights, the urban poor have limited political power; residents are easily removed from informal settlements within Indian cities to sites on the urban fringe (Chatterjee 2004; Ghertner 2015). Other scholars, however, have offered a more optimistic view of the power of India's urban poor to influence land use decisions, arguing that city government officials and developers are increasingly incorporating slum residents into decision-making processes or providing alternative housing options (Weinstein 2009).[20] Surprisingly, scholars have carried out little work that explains subnational variation in the influence of slum residents on land use planning.[21]

Policy case studies also suggest elites can capture land regulation in uncompetitive political systems, where poor voters exercise little power. In East Africa, slum-upgrading programs have primarily benefited middle-class areas rather than the urban poor (UN-HABITAT 2010). In Mali, mayors often take advantage of ambiguity in urban land-tenure systems to engineer land sales that serve as patronage for political supporters (Durand-Lasserve et al. 2015; Eghoff et al. 2007). Even in South Africa, a country with a well-developed system of land titling and registration, well-positioned developers can take advantage of underfunded local officials and knowledge of a complex regulatory system to undermine pro-poor urban land development schemes (Napier 2009). Similarly, a housing program in Bamako, Mali in which local municipal authorities determined whether to allow residents to live in upgraded slums or to resettle them elsewhere ended up benefiting well-positioned elites, who bought the upgraded land and dispossessed the poor, who often could not be resettled due to the fact that the resettlement land was already occupied (Durand-Lasserve et al. 2015). In East Asia, titling programs also offer limited prospects for improving access to adequate land for the poor, as often unregistered, occupied land is possessed by an absentee landowner (Childress 2004). In aggregate, academic case studies and policy evaluations suggest that decentralized land management in democratic contexts empowers the poor to demand land title, while elites capture land markets in less competitive political contexts.

These two sets of findings exemplify the trade-off posed by administrative decentralization in this policy area. On one hand, it is desirable for the poor to

---

elected officials may manage land market transactions even when they do not have the formal power to do so (e.g., in Uganda [Joireman 2011, p. 65]).

[20] Note that redevelopment policy is often dictated by state rather than municipal governments in India.

[21] Weinstein and Ren (2009) have explored cross-national variation in the political power of slum residents.

have access to decent housing. However, given the absence of quality, market-rate rental or public housing for the poor in much of the developing world, self-constructed homes in slums serve as an important source of housing.[22] Granting title to residents encourages investment in dwellings because it increases the security of the investment, and title often makes households eligible for or more likely to receive other services.[23] However, granting title can come at a cost: slums are often located on environmentally marginal land, and residents are thus exposed to serious health risks (Auyero 2009; Hardoy et al. 2001; UN-HABITAT 2016). Moreover, settlements may be located on land originally set aside for watershed preservation or other important purposes (Abers and Keck 2013). Decentralized land management in political settings that encourage politicians to court votes through granting title in such cases therefore creates significant impacts.

The policy literature devotes far more attention than the academic literature to the extraction of government revenue from urban land markets. Property taxes, along with transfers, constitute one of the principal revenue sources for local governments post-decentralization. Unfortunately for local governments, collecting property taxes requires a fair degree of state capacity (UN-HABITAT 2016; see also Rodden, Chapter 5 in this volume). A review of the African experience suggests that local governments have faced severe difficulties collecting property taxes (Kelly 2000; Paulais 2012; UN-HABITAT 2010, 2014) because of their inability to maintain cadastral systems and other obstacles (UN-HABITAT 2010).[24] Local governments also turn to land development for sources of revenue, with levels of success also appearing to correlate with state capacity. Latin American countries such as Brazil, Colombia, and Uruguay boast urban "land-value capture" schemes in which charges for development rights are used to finance public infrastructure (Magalhães et al. 2016; Sandroni 2014; Smolka 2013; Walters 2013). In China, city governments lease land for development or engage in development themselves (Lichtenberg and Ding 2009), but often do not capture the full value of the improved land (Anderson 2012; Peterson 2009). Efforts by African local governments to generate revenue by selling public land have often failed to generate revenue for the public coffers, with many sales occurring illegally and/or being mired in corruption; UN-HABITAT (2010b) reports that in Central Africa, corruption is so commonplace that these sales fail to generate funds for urban service provision.

---

[22] Rental housing is also present in some slums (e.g., Blanco et al. 2014 for evidence from Latin America), but this housing is often of low quality.

[23] For a review of work by economists on the effects of land titling, see Marx et al. (2013).

[24] Evidence from Indian cities offers a potential solution to issues of low levels of local state capacity. GPS mapping has allowed physical surveys of land that have not only increased resource mobilization, but have also decreased corruption (Jha 2003, p. 15).

Overall, the academic and policy literatures suggest that decentralization comes at important costs. Municipal officials largely fail to address the issues that accompany complex land markets and powerful private interests, except in politically competitive contexts with reasonable levels of state capacity, such as Latin America. Moreover, decentralization complicates efforts to address metropolitan interests and important environmental externalities. The tension between the benefits and costs associated with decentralized land management suggests that it may make sense to establish metropolitan institutions that can promote citywide interests such as managing watersheds effectively, locating new housing near existing transit routes, and preventing settlement in areas vulnerable to mudslides or flooding. Such agencies could coexist with more local, municipal institutions that would be more responsive to individual voters or poor communities, especially in more competitive contexts. Such coordinated land use planning and implementation efforts would help avoid unregulated sprawl, better equipping governments to administer basic services such as water and sanitation (UN-HABITAT 2016).

URBAN WATER AND SANITATION

Decentralization has also been widespread in the urban water and sanitation sector. Starting in the mid-1980s, a large set of developing countries transferred administrative responsibilities for the operation and management of urban water and sanitation systems to lower tiers of government, in many cases municipalities (Table 8.2). In doing so, they often reversed decisions to centralize services taken immediately following World War II or independence. Decentralization efforts typically passed on operations and maintenance functions to local governments, while higher tiers of government often continue to at least partially fund investments in basic infrastructure such as new treatment plants.

Analysis of the effects of decentralization on the quality of service provision, however, are complicated by at least two issues.[25] First, decentralization was frequently prompted by fiscal crises: national governments frequently decentralized during periods of tax shortfalls, as it became increasingly difficult to subsidize the operations of state providers that charged consumers rates that only covered a fraction of their costs. Decentralized providers were then expected to make do with fewer resources. Second, decentralization was often followed by institutional reforms intended to insulate service providers from direct political pressure, such as corporatization (i.e., establishing a legally independent, government-owned provider) or privatization. Policy analysts promoting corporatization and privatization assumed that protecting utility managers from day-to-day political pressures would allow them to introduce

---

[25] See Herrera and Post (2014) for more detail.

cost recovery measures such as reducing the number of employees, enforcing bill payment, and raising user charges in line with production costs.

Despite these complications, analysts do seem to concur that decentralization in this sector also involves trade-offs between the advantages of centralizing management at the metropolitan or state, rather than municipal, level, and the opportunities for greater public input and pressure when services are managed locally. The balance, however, is in favor of management by intermediate or metropolitan tiers of government, with provisions to insulate providers from direct political pressure because of the general unwillingness of voters to fund basic investment through service fees. Such fees are an important prerequisite for extending access while still providing quality services.

First, in examining the effects of decentralizing responsibility for water and sanitation to small cities and towns, rather than to states or large cities, the literature suggests that governments of smaller subnational units find it more difficult to address externalities and to provide services efficiently.[26] Policy studies suggest that networked infrastructure like water and sanitation often exhibits economies of scale; an analysis of data from providers in thirty-seven countries finds that a doubling in population size is associated with greater efficiency gains for small cities of fewer than 125,000 residents than for larger ones (Tynan and Kingdom 2005). Compact cities are also thought to generate lower costs for water and sewage than are cities that are more scattered (United Cities and Local Governments 2016). Evidence from 8,600 Latin American cities, for instance, suggests that density is strongly and positively correlated with water and sanitation coverage (Libertun de Duren and Guerrero Compeán 2016). A 2011 synthesis of reform experiences in Eastern Europe, the Caucasus, and Central Asia suggests that the overly small size of systems following decentralization has worked against scale economies and already prompted consolidation efforts (OECD 2011). Actual efficiency gains in a particular place would, of course, vary with a variety of local factors.

Second, academic and policy studies both stress that metropolitan or state-level organization provides greater opportunities for cross-subsidization. Metropolitan utilities can impose uniform or progressive prices across a metropolitan area, thereby cross-subsidizing consumption for low-income populations. This makes it more likely that utilities can cover operational costs through user fees and avoid conflicts over the allocation of system-wide development and maintenance costs (Kitonsa and Schwartz 2012; Mitchell 2000). A summary of the experiences of Latin American countries for the United Nations Economic Commission for Latin America and the Caribbean (ECLAC) argues that decentralization reduces opportunities for cross-subsidization across income groups, thereby detracting from the financial viability of local providers; decentralization to intermediate, rather than

---

[26] See Pierskalla's chapter in this volume (Chapter 6) for a more general discussion of the effects of administrative unit size on service provision.

municipal, tiers in Argentina and Chile allowed for the development of more effective regulatory frameworks (Lentini 2014). The World Bank had clearly reached similar conclusions by 2004 based on its experience: that year's *World Development Report* recommended amalgamating municipal water systems into larger units (Childress 2004). In addition, research on the Indian water sector suggests that state capacity in the sector is typically higher at the state or metropolitan than the municipal level (Asthana 2012) and that clientelism is more likely to affect service provision when decision making is highly decentralized (De and Nag 2016). As in the case of land regulation, there are costs to decentralizing urban water and sanitation to the very local level.

One might suppose that these costs of decentralizing to the municipal level would be outweighed by improved opportunities for citizens to hold providers to account, leading to improvements in service delivery.[27] A largely case study–based literature focused on the developing world suggests that decentralized water utilities are often more responsive to public opinion than centralized providers, but that the direction of this influence is not always positive.

Two types of water policies appeal to citizens: existing customers like low prices, and those without network connections want to receive them, presuming connection fees are reasonable. Because municipalities are responsible for fewer policy areas than national governments, water policy is more likely to be debated in local elections. Concerns regarding local public opinion therefore prompt politicians to pressure utility managers to keep prices low – not even raising rates in line with inflation, at least during election years – because large fractions of the population receive and pay for services. If services are of low quality, politicians can find it difficult to defend efforts to enforce bill payment for similar reasons. As a result, local utilities often collect little revenue with which to fund investment in basic infrastructure, much less operation and maintenance costs. Politicians also have incentives to expand water networks into new residential areas, in order to cement relationships with specific neighborhoods or groups.[28] This political context helps fuel a vicious cycle in which increasing numbers of

---

[27] See Devas (2005) for a full discussion of the trade-off between "scale" and "voice" in urban public services provision.

[28] On this general logic, see Savedoff and Spiller (1999, p. 14). See academic studies by Gilbert (2007, p. 1571) and Krause (2009, p. 103) on the Colombian case, Herrera (2014) and Pineda Pablos and Briseño-Ramírez (2012, p. 67) on Mexico, Onjala (2002, p. 19) on Kenya, and Post (2014, pp. 44–45, 84, 88, 93, 121) on the Argentine case, pre- and post-privatization. Within the policy literature, Fernández (2004, p. 7) observes such dynamics in small cities in Colombia. Analyzing Sri Lanka, McIntosh (2003, p. 80) notes that municipal providers not only failed to increase rates after decentralization but also preferred to hand back responsibility to the national government rather than to raise water rates. These dynamics explain why scholars such as Hiskey (2000, p. 3) and Cleary (2007) have observed that municipal political competition and other forms of political participation seem to be associated with higher levels of electricity and public utility coverage, respectively: citizens are pressuring for network expansion, and governments are responding. Vasconcellos (2014, p. 134) describes similar pressures to keep urban

households may receive services in theory, but many households receive water intermittently due to low water pressure; water is unsafe for drinking and households often turn to alternative, independent service providers such as tankers (Berg and Danilenko 2011; Kjellen and McGranahan 2006; Kooy 2014; Post, Bronsoler, and Salman, 2015).

Citizens tend to value water connections more than sewerage connections because fewer of the positive externalities associated with sewerage infrastructure – such as groundwater protection – are enjoyed at the household level; this means politicians face stronger political incentives to expand water access than sewerage access, leading to lags in sewer development.[29] These dynamics still seem to occur – though to a lesser extent – even if services have been insulated from elected officials via corporatization or privatization (Herrera and Post 2014). Under decentralized management, it appears, political incentives to cater to voters' immediate preferences in the short run can actually work against investments that could be in voters' long-term interests.[30]

In summary, urban land regulation and water and sanitation policy both exhibit the trade-offs associated with decentralization. On one hand, decentralization to the local level means that politicians and policymakers are less able to tackle important regional concerns and enjoy economies of scale. On the other hand, it provides citizens with easier access to decision makers and opportunities to affect policy. In land management, it appears that decentralization has thereby allowed the urban poor to pressure for the regularization of land title in more democratic, competitive contexts. In more closed political systems, however, elites "capture" land regulation. In the water sector, citizen influence over policy appears to increase following decentralization in a wide variety of contexts, though especially so in democracies. While popular pressure has contributed to water and sewerage network expansion, it has also increased the difficulty of charging users for services, and has thus eroded the providers' bottom lines. This has led to decreases in service quality, and even in providers' ability to further extend networks. This suggests that the argument for management by intermediate tiers of government – or at least pooling functions such as technical support across small municipalities – may be stronger in the case of water and sanitation and that recent efforts to insulate water providers from electoral pressures through "corporatization" may improve their ability to maintain systems and provide quality services.[31] Investments in

---

transit fares low and how they fuel a "regulatory cycle" in which private sector management becomes unviable, forcing the state to take over and subsidize providers.

[29] According to WHO-UNICEF Joint Monitoring Programme data, rates of household network connections are far higher for water than for sewerage in the developing world.

[30] Municipal term limits accentuate these dynamics across a variety of service areas in Mexico, where local governments are responsible for water distribution (Grindle 2007, pp. 5, 17–18, 22).

[31] It is equally important that national governments provide local water and sanitation service providers with sufficient capital for investment.

network expansion, in contrast, may be most effectively financed through transfer payments from higher tiers of government, with local elected officials playing a stronger role in decision making regarding network expansion priorities.

AVENUES FOR FUTURE RESEARCH

Reviewing the existing academic and policy literature on decentralization and urban governance suggests a number of important areas for future research. First, there is an almost complete lack of basic data. There are, for instance, no cross-country data on the timing and scope of decentralization in the developing world as it has affected cities. While the World Bank and United Cities (2008) report provides a good compendium on the government tiers responsible for different urban services, to the best of our knowledge there is no compilation of information regarding the timing, scope, and degree of implementation of decentralization in sectors like transportation, solid waste management, water and sanitation, and urban land market regulation.[32] Simply reviewing national policies is often not sufficient to determine whether decentralization has, in fact, occurred. Several analyses of urban land market regulation in Africa, for example, question the extent to which decentralization has occurred in practice (Paulais 2012; UN-HABITAT 2010b). Just as important, there are few data on urban service access and quality. While UN-HABITAT compiles some data, its city indicators are partial at best. International institutions could facilitate academic research by assembling more data of this sort. This would allow for more systematic testing of the theoretical propositions and empirical findings in the existing literature. It would also allow researchers to identify the scope conditions for conclusions drawn from extant case studies.

This review also shows that the bulk of relevant research does not focus explicitly on the effects of decentralizing reforms. This is understandable, given the research design challenges associated with assessing the effects of an institutional reform that can take on quite different forms in different contexts. Even within the qualitative literature, which is better placed to evaluate the effects of particular reforms in particular cases, urban governance and public services receive little attention. More deliberate collection of data prior to reform implementation would allow for more rigorous case study analysis. To the extent that aid organizations or multilateral institutions are involved with particular reforms, they could involve researchers from the outset so that appropriate data are identified and collected.

---

[32] For an exception, see Herrera and Post (2014).

Meanwhile, the research community could capitalize on new decentralization programs being phased in, such as that currently being undertaken by the Tunisian government, to conduct quantitative and qualitative studies.[33] Similarly, researchers could exploit city-sized thresholds, which are sometimes used to determine how and whether decentralization policies will be implemented, to analyze decentralization processes as natural experiments.[34] In the arena of urban public services, researchers could address concerns about statistical power by working closely with local governments to design interventions that could be randomly assigned at the neighborhood level. This unit of analysis would allow researchers to maintain an urban focus while potentially avoiding the classic problem of small samples that often accompanies the study of cities. Existing analyses tend to pool across both types of jurisdictions or focus only on villages. Researchers should also examine heterogeneous treatment effects to better understand how relationships of interest vary between rural and urban areas.

Finally, while some topics have received a fair amount of attention by both the scholarly and policy community, we know very little about others. Few studies have investigated how urban institutional design conditions the effects of political decentralization. Is political decentralization more likely to yield increases in political participation under ward-based or at-large elections? Under partisan or nonpartisan local elections? Research on these questions has been limited to American politics, where scholars examine how different electoral systems affect ethnic minority political participation.[35] Meanwhile, important urban services such as small business regulation (e.g., licensing, health inspection), mass transit, and solid waste management have received very little attention – at least in the developing world context.[36] We know very little about the politics of these sectors, which makes it very difficult to anticipate the political obstacles that may block reform initiatives. Last, our understanding of urban land markets is rudimentary at best. Ethnographic studies and policy analyses suggest important variation across regions – and even across neighborhoods within cities – in terms of which social groups can exercise influence, as well as the ability of city governments to raise revenue. Research aimed at understanding the drivers of this striking variation could potentially inform future policy interventions.

---

[33] Scholars have exploited the staged nature of the Indonesian decentralization program.

[34] See, for example, Rosenblatt, Bidegain, Monestier, and Rodríguez (2015).

[35] Davidson and Korbel (1981) suggest that ward elections are better at including a representative cross-section of city residents than are at-large elections (pp. 1003–1005). Also, examining the United States, Schaffner et al. (2001) find that nonpartisan elections depress turnout and lead to higher incumbency voting in the absence of partisan cues.

[36] For a review of existing work on mass transit, see Post, Bronsoler, and Salman (2015).

REFERENCES

Abers, R. 1998. "From Clientelism to Cooperation: Local Government, Participatory Policy, and Civic Organization in Porto Alegre, Brazil." *Politics and Society*, 26(4): 511–537.

Abers, R., and M. E. Keck. 2013. *Practical Authority: Agency and Institutional Change in Brazilian Water Politics*. Oxford: Oxford University Press.

Adam, A. G. 2014. "Tenure in the Changing Peri-Urban Areas of Ethiopia: The Case of Bahir Dar City." *International Journal of Urban and Regional Research*, 38(6): 1970–1984. Retrieved from http://doi.org/10.1111/1468-2427.12123

Anderson, J. E. 2012. "Collecting Land Value through Public Land Leasing." In G. K. Ingram and Y. Hong (eds.), *Value Capture and Land Policies*. Pp. 123–144. Boston, MA: Lincoln Institute of Land Policy.

Asthana, A. N. 2012. "Decentralisation, HRD and Production Efficiency of Water Utilities: Evidence from India." *Water Policy*, 14(1): 112–126. Retrieved from http://doi.org/10.2166/wp.2011.119

Auerbach, A. 2016. "Clients and Communities: The Political Economy of Party Network Organization and Development in India's Urban Slums – ERRATA." *World Politics*, 68(1): 189. Retrieved from http://doi.org/10.1017/S004388711500043X

Auyero, J. 2000. *Poor People's Politics*. Durham, NC: Duke University Press.

Auyero, J. 2009. *Flammable: Environmental Suffering in an Argentine Shantytown*. Oxford: Oxford University Press.

Avritzer, L. 2006. "New Public Spheres in Brazil: Local Democracy and Deliberative Politics." *International Journal of Urban and Regional Research*, 30(3): 623–637. Retrieved from http://doi.org/10.1111/j.1468-2427.2006.00692.x

Baiocchi, G., P. Heller, and M. K. Silva. 2008. "Making Space for Civil Society: Institutional Reforms and Local Democracy in Brazil." *Social Forces*, 86(3): 911–936.

Bardhan, P., and D. Mookherjee. 2006. *Decentralization and Local Governance in Developing Countries: A Comparative Perspective*. Cambridge, MA: MIT Press.

Benjaminsen, T. A., S. Holden, C. Lund, and E. Sjaastad. 2009. "Formalisation of Land Rights: Some Empirical Evidence from Mali, Niger and South Africa." *Land Use Policy*, 26(1): 28–35. Retrieved from http://doi.org/10.1016/j.landusepol.2008.07.003

Berenschot, W. 2010. "Everyday Mediation: The Politics of Public Service Delivery in Gujarat, India." *Development and Change*, 41(5): 883–905. Retrieved from http://doi.org/10.1111/j.1467-7660.2010.01660.x

van den Berg, C., and A. Danilenko. 2011. *The IBNET Water Supply and Sanitation Performance Blue Book: The International Benchmarking Network of Water and Sanitation Utilities Databook*. Washington, DC: World Bank Publications.

Bhavnani, R. R. 2009. "Do Electoral Quotas Work after They Are Withdrawn? Evidence from a Natural Experiment in India." *American Political Science Review*, 103(1): 23–35. Retrieved from http://doi.org/10.1017/S0003055409090029

Blanco, A., V. Fretes Cibils, A. Muñoz Miranda, A. Gilbert, S. Webb, E. Reese, and J. Kim. 2014. "Busco casa en arriendo: Promover el alquiler tiene sentido." Inter-American Development Bank. Retrieved from http://publications.iadb.org/handle/11319/6730

Carvalho, S., G. M. Perkins, A. G. Kapoor, H. N. White, C. Bahnson, and S. A. Weber-Venghaus. 2002. "Social Funds: Assessing Effectiveness" (No. 24615). The World Bank. Retrieved from http://documents.worldbank.org/curated/en/2002/05/1972083/social-funds-assessing-effectiveness

Chatterjee, P. 2004. *Politics of the Governed: Popular Politics in Most of the World.* New York, NY: Columbia University Press.

Childress, M. 2004. "Regional Study on Land Administration, Land Markets, and Collateralized Lending" (No. 37415) (pp. 1–64). The World Bank. Retrieved from http://documents.worldbank.org/curated/en/2004/06/7105185/regional-study-land-administration-land-markets-collateralized-lending

Cleary, M. R. 2007. "Electoral Competition, Participation, and Government Responsiveness in Mexico." *American Journal of Political Science, 51*(2): 283–299. Retrieved from http://doi.org/10.1111/j.1540-5907.2007.00251.x

Conning, J., and M. Kevane. 2002. "Community-Based Targeting Mechanisms for Social Safety Nets: A Critical Review." *World Development, 30*(3): 375–394. Retrieved from http://doi.org/10.1016/S0305-750X(01)00119-X

Dasgupta, A., and V. A. Beard. 2007. "Community Driven Development, Collective Action and Elite Capture in Indonesia." *Development and Change, 38*(2): 229–249. Retrieved from http://doi.org/10.1111/j.1467-7660.2007.00410.x

Davidson, C., and G. Korbel. 1981. "At-Large Elections and Minority-Group Representation: A Re-Examination of Historical and Contemporary Evidence." *Journal of Politics, 43*(4): 982–1005. Retrieved from http://doi.org/10.2307/2130184

De, I., and T. Nag. 2016. "Dangers of Decentralisation in Urban Slums: A Comparative Study of Water Supply and Drainage Service Delivery in Kolkata, India." *Development Policy Review, 34*(2): 253–276.

De Soto, H. 2000. *The Mystery of Capital: Why Capitalism Triumphs in the West and Fails Everywhere Else.* Basic Books.

Devas, N. 2005. "Metropolitan Governance and Urban Poverty." *Public Administration and Development, 25*(4): 351–361. Retrieved from http://doi.org/10.1002/pad.388

Dickovick, J. T. 2005. "The Measure and Mismeasure of Decentralisation: Subnational Autonomy in Senegal and South Africa." *Journal of Modern African Studies, 43*(2): 183–210.

Dietz, H. 1998. *Urban Poverty, Political Participation, and the State: Lima, 1970–1990.* University of Pittsburgh Press.

Donaghy, M. 2015. "Resisting Removal: The Impact of Community Mobilization in Rio de Janeiro." *Latin American Politics and Society, 57*(4): 74–96. Retrieved from http://doi.org/10.1111/j.1548-2456.2015.00288.x

Durand-Lasserve, A., M. Durand-Lasserve, and H. Selod. 2015. *Land Delivery Systems in West African Cities: The Example of Bamako, Mali.* Washington, DC: World Bank Publications.

Eaton, K. 2006. "The Downside of Decentralization: Armed Clientelism in Colombia." *Security Studies, 15*(4): 533–562. Retrieved from http://doi.org/10.1080/09636410601188463

Eghoff, C., C. Farvacque-Vitkovic, A. Casalis, and M. Diop. 2007. "Development of the Cities of Mali: Challenges and Priorities" (No. 41890) (pp. 1–79). The World Bank. Retrieved from http://documents.worldbank.org/curated/en/2007/09/8896976/development-cities-mali-challenges-priorities

Faguet, J.-P. 2014. "Decentralization and Governance." *World Development, 53,* 2–13. Retrieved from http://doi.org/10.1016/j.worlddev.2013.01.002

Fernández, D. 2004. "Colombia: Desarollo económico reciente en infraestructura: Balanceando las necesidades sociales y productivas de infraestructura." World Bank, Finance, Private Sector and Infrastructure Unit.

Ferraz, C., and F. Finan. 2011. "Electoral Accountability and Corruption: Evidence from the Audits of Local Governments." *American Economic Review*, 101(4): 1274–1311.

Fritzen, S. A. 2007. "Can the Design of Community-Driven Development Reduce the Risk of Elite Capture? Evidence from Indonesia." *World Development*, 35(8): 1359–1375. Retrieved from http://doi.org/10.1016/j.worlddev.2007.05.001

García-Guadilla, M. P., and C. Pérez. 2002. "Democracy, Decentralization, and Clientelism: New Relationships and Old Practices." *Latin American Perspectives*, 29(5): 90–109.

Gay, R. 1994. *Popular Organization and Democracy in Rio de Janeiro: A Tale of Two Favelas*. Philadelphia, PA: Temple University Press.

Ghertner, D. A. 2011. "Gentrifying the State, Gentrifying Participation: Elite Governance Programs in Delhi." *International Journal of Urban and Regional Research*, 35(3): 504–532. Retrieved from https://doi.org/10.1111/j.1468-2427.2011.01043.x

Ghertner, D. A. 2015. *Rule By Aesthetics: World-Class City Making in Delhi*. Oxford University Press.

Gilbert, A. 2007. "Water for All: How to Combine Public Management with Commercial Practice for the Benefit of the Poor." *Urban Studies*, 44(8): 1559–1579.

Goldfrank, B. 2007. "The Politics of Deepening Local Democracy: Decentralization, Party Institutionalization, and Participation." *Comparative Politics*, 39(2): 147–168. Retrieved from http://doi.org/10.2307/20434031

Gough, K. V., and P. W. K. Yankson. 2000. "Land Markets in African Cities: The Case of Peri-Urban Accra, Ghana." *Urban Studies*, 37(13): 2485–2500. Retrieved from http://doi.org/10.1080/00420980020080651

Grindle, M. S. 2007. *Going Local: Decentralization, Democratization, and the Promise of Good Governance*. Princeton, NJ: Princeton University Press.

Hardoy, J. E., D. Mitlin, and D. Satterthwaite. 2013. *Environmental Problems in an Urbanizing World: Finding Solutions in Cities in Africa, Asia and Latin America*. Routledge.

Hardoy, J. E., D. Mitlin, and D. Satterwhaite. 2001. *Environmental Problems in an Urbanizing World*. London: Earthscan.

Herrera, V. 2014. "Does Commercialization Undermine the Benefits of Decentralization for Local Services Provision? Evidence from Mexico's Urban Water Sector." *World Development*, 56, 16–31.

Herrera, V., and A. E. Post. 2014. "Can Developing Countries Both Decentralize and Depoliticize Urban Water Services? Evaluating the Legacy of the 1990s Reform Wave." *World Development*, 64, 621–641. Retrieved from https://doi.org/10.1016/j.worlddev.2014.06.026

Hiskey, J. 2003. "Demand-Based Development and Local Electoral Environments in Mexico." *Comparative Politics*, 36(1): 41–59.

Holland, A. 2016. "Forbearance." *American Political Science Review*, 110(2): 232–246.

Holston, J. 2009. "Insurgent Citizenship in an Era of Global Urban Peripheries." *City and Society*, 21(2): 245–267. Retrieved from http://doi.org/10.1111/j.1548-744X.2009.01024.x

Holston, J., and T. Caldeira. 2008. "Urban Peripheries and the Invention of Citizenship." *Harvard Design Magazine, 28.*

Interamerican Development Bank. 2012. "Room for Development: Housing Markets in Latin America and the Caribbean." Summary. Retrieved from http://publications. iadb.org/handle/11319/447

Islam, N. 2003. "Reforming Governance in Dhaka, Bangladesh." In R. Stren and P. McCarney (eds.), *Governance on the Ground: Innovation and Discontinuities in Cities of the Developing World.* Pp. 194–219. Washington, DC: Woodrow Wilson Center Press.

Jha, G. 2003. "Municipal Financial Resource Mobilisation Status, Concerns and Issues." Paper prepared for the National Seminar on Municipal Finance, 12th Finance Commission, Indian Institute of Public Administration, New Delhi, December 29–30, 2003.

Jha, S., V. Rao, and M. Woolcock. 2007. "Governance in the Gullies: Democratic Responsiveness and Leadership in Delhi's Slums." *World Development, 35*(2): 230–246. Retrieved from http://doi.org/10.1016/j.worlddev.2005.10.018

Joireman, S. F. 2011. *Where There Is No Government: Enforcing Property Rights in Common Law Africa.* Oxford University Press.

Keefer, P. 2007. "Clientelism, Credibility, and the Policy Choices of Young Democracies." *American Journal of Political Science, 51*(4): 804–821.

Kelly, R. 2000. "Designing a Property Tax Reform Strategy for Sub-Saharan Africa: An Analytical Framework Applied to Kenya." *Public Budgeting & Finance, 20*(4): 36–51.

Kitonsa, W., and K. Schwartz. 2012. "Commercialisation and Centralisation in the Ugandan and Zambian Water Sector." *International Journal of Water, 6*(3/4): 176–194.

Kjellen, M., and G. McGranahan. 2006. "Informal Water Vendors and the Urban Poor" (Human Settlements Discussion Paper Series No. 978-1-84369-586-8). London: International Institute for Environment and Development. Retrieved from www. mumbaidp24seven.in/reference/informal_water_vendors.pdf

Kooy, M. 2014. "Developing Informality: The Production of Jakarta's Urban Waterscape." *Water Alternatives, 7*(1): 35–53.

Krause, M. 2009. *The Political Economy of Water and Sanitation.* New York, NY: Routledge.

Krishna, A. 2013. "Stuck in Place: Investigating Social Mobility in 14 Bangalore Slums." *Journal of Development Studies: JDS, 49*(7): 1010–1028.

Lentini, E. 2014. "Servicios de agua potable y saneamiento: lecciones de experiencias relevantes" [Text]. Retrieved from www.cepal.org/es/publicaciones/3851-servicios-agua-potable-saneamiento-lecciones-experiencias-relevantes

Levitsky, S. 2003. *Transforming Labor-Based Parties in Latin America: Argentine Peronism in Comparative Perspective.* Cambridge University Press.

Libertun de Duren, N., and R. Guerrero Compeán. 2016. "Growing Resources for Growing Cities: Density and the Cost of Municipal Public Services in Latin America." *Urban Studies, 53*(14): 3082–3107. Retrieved from https://doi.org/ 10.1177/0042098015601579

Lichtenberg, E., and C. Ding. 2009. "Local Officials as Land Developers: Urban Spatial Expansion in China." *Journal of Urban Economics, 66*(1): 57–64. Retrieved from https://doi.org/10.1016/j.jue.2009.03.002

Lusugga Kironde, J. M. 2006. "The Regulatory Framework, Unplanned Development and Urban Poverty: Findings from Dar es Salaam, Tanzania." *Land Use Policy*, 23(4): 460–472. Retrieved from http://doi.org/10.1016/j.landusepol.2005.07.004

Magalhães, F., P. Acosta Restrepo., F. Lonardoni, and R. Moris. 2016. "Slum Upgrading and Housing in Latin America." Retrieved from http://publications.iadb.org/handle/11319/7879

Marx, B., T. Stoker, and T. Suri. 2013. "The Economics of Slums in the Developing World." *Journal of Economic Perspectives*, 27(4): 187–210.

McIntosh, A. C. 2003. "Asian Water Supplies: Reaching the Urban Poor." Asian Development Bank. Retrieved from www.adb.org/publications/asian-water-supplies-reaching-urban-poor

Meagher, K. 2011. "Informal Economies and Urban Governance in Nigeria: Popular Empowerment or Political Exclusion?" *African Studies Review*, 54(2): 47–72. Retrieved from http://doi.org/10.1353/arw.2011.0026

Mitchell, J. 2000. "Political Decentralization, Municipal Fragmentation, and the Geography of Real Estate Investment in Caracas, Venezuela." *Urban Geography*, 21 (2): 148–169. Retrieved from http://doi.org/10.2747/0272-3638.21.2.148

Napier, M. 2009. "Making Urban Land Markets Work Better in South African Cities and Towns: Arguing the Basis for Access by the Poor." In S. V. Lall, M. Freire, B. Yuen, R. Rajack, and J.-J. Helluin (eds.), *Urban Land Markets* (pp. 71–97). Springer Netherlands. Retrieved from http://link.springer.com/chapter/10.1007/978-1-4020-8862-9_4

Nathan, N. 2016. "Does Participation Reinforce Patronage? Policy Preferences and Turnout in Urban Ghana." *British Journal of Political Science*. 1–27. doi:10.1017/S0007123416000351

Nickson, A. 1995. *Local Government in Latin America*. Boulder, CO: Lynne Rienner Publishers.

Novaes, L. M. 2015. "Disloyal Political Brokers and the Problem of Clientelistic Party Building." University of California, Berkeley. Retrieved from http://ebape.fgv.br/sites/ebape.fgv.br/files/promiscPoliticians+1.pdf

OECD. 2011. *Ten Years of Water Sector Reform in Eastern Europe, Caucasus and Central Asia*. OECD Publishing.

Olken, B. A. 2010. "Direct Democracy and Local Public Goods: Evidence from a Field Experiment in Indonesia." *American Political Science Review*, 104(2): 243–267. Retrieved from http://doi.org/10.1017/S0003055410000079

Onjala, J. 2002. "Good Intentions, Structural Pitfalls: Early Lessons from Urban Water Commercialisation Attempts in Kenya" (2). Retrieved from www.africabib.org/rec.php?RID=238984737

Pasotti, E. 2010. *Political Branding in Cities: The Decline of Machine Politics in Bogotá, Naples, and Chicago*. Cambridge University Press.

Paulais, T. 2012. *Financing Africa's Cities: The Imperative of Local Investment*. Washington, DC: World Bank Publications.

Peterson, G. E. 2009. *Unlocking Land Values to Finance Urban Infrastructure*. Washington, DC: World Bank Publications.

Pineda Pablos, N., and H. Briseño Ramírez. 2012. "¿Por qué son mejores los organismos de agua de Baja California que los de Sonora? Instituciones locales y desempeño de los organismos públicos." *Región Y Sociedad*, 24(SPE.3): 181–212.

Post, A. E. 2014. *Foreign and Domestic Investment in Argentina: The Politics of Privatized Infrastructure*. New York, NY: Cambridge University Press.

Post, A. E., V. Bronsoler, and L. Salman. 2017. "Hybrid Regimes for Local Public Goods Provision: A Framework for Analysis." *Perspectives on Politics.* 15(4): 952–966.

Pradhan, M., V. Rao, and C. Rosenberg. 2009. *The Impact of the Community Level Activities of the Second Urban Poverty Project.* Washington, DC: World Bank Publications.

Rao, V., and A. M. Ibáñez. 2003. *The Social Impact of Social Funds in Jamaica: A Mixed-Methods Analysis of Participation, Targeting, and Collective Action in Community-Driven Development.* Washington, DC: World Bank Publications.

Resnick, D. 2014. "Urban Governance and Service Delivery in African Cities: The Role of Politics and Policies." *Development Policy Review, 32*(s1): s3–s17. Retrieved from http://doi.org/10.1111/dpr.12066

Rodriguez-Acosta, C., and A. Rosenbaum. 2008. "Metropolitan Governance in Latin America." In M. S. de Vries, M. S. Haque, and P. S. Reddy (eds.), *Improving Local Government: Outcomes of Comparative Research* (pp. 9–31). Basingstoke, NY: Palgrave Macmillan.

Rosenblatt, F., G. Bidegain, F. Monestier, and R. P. Rodríguez. 2015. "A Natural Experiment in Political Decentralization: Local Institutions and Citizens' Political Engagement in Uruguay." *Latin American Politics and Society, 57*(2), 91–110. Retrieved from https://doi.org/10.1111/j.1548-2456.2015.00268.x

Sandroni, P. 2014. "A New Financial Instrument of Value Capture in São Paulo: Certificates of Additional Construction Potential." In G. K. Ingram and Y. Hong (eds.), *Municipal Revenues and Land Policies* (pp. 218–237). Boston, MA: Lincoln Institute of Land Policy.

Savedoff, W., and P. Spiller (eds.). 1999. *Spilled Water: Institutional Commitment in the Provision of Water Services.* Washington, DC: Inter-American Development Bank.

Schaffner, B. F., M. Streb, and G. Wright. 2001. "Teams without Uniforms: The Nonpartisan Ballot in State and Local Elections." *Political Research Quarterly, 54* (1): 7–30. Retrieved from http://doi.org/10.1177/106591290105400101

Smolka, M. O. 2013. *Implementing Value Capture in Latin America.* Boston, MA: Lincoln Institute of Land Policy.

Stokes, S. C. 1995. *Cultures in Conflict: Social Movements and the State in Peru.* Berkeley, CA: University of California Press.

Szwarcberg, M. 2015. *Mobilizing Poor Voters: Machine Politics, Clientelism, and Social Networks in Argentina.* New York, NY: Cambridge University Press.

Tynan, N., and B. Kingdom. 2005. "Optimal Size for Utilities?" (No. 31562) (pp. 1–4). The World Bank. Retrieved from http://do.worldbank.org/curated/en/2005/01/5628543/optimal-size-utilities

Ubink, J. 2007. "Traditional Authority Revisited: Popular Perceptions of Chiefs and Chieftaincy in Peri-Urban Kumasi, Ghana." *Journal of Legal Pluralism and Unofficial Law, 39*(55): 123–161. Retrieved from http://doi.org/10.1080/07329113.2007.10756610

UN-HABITAT. 2005. Global Report on Human Settlements 2005 – Financing Urban Shelter.

UN-HABITAT. 2010a. *State of the World's Cities 2010–2011: Cities for All: Bridging the Urban Divide.* Routledge.

UN-HABITAT. 2010b. *The State of African Cities 2010: Governance, Inequality and Urban Land Markets.* UN-HABITAT.

UN-HABITAT. 2012. *State of Latin American and Caribbean Cities.* UN-HABITAT.

UN-HABITAT. 2014. "State of African Cities 2014: Re-Imagining Sustainable Urban Transitions." Retrieved from https://unhabitat.org/books/state-of-african-cities-2014-re-imagining-sustainable-urban-transitions/state-of-african-cities-2014-re-imagining-sustainable-urban-transitions/

UN-HABITAT. 2015. Issue Paper on Informal Settlements. Retrieved from https://unhabitat.org/wp-content/uploads/2015/04/Habitat-III-Issue-Paper-22_Informal-Settlements.pdf.

UN-HABITAT. 2016. *World Cities Report 2016*.

United Cities and Local Government, and World Bank. 2008. "Decentralization and Local Democracy in the World: 2008 First Global Report by United Cities and Local Governments [*sic*]" (No. 47811) (pp. 1–350). The World Bank. Retrieved from http://documents.worldbank.org/curated/en/2009/01/10362467/decentralization-local-democracy-world-2008-first-global-report-united-cities-local-governments

United Cities and Local Governments. 2016. *UCLG Policy Paper on Local Finance*. Retrieved from: www.uclg.org/sites/default/files/background_paper_of_lrgs_on_ffd3.pdf.

United Nations. 2015. *World Urbanization Prospects 2014*. United Nations Publications.

Vasconcellos, E. A. 2014. *Urban Transport Environment and Equity: The Case for Developing Countries*. London: Routledge.

Walters, L. C. 2013. "Land Value Capture in Policy and Practice." *Journal of Property Tax Assessment & Administration*, April: 5–21.

Wampler, B. 2008. "When Does Participatory Democracy Deepen the Quality of Democracy? Lessons from Brazil." *Comparative Politics*, 41(1): 61–81. Retrieved from http://doi.org/10.2307/20434105

Weinstein, L. 2009. "Democracy in the Globalizing Indian City: Engagements of Political Society and the State in Globalizing Mumbai." *Politics & Society*, 37(3), 397–427. Retrieved from https://doi.org/10.1177/1049731509338926

Weinstein, L., and X. Ren. 2009. "The Changing Right to the City: Urban Renewal and Housing Rights in Globalizing Shanghai and Mumbai." *City and Community*, 8(4): 407–432. Retrieved from http://doi.org/10.1111/j.1540-6040.2009.01300.x

Weitz-Shapiro, R. 2014. *Curbing Clientelism in Argentina: Politics, Poverty, and Social Policy*. Cambridge University Press.

World Bank. 2003. *World Development Report 2004: Making Services Work for Poor People*. Washington, DC: World Bank Publications.

World Bank. 2013. *Urbanization beyond Municipal Boundaries: Nurturing Metropolitan Economies and Connecting Peri-Urban Areas in India*. Washington, DC: World Bank Publications.

World Bank. 2015. *East Asia's Changing Urban Landscape: Measuring a Decade of Spatial Growth*. Washington, DC: World Bank Publications.

9

Decentralization in Post-Conflict Settings

Assessing Community-Driven Development in the Wake of Violence

Fotini Christia

INTRODUCTION

The past twenty years have witnessed an accumulation of valuable social scientific inquiries into the effects of decentralizing political power in advanced societies (Broadway and Shah 2009; Treisman 2006) and in the developing world (Bardhan 2002; Enikolopov and Zhuravskaya 2007). Nevertheless, there is little consensus in either literature as to whether devolution improves governance (Treisman 2007).[1] Similar disagreement exists in the comparatively thin body of work on decentralization in post-conflict settings, where research is often hindered by limited state capacity, institutional weakness, and instability. The frequency and spread of conflict around the globe, and its deep and undisputed negative effects on development (Cameron et al. 2015; World Bank 2011), have recently inspired new work by academics and practitioners to fill this gap (Beath et al. 2013a, 2013b; Casey et al. 2012; Fearon et al. 2009, 2015; Humphreys et al. 2015).[2] These initiatives have capitalized on the opportunities for institutional change that often arise in

---

[1] Studies of decentralization often distinguish among three different types of institutional arrangements: "devolution" (or "democratic decentralization"), which implies a "transfer of power and resources to subnational authorities that are both (relatively) independent of central government and democratically elected"; "deconcentration," which implies a "transfer of authority to subnational branches of the central state"; and "fiscal decentralization," which implies that local officials, elected or appointed, have authority to draft their own budgets, collect their own taxes, and/or spend these revenues as they see fit (Crawford and Hartmann 2008, p. 9). The focus of this chapter is largely on devolution, not deconcentration or fiscal decentralization.

[2] An estimated 70% of fragile states have been plagued by violent conflict in the past twenty-five years, leading to high levels of poverty and low levels of development (Cameron et al. 2015). Aid is thus integral to post-conflict governance as it is intended to help recreate a state and to rebuild institutions that can provide goods and services.

the wake of violence to evaluate the role of aid and decentralization using innovative methods (King and Samii 2014).

This chapter reviews the evidence linking decentralization with peace, stability, and development after the termination of violent conflict. In doing so it focuses specifically on the role of foreign aid and community-driven development (CDD). It also discusses what remains contested in this literature and attempts to explain what may account for the conflicting results – including differences in context, research design, and measurement. CDD initiatives may vary in their degree of integration with the formal public sector and local government structures. They are nevertheless worthy of consideration in their own right in a discussion on decentralization in post-conflict settings given their role as one of the leading bottom-up development interventions in such contexts.

Given the state of knowledge, the chapter seconds recent calls for more theoretically motivated studies of post-conflict decentralization that better assess the relevance of the community approach to development (Bennett and D'Onofrio 2015). For development practitioners, it highlights the need to integrate rigorous program assessment in the program design phase. This involves launching clear and straightforward interventions and requires closely considering how aid-targeting decisions are affecting outcomes. Though many decentralization interventions are informed by the same principles and theories, different regional contexts, institutional legacies, conflict histories, and levels and types of aid can all affect results.

This chapter also calls for future scholarship to employ mixed-method designs and carefully crafted measurement strategies that permit estimation of precise, well-contextualized effects. It closes by highlighting promising current initiatives to improve collaboration between academics and policymakers, and between academics pursuing similar studies in different parts of the world. Coordination of this type enables pre-analysis planning that enhances hypotheses testing without stifling discovery, while also facilitating replication and the efficient accumulation of knowledge.

GENERAL FINDINGS ON POST-CONFLICT DECENTRALIZATION

The main objective of decentralization is to improve governance and service delivery through competent and accountable leadership at the local level. It is based on the premise that certain fiscal and administrative powers are best vested with local officials because they are well placed to ascertain local needs and preferences. Decentralization is also thought to minimize opportunities for public resources to be misappropriated. The findings from both theoretical and empirical discussions of the effects of decentralization, however, are mixed, as such reforms may introduce local resource capture, i.e., theft, that exacerbates preexisting issues of governance and service delivery. Implementing such far-reaching institutional reforms is even more challenging in the wake of violent conflict. War inevitably impairs economies, disrupts institutions, compromises service delivery, and delegitimizes prewar power structures. As a result, the degree to which institutional change can be dictated from the top down is limited.[3]

Decentralization, though it may mitigate inefficiencies in service provision, also involves an array of power struggles. Often these occur when new local institutions are granted powers that overlap with, or supersede, those of traditional authorities (Beath et al. 2013c). Reform may be further constrained by the need to sustain a post-conflict agreement between former warring parties that are expected to share power. Local power-holders whose position has improved through war represent yet another threat to successful reform. Many face strong incentives to capture devolved assets for the purpose of redistributing skimmed funds to local constituents (ex-combatants among them) or for simple self-enrichment (Blum et al. 2015).

Decentralization can thus be a tool of political gamesmanship as well as a best practice in public administration. Where it is enacted for the former purpose, it can readily lead to poor governance and instability. Cunningham (2011), who explores the instrumental use of decentralization as a type of concession to rebellious self-determination movements, finds that a state is more likely to offer such an inducement to a movement that is internally divided than to one that is unified. The reason, she posits, is that states prefer to offer modest concessions, with the goal of creating friction between moderate and radical factions, rather than to relinquish the larger stakes that would be necessary to cow a more tightly organized rebellion. As a result, decentralization that is initiated as part of the end of rebellion often does little to reduce the time until conflict recurs.

Decentralization also entails a de facto shift of public resources away from the political center that in turn changes the intranational balance of power. Compared to a more unitary system, public monies and material are more available for capture by dissidents on the periphery. Where decentralization accentuates the attractiveness of exploiting such an opportunity, it may have more conflict-inducing than conflict-mitigating effects. This danger, mainly discussed in studies of ethno-federalism, is thought to be most acute where ethnic groups with increased access to public resources at the subnational level are dissatisfied with the representation awarded to them by the central state. One study finds that in post-conflict settings, regional autonomy alone is associated with a higher incidence of renewed rebellion than autonomy combined with power sharing at the national level (Cederman et al. 2015).

---

[3] Particularly in sub-Saharan Africa, where the zeal to promote decentralization in the late 1990s and early 2000s was greatest, a clear pattern of foot-dragging and slow-rolling on the part of the central governments emerged (Van de Walle 2001). The result was that decentralization often simply did not occur in practice or was steadily reversed (i.e., authority was "recentralized") despite appropriate laws having been passed (Dickovick 2014; Kimenyi and Meagher 2004).

A similar study shows that de facto grand coalitions involving former rebels are associated with a lower likelihood of conflict recurrence following the termination of civil wars, while de facto autonomy is associated with a higher probability of territorial conflict (Pospieszna and Schneider 2013). Incentives for violent remobilization can therefore increase as the share of public resources and the balance of power between subnational units and the center moves increasingly in favor of the former.

Conversely, this same devolution of power and resources may increase a government's proximity to its citizens by enhancing participation in community affairs and by rendering decision making more inclusive. To the extent that decentralization increases local institutions' accountability and enables public expenditure to match citizens' preferences more closely, it is expected to improve service delivery, increase aggregate welfare, and mitigate conflict (Besley and Coate 2003; Oates 1972).

Urgent needs for service delivery in these post-conflict contexts are rarely met through central government budgets alone. More often than not, they are satisfied in part by international aid. The formal intent of aid agencies is to build peace by building capacity. Achieving this objective requires that local governments possess capable bureaucracies, and that these bureaucracies answer as much to citizens as to higher levels of government.[4] Donors, however, bring to recipient countries their own agendas, sources of influence, and means of delivering resources, each of which may undermine rather than strengthen the state (Barron 2010; Blum et al. 2015). Given the capacity deficits in post-conflict environments and resultant high levels of aid infusion, more attention is often paid to using decentralization as a vehicle for the expenditure of incoming aid than to building human capital or improving local governance and service provision.

These observations have important implications for the potential utility of foreign aid in decentralization initiatives. The evidence suggests that aid is most successful where conflict results in a negotiated settlement, where both parties have a stake in decentralization, where the means exist to build capable and locally accountable subnational governments, and where donors can bring into agreement the interests of the central government, local governments, and traditional authorities.[5]

---

[4] Mansoob Murshed et al. (2009) show that in Indonesia ordinary criminal violence decreased more where subnational governments created between 1998 and 2001 were larger and wealthier. In Sierra Leone, Sacks and Larizza (2012) present results indicating that citizens' trust in government officials and their willingness to comply with government instructions is strongly associated with their perception of local officials' performance.

[5] Dickovick (2014) notes with respect to center–periphery relations that it is important that donors build capacity at both levels in a coordinated fashion. Often reforms in the ministries of national government outpace the creation of local government, leading the former to assume the responsibilities of the latter preemptively. Carefully delineating the authority of ethnic or tribal rulers vis-à-vis that of the local government is equally important for defusing potential conflict. This is

One major weakness in the literature discussed earlier is that it does not feature robust empirical analysis of the service-related outcomes of decentralization. In other words, it does not measure systematically or directly the degree to which access to services changes as a result of decentralization initiatives. Equivalent analyses of the effect of decentralization on democratic participation, faith in government, or conflict are more prevalent but generally unsatisfactory for methodological reasons, as they only rarely pay attention to parsing causality from correlation. Recent research on CDD in post-conflict contexts represents an exception to this pattern. Though there is not yet unqualified proven impact of such post-conflict interventions, CDD has been singled out in recent assessments of the literature on post-conflict reconstruction as a uniquely consistent body of work for which an evidence synthesis is possible (Brown et al. 2015; Cameron et al. 2015; Gisselquist 2015; King and Samii 2014; Casey 2018). For this reason, it is a point of emphasis in this chapter.

Community-driven development, which focuses on improving levels of civic engagement, service provision, and economic well-being, is broadly seen as an effective way to decentralize political and fiscal authority.[6] CDD projects employ participatory processes to elect local development councils. With input from the community, these bodies identify development needs, select particular projects, and see them to completion. The high level of civic engagement that is part of CDD is considered more likely to enhance social capital, effectively meet local needs, and limit aid theft. It has therefore become an attractive way to disburse development aid (Barron 2010; Wong and Guggenheim 2005). It is also particularly attractive in the post-conflict context, where weak central governments often lack access to the periphery, and there is increased risk of graft that prevents aid from reaching its intended beneficiaries (de Regt et al. 2013; USAID 2007; World Bank 2006). Tens of billions of dollars have been directed to this form of decentralized post-conflict development in recent years (de Regt et al. 2013; King and Samii 2014; Mansuri and Rao 2012; Wong 2012).[7]

---

especially true on matters relating to tax collection and land usage – two issues that in many postcolonial countries tended to be the remit of designated traditional elites (Fanthorpe 2006).

[6] Community-driven development is often called community-driven reconstruction (CDR) in the post-conflict context. The more general term *community-driven development* is used in this chapter.

[7] King and Samii (2014) note that the World Bank has been the pioneer and strongest proponent of CDD but that the United States, the United Kingdom, and other bilateral donors have also been actively involved. They state specifically that by 2012 the World Bank had sponsored more than 400 projects in 94 countries (Wong 2012, p. iv) including 167 CDD projects in 29 fragile or violent countries from 2000 to 2010 (de Regt et al. 2013, p. 5); they also reference US CDD-related assistance to Afghanistan, Iraq, and Pakistan, among others, and UK CDD-supported projects in Nigeria, India, and Bangladesh (King and Samii 2014, p. 740).

Existing findings on the CDD approach generally (e.g., Mansuri and Rao 2012; Wong 2012; Casey 2018) and on its effects in the post-conflict setting more specifically (e.g., de Regt et al. 2013; Guggenheim 2010; King and Samii 2014) suggest some strong effects on service delivery and weaker evidence of short-term improvements in economic well-being. Results pertaining to governance and social cohesion are mixed. There are several differences in the studies – including program design, timing, measurement strategy, context, and the type and magnitude of the intervention considered – that make it hard to conclusively say whether and how CDD works in post-conflict settings. These potential sources of disagreement are discussed in more detail in what follows.

WHAT WE KNOW ABOUT POST-CONFLICT COMMUNITY-DRIVEN DEVELOPMENT

Since the mid-1980s, development agencies have increasingly utilized decentralized approaches to aid delivery (Dongier et al. 2002; Mansuri and Rao 2012; Wong 2012; Casey 2018). This modus operandi is focused on direct community involvement not only in identifying development needs but also in planning projects, implementing them, and maintaining them over time. As such, these approaches are consistent with academic findings suggesting that communities are best suited to mobilize the resources necessary to solve local challenges (Sen 1999). They were also seen as an appropriate reaction to calls for decentralization prompted by "top-down" development, and its related lack of responsiveness to local beneficiaries (Scott 1998). Finally, CDD is considered good for local institution building as it is meant to be more representative, transparent, and accountable, while also being adaptable and scalable (Pritchett and Woolcock 2004; Wong and Guggenheim 2005).

Following violent conflict there is a heightened need to rebuild communities' social cohesion as well as their economic well-being (Cliffe et al. 2003). This has motivated aid agencies to focus their CDD programming on conflict-affected areas (de Regt et al. 2013; USAID 2007; World Bank 2006). In these circumstances, programming features collective action initiatives to rebuild trust and promote peace building as well as long-term institutional change (Barron 2010). Post-conflict CDD has been used in Afghanistan, the Democratic Republic of Congo, Indonesia, Liberia, Philippines, Sierra Leone, Timor-Leste, Yemen, and other countries. Despite notable variability in context, as well as in the length and intensity of the intervention, all these CDD programs have shared the principle that decentralized development aid should contribute to peace building.

The bulk of the impact assessments of CDD interventions to date have relied on qualitative methodologies and case studies (for a review, see Mansuri and Rao 2012; Wong 2012). Case studies have tended to portray CDD very flatteringly, highlighting success stories and lauding the civic engagement it creates. This is also the case for assessments of post-conflict CDD programs (for a discussion, see Gisselquist 2015). An example is Yemen's Social Fund for Development, whose success on all levels – governance, economic well-being, and civic engagement, among others – has been attributed to its stakeholder ownership approach, the relevance of its interventions for beneficiaries, its political neutrality in terms of resource allocation, and its flexibility in project funding (Al-Iryani et al. 2015).

Because case studies intended to evaluate CDD in general, and specifically in post-conflict settings, are skewed toward validation, researchers have recently turned to experimental and quasi-experimental methods for more conclusive, evidence-based answers. The first wave of these studies considered CDD programs in Southeast Asia. Voss (2008) uses difference-in-differences estimation to evaluate the Kecamatan Development Program (KDP) in Indonesia. He finds substantive increases in consumption and poverty reduction in the poorest communities, but no impact on economic outcomes in more affluent areas. KDP also produced a general reduction in unemployment, while increasing access to health care services as well. Barron et al. (2009) evaluate the Community-Based Reintegration Assistance for Conflict Victims (BRA-KDP) program in Aceh, Indonesia. Their study, which uses propensity-score matching and an instrumental variables approach, concludes that BRA-KDP increased asset ownership, agricultural activity, and economic perceptions, but had no impact on employment, access to health care and education, or the level of community infrastructure. It also presents no evidence that BRA-KDP influenced associational activity, trust in institutions, acceptance of returning groups, social tensions, conflict, or perceptions of community efficacy. Edillon et al. (2011) evaluate the Kapit-Bisig Laban Sa Kahirapan(KALAHI-CIDSS)-Comprehensive and Integrated Delivery of Social Services program in the Philippines using panel survey data. They find that participation in the program is associated with increased per capita consumption, employment, income diversification, access to markets for agricultural produce, visits to local health care facilities, and use of clean drinking water. The program also heightened participation in local governance activities, knowledge of public affairs, organizational membership, and interpersonal trust, but negatively affected collective action.

These analyses, though offering a marked improvement over inferences from purely observational studies, still encounter potential identification challenges.[8] A recent wave of randomized controlled trials (RCTs) intended to measure the effects of CDD initiatives in post-conflict settings have sought to convey more convincing causal estimates. These RCTs were possible thanks to the large scale

---

[8] Obstacles include an absence of evidence indicating parallel trends between treated and control units in studies using difference-in-differences estimation, possible specification errors in propensity score models, and the inevitable difficulty of satisfying the exclusion restriction when using instrumental variables analysis.

of the interventions under study across several communities as well as the programs' gradual rollouts. Evaluated CDD interventions include those in Liberia (Fearon et al. 2009, 2015), Sierra Leone (Casey et al. 2012), Afghanistan (Beath et al. 2013a, 2013b), and the Democratic Republic of Congo (Humphreys et al. 2012, 2015).

Fearon et al. (2009, 2015) carried out a randomized impact evaluation of a community-driven reconstruction (CDR) program in Liberia. The study finds strong evidence that the program improved access to local public goods and education, but only weak evidence that it increased employment and asset holdings. Though there was no impact on decision making or villagers' sense of personal efficacy, there was an increase in democratic processes for selection of community representatives and of projects, as well as a heightened trust in community leaders, reduced social tension, and increased acceptance of marginalized groups. Casey et al. (2012) conduct a randomized assessment of a CDD program in Sierra Leone and find that the program had a positive effect on economic well-being by increasing market activity and asset ownership, and improving the quality and quantity of public goods provision. There was, however, no identified impact on trust or collective action beyond the sphere of the project or any increase in participation or empowerment of women or youths in local affairs. Humphreys et al. (2012) and Humphreys et al. (2015) find no evidence of impact on services or economic well-being in a randomized evaluation of a CDD program in the Democratic Republic of Congo. Although the program was found to increase trust in ex-combatants, there were no other notable civic or governance effects. Beath et al. (2013a, 2013b) carried out a randomized impact evaluation of a CDD program in Afghanistan and found positive effects on access to services and perceptions of economic well-being, as well as increased female community participation. The program's effects on objective measures of economic well-being and governance, however, were mixed.

These programs took place in national contexts that varied in their historical and customary norms, preexisting institutions, and legacies of conflict, to name just a few relevant dimensions. Each also differed on a structural level, including the number and size of affected communities and the degree of government involvement. The programs themselves represented another source of variation. For example, each spent different amounts of development aid per capita,[9] delivered monetary aid in different ways,[10] took place on different timelines, and used different decision rules for implementation.[11]

---

[9] Total investment per capita was estimated to be $8.00 in Liberia, $16.00 in Sierra Leone, $10.00 in the Democratic Republic of Congo, and $20.40 in Afghanistan (King and Samii 2014, p. 743).

[10] For example, some programs utilized cash transfers, while others delivered aid via infrastructural projects.

[11] Programs in the Democratic Republic of Congo and Afghanistan mandated elections and women's participation in development councils (Beath et al. 2013a, 2013b; Humphreys et al.

Largely qualitative assessments of the effects of CDD interventions on violence in Southeast Asia suggest, contra extant theory, little evidence that CDD reduces levels of violence (Barron 2010; Barron et al. 2004). However, results from a recent quasi-experimental study of a CDD program in the Philippines and a randomized controlled trial of a CDD program in Afghanistan diverge.[12] In the former case, CDD not only had no effect on violence in the long run but even led to heightened insurgent attacks during the program's setup and preparation (Crost et al. 2014). A randomized impact evaluation of a similar program in Afghanistan, however, shows that there is heterogeneity in program impact depending on the location of the areas receiving aid (Beath et al. 2018). Specifically, CDD led to a notable reduction in violent incidents and improved perceptions of the government in areas not bordering Pakistan, but had no effect along the Pakistani border.[13] Viewed in juxtaposition, these results suggest that the effect of decentralized aid initiatives on violence varies considerably with structural and contextual factors (Berman et al. 2013; Dube and Vargas 2013).

Across all rigorous studies of post-conflict CDD programs there is relatively consistent evidence of positive effects on service delivery and somewhat weaker evidence of improved socioeconomic well-being over the short term. Though there is also reason to believe that community participation increases as well, this finding seems to vary by intervention and does not translate into longer-lasting governance-related effects (Barron 2010; Bennett and D'Onofrio 2015; King and Samii 2014), a pattern that is reflected in assessments of CDD programs outside of conflict zones as well (Mansuri and Rao 2012; Wong 2012). Effects regarding violence are highly mixed and context-specific.

ADVANCING THE FRONTIER

Several scholars have attributed the mixed and, in some respects, underwhelming results from CDD programs in post-conflict settings to unrealistic expectations, relatively low levels of aid, and limited time horizons for implementation.

2012, 2015), while those in Sierra Leone and Liberia did not (Casey et al. 2012; Fearon et al. 2009, 2015).

[12] This divergence in results is consistent with existing observational work on the effectiveness of more general forms of aid (other than CDD) in mitigating conflict. For instance, though some studies find that a reduction in aid increases conflict onset (Nielsen et al. 2011), others show that aid (in the form of US food assistance) can prolong conflict duration (Nunn and Qian 2014), while others find that short-term US military-funded infrastructure projects led to a decrease in insurgent attacks (Berman et al. 2011).

[13] Other differences between districts on and off the Pakistan border, such as ethnic composition, levels of violence, and opium production before the program's start, cannot explain this variation (Beath et al. 2018).

The following discussion aims to highlight the opportunities and challenges specific to decentralization and development aid initiatives in the post-conflict context. In doing so, it emphasizes the importance of being sensitive to the realities of local context and tailoring interventions accordingly, while also staying aware of what remains broadly applicable. More specifically, interventions must be informed by theories linking decentralization with improvements in governance and security; identify mechanisms and channels through which these effects are meant to occur; and integrate a robust, mixed-methods approach of impact evaluation with aid programming. This discussion also references innovative collaboration initiatives of development practitioners with academics.

Distinguish Decentralization Initiatives from Humanitarian Aid

The recent violence, social dislocation, and political instability associated with post-conflict environments all pose a serious challenge to successful institutional reform. However, post-conflict contexts also present a real opportunity for change precisely because war wreaks such thorough institutional disruption. This often makes recently war-torn areas particularly interesting laboratories for new development interventions and social science.

Though no good opportunity to build knowledge around development should be missed, practitioners and scholars need to be particularly careful about distinguishing development interventions that contribute to decentralization from more limited humanitarian initiatives. Often the two can be blurred. In the aftermath of conflict, aid delivered through local government bodies frequently comes with its own priorities (e.g., it is intended for the most vulnerable and needy) and with specific targeting restrictions. Its impact is meant to be transitional and short term. Development interventions linked to decentralization, by contrast, come not just with infusions of monetary aid, but with clear civic engagement and institutional components intended to have lasting effects. Distinguishing to the greatest possible degree what assistance is intended for immediate humanitarian purposes versus longer-term development will permit better programming around the effects of decentralization initiatives and clearer assessment of its impact on institutions and economic well-being.

Actually parsing these two forms of assistance can be complicated. The tenure of development practitioners in many post-conflict areas is short, making it tempting to focus on limited interventions that can be implemented quickly rather than more ambitious, longer-term initiatives. It is the latter, however, that are actually required for effective decentralization to take root. Robust methods of assessing the impact of development interventions associated with decentralization, such as randomized controlled trials, also require extended time horizons and relatively costly measurement strategies to which only interventions of a more systematic character are amenable.

Unbundle the Intervention

The ample opportunity for intervention and the acute need for development aid associated with post-conflict settings can also lead to overambitious aid initiatives. As discussed earlier in this chapter, development interventions grounded in decentralization, such as CDD programs, tend to have an array of broad objectives and mandates. They involve not just improved service delivery, but also increased civic engagement, as well as more representative, effective, and accountable governance through the introduction of new local institutions. This bundling of institutional change with civic engagement and monetary infusions is often considered a "super treatment" that is not intended just to inoculate against weak governance–related pathologies, but to treat them as well. Specifically, it is intended to lead to higher levels of overall political participation; more involvement of women and minorities; more equal access to services; and higher levels of transparency and accountability of local governance actors, which in turn lead to higher levels of satisfaction with community leadership. These are lofty expectations in any setting, particularly one that has recently experienced war.

Bundling treatments, and their associated expectations, also makes it hard to assess what exactly may be driving change if it occurs. As a result, there have been increasing calls to unpack these complex development packages to make them as straightforward as possible. This is intended to facilitate implementation and delivery, as well as to enhance our ability to understand which aid interventions may be working, be they monetary, institutional, or an interaction of the two. Nevertheless, convincing practitioners and aid agencies to keep interventions simple in such complex environments is a difficult proposition. This is particularly the case since the level of need and demands from the host government and other local partners on the ground tends to be extensive.

Account for Local Context

The imperative to keep decentralization initiatives simple creates a further need to understand what decentralization amounts to in specific contexts. This involves assessing the level of institutional change the treatment introduces and the size of the donation it delivers. It also requires a solid understanding of governance and economic well-being at baseline and the concrete changes decentralization aims to effect. Finally, it must also be clear whether community engagement can be effectively mandated on the decision side (i.e., assessing and selecting what the community needs) and/or on the implementation side (i.e., community contributions in cash or in kind toward the delivery and management of a project).

Appreciating what intervention means for preexisting local institutions is equally, if not more, important than gauging its practical scope. Institutions that predate a conflict, particularly if they were not instrumental in fomenting it, are likely to play an important role in post-conflict institution building in spite of any disruption they may have experienced. Formal and informal norms of political, social, and economic interaction may also coexist with other behavioral conventions that evolved in the course of war or were introduced by foreign donors. This institutional layering, in turn, raises legitimate questions about the depth of institutional change the proposed reforms should seek.

Before introducing new arrangements, donor agencies must, at a minimum, be aware of existing institutional legacies and structures, account for them, and engage with relevant stakeholders, whether they are part of the de jure government or the de facto local authority. Donors also need to consider whether the service delivery they envision and implement at the local level builds on or undermines local capacity and governance. If newly introduced local governance structures, such as community development councils, compete with preexisting institutional arrangements, there is an increased possibility of conflict, aid skimming, and unwitting negative interference with community welfare.

Recent CDD studies pertaining to Afghanistan (Beath et al. 2013c) and the Democratic Republic of Congo (Humphreys et al. 2015) highlight the need to critically assess such local governing bodies. Beath et al. (2013c) find that though democratically elected local bodies can more equitably target local aid than customary institutions, leakages in the form of embezzlement are exacerbated as overlapping mandates between new and existing institutions result in increased rent-seeking. Humphreys et al. (2015) in turn find little to no evidence that local development councils have any effect, and express their view that the aid community's optimism about the introduction of such local representative institutions may be misguided.

Have a Clear Theory of Change

In tailoring decentralization to particular post-conflict contexts, it is important to remain cognizant of what is broadly true about these initiatives. More specifically, existing theories and motivating principles must be actively utilized for the purpose of developing precise ex ante answers to important overarching questions. For example, why and how should a new local institution, and the infusion of aid that accompanies it, influence local governance and service delivery? What is the anticipated direction and size of this effect and what are the underlying mechanisms? In other words, development interventions for post-conflict decentralization must be guided by a theory of change that moves beyond aspirations of what CDD programs should deliver. This theory must clearly explain what decentralization can be expected to achieve and why. In doing so, it must also be tightly linked to the actual nature of the intervention in question and the context in which it is taking place (as discussed earlier in this chapter).[14]

One manifestation of the theoretical deficit that often afflicts the design of post-conflict CDD concerns popular representation. Much of the motivation behind decentralization resides in the assumption that greater representation is better because it leads to higher levels of political participation, higher levels of ownership, and more transparency and accountability. This view is a noble one, but it may also be too simplistic. Most problematic, it is not sensitive to the possibility that legacies of violence or preexisting local governance structures will make greater representation a catalyst for competition and conflict (Brancati 2006) or create new opportunities for graft and expropriation (Bardhan and Mookherjee 2006). It also provides no indication of how these newly introduced institutional structures can be sustained after an initial influx of development resources or what the intended purposes of such structures are for governance (Beath et al. 2013c).

Choose Program Implementation Rules Wisely

Whether a post-conflict CDD intervention will effect changes in governance, economic well-being, and civic engagement depends not only on context but – as discussed earlier in this chapter – also on the specific nature of the intervention and the associated theory of change on which it is based. The way the program is implemented and the decision rules associated with it have also proven quite significant. First, the procedures that govern how members of decentralized local institutions are chosen are likely to affect how competent the selected individuals are and their performance in office. For example, Beath et al. (2016), using a theoretical model and data from a CDD program in Afghanistan, find that anticipation of bargaining over policy causes voters in elections with multiple single-member districts to prefer candidates with polarized policy positions over more competent candidates. As a result, representatives elected in elections with a single multimember district prove better educated and exhibit less extreme policy preferences.

Second, the way infrastructural development aid projects are proposed, selected, and prioritized may either mitigate or exacerbate the degree to which resources are captured by elites. Studies examining CDD in Indonesia and Afghanistan, respectively, find that in villages where projects were selected by popular vote rather than in consultation with village elites, satisfaction with projects and their perceived benefits was greater (Beath et al. 2017; Olken

---

[14] This approach, apart from having deductive merits, has also been expressly recommended by practitioners in light of conflicting results from recent CDD programming in post-conflict contexts (Bennett and D'Onofrio 2015).

2010). Nevertheless, there were no notable changes in the types of selected projects or the average impact of such projects.

Whether and how projects get audited represents an additional set of relevant procedures, which Olken (2007) shows is a determinant of aid leakage (i.e., theft). In his randomized experiment spanning more than 600 Indonesian village road projects, increased top-down monitoring in the form of government audits, rather than grassroots participation in monitoring, was more effective in reducing missing expenditures.

Another study related to the CDD program in Afghanistan demonstrates that civic participation and social engagement are affected by the rules and quotas regarding the involvement of women (Beath et al. 2013a). A CDD program that mandates female participation improves outcomes specific to female participation in economic, social, and political activities, including increased mobility and income generation. There is, however, no change in more entrenched gender roles linked to family decision making or in attitudes toward the general role of women in society.

Insofar as these decision rules pertain to a large number of communities or individuals participating in an intervention, they may also present opportunities for additional social scientific inquiry in the form of sub-treatment randomized evaluations and assessments as in the works discussed earlier in this chapter. These analyses, in turn, would allow researchers and practitioners to not just answer whether an intervention works and how but also to understand more fully the role of the operational rules and how they can be made more effective.

Integrate Impact Evaluation into Program Design

To verify that decentralization interventions after the termination of violent conflict are effective, it is important to make impact evaluation an integral part of a development program's plan. Beyond an appropriate budget allocation, this means streamlining the intervention to ensure it is based on a clear theory of change with straightforward objectives; identifying appropriate units of analysis; and devising sound mixed methods of assessment and measurement. In that spirit, the World Bank and USAID have increasingly been trying to integrate evaluation design into program design prior to the start of implementation.

Randomized controlled trials are considered the gold standard for impact evaluation from an econometric perspective (Angrist and Pischke 2008); however, they are not always feasible or appropriate. They may not be feasible when interventions are targeted to a sample that is too small, data collection costs are too high, or programming priorities dictate a nonrandom target community (e.g., the neediest or most distressed). There is therefore also space for observational and quasi-experimental work involving instrumental variables, regression discontinuity designs, matching, difference-in-differences, and other related methods (Dehejia

2015). These alternate inferential approaches may also be more appropriate for identifying underlying mechanisms, as well as determining how broadly estimated effects apply.

Employ Multi-Method Measurement Strategies to Assess Impact

Assessing the effect of post-conflict decentralized interventions and their underlying mechanisms requires rigorous measurement in addition to a carefully conceived inferential plan. Indicators must capture both subjective and objective change, as well as variation in attitudes and behaviors. Researchers and practitioners would be well served to supplement survey instruments, which can readily tap opinions, with monitoring tools that record behaviors related to infrastructure, governance, and relevant public services at the appropriate unit of analysis. Stylized behavioral assessments of an intervention's impact, including dictator, ultimatum, or public goods games, remain relevant; however, cellphones, SMS, and fast-spreading smartphones are creating an array of new monitoring and measurement strategies that should be actively considered. A noteworthy advantage of these new tools is that they enable practitioners to assess whether and to what extent self-reported outcomes measured via surveys diverge from behavioral ones captured by a phone.

There is also a need for qualitative evidence that elucidates the causal mechanisms driving estimated effects. This is particularly true in the context of post-conflict CDD, as interventions very often group together institutional changes, capital infusions, and programming for civic engagement. Teasing out which of these facets is responsible for observed treatment effects is an important task. Using multiple different measurement strategies to tap the same concept could also help researchers examine whether attitudes and behaviors, and objective and subjective measures, tell a consistent story. For these reasons, collecting data about mechanisms cannot be a methodological afterthought for when principal quantitative measures indicate conflicting or counterintuitive effects. Rather, these measures must be part of the original impact evaluation design.

Coordinate with the Host Government and Other Development Initiatives

Donor and aid agencies have prescribed time horizons for their interventions that in turn dictate a focus on more short- or medium-term outcomes than what is often desired by the local communities and/or the host government. In terms of CDD programming, existing findings suggest that unless communities receive resources over a long period of time, any positive effects are likely to taper off. This speaks directly to issues of program sustainability, which in turn mandates coordination with both the host government and other development initiatives.

The post-conflict setting is, however, a particularly complex environment. As discussed earlier in this chapter, the host government is often overburdened and administratively weak. Under these circumstances, it is important to avoid disbursing aid via channels from which the government is excluded. Working through the government to effect decentralization not only allows more sustainable institutions to take root, it also builds local human capital and contributes to the creation of a competent civil service. Though there will undoubtedly be a need to employ foreign experts and staff, it is important to partner them with government employees so that decentralization both improves the faculties of the civil service and facilitates robust connections between the center and the periphery (Blum et al. 2015).

Donors also need to coordinate among themselves. Frequently, numerous different agencies are simultaneously active in one or more facets of decentralized post-conflict governance and service delivery. Issue areas on which there might be overlap range from water and sanitation, to roads and transportation, and democratization and governance. Donors' efforts in these domains and others may not be rationalized at the local level. Interventions at different levels of analysis, or that involve different clusters or catchment areas, may impede one another. It is therefore particularly important for CDD programming and decentralized governance initiatives more broadly to coordinate with other local service provision or institutional interventions to avoid duplicating efforts. It is also important to think more broadly about how CDD programming interacts with other decentralized interventions such as cash-for-work, civil service reform, or disarmament, demobilization, and reconciliation projects. From the researcher's perspective, transparent coordination is vital to assessing correctly an intervention's impact, since other infusions of aid, if unaccounted for, can radically distort outcomes.

Development initiatives intended to build decentralized institutions for the host government must also be distinguished from development initiatives run by peacekeepers or foreign troops. Again, multiple donors in these complex post-conflict environments may be operating in the same sphere but with diverging agendas. Recent examples out of Afghanistan and Iraq include Provincial Reconstruction Teams, Commander's Emergency Response Projects, donor-funded and government-run decentralization projects such as the National Solidarity Program in Afghanistan, and donor-funded projects implemented directly by nongovernmental organizations independent from the government. Which entity is providing aid and how, in a context of decentralized interventions, is often as important as the aid itself. Local ownership may be the most promising means by which these interventions can have a lasting influence.

Collaborate with Academics

Innovations for Poverty Action (IPA), Evidence in Governance and Politics (EGAP), the Abdul Latif Jameel Poverty Action Lab (J-PAL), and the World Bank's Development Impact Evaluation (DIME) all organize targeted workshops that pair academics with practitioners possessing similar regional and subject matter expertise. These workshops involve meetings with large development agencies, including USAID and DFID, to encourage interventions and program evaluations that allow for learning, as well as efficiency and optimized outcomes. Local governance interventions in post-conflict settings are increasingly becoming part of the agenda.

There is ample room for collaboration between academics and practitioners in assessing the impact of post-conflict decentralization. To date there have been several fruitful synergies of this type that have facilitated discussions about the separation of the intervention and program design and theories of change, as well as impact evaluation design and measurement. Such collaborations have also brought into the forefront pre-analysis planning, a method of evaluating CDD interventions that avoids data mining and specification searching. This is especially relevant for interventions linked to decentralization and local governance, including CDD programs, given the multitude of different outcomes and varied dimensions that are often assessed.[15] Recent works on local governance RCTs have centrally featured preregistration of the trials' research plans (Beath et al. 2013b, 2013c; Casey et al. 2012; Humphreys et al. 2013, 2015; Olken 2007, 2010).[16]

Beyond creating academic transparency and mitigating publication bias, preregistration plans are excellent for keeping development agencies and policymakers honest. In effect, each plan acts as an agreement that binds both academics and their practitioner counterparts to transparency. The latter, in particular, are prevented from trying to stifle the publication of unfavorable results. That said, a pre-analysis plan is not inviolable: it is meant to maintain transparency but not to limit knowledge or scholarship by preventing results from being disclosed or reported just because they were not anticipated (Olken 2015).[17] In general, deviations from a pre-analysis plan are acceptable if explicit reasons are given and if results from both the pre-analysis plan and the new specifications are presented.

Innovate While Replicating

Despite their many attractive features as tools for the evaluation of development interventions, randomized controlled trials are no magic bullet. An absence of external validity is often cited as a major drawback. Yet even

[15] As an example, Casey et al. (2012) look at 334 different outcomes that, if cherry-picked, would have yielded diametrically opposite conclusions about a program's effect on institutions.

[16] There is preregistration of dated and time-stamped designs at EGAP or at the American Economic Association RCT Registry. JPAL started a registry back in 2009, which operated until 2013. It has since been referring people to preregister with the AEA registry at www .socialscienceregistry.org. The EGAP registry can be found at http://egap.org/content/ registration.

[17] See Bill Easterly's blog on preregistration and surprise findings: www.nyudri.org/2012/10/if-christopher-columbus-had-been-funded-by-gates/.

this limitation can be surmounted by the accumulation of analogous studies. Consider, by way of illustration, the CDD evaluations referenced in this chapter regarding programs in Liberia, Sierra Leone, Afghanistan, and the Democratic Republic of Congo. Though these studies are far from identical, not least because of differences in local context and historical legacies, program modalities, monetary influxes, and measurement strategies, some findings seem to converge. Across the board, one finds that interventions positively affect service provision and perceived short-term material well-being. At the same time, effects on governance and collective action are far less consistent. To understand the effects of development programming, as well as whether a specific model can succeed across multiple post-conflict contexts, further replication is crucial.

While academics aspire to original research designs that can yield publishable results over a relatively short period of time, practitioners are more interested in understanding the long-term impacts of development programming. The latter are also interested in whether a specific model can succeed across multiple post-conflict contexts. By contrast, replication offers little social scientific excitement or reward for academics, even if it is an important component of knowledge accumulation.

Academics, however, also face pressure to produce original research designs that can yield publishable results over a prescribed (and ideally short) period. To bring the imperatives to innovate and replicate into agreement, academics have initiated new collaborative efforts to promote integrated research programs that yield generalizable results on questions of academic and policy relevance. A prime example comes from Evidence in Governance and Politics (EGAP) and the University of California, Berkeley's Center on the Politics of Development. Their "metaketa" initiative, which brings together projects on the same topic area, aims to coordinate research designs, hypotheses, treatments, instruments, and measurement strategies to allow for more comparable findings, which in turn should enable more generalizable inferences.[18] The first metaketa awarded $1.8 million across seven projects that focus on the role of information on voter choices during elections and their effects on political accountability.[19] Another metaketa with a focus on the effects of development interventions on mitigating violence and enhancing security through community policing is also under way, and is likely to generate important learning for post-conflict reconstruction development initiatives.

---

[18] For more, see "Replicate It! A Proposal to Improve the Study of Political Accountability," *Washington Post*, Monkey Cage, May 16, 2014, www.washingtonpost.com/blogs/monkey-cage/wp/2014/05/16/replicate-it-a-proposal-to-improve-the-study-of-political-accountability/.

[19] For more on this metaketa, see http://egap.org/metaketa/metaketa-information-and-accountability.

CONCLUSIONS

This chapter's first objective was to review the state of knowledge on the effects of decentralization, and community-driven development initiatives specifically, in post-conflict circumstances. It found with respect to both literatures that the positive effects of devolving political power to local institutions are not universal. Where power-sharing arrangements do not adequately accommodate former dissident communities or key domestic actors are opposed to reform, increased opportunities to capture resources on the periphery may outweigh efficiency gains in the allocation of public funds. CDD, despite having been evaluated much more rigorously than post-conflict decentralization initiatives writ large, also is not strictly beneficial. Though service provision and some measures of material well-being generally improve, positive social outcomes, such as trust in government or political participation, are less consistently evinced.

A second goal of this chapter was to identify best practices for CDD interventions with respect both to optimizing short-term project outcomes and, over the long term, to efficiently accumulating knowledge about aid-assisted decentralization. Toward this end, the chapter provides ten recommendations:

1. *Distinguish decentralization initiatives from humanitarian aid.* CDD should be kept separate from humanitarian efforts so that it can be conducted in a way that builds local capacity instead of substituting for it.
2. *Unbundle the intervention.* Multifaceted interventions should be disentangled so that it is possible to discern which components are effective with respect to specific outcomes.
3. *Account for local context.* The scale and scope of CDD initiatives should reflect localities' capacity to absorb new resources and political initiatives, as well as existing institutional arrangements.
4. *Have a clear theory of change.* CDD should not be a strictly aspirational enterprise; it should be informed by social scientific theories that clearly elucidate why a certain intervention should have particular effects.
5. *Choose program implementation rules wisely.* The procedures by which aid and reform are implemented can be significant and should be crafted with attention to relevant scholarly work.
6. *Integrate impact evaluation into program designs.* Randomized controlled trials, the gold standard of impact evaluation, should be accommodated in the plans for CDD initiatives if this method of assessment is appropriate and feasible for the respective program.
7. *Employ multi-method measurement strategies to assess impact.* Plans to evaluate CDD initiatives should include efforts to collect a variety of data, including behavioral measures and other evidence that can be used to understand causal mechanisms.

8. *Coordinate with the host government and other development initiatives.* Donors in a single post-conflict setting should coordinate their respective interventions, while also seeking to include the host government in their efforts as fully as possible.

9. *Collaborate with academics.* Interaction between academics and practitioners promises to increase the effectiveness of project assessments and further the dissemination of unbiased scholarship.

10. *Innovate while replicating.* Academics should continue coordinating research designs across similar program assessment projects.

Current developments suggest that the international community will be confronted with an array of complex conflict and post-conflict environments for years to come. Efforts to reestablish stability and governance in the aftermath of such incidents will therefore only become more crucial. The suggestions given earlier in this chapter, despite being undoubtedly demanding, are by no means merely aspirational. Academic research initiatives in collaboration with development agencies are becoming increasingly aware of the benefits in learning from using such protocols. Though specifically applicable to decentralization initiatives, these recommendations are also intended to provide a general framework relevant to advancing both the study and the practice of post-conflict community-driven development.

REFERENCES

Al-Iryani, L., A. de Janvry, and E. Sadoulet. 2015. "The Yemen Social Fund for Development: An Effective Community-Based Approach amid Political Instability." *International Peacekeeping* 22(4): 321–336.

Angrist, J. D., and J.-S. Pischke. 2008. *Mostly Harmless Econometrics: An Empiricist's Companion.* Princeton, NJ: Princeton University Press.

Bardhan, P. 2002. "Decentralization of Governance and Development." *Journal of Economic Perspectives* 16(4): 185–205.

Bardhan, P., and D. Mookherjee. 2006. "Decentralization, Corruption and Government Accountability." *International Handbook on the Economics of Corruption* 6: 161–188.

Barron, P. 2010. "CDD in Post-Conflict and Conflict-Affected Areas: Experiences from East Asia." World Development Report Background Paper, World Bank, Washington, DC.

Barron, P., R. Diprose, C. Q. Smith, K. Whiteside, and M. Woolcock. 2004. "Applying Mixed Methods Research to Community Driven Development Projects and Local Conflict Mediation: A Case Study from Indonesia." Technical report, World Bank, Washington, DC.

Barron, P., M. Humphreys, L. Paler, and J. Weinstein. 2009. *Community-Based Reintegration in Aceh: Assessing the Impacts of BRA-KDP.* Washington, DC: World Bank Publications.

Beath, A., F. Christia, G. Egorov, and R. Enikolopov. 2016. "Electoral Rules and Political Selection: Theory and Evidence from a Field Experiment." *Review of Economic Studies* 83(3): 932–968.

Beath, A., F. Christia, and R. Enikolopov. 2018. Can Development Programs Counter Insurgencies?: Evidence from a Field Experiment in Afghanistan. MIT Political Science Department Research Paper No.2011–14.

Beath, A., F. Christia, and R. Enikolopov. 2013a. "Empowering Women through Development Aid: Evidence from a Field Experiment in Afghanistan." *American Political Science Review* 107(3): 540–557.

Beath, A., F. Christia, and R. Enikolopov. 2013b. Randomized Impact Evaluation of Afghanistan's National Solidarity Programme: Final Report. Technical Report 81107, World Bank, Washington, DC.

Beath, A., F. Christia, and R. Enikolopov. 2013c. "Do Elected Councils Improve Governance? Experimental Evidence on Local Institutions in Afghanistan." Research Paper 2013–24, MIT Political Science Department.

Beath, A., F. Christia, and R. Enikolopov. 2017. "Direct Democracy and Resource Allocation: Experimental Evidence from Afghanistan." *Journal of Development Economics*, 124, 199–213.

Bennett, S., and A. D'Onofrio. 2015. "Community-Driven? Concepts, Clarity and Choices for CDD in Conflict-Affected Contexts." Technical report, International Rescue Committee.

Berman, E., J. H. Felter, J. N. Shapiro, and E. Troland. 2013. "Modest, Secure, and Informed: Successful Development in Conflict Zones." *American Economic Review* 103(3): 512–517.

Berman, E., J. N. Shapiro, and J. H. Felter. 2011. "Can Hearts and Minds Be Bought? The Economics of Counterinsurgency in Iraq." *Journal of Political Economy* 119(4): 766–819.

Besley, T., and S. Coate. 2003. "Centralized versus Decentralized Provision of Local Public Goods: A Political Economy Approach." *Journal of Public Economics* 87(12): 2611–2637.

Blum, J., F. Christia, and D. Rogger. 2015. "Civil Service Reform in Post-Conflict Societies." Fragile and Conflict State Impact Evaluation Research Program, World Bank, Washington DC.

Brancati, D. 2006. "Decentralization: Fueling the Fire or Dampening the Flames of Ethnic Conflict and Secessionism?" *International Organization* 60(3): 651–685.

Broadway, R. and A. Shah. 2009. *Fiscal Federalism: Principles and Practice of Multiorder Governance*. Cambridge: Cambridge University Press.

Brown, A. N., F. McCollister, D. B. Cameron, and J. Ludwig. 2015. "The Current State of Peacebuilding Evidence and Policy." Technical report, International Initiative for Impact Evaluation.

Cameron, D. B., A. N. Brown, A. Mishra, M. Picon, H. Esper, F. Calvo, and K. Peterson. 2015. "Evidence for Peacebuilding: An Evidence Gap Map." Technical report, International Initiative for Impact Evaluation.

Casey, K., R. Glennerster, and E. Miguel. 2012. "Reshaping Institutions: Evidence on Aid Impacts Using a Preanalysis Plan." *Quarterly Journal of Economics* 127(4): 1755–1812.

Casey, K. 2018. "Radical Decentralization: Does community driven development work?" *Annual Review of Economics* 10:139–165.

Cederman, L.-E., S. Hug, A. Schädel, and J. Wucherpfennig. 2015. "Territorial Autonomy in the Shadow of Conflict: Too Little, Too Late?" *American Political Science Review* 109(2): 354–370.

Cliffe, S., S. Guggenheim, and M. Kostner. 2003. *Community-Driven Reconstruction as an Instrument in War-to-Peace Transitions.* Washington, DC: Conflict Prevention and Reconstruction Unit, World Bank.

Crawford, G., and C. Hartmann. 2008. *Decentralisation in Africa: A Pathway Out of Poverty and Conflict?* Amsterdam: Amsterdam University Press.

Crost, B., J. Felter, and P. Johnston. 2014. "Aid under Fire: Development Projects and Civil Conflict." *American Economic Review* 104(6): 1833–1856.

Cunningham, K. G. 2011. "Divide and Conquer or Divide and Concede: How Do States Respond to Internally Divided Separatists?" *American Political Science Review* 105 (2): 275–297.

de Regt, J., S. Majumdar, and J. Singh. 2013. "Designing Community-Driven Development Operations in Fragile and Conflict-Affected Situations: Lessons from a Stocktaking." Technical report, World Bank, Washington, DC.

Dehejia, R. 2015. "Experimental and Non-Experimental Methods in Development Economics: A Porous Dialectic." *Journal of Globalization and Development* 6(1): 47–69.

Dickovick, J. T. 2014. "Foreign Aid and Decentralization: Limitations on Impact in Autonomy and Development." *Public Administration and Development* 34(3): 194–206.

Dongier, P., J. Van Domelen, E. Ostrom, A. Rizvi, W. Wakeman, A. Bebbington, S. Alkire, T. Esmail, and M. Polski. 2002. *A Sourcebook for Poverty Reduction Strategies, Volume 1: Core Techniques and Cross-Cutting Issues,* Chapter 9: Community-Driven Development. Washington, DC: World Bank Publications.

Dube, O. and J. F. Vargas. 2013. "Commodity Price Shocks and Civil Conflict: Evidence from Colombia." *Review of Economic Studies* 80(4): 1384–1421.

Eaton, K. 2006. "The Downside of Decentralization: Armed Clientelism in Colombia." *Security Studies* 15(4): 533–562.

Edillon, R., S. F. Piza, and C. A. Santos. 2011. "Final Survey for the KALAHI-CIDSS Impact Evaluation." Technical report, World Bank, Washington, DC.

Edwards, B., S. Yilmaz, and J. Boex. 2015. "Decentralization as a Post-Conflict Strategy: Local Government Discretion and Accountability in Sierra Leone." *Public Administration and Development* 35(1): 46–60.

Enikolopov, R. and E. Zhuravskaya. 2007. "Decentralization and Political Institutions." *Journal of Public Economics* 91(11): 2261–2290.

Fanthorpe, R. 2006. "On the Limits of Liberal Peace: Chiefs and Democratic Decentralization in Post-War Sierra Leone." *African Affairs* 105(418): 27–49.

Fearon, J. D., M. Humphreys, and J. M. Weinstein. 2009. "Can Development Aid Contribute to Social Cohesion after Civil War? Evidence from a Field Experiment in Post-Conflict Liberia." *American Economic Review* 99(2): 287–291.

Fearon, J. D., M. Humphreys, and J. M. Weinstein. 2015. "How Does Development Assistance Affect Collective Action Capacity? Results from a Field Experiment in Post-Conflict Liberia." *American Political Science Review* 109(3): 450–469.

Gisselquist, R. M. 2015. "Good Aid in Hard Places: Learning from 'Successful' Interventions in Fragile Situations." *International Peacekeeping* 22(4): 283–301.

Green, E. D. 2008. "Decentralisation and Conflict in Uganda." *Conflict, Security & Development* 8(4): 427–450.

Grossman, G., and J. I. Lewis. 2014. "Administrative Unit Proliferation." *American Political Science Review* 108(1): 196–217.

Guggenheim, S. 2010. "Community-Driven Development versus Flexible Funding to Communities in Conflict and Post-Conflict Environments." World Development Report Background Paper, World Bank, Washington, DC.

Hartmann, C. 2008. *Decentralisation and the Legacy of Protracted Conflict – Mauritius, Namibia, and South Africa*, Chapter 6, pp. 169–190. Amsterdam: Amsterdam University Press.

Heller, P. 2001. "Moving the State: The Politics of Democratic Decentralization in Kerala, South Africa, and Porto Alegre." *Politics and Society* 29(1): 131–163.

Humphreys, M., R. S. de la Sierra, and P. Van Der Windt. 2012. "Social and Economic Impacts of Tuungane: Final Report on the Effects of a Community Driven Reconstruction Program in Eastern Democratic Republic of Congo." Unpublished manuscript, Department of Political Science, Columbia University.

Humphreys, M., R. S. de la Sierra, and P. Van der Windt. 2013. "Fishing, Commitment, and Communication: A Proposal for Comprehensive Nonbinding Research Registration." *Political Analysis* 21(1): 1–20.

Humphreys, M., R. S. de la Sierra, and P. Van der Windt. 2015. "Social Engineering in the Tropics: A Grassroots Democratization Experiment in the Congo." Unpublished manuscript.

Kauzya, J.M. 2007. "Political Decentralization in Africa: Experiences of Uganda, Rwanda and South Africa." Discussion paper, Department of Economic and Social Affairs, United Nations, New York, NY.

Kimenyi, M. S., and P. Meagher. 2004. *Devolution and Development: Governance Prospects in Decentralizing States*. Farnham, UK: Gower Publishing, Ltd.

King, E., and C. Samii. 2014. "Fast-Track Institution Building in Conflict-Affected Countries? Insights from Recent Field Experiments." *World Development* 64 (December), 740–754.

Mansoob Murshed, S., M. Zulfan Tadjoeddin, and A. Chowdhury. 2009. "Is Fiscal Decentralization Conflict Abating? Routine Violence and District Level Government in Java, Indonesia." *Oxford Development Studies* 37(4): 397–421.

Mansuri, G., and V. Rao. 2012. *Localizing Development: Does Participation Work?* Washington, DC: World Bank Publications.

Nielsen, R. A., M. G. Findley, Z. S. Davis, T. Candland, and D. L. Nielson. 2011. "Foreign Aid Shocks As a Cause of Violent Armed Conflict." *American Journal of Political Science* 55(2): 219–232.

Nunn, N., and N. Qian. 2014. "U.S. Food Aid and Civil Conflict." *American Economic Review* 104(6): 1630–1666.

Oates, W. E. 1972. *Fiscal Federalism*. New York, NY: Harcourt Brace Jovanovich.

Olken, B. A. 2007. "Monitoring Corruption: Evidence from a Field Experiment in Indonesia." *Journal of Political Economy* 115(2): 200–249.

Olken, B. A. 2010. "Direct Democracy and Local Public Goods: Evidence from a Field Experiment in Indonesia." *American Political Science Review* 104(2): 243–267.

Olken, B. A. 2015. "Promises and Perils of Pre-Analysis Plans." *Journal of Economic Perspectives* 29(3): 61–80.

Pospieszna, P., and G. Schneider. 2013. "The Illusion of 'Peace through Power-Sharing': Constitutional Choice in the Shadow of Civil War." *Civil Wars* 15 (suppl. 1): 44–70.

Pritchett, L., and M. Woolcock. 2004. "Solutions When *the* Solution Is the Problem: Arraying the Disarray in Development." *World Development* 32(2): 191–212.

Sacks, A., and M. Larizza. 2012. "Why Quality Matters: Rebuilding Trustworthy Local Government in Post-Conflict Sierra Leone." Technical Report 6021, World Bank, Washington, DC.

Sánchez, F., and M. Chacón. 2005. "Conflict, State and Decentralisation: From Social Progress to an Armed Dispute for Local Control, 1974–2002." Working Papers Series 1, No. 70, Crisis States Research Centre, London School of Economics and Political Science.

Schelnberger, A. K. 2008. *Decentralisation and Conflict in Kibaale, Uganda*, Chapter 7, pp. 191–212. Amsterdam: Amsterdam University Press.

Scott, J. C. 1998. *Seeing Like a State: How Certain Schemes to Improve the Human Condition have Failed*. New Haven, CT: Yale University Press.

Sen, A. 1999. *Development As Freedom*. Oxford: Oxford University Press.

Treisman, D. 2006. "Fiscal Decentralization, Governance, and Economic Performance: A Reconsideration." *Economics & Politics* 18(2): 219–235.

Treisman, D. 2007. *The Architecture of Government: Rethinking Political Decentralization*. Cambridge: Cambridge University Press.

USAID 2007. *Community-Based Development in Conflict-Affected Areas: An Introductory Guide for Programming*. Washington, DC: US Agency for International Development.

Van de Walle, N. 2001. *African Economies and the Politics of Permanent Crisis, 1979–1999*. Cambridge: Cambridge University Press.

Voss, J. 2008. "Impact Evaluation of the Second Phase of the Kecamatan Development Project in Indonesia." Technical Report 45590, World Bank, Washington, DC.

Wong, S. 2012. "What Have Been the Impacts of World Bank Community-Driven Development Programs? CDD Impact Evaluation Review and Operational and Research Implications." Technical Report 69541, World Bank, Washington, DC.

Wong, S., and S. Guggenheim. 2005. *East Asia Decentralizes: Making Local Government Work*, Chapter 12: Community-Driven Development: Decentralization's Accountability Challenge. Washington, DC: World Bank Publications.

World Bank. 2006. "Community-Driven Development in the Context of Conflict-Affected Countries: Challenges and Opportunities." Technical Report 36425, World Bank, Washington, DC.

World Bank 2011. *World Development Report 2011: Conflict, Security, and Development*. Washington, DC: World Bank Publications.

Zhou, Y., ed. 2009. *Decentralization, Democracy, and Development: Recent Experience from Sierra Leone*. Washington, DC: World Bank Publications.

Clientelism in Decentralized States

Gianmarco León and Leonard Wantchekon

INTRODUCTION

Growing evidence suggests that targeted redistribution and clientelism are central parts of electoral politics in both developed and developing countries. Under these electoral strategies, politicians tend to use public resources for political gain, and voting behavior is shaped by short-term benefits rather than broad policy considerations. As such, clientelism and targeted redistribution entail significant welfare costs to societies (Bardhan 2002). This contrasts with programmatic electoral politics where redistributive policies are designed to maximize voters' welfare and economic performance at the national level (Dixit and Londregan 1998; Wantchekon 2003).

In most of the current scholarship on the topic, clientelism is defined as "giving material goods in return for electoral support, where the criterion of distribution that the patron uses is simply: did you/will you support me?" (Stokes 2009, p. 2). As such, it is viewed as a two-party relationship between a patron and a client. However, decentralized states are the norm in the developing world, and clientelistic networks are imbedded in government structures with vertical as well as horizontal power relations, which makes dyadic relationships less realistic. As a result, a central part of a clientelistic organizational structure today is the intermediary or broker, whose role is to mobilize a network of local voters in exchange for financial payment or patronage jobs. Understanding the behavior and strategy of a broker and the two-part contractual arrangement with the national politician and voters is key in analyzing inefficiency and corruption under clientelistic systems.

Zara Riaz and Tania Mathurin provided outstanding research assistance. León acknowledges the financial support of the Spanish Ministry of Economy and Competitiveness (through the Severo Ochoa Program for Centers of Excellence in R&D (SEV-2011-0075) and grant ECO2014-55555-P. The views expressed in this chapter are solely the authors'.

One particular institutional design that has been at the center of state reform initiatives in the developing world in the past three decades and that bolsters the presence of local politicians as political brokers, is the devolution of power and fiscal capacity to lower levels of the government. Many multilateral organizations, in particular the World Bank, have pushed decentralization as one of the main points in their reform agendas (Burki et al. 1999; World Bank 2000). How decentralization affects political structures, public goods provision, corruption and welfare has been widely studied and we have a fairly clear idea of its potential costs and benefits (Bardhan 2002; Gadene and Singhal 2014). However, there is a nascent but still small literature analyzing the way decentralization of political power and fiscal autonomy shapes the various clientelistic strategies adopted by political actors and the consequences of those strategies.

Clientelistic networks and decentralization share common organizational features and interact in different ways. They are both multitiered structures plagued with agency issues. In this chapter, we study these links, reviewing the current scholarship and emphasizing how the different features of political decentralization affect clientelistic politics and point to avenues for future research. In particular, we emphasize the role clientelistic networks and upward and downward accountability play in undermining programmatic politics. We finally provide a brief analysis of the role local bureaucracies can play in counterbalancing the efficiency losses introduced by clientelistic politics in decentralized states.

The next section provides the working definition of clientelism, explains different clientelistic strategies and emphasizes the costs and benefits that clientelistic practices generate for society. Section 3 reviews varieties of decentralization and evidence on the effects of decentralization on public services provision, political accountability and personnel structures. Section 4 looks at the information advantages of decentralization and how they can be undermined by clientelism. Section 5 reviews the small but growing literature that studies clientelistic networks within decentralized settings, focusing specifically on how career-concerned politicians face different incentives in a decentralized structure. Section 6 provides insights on the role local bureaucracies can play in these settings and Section 7 concludes by providing new directions for future research.

CLIENTELISM

Clientelism has been traditionally defined as a dyadic relationship between a patron and client, in which the patron provides the potential supporter with goods or services in exchange for a promise of political support (Hicken 2011; Stokes et al. 2013). This implies a hierarchical relationship in which a person holding power (economic or political) uses his/her own influence and resources to provide protection or benefits (or both) for a person of lower status (Scott

1972). Further, one of the key factors of clientelism is that it relies on repeated interactions, which provide both the patron and the client with information about the reliability of the other and gives each party the opportunity to punish the other for defecting. However, even in developing countries, political processes are increasingly competitive; voters are better informed, politically savvy and organized.[1] As a result, voters are more informed about different types of politicians and their offers and strategies and are less likely to accept or comply with relational contracts that limit voters' future actions. Under this scenario, the assumption of two-way, repeated and exclusive relationships between voters and politicians is more likely to break down.

There are broad categories of different clientelistic practices and we adopt the modern view of clientelism as standard targeted redistributive politics, while putting the broker (local political agents) at the center of these relationships.

Extensive literature has examined the role of the broker in the modern view of clientelism (see, e.g., Finan and Schechter 2012). Politicians rely on vote brokers because they assume that they are more likely to have knowledge about voters' preferences and their characteristics, e.g., they know who they are more or less likely to vote for and how intense their preferences are. Politicians usually employ brokers to gather information on their constituents' political affiliations, to monitor votes, survey local needs and demands and provide goods and benefits to voters. Brokers are tasked with tremendous responsibilities, since votes are cast in secret and election results are usually uncertain.

Despite the assumption that brokers are equipped with better and more accurate information about local voters' preferences, there is not much evidence to support this. In an extensive study on the role of brokers in local politics, specifically their ability to guess the preferences of their voters in rural Rajasthan, India, a poor state where clientelism is widespread, Sneider developed a measure, *guessability*, which indicated whether local leaders, who act as brokers in this instance, could correctly guess villagers' intended vote in the next election (Sneider 2016). In a cross-referenced survey of 1,000 voters and 200 local politicians across ninety-six village councils, Sneider found that brokers did not do a better job at identifying voters' preferences than low-information benchmarks. In fact, brokers incorrectly guessed voter preferences 35.5% of the time. However, they could identify preferences of voters who belong to the same ethnic groups. This may be due to the fact that those voters are more likely to vote for co-ethnic politicians.

---

[1] Partially, this change in voter behavior in the developing world is explained by the growth in nongovernmental organizations (NGOs) and international organizations that have been increasingly developing programs and projects focused on disseminating information about politicians' performance in office, i.e., scorecards (Banerjee et al. 2011; Humphreys and Weinstein 2014). Additionally, the expansion of information technologies, including cell phones and social media, has contributed to generating more active, informed, and critical voters.

However, there is evidence that political brokers target specific types of voters when giving out benefits. A study in Paraguay analyzed the role brokers play in politicians' clientelistic strategies (Finan and Schechter 2012). Brokers are in charge of distributing benefits among voters in exchange for the promise of their vote. In this instance, brokers target reciprocal voters, i.e., those who are more likely to commit to an action in response to a gift despite the fact that this action is unobservable. An increase of one standard deviation in the level of reciprocity results in an increase of forty-four percentage points in the likelihood of being targeted by the political broker. The researchers argue that, given that ballots are secret, brokers target gifts and favors to reciprocal voters since they are more likely to comply with an oral contract that can't be enforced. To be able to carry out this strategy, brokers must hold a large amount of information about voters' preferences. To further demonstrate the connection between brokers and villagers, the researchers conducted several surveys to identify villagers' characteristics and social preferences, then to see if the brokers could correctly guess the villagers' answers to those questions. They found a high correlation between the brokers' and villagers' responses, not just on specific characteristics but also regarding social preferences. This study has important implication for Sneider's Rajasthan findings. It shows that by targeting specific reciprocal individuals, brokers can ensure that targeted individuals are likely to commit their vote to the intended politician.

While the literature on the role of brokers is mostly focused on vote-buying, we want to stray from this specific type of clientelism and examine the broader ties between clientelism and decentralization.[2]

Consequences of Clientelism

Clientelistic politics leads to large welfare losses to society. For example, they have the potential to reverse standard accountability mechanisms, which are central to democracy. When politicians provide favors to voters in exchange for voters' support, voters lose the ability to effectively hold politicians and parties accountable for their behavior in office and instead, become the ones held accountable by parties and politicians (Hicken 2011). This lack of accountability could lead to increased corruption and more generally, lower empowerment of civil society. For example, Lederman et al. (2005) note that the literatures of both political science and economics have extensively studied the relationship between political accountability and reduced corruption (Fackler

---

[2] As Kitschelt (2012) mentions, politicians may offer goods before or after an election or through the election cycle. In their work, Robinson and Verdier (2013) focused on clientelism as redistributive politics in employment as they found that it is jobs that are exchanged the most for votes in clientelism. Politicians promise jobs because it is one method to ensure that politicians can have the support of voters. Robinson and Verdier found this type of clientelism to be more prevalent in monopolistic states – in areas where the state dominates and controls a wide range of goods and services.

and Lin 1995; Linz and Stepan 1996; Nas et al. 1986; Bailey and Valenzuela 1997; Persson et al. 1997; Rose-Ackerman 1999; Djankov et al. 2001; Laffont and Meleu 2001). They note that the common argument of these studies is that increased political accountability aligns politicians' preferences with those of their citizens by punishing politicians who adopt policies unfit for their constituents. As we describe in more detail later, accountability structures are central to the functioning of decentralized states. Further, the closeness of political power to their constituencies allows these structures to make use of an information advantage to hold local-level politicians accountable and reduce the incidence of clientelism and corruption.

Furthermore, clientelism has been linked to larger public deficits and public sector inefficiencies (Hicken 2011). In clientelistic systems, non-targeted public goods are undersupplied, while there is an overprovision of goods and services targeted to narrow constituencies. This implies an unequal allocation of resources, which leads to slower economic development and efficiency losses. An unusual data set reveals the political preferences in favor or against the Hugo Chavez regime in Venezuela to document how the government took action against political detractors, limiting their possibilities of accessing public sector jobs (Hsieh et al. 2011). This led to large misallocations and to productivity losses between 2 and 5%. Another study shows that providing public sector jobs represents an incentive-compatible strategy to overcome the commitment problems imbedded in clientelism (Robinson and Verdier 2013). This leads to inefficiencies in public goods provision. Such inefficiencies are worse when the political stakes are high, when inequality is high, and when money matters less than ideology in politics. In cases where budget constraints are soft, as, for example, in countries where central government grants and transfers fund much of local government expenditure, the potential for public funds to be used for political purposes might be higher (Bordignon 2004).

In addition to welfare losses and public sector inefficiencies, clientelism also affects party systems. In non-democracies, clientelistic strategies weaken party structures, allowing dictators to hold onto power longer. Autocrats prevent voters from expressing their preferences due to fear of retaliation, or of losing the conditional benefits provided by the government (Stokes 2009). For example, in Singapore, clientelistic strategies, such as the construction of public housing in exchange for political support, created socioeconomic dependence on the regime. To vote against the ruling party would mean to risk losing such benefits (Hicken 2011). On the other hand, programmatic systems tend to have lower electoral volatility, lower party-system fragmentation, and higher levels of party-system institutionalization (Kitschelt et al. 2010). For example, Hagopian et al. (2009) discuss the shift from an inchoate and volatile party system characterized by clientelism and patronage to one that slowly became more programmatic and thus institutionalized over the course of the 1990s and 2000s.

DECENTRALIZATION

Before discussing any of decentralization's benefits, it is important to distinguish between its three main forms. *Political* decentralization is the transfer of political authority from the central government to subnational governments, which takes place through constitutional amendments or electoral reform (USAID 2009). *Administrative* decentralization involves the transfer of responsibility for the planning and management of public functions from the national government to subnational units or governments. Finally, *fiscal* decentralization refers to "policies designed to increase the revenues or fiscal autonomy of subnational governments" (Falleti 2005). This form of decentralization expands the authority of subnational officials by giving them responsibilities for collecting tax revenues or by directly involving them in expenditure policy (USAID 2009). Though each type of decentralization affects relationships between central-level officials, local politicians, and citizens, we focus specifically on political decentralization and its effects on local politicians' incentives and payoffs for engaging in clientelistic behavior.

CLIENTELISM AND THE INFORMATION ADVANTAGES OF DECENTRALIZATION

Some argue that decentralization has the potential to improve public services provision. The decentralization of political power brings politicians closer to voters, allowing them to get a better assessment of voters' preferences and thus provide the public goods preferred by the majority of voters (Bardhan and Mookherjee 2000, 2006; Seabright 1996). However, these benefits can easily be lost when clientelistic politics dominate the local political arena.

Politicians in decentralized states are able to deliver public goods that are closer to the preferred policies of the electorate (Alesina and Spolaore 2003; Hayek 1945). When preferences are heterogeneous across geographic areas, having smaller and geographically concentrated constituencies makes it easier to target the types of public goods that maximize welfare and thus welfare gains can be achieved by decentralizing power (Besley and Coate 2003; Oates 1972). Decentralization makes government more responsive to local needs by "tailoring levels of consumption to the preferences of smaller, more homogenous groups" (Shah 1998; Wallis and Oates 1988; World Bank 1994).

Several studies empirically examine decentralization's ability to lead to improved service delivery: for example, one shows that the decentralization of public services provision in Albania allowed local governments to improve targeting of social programs by making use of local information (Alderman 2002). Another uses information from the Bangladeshi Food and Education Program, and notes that communities do a much better job than the government at identifying the poor (Galasso and Ravallion 2005). And a third shows that the network structures in Indonesian villages affect the way information is aggregated for targeting a cash-transfer program (Atalas et al. 2012).

Furthermore, using data from the decentralization reforms in Bolivia in the late 1980s that doubled public revenues allocated to local governments, Faguet (2004) shows that it led to an increase in the proportion of the budget allocated to education and health care. These areas had large demands from the population. Evidence from Indonesia shows that the 2001 decentralization reform led to higher infrastructure investment in places that had a larger infrastructure deficit (Kis-Katos and Sjahrir 2017), while the Argentine decentralization led to significant gains in test scores, although these gains were concentrated among the non-poor (Galiani et al. 2008).

However, the advantages that political decentralization can bring in aligning the government's choices more closely with voters' preferences and implementing programmatic politics can break down in the presence of clientelism. Under which conditions would politicians engage in programmatic rather than clientelistic politics? Officials in power will have better chances of being reelected when they accommodate voters' preferences. Likewise, candidates running for office will succeed when they make credible promises. Keefer and Vlaicu (2008) propose a model of electoral competition in which candidates have different ways of gaining credibility with the electorate. They can spend resources to communicate directly with voters, rely on preexisting patron-client networks, or allow patrons to make credible promises for them. This model can be used to examine the relationship between decentralization and clientelism. With these quandaries on how to win votes, national politicians are more likely to engage in patronage politics to reward their local brokers, but meritocratic appointment procedures can limit these incentives. Likewise, more political competition or strong political parties with known policy stances provide politicians with greater credibility, which can aid a transition toward programmatic politics. Experimental evidence from Benin and the Philippines suggests that policy deliberation (town hall meetings) and two-way communication can overcome clientelism and facilitate the transition to programmatic politics by enabling candidates to commit to specific post-election policy agendas (Fujiwara and Wantchekon 2013; Wantchekon et al. 2016).

Programmatic politics can break clientelistic networks in Mexico (Larreguy et al. 2015). Turning to Mexico's federal structure and changes in incumbency over time in the context of a federal land-titling program, the authors provide empirical evidence that municipal incumbents, who often relied on weak property rights to enforce clientelistic exchanges, experienced a large decrease in their vote share in precincts where the national land-titling program was implemented. Meanwhile, *federal* incumbents' loss of clientelistic capacity was more than compensated for by increased votes from the land-titling program's beneficiaries. This shows that programmatic reforms can reduce clientelism while rewarding incumbents for the policies in office.

All in all, decentralization has the potential of aligning public goods provision with voter's preferences due to its informational advantages. However, the presence of clientelistic networks threatens this advantage, mainly through three channels, which we describe next: (i) absent accountability mechanisms, politicians could be more responsive to national political interests, becoming de facto political brokers; (ii) when there is lack of citizen control, politicians can respond more actively to the interests of local elites, thus transforming horizontal accountability in corruption networks; and (iii) career incentives for local politicians can make them more accountable to national parties, rather than their constituencies.

Clientelism, Decentralization and Accountability

The agency problem in a centralized government is one between the citizens, local bureaucrats and the central government. Political decentralization reforms change this by making local elected politicians accountable to the population. Voters can more easily observe politicians' types and actions, which allows citizens to hold elected officials accountable (Bardhan and Mookherjee 2005, 2006). Further, if decentralized units are responsible only for the performance of their own jurisdictions (i.e., no spillovers), then voters can compare the performance of the different units and hold them accountable through yardstick competition (Besley and Coate 2003). This increased accountability is generally thought to reduce corruption and allow less theft of public funds (Fisman and Gatti 2002). While decentralization has the potential to make politicians more accountable and reduce politicians' moral hazards, this can be undermined by weak institutions, which favor clientelistic practices and elite capture.[3] In this section, we focus precisely on this issue, particularly emphasizing the role played by clientelistic networks.

Clientelistic Networks in Decentralized Structures

In many weak states, politicians may lack the capacity to mobilize resources, monitor problems, or encourage participation at the local level. In these contexts, the ability of politicians to respond to local needs or to be able to get political support from the population relies on their capacity to establish a network. This network can be composed of political brokers or local politicians. Most of the literature analyzing political clientelism has focused on the former, i.e., how political brokers operate at the local level (Finan and Schechter 2012; Larreguy et al. 2015; Vicente 2014, among others).

---

[3] While there is a clear distinction between elite capture and clientelism, several scholars suggest that elite capture can be linked to higher levels of clientelism. For example, Bardhan et al. (2010) use a household survey in rural West Bengal and find that the elite capture of goods also supports the delivery of goods or benefits to the poor that elites themselves do not have much use for.

With clientelism, local politicians in decentralized states become part of a larger structure and their interactions with voters cannot be analyzed independently from national politics. In this context, local politicians can end up acting as de facto political brokers for the national parties, facing a completely different set of incentives that have to be factored in when analyzing their behavior. Thus, although decentralization is aimed at enhancing local politicians' accountability to citizens, this downward accountability is limited by the fact that local politicians have to respond to their party patrons (i.e., upward accountability) once clientelism comes into play.

Downward Accountability

Under centralization, immediate accountability for local officials, selected by higher-level authorities, is upward, i.e., to the central government and they face strong incentives to respond to the central government's priorities and concerns. This weakens incentives to respond to local citizens' needs. Under decentralization, however, local officials' tenure and career are in the hands of citizens who elect them, tightening the loop between those who produce public goods and those who consume them (Faguet 2012).

Reelection incentives are key in addressing the moral hazard problem in politicians' efforts to provide public goods. A quasi-experiment in Brazilian municipalities chose a random sample of municipalities to audit and the results of these audits were made public either before or after the elections (Ferraz and Finan 2008). Using a difference-in-difference strategy, the researchers show that the availability of information about poor management of local governments reduced mayors' reelection probabilities. Another study of the same setting finds that mayors facing a higher chance of being audited work harder and are more efficient in providing public goods (Litschig and Zamboni 2018). Other studies also show empirically that when local populations can easily observe politicians' actions, they hold elected politicians accountable and public services delivery improves (Banerjee et al. 2011; Besley and Burgess 2002; Olken and Pande 2012). If decentralization increases the flow of information, the evidence shows that it can potentially improve the level of information voters have about their politicians and hold them accountable, thus reducing corruption and improving public goods provision.[4]

---

[4] Other scholars contend that relative to centralized structures, decentralization undermines accountability. Ponzetto et al. (2016) develop a political-agency model with voters who differ in their ability to monitor rent-seeking politicians, and find that while voter information improves monitoring, it also reduces the appeal of holding office. Rent extraction is thus a decreasing and inverse function of the share of informed voters. As a result, with information heterogeneity, rent extraction falls in less-informed regions and generally remains constant in better-informed regions, resulting in aggregate efficiency gains. For centralization to maximize welfare, however, the central government must be required to provide identical public goods to all regions rather than favor informed regions at the expense of others. Their study highlights a trade-off between

This downward accountability breaks down under weak institutions that lead to either elite resource capture or patronage and clientelism. In settings with weak accountability mechanisms and institutions, local elites can take advantage of their power and capture budgets and public goods (Bardhan and Mookherjee 2005, 2006). If communities can't take actions against the elites, or the elites can influence the enforcement or lawmaking process, politicians end up being accountable to local elites rather than to the local population. For example, many decentralization statutes in West Africa failed to enfranchise local populations, and laws have been structured to make local authorities upwardly accountable to the central state rather than downwardly accountable to the community (Agrawal and Ribot 1999). The literature also shows that ethnic majorities can gain control over local officials and this has been particularly the case in Africa and South Asia. Ethnic diversity is negatively related to efficient public goods provision (Alesina and La Ferrara 2005; Burgess et al. 2015; Easterly and Levine 1997; Miguel and Gugerty 2005).

Decentralization in weakly institutionalized settings is conducive to what Kent Eaton calls "armed clientelism" (Eaton 2006). Studying the Colombian setting, he argues that both guerillas and paramilitaries used devolved structures to expand their authority over state-financed goods and services, which were exchanged for political support. The central government failed to provide public order and central government representatives were too weak to enforce the decentralizing measures – suggesting a sequenced approach to decentralization is particularly important in weak states. An empirical study of the Employment Assurance Scheme (EAS) in rural West Bengal in India examined interactions between the community, elected officials, and civil servants that enables the theft of funds from the EAS in two localities (Véron et al. 2006). The researchers show that in decentralized settings, when vertical accountability is weak, horizontal accountability structures between local civil society and officials can mutate into networks of corruption.

Upward Accountability

When strong national political parties dominate the arena, local politicians' careers are in the hands of national leaders, leading them to enact policies that will lead to their advancement within the party structure rather than those that will benefit the community (Ahmed et al. 2017).

In his seminal work from 1964, Riker argues that strong national parties often align local politicians' political incentives with national objectives by exploiting local politicians' career concerns (leverage over their promotions to national-level politics). Enikolopov and Zhuravskaya (2007) use cross-country data to test Riker's classical hypotheses about decentralization. Their findings

decentralization's ability to better match goods to local preferences and centralization's improved accountability.

highlight the importance of national parties in disciplining local politicians to achieve economic growth, quality of government, and public goods provision. On the other hand, they show that administrative subordination (i.e., appointing local politicians rather than electing them) may not improve the results of fiscal decentralization.

Creating and sustaining upward accountability through a patron–client relationship allows the central political leadership to dominate political power and resources throughout the society by positioning loyal clients at subnational levels. Loyal political leaders benefit, as they have access to rewarding positions in the subnational government. For example, a clientelistic intraparty relationship in Ethiopia has undermined the virtues of decentralization (allocative and production efficiencies, accountability, responsiveness, etc.) (Chanie 2007). Although the ruling Tigrayan People's Liberation Front (TPLF) ensures that both regional leaders and the populace feel there is no special treatment for any region, at least in terms of documented fiscal performance, new patronage or unofficial mechanisms for maintaining traditional clientelism exist. Regional political leaders cannot raise issues concerning the new patronage mechanisms, as this would endanger their political position in relation to the central government.

Several country cases exhibit how incentives to gain higher positions in national or subnational governments can inhibit downward accountability. Local elections that occurred on a partisan basis in several Latin American countries including Bolivia, Brazil, Costa Rica, Honduras, and Nicaragua diminished the capacity of local actors to demand accountability from local elected officials (Larson 2003). Larson argues that this was mostly due to the fact that national parties were the ones appointing candidates to local offices, thereby limiting citizens' opportunities to select representatives. In Senegal, only nationally registered political parties can present candidates for rural councils for election; as a result, there is little competition and no formal mechanisms that make local representatives accountable to the population (Agrawal and Ribot 1999).

Upward accountability is also influenced by whether the central or subnational governments have discretion over decentralizing measures. While decentralization is often advanced for its ability to increase the independence of local decision makers and bringing government closer to the people, Bohlken (2012) argues that when government elites have discretion over the implementation of decentralization, they can use it as an instrument to control local politicians. Bohlken tests the argument that local politicians have an incentive to work toward the success of their party by acting as intermediaries when party leaders implement decentralization with a great degree of executive discretion. Using variation in the degree to which parties had discretion over the allocation of resources to local governments in the Indian state of Kerala, she finds that local politicians are more likely to encourage voting for their party's candidates in state elections when state party leaders exercise discretion over decentralizing reforms, as this provides local politicians with opportunities to extract private rewards for themselves.

Additionally, the ability of the central government or national party leaders to monitor local officials shapes upward accountability. In the same study on village-level incumbents in Kerala, Bohlken finds that local politicians are also more likely to encourage their supporters to vote for their party when state-level governments have greater ability to selectively monitor village politicians. Furthermore, empirical evidence shows that the Institutional Revolutionary Party (PRI) in Mexico uses electoral results to monitor the performance of local political brokers to make sure they deliver the votes of its clientelistic networks (Larreguy 2013).[5]

Overall, local politicians' incentives in clientelistic settings reveal that upward accountability is influenced by several factors, including the partisan or nonpartisan nature of local politics, discretion over decentralizing resources, and the strength of monitoring by national parties.

Balancing Incentives

Martinez-Bravo (2014) argues that having local politicians accountable to the population can balance their incentives for upward mobility and reduce the incidence of clientelistic practices. Using a model of career-concerned politicians to guide the analysis and a natural experiment from Indonesia's first democratic election, where some villages had appointed leaders while in others they were elected, Martinez-Bravo shows that appointed officials have stronger incentives to influence voters during national-level elections because of their career concerns. Given that the appointed officials' jobs depend on decisions from the central government, they have stronger incentives to support the national party and to deliver votes for it. On the other hand, elected officials stay in their positions mainly due to their local constituents' decisions. The alignment patterns of electoral results support the model's predictions, suggesting that clientelistic politics is more widespread when local authorities are only accountable upward.

The arguments for balancing politicians' incentives with upward and vertical accountability are also developed in Myerson (2015), who shows how political centralization of government can raise the economic costs of moral hazard in public spending. He analyzes a model of moral hazard in local public services that could be efficiently managed by officials under local democratic accountability but not by officials who are appointed by the ruler of a centralized autocracy. The main result is that agency problems have efficient solutions requiring some constitutional decentralization of power.

---

[5] Larreguy (2013) also shows that municipalities with larger communal lands, where the control of political brokers is less costly, were associated with both larger PRI vote shares and lower levels of public goods provision.

In summary, politically decentralized states carry an inherent tension between upward and downward accountability. In institutionalized settings with reelection incentives, the latter should dominate, even for career-concerned politicians.

THE ROLE OF LOCAL BUREAUCRACIES IN DECENTRALIZED STATES

One key question underlying the discussion on the extent to which upward or downward accountability prevails in decentralized states in the presence of clientelism is whether we can design safeguards to ensure that whatever public goods are provided, are provided efficiently. In order to do this, we need to think about local bureaucrats and the incentives they face (Finan et al. 2017).

In a world in which reelection incentives are present, local politicians should have the incentives to efficiently deliver public goods, since this will gain them the support of the population. However, when local politics are plagued with ethnic voting and clientelism, the continuation value of being in office does not depend on the utility of citizens and thus local governments do not have the incentives to recruit efficient bureaucrats or enforce high levels of effort.

One argument commonly cited for the lack of efficiency in the local management of public services provision is the lack of human, financial, and technical resources to manage a large number of local governments (Crook and Sverrisson 2001; Smith 1985). Some have argued that local governments often fail to attract highly trained bureaucrats, since the rewards at the local level are lower than at the national level (Prud'homme 1995; Tanzi 1996). This translates into a lack of management capacity, poor public services provision, and high corruption in decentralized states. However, to a large extent this could be explained by the poor incentives politicians have to recruit able bureaucrats. Instead, it might be more politically profitable to use public sector jobs as a patronage tool (Robinson and Verdier 2013).[6]

Most developing countries lack professional civil services and instead rely on short-term contracts to staff different personnel in the government. This generates opportunities to use public sector jobs as a patronage tool. Generating a professional civil service can potentially limit local politicians' ability to use public sector jobs as part of their clientelistic network. Alternatively, there is much to be done to design recruitment strategies that manage to attract motivated bureaucrats to work in local governments, as well

---

[6] An alternative argument for local governments' poor performance is that the large number of contracts that have to be managed at the local level makes the number of opportunities for corruption more widespread in decentralized governments, and local politicians and bureaucrats are likely to be more subject to pressing demands from local interest groups. Additionally, local officials usually have more discretionary power than national decision makers, and monitoring and auditing are usually more developed at the national level (Manor 1999).

as to design incentives that deter corruption, limit clientelism, and motivate bureaucrats to exert effort and enhance local public goods provision.

A nascent empirical literature investigates different ways in which we can design recruitment strategies and contracts for public sector workers (reviewed in Finan et al. 2017). Following this literature, ongoing work tests whether centrally implemented, performance-based, group incentives can extract a high level of effort from local-level bureaucrats, while at the same time reducing the negative effects of political appointees on local-level productivity (Bobba et al. ongoing).

CONCLUSIONS

The large decentralization drive that took place in the developing world in the past thirty years represents a big step toward the alignment of public policies with preferences of local populations. However, in weak institutional environments, the hierarchical structure of decentralized government is likely to overlap with that of clientelistic networks. This introduces risks in terms of breaking down the advantages of decentralization and instead consolidating clientelistic networks that prevent the resurgence of programmatic politics.

In this chapter, we have described the benefits of political decentralization in terms of information advantages of local politicians and downward and upward accountability and pointed out an overlooked dimension of decentralization that is commonplace in developing countries: clientelistic networks. The combination of these two elements can distort the incentives and lead to unexpected outcomes and instead of reinforcing the information advantage and accountability channels of decentralization, they bolster the strength of patronage and clientelistic networks. However, decentralization also presents an opportunity for national politicians' local brokers to turn into elected officials in local governments, with their own independent political agendas and career objectives, thereby freeing them for clientelistic dependency. In other words, by turning the broker from a patronage job seeker into a mayor or a governor whose political career depends on the will of the people, decentralization may weaken the demand side of clientelism and help promote programmatic electoral politics and good governance. This is more likely if decentralization includes accountability-enhancing reforms such as auditing and participatory budgeting.[7]

Despite some theoretical contributions and the few empirical ones mentioned earlier, evidence is still limited on how vertical relations between politicians in a decentralized setting can be shaped by clientelistic politics. In particular, the literature has largely overlooked how decentralization changes politicians' incentives and the extent to which clientelistic practices can be useful for career advancements in such institutional settings. More important, this

---

[7] See Ferraz and Finan (2008) for evidence on the effect of auditing on accountability.

evidence will allow us to have a better understanding of the checks and balances that should be incorporated to make sure the changes create incentives for decentralization to result in improved local governance.

REFERENCES

Agrawal, Arun, and Jesse Ribot (1999). "Accountability in Decentralization: A Framework with South Asian and West African Cases." *Journal of Developing Areas* 33 (4): 473–502.

Ahmed, Mirza Ashfaq, Suleman Aziz Lodhi, and Zahoor Ahmad (2017). "Political Brand Equity Model: The Integration of Political Brands in Voter Choice." *Journal of Political Marketing* 16(2): 147–179.

Alatas, Vivi, Abhijit Banerjee, Rema Hanna, Benjamin A. Olken, and Julia Tobias (2012). "Targeting the poor: evidence from a field experiment in Indonesia." *American Economic Review*, 102(4): 1206–40.

Alderman, Harold (2002). "Do Local Officials Know Something We Don't? Decentralization of Targeted Transfers in Albania." *Journal of Public Economics* 83: 375–404.

Alesina, Alberto, and Eliana La Ferrara (2005). "Ethnic Diversity and Economic Performance." *Journal of Economic Literature* 43 (3): 762–800.

Alesina, Alberto, and Enrico Spolaore (2003). *The Size of Nations.* Cambridge, MA: MIT Press.

Bailey, John, and Arturo Valenzuela (1997). "The Shape of the Future." *Journal of Democracy* 8: 43–57.

Banerjee, Abhijit, Selvan Kumar, Rohini Pande, and Felix Su (2011). "Do Informed Voters Make Better Choices? Experimental Evidence from Urban India." Mimeo, Harvard University.

Banerjee, Abhijit V., Esther Duflo, Rohini Pande, and Clement Imbert (2012). "Enhancing Local Public Service Delivery: Experimental Evidence on the National Rural Employment Guarantee Scheme in Bihar." International Growth Center Policy Brief 6010.

Bardhan, Pranab (2002). "Decentralization of Governance and Development." *Journal of Economic Perspectives* 16 (4): 185–205.

Bardhan, Pranab, and Dilip Mookerjee (2000). "Corruption and Decentralization of Infrastructure Delivery in Developing Countries." Working paper, University of California, Berkeley.

Bardhan, Pranab, and Dilip Mookherjee (2005). "Decentralizing Antipoverty Program Delivery in Developing Countries." *Journal of Public Economics* 89 (4): 675–704.

Bardhan, Pranab, and Dilip Mookherjee (2006). "Decentralisation and Accountability in Infrastructure Delivery in Developing Countries." *Economic Journal* 116 (508): 101–127.

Bardhan, Pranab, Dilip Mookherjee, and Monica Parra Torrado (2010). "Impact of Political Reservations in West Bengal Local Governments on Anti-Poverty Targeting." *Journal of Globalization and Development* 1(1): 1–38.

Besley, Timothy J., and Robin Burgess (2002). "Can Labour Regulation Hinder Economic Performance? Evidence from India." CEPR Discussion Paper No. 3260.

Besley, Timothy, and Stephen Coate (2003). "Centralized versus Decentralized Provision of Local Public Goods: A Political Economy Approach."*Journal of Public Economics* 87: 2611–2637.

Bobba, Matteo, Gianmarco Leon, Damase Sossou, and Leonard Wantchekon (ongoing) "Group Incentives in Local Governments: Evidence from Benin."

Bohlken, Anjali (2012). "Upward Accountability: Village Politicians, Decentralization, and the Electoral Success of Party Machines in India." University of British Columbia Working Paper.

Bordignon, Masimo (2004). "Fiscal Decentralization: How to Achieve a Hard Budget Constraint." Workshop on Fiscal Surveillance in EMU: New Issues and Challenges: Brussels.

Burgess, Robin, Remi Jedwab, Edward Miguel, Ameet Morjaria, and Gerard Padró i Miquel (2015). "The Value of Democracy: Evidence from Road Building in Kenya." *American Economic Review* 105(6): 1817–1851.

Burki, Shahid Javed, Guillermo E. Perry, and William R. Dillinger (1999). *Beyond the Center: Decentralizing the State*. Washington, DC: World Bank.

Chanie, Paulous (2007). "Clientelism and Ethiopia's Post-1991 Decentralization." *Journal of Modern African Studies* 45 (3): 355–384.

Crook, Richard C., and Alan S. Sverrisson (2001). "Decentralisation and Poverty-Alleviation in Developing Countries: A Comparative Analysis *or*, Is West Bengal Unique?" Institute of Development Studies Working Paper 130.

Cruz, Ceci (2013). "Social Networks and the Targeting of Illegal Electoral Strategies." American Political Science Association Annual Meeting Paper.

Dixit, Avinash, and John Londregan (1998). "Ideology, Tactics and Efficiency in Redistributive Politics." *Quarterly Journal of Economics* 113 (2): 497–529.

Djankov, Simeon, Caralee McLiesh, Tatiana Nenova, and Andrei Shleifer (2001). "Who Owns the Media?" World Bank Policy Research Working Paper No. 2620, Washington, DC: World Bank.

Easterly, William and Ross Levine (1997). "Africa's Growth Tragedy: Policies and Ethnic Divisions." *Quarterly Journal of Economics* 112 (4): 1203–1250.

Eaton, Kent (2006). "The Downside of Decentralization: Armed Clientelism in Colombia." *Security Studies* 15 (4): 533–562.

Enikolopov, Ruben, and Ekaterina Zhuravskaya (2007). "Decentralization and Political Institutions." *Journal of Public Economics* 91 (11–12): 2261–2290.

Fackler, Tim, and Tse-min Lin (1995). "Political Corruption and Presidential Elections 1929–1999." *Journal of Politics* 57: 971–993.

Faguet, Jean-Paul (2004). "Does Decentralization Increase Responsiveness to Local Needs? Evidence from Bolivia." *Journal of Public Economics* 88(4): 867–894.

Faguet, Jean-Paul (2012). *Decentralization and Popular Democracy: Governance from Below in Bolivia*. Ann Arbor, MI: University of Michigan Press.

Falleti, Tulia (2005). "A Sequential Theory of Decentralization: Latin American Cases in Comparative Perspective." *American Political Science Review* 99: 327–346.

Ferraz, Claudio, and Frederico Finan (2008) "Exposing Corrupt Politicians: The Effects of Brazil's Publicly Released Audits on Electoral Outcomes." *Quarterly Journal of Economics* 123(2): 703–745.

Ferraz, Claudio, and Frederico Finan (2011). "Electoral Accountability and Corruption: Evidence from the Audits of Local Governments." *American Economic Review* 101 (4): 1274–1311.

Ferraz, Claudio, Frederico Finan, and Dimitri Szerman (2015). "Procuring Firm Growth: The Effects of Government Purchases on Firm Dynamics." NBER Working Paper 21219.

Finan, Federico, and Laura Shecter (2012). "Vote Buying and Reciprocity." *Econometrica* 80 (2): 863–882.

Finan, Frederico, Benjamin Olken, and Rohini Pande (2017). "The Personnel Economics of the Developing State." In Abhijit Banerjee and Esther Duflo (eds.) *Handbook of Economic Field Experiments*, Vol. 2. Amsterdam: North Holland, pp. 467–514.

Fisman, Raymond, and Roberta Gatti (2002). "Decentralization and Corruption: Evidence across Countries." *Journal of Public Economics* 83: 325–345.

Fujiwara, Thomas, and Leonard Wantchekon (2013). "Can Informed Public Deliberation Overcome Clientelism? Experimental Evidence from Benin." *American Economic Journal: Applied Economics* 5 (4): 241–255.

Gadenne, Lucie, and Monica Singhal (2014). "Decentralization in Developing Economies." *Annual Review of Economics* 6: 581–604.

Galasso, Emanuela, and Martin Ravallion (2005). "Decentralized Targeting of an Antipoverty Program." *Journal of Public Economics* 89 (4): 705–727.

Galiani, Sebastien, Paul Gertler, and Ernesto Schargrodsky (2008). "School Decentralization: Helping the Good Get Better, but Leaving the Poor Behind." *Journal of Public Economics* 92 (10–11): 2106–2120.

Gans-Morse, Jordan, Sebastiàn Mazzuca, and Simeon Nicheter (2014). "Varieties of Clientelism: Machine Politics during Elections." *American Journal of Political Science* 58 (2): 415–432.

Hagopian, Frances, Carlos Gervasoni, and Juan Andrés Moraes (2009). "From Patronage to Program: The Emergence of Party-Oriented Legislators in Brazil." *Comparative Political Studies* 3: 360–391.

Hayek, Friedrich A. (1945). "The Use of Knowledge in Society." *American Economic Review* 35 (4): 519–530.

Hicken, Allen (2011). "Clientelism." *Annual Review of Political Science* 14: 289–310.

Hsieh, Chang-Tai, Edward Miguel, Daniel Ortega, and Francisco Rodriguez (2011). "The Price of Political Opposition: Evidence from Venezuela's *Maisanta*." *American Economic Journal: Applied Economics* 3(2): 196–214.

Humphreys, Macarthan and Jeremy Weinstein (2014). "Failing Grade: How Transparency Shapes the Performance of Politicians in Uganda." Mimeo, Stanford University.

Keefer, Philip, and Razvan Vlaicu (2008). "Democracy, Credibility, and Clientelism." *Journal of Law, Economics and Organization* 24 (2): 371–406.

Kis-Katos, Bambang, and Suharnoko Sjahrir (2017). "The Impact of Fiscal and Political Decentralization on Local Public Investments in Indonesia." *Journal of Comparative Economics* 45(2): 344–365.

Kitschelt, Herbert (2012). "Parties and Interest Intermediation." In Edwin Amenta, Kate Nash, and Alan Scott (eds.) *The Wiley-Blackwell Companion to Political Sociology*. Hoboken, NJ: Wiley-Blackwell, pp. 144–157.

Kitschelt, Herbert, Kirk A. Hawkins, Juan Pablo Luna, Guillermo Rosas, and Elizabeth J. Zechmeister (2010). *Latin American Party Systems*. Cambridge: Cambridge University Press.

Laffont, Jean-Jacques, and Mathieu Meleu (2001). "Separation of Powers and Development." *Journal of Development Economics* 64: 129–145.

Gianmarco León and Leonard Wantchekon

Larreguy, Horacio (2013). "Monitoring Political Brokers: Evidence from Clientelistic Networks in Mexico." Mimeo, Harvard University.

Larreguy, Horacio, John Marshall, and Laura Trucco (2015). "Breaking Clientelism or Rewarding Incumbents? Evidence from an Urban Titling Program in Mexico."

Larson, Anne (2003). "Decentralization and Forest Management in Latin America: Towards a Working Model." *Public Administration and Development* 23: 211–226.

Lederman, Daniel, Norman Loayza, and Rodrigo R. Soares (2005). "Accountability and Corruption: Political Institutions Matter." *Economics and Politics* 17(1): 1–35.

Linz, Juan (1990). "The Virtues of Parliamentarism." *Journal of Democracy* 1: 84–92.

Linz, Juan, and Alfred Stepan (1996). "Towards Consolidated Democracies." *Journal of Democracy* 7: 14–33.

Manor, James (1999). *The Political Economy of Democratic Decentralization*. Washington DC: World Bank.

Mares, Isabela, and Lauren Young (2016). "Buying, Expropriating, and Stealing Votes." *Annual Review of Political Science* 19: 15.1–15.22.

Martinez-Bravo, Monica (2014). "The Role of Local Officials in New Democracies: Evidence from Indonesia." *American Economic Review* 104 (4): 1244–1287.

Miguel, Edward, and Mary Kay Gugerty (2005). "Ethnic Diversity, Social Sanctions, and Public Goods in Kenya." *Journal of Public Economics* 89 (11–12): 2325–2368.

Myerson, Roger (2015). "Local Agency Costs of Political Decentralization." University of Chicago Working Paper.

Nas, Tevfik, Albert Price, and Charles Weber, (1986). "A Policy-Oriented Theory of Corruption." *American Political Science Review* 80: 107–119.

Oates, Wallace E. (1972). *Fiscal Federalism*. New York, NY: Harcourt Brace Jovanovich.

Olken, Benjamin, and Rohini Pande (2012). "Lifting the Curtain on Corruption in Developing Countries." VOX.eu [https://voxeu.org/article/lifting-curtain-corruption-developing-countries].

Panzetto, Giacomo A. M., Frederico Boffa, and Amedeo Piolatto (2016). "Political Centralization and Government Accountability." *Quarterly Journal of Economics* 131: 381–422.

Persson, Petra, and Ekaterina Zhuravskaya (2015). "The Limits of Career Concerns in Federalism: Evidence from China." *Journal of the European Economic Association* 14 (2): 1–37.

Persson, Torsten, Gérard Roland, and Guido Tabellini (1997). "Separation of Powers and Political Accountability." *Quarterly Journal of Economics* 112: 163–1202.

Prud'homme, Remy (1995). "The Dangers of Decentralization." *World Bank Research Observer* 10 (2): 201–220.

Riker, William (1964). *Federalism: Origin, Operation, Significance*. Boston, MA: Little Brown.

Robinson, James, and Thierry Verdier (2013). "The Political Economy of Clientelism." *Scandinavian Journal of Economics* 115 (2): 260–291.

Rose-Ackerman, Susan (1999). *Corruption and Government: Causes, Consequences, and Reform*. Cambridge: Cambridge University Press.

Scott, James C. (1972). "Patron-Client Politics and Political Change in Southeast Asia." *American Political Science Review* 66 (1): 91–113.

Seabright, Paul (1996). "Accountability and Decentralization in Government: An Incomplete Contracts Model." *European Economic Review* 40: 61–89.

Shah, Anwar (1998). "Balance, Accountability, and Responsiveness: Lessons about Decentralization." World Bank Policy Research Working Paper 2021.

Smith, B. C. (1985). *Decentralization: The Territorial Dimension of the State*. London: George Allen & Unwin.

Sneider, Mark (2016). "Do Brokers Know Their Voters? A Test of Guessability in India." Working paper, University of California, Berkeley.

Stephan, Alfred C. (1996). "Toward Consolidated Democracies." *Journal of Democracy* 7: 14–33.

Stokes, Susan (2009). "Political Clientelism." In Charles Boix and Susan Stokes (eds.) *The Oxford Handbook of Comparative Politics*, Oxford: Oxford University Press, pp. 1–27.

Stokes, Susan, Thad Dunning, Marcelo Nazareno, and Valeria Busco (2013). *Brokers, Voters and Clientelism: The Puzzle of Distributive Politics*. Cambridge: Cambridge University Press.

Tanzi, Vito (1996). "Fiscal Federalism and Decentralization: A Review of Some Efficiency and Macroeconomic Aspects." International Bank for Reconstruction and Development.

US AID (2009). *Democratic Decentralization Programming Handbook*. Washington DC: USAID.

Véron, René, Glyn Williams, Stuart Corbridge, and Manoj Srivastava (2006). "Decentralized Corruption or Corrupt Decentralization? Community Monitoring of Poverty-Alleviation Schemes in Eastern India." *World Development* 34 (11): 1922–1941.

Vicente, Pedro. (2014) "Is Vote Buying Effective? Evidence from a Field Experiment in West Africa." *Economic Journal* 124 (574): F356–F387.

Vicente, Pedro, and Leonard Wantchekon (2009). "Clientelism and Vote Buying: Lessons from Field Experiments in West Africa." *Oxford Review of Economic Policy* 25 (2): 292–305.

Wallis, John J., and Wallace E. Oates (1988). "Decentralization in the Public Sector: An Empirical Study of State and Local Government." in Harvey Rosen (ed.) *Fiscal Federalism: Quantitative Studies*. Chicago, IL: University of Chicago Press, pp. 5–32.

Wantchekon, Leonard (2003). "Clientelism and Voting Behavior: Evidence from a Field Experiment in Benin." *World Politics* 55 (3): 399–422.

Wantchekon, Leonard, Gabriel Lopez-Moctezuma, Thomas Fujiwara, Cecilia Lero, and Daniel Rubenson (2016). "Policy Deliberation and Voter Persuasion: Experimental Evidence from an Election in the Philippines." Working paper, Princeton University.

World Bank (1994). *World Development Report 1994: Infrastructure for Development*. New York, NY: Oxford University Press for the World Bank.

World Bank (2000). "Decentralization and Health Care." Decentralization Thematic Group. Washington, DC.

Zamboni, Yves, and Stephan Litschig (2018) "Audit risk and rent extraction: Evidence from a randomized evaluation in Brazil." *Journal of Development Economics*, 134: 133–149.

Decentralization and Ethnic Diversity

Thad Dunning

Political decentralization allegedly eases basic problems of governance in ethnically diverse societies. According to fiscal federalism theory, varying preferences associated with ethnic divisions promote conflict over the nature of public goods and the distribution of private benefits. Reduction in the local heterogeneity of preferences via decentralization may thus foster greater horizontal cooperation and thereby produce welfare gains (Oates 1999). Decentralization may also boost equity and accountability; for example, it may be a vehicle for institutions that empower marginalized or disadvantaged ethnic groups at the local level. This theory of change motivates substantial development programming by USAID and other international donors. Yet to what extent, and under what conditions, has decentralization fostered improvements in governance? What are the challenges to public goods provision in diverse localities, and what interventions may minimize these problems?

In this chapter, I make several observations that challenge and extend this standard theory of change – and call into question donors' focus on devolution as a matter of absolute normative preference. While devolution can conceivably have positive effects on accountability or public goods provision, it can also worsen some forms of ethnic division. The dynamics of devolution can also render associated development programming ineffective for boosting local accountability. Local and national circumstances may determine the extent to which decentralization does or does not improve governance outcomes. I argue that two dimensions of variation insufficiently discussed by fiscal federalism theory may condition the effects of decentralizing reforms and related development programming.

First, we may draw a stylized distinction between settings in which subnational units are ethnically homogenous – as in many parts of sub-Saharan Africa, where ethnic groups are identified with particular rural home regions – and those that are locally heterogeneous – such as Indian villages, which are typically home to numerous castes or religious communities. In the former case, devolution approaches ethnic partition. Fiscal federalism theory applies most clearly in this context. One might therefore expect the gains from decentralization to be greater in the case of local homogeneity. An important caveat is that even if devolution locally mitigates distributive or social choice problems, it could also exacerbate conflicts *between* homogenous communities in an otherwise heterogeneous society. In the latter case, by contrast, local governments may encounter many of the governance tensions associated with ethnic diversity, but on a smaller scale. Theories of decentralization and diversity should distinguish these very different settings.

Second, and especially important for my argument, while political decentralization extends spheres of autonomous action to subnational governments, it also involves continued interaction between subnational and national actors – and can even create new opportunities for the penetration of central government actors in local affairs. For example, subnational elections can give rise to bottom-up political movements that then scale up to the national level. They can also provide novel vehicles for incursion of national parties at the grassroots. Elected subnational leaders are natural brokers for national political parties seeking to curry local favor – or even to buy local votes. Thus, subnational elections can allow for forms of local–national linkage that would not have existed in their absence. Even in semi-authoritarian settings without national elections, local elections can provide new avenues for national–local linkage. This observation shifts our attention from the independent spheres of action that devolution allows toward a focus on the links between governmental units that are retained post-devolution – and that sometimes develop in response to devolution. Of course, devolution may strengthen local–national linkages differently in distinct cases: for example, in systems with weak national parties (or strong local/regional parties), national organizations may not penetrate subnational elections effectively. In this case, devolution could bolster horizontal responsiveness more than vertical accountability. A second key dimension of variation is therefore the strength or weakness of local–national ties in the wake of devolution.

Crossing these two dimensions of variation gives a 2 x 2 typology based on local ethnic diversity and the strength of local–national linkages (Table 11.1). Different combinations of conditions may suggest contrasting impacts of devolution. Taking the top-left cell of Table 11.1 first, in the case of weak local–national linkages, limited diversity might indeed smooth the path of some forms of local governance – for instance, the provision of in-kind donations to small-scale public goods. This setting approaches the situation envisioned by much fiscal federalism theory. Nonetheless, as a large literature related to residential sorting suggests, and as I detail further later, segregation into homogenous, self-governing communities could also inflame cross-community conflict.

TABLE 11.1 *Decentralization and Diversity: A Typology*

		Local Ethnic Diversity	
		Homogenous	Heterogeneous
Local–National Linkages	Weakened	Improved local governance (but possible cross-community conflict)	Local reproduction of governance challenges
	Strengthened	Empowerment of "wholesale" ethnic brokers	Empowerment of "retail" partisan brokers; may undercut ethnic empowerment

In the lower-left cell of Table 11.1 – where strong local–national linkages exist after devolution – devolved governance to a homogeneous setting could still mitigate local conflict over private or public goods. Yet local homogeneity may also foster the emergence of "wholesale" ethnic brokers, who can deliver the support of their ethnically homogenous constituents to national parties and leaders in exchange for policy favors. These brokers may be unelected (e.g., chiefs in sub-Saharan Africa), but federalism can also create opportunities for election of ethnic leaders of previously unrepresented groups (e.g., indigenous mayors in southern Mexico or Peru). Such leaders may have substantial bargaining power vis-à-vis national leaders, since they sometimes command blocs of voters who may be mobile between different partisan options and can therefore be offered to the highest bidder. Yet ethnic brokers may retain rents rather than diffuse them broadly to constituents. The consequences of devolution for equity, accountability, and other governance outcomes are therefore an open question in the presence of local homogeneity and strong local–national linkages (lower-left cell of Table 11.1).

Moving to the upper-right cell of Table 11.1, we have both local ethnic heterogeneity and weak local–national linkages. Here, devolution may simply duplicate at the local level many of the governance problems associated with heterogeneity at the national level. Indeed, ethnic inequities may be as or more severe locally than they are nationally, so decentralization could worsen horizontal cooperation. However, many instances of devolution are also accompanied by explicit institutional interventions designed to redress such local inequalities. For example, the 73rd Amendment in India mandated the holding of elections for village councils, created new powers for those subnational governments, and also decreed the reservation of certain elected positions for members of marginalized castes and tribes as well as women. Those elected leaders may promote the material welfare and security of their constituents and also generate broader symbolic benefits for their communities.

Yet the Indian case – and many other cases in which reforms seek to bolster the power of marginalized groups in subnational governments – should in fact be situated in the lower-right cell of Table 11.1. Here we have both local ethnic diversity and strong local–national linkages. This final case deserves special attention, because it is empirically common yet understudied. Much of the literature on decentralization and diversity assumes a setting in which preference heterogeneity is reduced by bringing government "closer to the people." Yet in many settings that assumption does not hold. Moreover, the perpetuation and even strengthening of local–national linkages in the wake of political decentralization – often though not exclusively via the channels of party organization and partisan competition – is substantially more important than much of the literature on devolution would presume.

In this final context, efforts to improve local equity and accountability can have unexpected consequences. For example, local elections – accompanied by the reservation of offices for particular groups, or other policies designed to empower marginalized citizens – can give state and national parties new inroads at the grassroots. Such elections allow national leaders readily to identify influential local leaders from a range of ethnic backgrounds. As in the case of local homogeneity and strong local–national linkages, elected leaders may therefore become important brokers. Yet, in part because local heterogeneity may not exactly reproduce national demographics, and in part because national politics is about broader issues not directly salient at the local level, grassroots ethnic splits may not map onto broader partisan divides. Rather than serving solely as ethnic intermediaries at the local level, influential leaders may tend to work for the benefit of national parties or other national organizations. This may have important consequences for the capacity of political decentralization to minimize governance problems associated with ethnic diversity, as well as to boost equity and accountability.

In the rest of this chapter, I seek to accomplish two related objectives. First, I extend my discussion of the typology in Table 11.1, focusing particularly on building theory about the consequences of decentralization in settings of local heterogeneity and strong local–national linkages. In the next section, I develop the idea that decentralization can foster new kinds of such connections: for example, devolution of powers (especially but not only involving subnational elections) may empower local brokers who mediate between national or state politicians and citizens. I then turn to some implications for the capacity of decentralization to solve basic governance problems, as well as to remedy problems of inequity and lack of accountability. This theory-building exercise may open a path for USAID and other donors to reconsider thinking about the effects of decentralization programming.

Next, I turn to empirical testing of several propositions that emerge from this theory-building exercise. India is particularly useful for empirical assessment, both because decentralization occurred in a context of local heterogeneity and strong national–subnational linkages and because an institution designed to

empower marginalized groups was created in a way that allows credible
identification of its causal effects. While the details of electoral reservation – i.e.,
quotas that reserve seats for particular caste or tribal groups in local elections – are
specific to the Indian case, lessons from this analysis extend to other contexts in
which USAID and other donors design programs to improve governance
outcomes. This analysis replicates and extends my previous work on the impact
of electoral quotas in this context (Dunning and Nilekani 2013). My results
indicate the difficulties of using such institutions to remedy problems of ethnic
marginalization at the local level. In particular, the evidence underscores the
importance of formal and informal links between levels of government,
especially partisan ties, in driving null effects of quotas (that is, the finding that
quotas do not materially improve outcomes for marginalized groups). In the
conclusion, I address conditions under which devolution may and may not
foster better governance outcomes.

LOCAL–NATIONAL LINKAGES AFTER DEVOLUTION

Per USAID's definition – which follows that of many scholars of decentralization
– devolution "is the most expansive form of decentralization, in that it
requires subnational governments to hold defined spheres of autonomous
action, which typically means the use of subnational elections" (Rodden
and Wibbels 2015). After devolution, separately elected decision makers
in subnational governments may thus be independent of the national
government in many ways.

Yet devolved units "are still bound by the provisions of national laws (such
as those regarding political rights and civil liberties), national policy priorities
(including meeting basic needs and reducing poverty), and national standards
(in such areas as fiscal responsibility, healthcare, and water quality)" (Rodden
and Wibbels 2015). The links between national and subnational governments –
and the ultimate responsibility of the former for the latter – is the source of the
lack of fiscal discipline in multitiered systems of government, engendering as it
does the moral hazard faced by subnational units (Rodden 2006). Even more to
the point, subnational actors interact politically with national leaders not only
for reasons of governing but also for contesting and financing electoral
campaigns, interacting with the bureaucracy, and more generally for serving,
rallying, persuading, cajoling, and mobilizing citizens to different ends. Much of
the literature on decentralization has focused on the independent spheres of
action that devolution allows – rightly so, because this independence is partly
decentralization's raison d'être. Yet this should not belie the importance of the
many continued links between subnational and national levels, as in federal
systems generally (Wibbels 2012).[1]

---

[1] Wibbels analyzes the representation of regional interests in national politics and also the partisan
influence of national leaders over subnational politicians.

Not only are such connections maintained after devolution; devolution may itself engender novel forms of local–national linkage. One illustration is the tendency of subnational elections to spawn regional movements or parties that can, under some conditions, become national political forces. But beyond this "bottom-up" form of linkage, subnational elections can also provide new openings for "top-down" penetration at the grassroots, for example, in enhancing the capacity of existing national forces to boost their local influence. One critical issue for national parties concerns the identification of effective local brokers who intermediate between parties or national leaders and citizens. In clientelist systems, where parties exchange material benefits in a quid pro quo for political support, such brokers are sine qua non: they provide the local knowledge that is crucial for identifying receptive voters and monitoring their compliance with the clientelist contract (Stokes, Dunning, Nazareno, and Brusco 2013). Even where conditions are not always enforced, local brokers can prove extremely valuable to national leaders by providing the local knowledge or authority to make national policies effective. Baldwin, for example, describes the legitimating functions of local chiefs in sub-Saharan Africa, who can pair with national politicians (such as Members of Parliament) to make development projects more efficacious (Baldwin 2015).

Subnational elections are often extremely helpful for identifying effective brokers, as they provide an observable measure of local popularity and influence. Electoral success may indicate not only that a local politician is hard-working and competent but also that she targets resources in a politically efficacious way – always an important issue in a setting with agency problems, in which local brokers may not target resources to optimize the political interests of national leaders (Camp 2017). Effective brokers can in turn be highly valuable electoral assets for higher-level politicians. As shown in a series of close-election analyses, electoral success at the state and national levels of government allows Brazilian parties to "hire" mayors, whose success in turn boosts the electoral fortunes of gubernatorial or congressional candidates of the hiring party (Novaes 2015). Such connections between elected politicians at different tiers of the political system are critical after devolution – indeed, in federal systems generally. In Argentina, city councilors work as brokers for mayors on the outskirts of metropolitan Buenos Aires, and mayors themselves are brokers for gubernatorial or national candidates. In India, members and especially the presidents of local village councils can serve as vote brokers for members of state assemblies or the national parliament (Dunning and Nilekani 2013). Even in authoritarian systems without national elections, such as China's, local elections can play important roles in developing intermediaries and providing higher-ups with useful information (Manion 2016).

However, local elections are not necessary for brokerage after devolution, as effective brokers can be identified through other mechanisms. Traditional authorities or leaders of religious communities, though not elected by citizens, may possess the moral authority required to deliver votes or enhance service delivery (Baldwin 2015 on traditional authorities; Koter 2013 on religious leaders). Baldwin argues that democratization in sub-Saharan Africa bolstered the constitutional status of traditional areas governed by chiefs and devolved defined spheres of autonomous action to those subnational units. These chiefs in turn proved valuable to national MPs for promoting development and retaining office. Here too, devolution created new opportunities for the penetration of national politics at the local level. At the micro level at which many intermediaries engage face to face with their clients, brokers are often not themselves electoral candidates, but are simply citizens who specialize in solving the problems of their neighbors (e.g., *punteros* in Argentina or *naya netas* in India) (Auyero 2001; Krishna 2011), and can build relationships with higher-ups in political parties. Political leaders may then use indicators other than or in addition to election results to identify effective brokers – such as the size of the crowd that a neighborhood leader has managed to turn out to a political rally (Scwartzberg 2015).

One critical feature of the local–national nexus, especially in settings with elected brokers, is the local penetration of national parties. Thus, parties often recruit brokers who work for the benefit of the party ticket – even if those brokers are by no means committed to a single party over time. In contexts like Brazil and India, there is often considerable party-switching by brokers. (After all, there are some brokers one cannot buy – only rent). An especially striking illustration comes from the aftermath of the 73rd Amendment in India. Notwithstanding the fact that mandated local council elections almost everywhere in India are officially nonpartisan (candidates do not affix party symbols or logos to their name on the ballot), partisanship is rife in such councils. Well over 90% of sampled citizens in three Indian states could name the party of their council president, and elected members of councils could readily name the partisan orientation of all other council members; knowledge of councilors' party was at least as widespread at the village level as knowledge of caste (Dunning and Nilekani 2013). While major Indian parties have long had some form of organization at the grassroots, decentralization gave them a new kind of toehold: competing for elections revealed and ratified the influence of local leaders, while the cost of local elections and the need to raise campaign finance often put them in direct conversation with party higher-ups, for whom they would also serve as brokers in state and national elections (Bohlken 2016).[2]

In sum, devolution extends spheres of autonomous action to subnational units, who therefore work independently in a number of domains. Yet in federal systems, both formal and informal mechanisms continue to link subnational actors to national leaders – and devolution even allows new forms of national penetration at the grassroots. One of the most important of these arises through

---

[2] Decentralization also provided national parties with new tools for competing with state parties at a third tier of governance; see Bohlken (2016).

party organization. National elections depend on subnational mobilization, and so national party leaders have strong incentives to recruit local brokers who can assist them in the tasks of local persuasion and mobilization. Devolution can produce ideal intermediaries. Often, these are elected leaders at the subnational (especially village or municipal) level; sometimes, they are nonelected leaders (such as traditional authorities) to whom new powers are devolved. In either case, it is important to recognize that just as decentralization involves a certain degree of subnational units' independence from national units, it can also engender new forms of local–national linkages, and sometimes even more intensive national penetration into local affairs.

DEVOLUTION AND DIVERSITY

What, then, are the implications of such local–national linkages for governance in ethnically diverse societies? How do these connections affect devolution's capacity to solve problems of collective action or to boost equity and accountability in the face of ethnic heterogeneity?

As discussed in the introduction, we can distinguish four settings, according to the extent of local ethnic diversity and the nature of local–national linkages in the wake of decentralization. These are of course ideal types, and one can think about continuums that link these poles. But they also correspond substantially to concrete empirical cases. In many contexts, ethnic groups are associated with particular home regions, and so the devolution of power to rural bodies in those regions generates subnational polities with much greater ethnic homogeneity than the national polity as a whole. Examples include subnational constituencies (not just provincial assembly units but also chiefly kingdoms) in sub-Saharan Africa, as well as certain indigenous regions in parts of the Americas, where native councils are given authority over circumscribed actions within delimited, ethnically homogeneous homelands. In other settings, by contrast, the local constituencies are themselves ethnically diverse. This is true in some rural settings (such as Indian villages) and also tends to characterize devolution to municipal/urban governments. In considering the possible impacts of devolution for governance in ethnically diverse societies, it is useful to consider these settings separately – with an eye to the moderating influence of the local–national linkages traced earlier. In this section, I expand on the theory-building discussion in the introduction.

Consider first the case of local homogeneity with weak local–national linkages (top-right cell of Table 11.1). This is perhaps the emblematic case for the fiscal theory of federalism, according to which homogeneity of tastes can lead to more efficient local outcomes after devolution. Oates, for example, summarizes this theory as follows:

By tailoring outputs of such goods and services to the particular preferences and circumstances of their constituencies, decentralized provision increases economic welfare above that which results from the more uniform levels of such services that are likely under national provision. The basic point here is simply that the efficient level of output of a "local" public good ... is likely to vary across jurisdictions as a result of both differences in preferences and cost differentials. To maximize overall social welfare thus requires that local outputs vary accordingly. (Oates 1999)

The conjecture that ethnic heterogeneity impedes cooperation and therefore leads to worse governance – for example, diminished public goods provision – is plausible enough, and is backed by a range of associational evidence in the form of a very large body of regressions. There are also many ways that ethnic heterogeneity may impede public goods provision, including not only differences in tastes but also barriers to cross-group communication, or distinct assumptions about the strategies that members of other groups will follow (Habyarimana, Humphreys, Posner, and Weinstein 2007). As a large political economy literature suggests, ethnic diversity can also affect a wide range of outcomes beyond public goods provision; see, for instance, work by Spolaore and Wacziarg on relatedness and war (2009), Michalopoulos on the causes, persistence, and implications of ethnic diversity (2008), and Posner on political influences on interethnic cooperation in realms such as marriage (2004). To be sure, the causal link between diversity and governance is in fact extremely difficult to identify and prove empirically. Yet if it exists, local ethnic homogeneity should foster cooperation for public goods provision, and so devolution in this setting should offer a solution to basic problems of governance, at least locally.

Notwithstanding this conjecture, devolving governance to homogenous local entities could also exacerbate distributive conflicts *between* communities in an otherwise heterogeneous society – and could also increase overall poverty or inequality and worsen broader governance outcomes. In developed countries such as the United States, scholars of residential sorting focus on such broader impacts of ethnic segregation (Bruch 2014). Kasara presents evidence that ethnic segregation in Kenya both diminishes interethnic trust and fosters intergroup conflict (2013, 2017). The dynamics through which local homogeneity exaggerates conflict between localities may plausibly be only heightened by the devolution of self-governing powers to ethnic homeland-like subnational units. Moreover, the tendency for conflict between these units could also be increased when formal or informal local–national links are weak, so that subnational units are not as integrated into a national political sphere.

Yet if strong integration of ethnically homogenous units into the national sphere might inhibit horizontal conflict between units, it can also pose different kinds of risks to equity and accountability. To consider this case of local homogeneity with strong local–national linkages (bottom-left cell of Table 11.1), one can profitably distinguish between the kind of horizontal cooperation on which this literature tends to focus – for example, in-kind contributions to the upkeep of water wells or roads – and vertical relations between citizens and their local leaders that also impact the quality of governance – in particular, the degree of accountability (Lierl 2015).[3] Here the tendency of homogeneous ethnic regions to produce leaders who serve as "wholesale" brokers – delivering the votes of an entire community to national political leaders in exchange for benefits or rents – appears especially germane. Indeed, this tendency was identified by Bates as one of the basic sources of group identification in Africa, according to which political entrepreneurs turned home regions into "ethnic" bases of power (Bates 1983).

What are the consequences of such wholesale group representation by ethnic brokers? Local bodies may produce leaders who are exceptionally secure in their tenure, either because their resources as local elites allow them to obtain electoral advantages or because of their non-electoral resources (such as hereditary authority in the case of chiefs). Because they can promise to deliver their ethnic or religious followers in a wholesale manner to the highest bidder, this can generate substantial payoffs from political higher-ups, as documented for the case of Senegal (Koter 2013). Ironically, co-ethnicity of these local brokers and their clients could undermine accountability by allowing brokers to retain a large portion of these payoffs they obtain through subnational-national bargains. To my knowledge, empirical work has not focused on this possibility or linked it to devolution patterns, but this appears to be an important area for further research.[4]

In sum, with local ethnic homogeneity, devolution could have contrasting impacts through diverse means. It may lead to more horizontal cooperation, consistent with the theory that ethnic diversity impedes contributions to public goods: rather than contributing in a diverse national constituency, citizens in a subnational unit face local ethnic similarity. Through this channel, devolution could contribute to solving basic problems of governance. Yet devolution in a context of ethnic segregation could also inflame cross-community conflict. And devolution could also potentially undermine vertical accountability, if it empowers local brokers or leaders who can take the support of their ethnically homogeneous constituents for granted. Through this channel, devolution could exacerbate other basic governance challenges.

Consider now the case of local ethnic heterogeneity. As mentioned previously, where subnational and national diversity are the same, devolution in this context may simply reproduce problems of governance associated with ethnic difference, albeit at a smaller scale, particularly in the case of weak local-national linkages (top-right cell of Table 11.1). It is particularly in such small-

---

[3] Lierl (2015) uses lab-in-the-field experiments to investigate contrasting problems of horizontal cooperation and vertical accountability in relatively homogeneous Tanzania.

[4] In a somewhat distinct vein, Kasara (2007) finds that national leaders in Africa tend to deny their co-ethnic regions favorable tax policies, relative to non-co-ethnics; local brokers play an important role in her interpretation. See also Padro i Miquel (2007).

scale settings that ethnic diversity seems negatively related to the provision of public goods.[5] Thus, devolution in this setting might not necessarily be expected to foster greater in-kind contributions to public goods or more generally to promote horizontal cooperation. Of course, this could be conditional on the nature of local hostility between groups, which, while substantial in many cases, is not in others; ethnic integration in Kenya is associated with trust, a finding also suggested by the "contact" hypothesis (Allport 1954; Kasara 2013). In some settings, identity-based heterogeneity might simply be easier to manage at the local level – perhaps because people are much more likely to personally interact with ethnic others. This may be less likely the case in what Horowitz called "ranked" systems in which ethnicity establishes a hierarchy of rights and privileges, such as the case of caste in India (Horowitz 1985). Even there, it is possible that priming ethnic identities is more costly locally than it would be nationally – e.g., for a politician such as Prime Minister Narendra Modi of the Bharatiya Janata Party (BJP), who has been affiliated with Hindutva nationalist groups (and is alleged to have permitted ethnic rioting targeted at Muslims while chief minister of the state of Gujarat), but who may at the national level be able to avoid many of the negative political consequences of fomenting violence in specific localities. Thus, devolution could conceivably have positive as well as negative consequences for horizontal interethnic cooperation.

Yet can devolution improve vertical accountability in this setting of local heterogeneity? Here, it is especially important to consider the case of strong local–national linkages (bottom-right cell of Table 11.1). Devolution in such settings has often been accompanied by formal mechanisms designed to rectify local imbalances in political power, in particular, to bolster the voice and policy influence of marginalized groups. For example, I discuss extensively in what follows the case of electoral quotas in India, which mandate the descriptive representation of marginalized castes and tribes as well as women on village councils. One can also point to reforms or interventions in other contexts that facilitate the political participation of marginalized groups. For example, much programming of international donors, including USAID, aims to bolster the participation of disadvantaged groups in local government. Political participation and leadership by historically marginalized groups may have several kinds of salutary effects. It can deeply shape perceptions of the balance of power in local contexts, allowing disadvantaged communities to confront local elites as relative equals for the first time. Some of these benefits can be symbolic, though not the less important for this reason: in India, electoral quotas are sometimes seen in terms of the "politics of dignity" that empower communities subject to the strictures of untouchability. Yet descriptive representation can also breed substantive representation: quotas may allow members of disadvantaged groups to influence policy outcomes through more

---

[5] See the evidence reviewed in Habyarimana et al. (2007, chapter 2).

vertical accountability, for example, to induce politicians to deliver material benefits to members of their poor and excluded communities.

In many of these settings, however, the subnational context is not simply a microcosm of the larger environment. This is not only because the grassroots could be a particularly propitious setting for generating participation by disfavored citizens in ways that may not be possible at the national level, but also because of substantial linkages between subnational and national organizations that structure the context in which these reforms and interventions take place – and can be key for determining whether such outcomes materialize. Like devolution generally, electoral quotas help party elites identify influential local intermediaries from a range of ethnic groups (because reserved seats require local candidates from marginalized groups). Thus, local leaders from marginalized as well as dominant local communities come into contact with party higher-ups, who may use them for electoral mobilization and reward them with private gains. To reiterate, such individuals become party brokers: that is, they are paid or otherwise rewarded by the national or state party, and their mobilization efforts tend to take place as members of parties rather than as members of ethnic groups (even if in practice they target voters from their respective communities).

In part because of these dynamics, ethnicity and party tend to become somewhat decoupled, in a context of local heterogeneity. In the case of quotas, each party seeks to identify local allies from marginalized groups to support as candidates.[6] Even without formal quotas, efforts to encourage the political participation of marginalized groups (as in much development programming by USAID and other donors) do not determine partisan affiliations. Competing local leaders from the same group may ally with different factions or parties. Party and ethnicity can therefore become crosscutting divides, with candidates and voters of marginalized as well as dominant groups represented in each competing party.

What are the consequences of this crosscutting of party and ethnic ties? As my case study of Indian local councils presented later in this chapter suggests, when a party is the dominant organizing force of political competition and members of different communities are incorporated in the same party (while members of the same group join different parties), reservation of a council seat or presidency can have little impact on policy outcomes. A quota changes the ethnic identity of a seat's occupant, but does not necessarily change the party that holds the seat. This persistence in incumbents' partisan orientations can diminish the contrast between policy outcomes with and without quotas.

To be sure, local–national linkages via party organization can aid historically disadvantaged groups. For example, ties to party higher-ups can help ease

---

[6] Again, candidates for village councils do not run on formal party tickets in most Indian states, but as I detail later, many local elections are de facto partisan contests in which party higher-ups provide significant campaign finance and other support.

access to public services outside of the village council's direct control, such as those offered by the state police and bureaucracy; party higher-ups often have formal or informal influence over such authorities through sway over transfers from favorable to unfavorable postings, among other means (Bussell 2012). Influence over the police is especially important for righting local injustices – such as ritual beatings and murders of lower-caste citizens. Thus the impact of policies such as quotas, in the context of the new local–national linkages that devolution fosters, may be far from straightforward or unidirectional for every outcome. (It is also generally exceptionally difficult to estimate empirically, posing difficulties that I discuss in the next section.)

To summarize, policies such as electoral quotas – or development programs aimed at supporting political participation of disadvantaged citizens – often seek to shift the balance of power in favor of marginalized groups and therefore boost equity and accountability. These policies have arisen especially in the context of decentralization and devolution, perhaps because countering exclusion through greater political participation seems especially feasible at the grassroots. Yet it is critical to recognize that in the settings of local ethnic heterogeneity in which such programs are developed, formal or informal mechanisms often continue to connect the subnational and national spheres. In these contexts, the specific nature of local–national connections after devolution can substantially influence the effectiveness of interventions designed to bolster equity and accountability.

A CASE STUDY: DEVOLUTION AND ETHNIC QUOTAS IN INDIA

I now turn to empirical testing of several propositions developed in the previous sections. A particularly informative case is the devolution of power to rural village councils in India, as mandated by the 73rd Amendment to the Indian Constitution passed in 1993–1994. The case is useful for a few reasons. First, it exemplifies the common but understudied setting of decentralization with local ethnic heterogeneity and strong local–national linkages, where the impact of devolution is not clearly predicted by existing theories. Second, this devolution made concrete provisions for the rotation of electoral quotas across councils, allowing empirical study of the impact of the presence of a local quota – one key mechanism that could in principle boost vertical accountability and therefore improve the quality of governance. Finally, the reform was intended at least on its face to decouple village governance from state and national politics, consistent perhaps with Gandhian idealizations of apolitical village life; for example, in almost every Indian state, candidates for village councils cannot run explicitly on party labels. The degree of local–national political ties in the wake of such a devolution – while substantial, as I show in what follows – could therefore be thought of as a kind of lower bound on the linkages likely to be found elsewhere.

I report results here of a replication and extension of a 2013 study of the impact of local quotas for council presidencies in the states of Karnataka, Rajasthan, and Bihar (Dunning and Nilekani 2013). In that study, we used the rotation of presidencies reserved for Scheduled Castes and Scheduled Tribes across village councils to identify the effect of quotas in the following manner. Within administrative units at the subdistrict level called blocks (or *taluks* or *mandals*), bureaucrats rank village council constituencies according to the proportion or number of Scheduled Caste or Scheduled Tribe residents.[7] Since the number of council presidencies to be reserved in a given electoral term depends on the overall proportion of each group in the block, a number smaller than the ranked list is reserved in each term. To assign reservation, bureaucrats rotate reservation down the list, starting at the top in one electoral term and moving down sequentially across terms. Near the threshold for reservation (that is, the bottom of the set of councils assigned to quotas in a particular term), whether a council receives a quota or not in a given term can be considered as good as random (a conjecture consistent with the available evidence). As we describe in more detail (Dunning and Nilekani 2013), we therefore select for our study group pairs of councils near the threshold for reservation (one just above and one just below) in a given electoral term in sampled blocks in Karnataka, Rajasthan, and Bihar. We are interested here in the policy consequences of reservation, and in particular if quotas lead to greater material benefits (in the form of access to schemes such as the employment program MGNREGA) for Scheduled Castes and Scheduled Tribes. A nearly identical identification strategy in Rajasthan was used to study the effects of reservation on symbolic stereotyping, perceptions of ethnic threat, and the propensity of dominant castes to victimize members of marginalized groups (Chauchard 2014).

We found no evidence that electoral quotas improve material outcomes for marginalized groups, in a large and well-powered study. Using data on council spending priorities as well as detailed household surveys, we found some evidence that quotas shape perceptions, for instance, of the priority that the village council affords to marginalized groups. Yet reservation did not shape the actual spending priorities of councils, nor did it increase the propensity of members of Scheduled Castes and Scheduled Tribes to benefit from that spending. What explains these null effects? We conjecture that local–national linkages, especially ties between council presidents and the state and national parties for which they serve as brokers, can help to explain why policies vary little in the presence of an electoral quota. Since local leaders are recruited as party members and run implicitly on party tickets (I noted earlier the strong relevance of partisanship in these local elections, despite the formal prohibition

---

[7] State-level lists (or "schedules") include the particular castes or tribes eligible for the benefits of Scheduled Caste or Scheduled Tribe reservation; Scheduled Castes include Dalit (formerly "untouchable") castes.

on party labels), their spending allegiances are often oriented toward party members or those persuadable as party members. The replacement of a party member of one caste by a party member of another caste due to the presence of an electoral quota does not therefore result in a major reorientation of council spending, despite the president's formal and informal ability to target beneficiaries (Dunning and Nilekani 2013).

This does not imply that quotas have no effect on other outcomes. The symbolic benefits of descriptive representation for minority groups can be substantial and real, consistent with a large literature on the importance of the "politics of dignity." Chauchard provides evidence of tangible benefits of this empowerment. Studying members of dominant castes, and using survey techniques including vignettes over MP3 players that may allow for reliable elicitation of sensitive attitudes, he finds that electoral quotas do not reduce stereotyping of minority groups, but they do reduce the propensity to engage in or support atrocities against those groups. One interpretation of these findings, alluded to earlier in this chapter, is that local–national linkages foster perceptions of the power of the village council president to intervene with the police or the bureaucracy to punish atrocities. For example, the presence of a quota in a given village significantly increases the propensity of dominant castes to agree with the statement, "If a member of the upper castes gets into a dispute with an SC [Scheduled Caste] villager, then he will be in a lot of trouble with the police" (Chauchard 2015). Thus, Chauchard's findings appear consistent with the idea that the impact of quotas depends on the kinds of linkages across levels of government that devolution may sustain or generate – though in his case those linkages promote better outcomes from the perspective of marginalized groups than for the targeted distributive spending. The null findings on targeted distributive spending should not distract from evidence of effects on these other important outcomes – and they do not belie the connection between descriptive and substantive representation in other contexts (e.g., Grossman, Gazal-Ayal, Pimentel, and Weinstein 2016).

In addition, other mechanisms are consistent with the available evidence, especially our null findings (Dunning and Nilekani 2013). Our identification strategy leverages the rotation of quotas across village councils and therefore allows them to estimate the effect of the presence of a quota, relative to its absence, in any electoral term, but it cannot estimate the effect of the overall system of rotation, i.e., the institution of reservation itself. Indeed, the effects we estimate are conditional on the overall system of reservation; the fact that the absence of reservation today implies its future presence, or its presence today its future absence, may even foment the kind of intraparty compromises over time (for example, across different council electoral terms) that our theory highlights. However, even in the absence of partisan ties that crosscut ethnic divisions, the dynamics of rotation could moderate shifts in spending outcomes from one electoral term to the next (Dixit, Grossman, and Gul 2000). Our findings also imply that quotas may induce a bigger shift in outcomes when party and caste are more tightly linked than they are in the states we examined – since then a caste quota may tend to result in the change of the partisanship as well as the caste of the village council president.

To explore these possibilities, I precisely replicated Dunning and Nilekani's (2013) approach in two additional Indian states, Jharkhand and Uttar Pradesh. These states are useful for distinct reasons. First, Jharkhand was subject to extreme delays in the implementation of village council elections after the passage of the 73rd Amendment, due mainly to a series of court cases that challenged the method of allocating reservation in so-called Scheduled Areas (home to a majority of tribal groups). Indeed, the first council elections took place in 2010. Because I gather outcome data after these elections, but before the second set of elections took place five years later, I can estimate effects in a setting where the consequences of quota rotation is plausibly less than in the other Indian states we studied in 2013. (To be sure, council members in Jharkhand during the study period may anticipate that future rotation will occur with some probability, but the certainty may be much less, given the lack of regularity of elections in that state.) Second, Uttar Pradesh is a state with well-known connections between party and caste at the state level and, in particular, one in which Scheduled Castes tend to be associated with one party, the Bahujan Samaj Party (which was the party of Chief Minister Mayawati at the time of the study). The question thus arises as to whether the impact of quotas is in consequence greater in that state. These replications can also further bolster confidence in our overall 2013 findings, given that pooling data from Karnataka, Rajasthan, Bihar, Jharkhand, and Uttar Pradesh will imply a very large study group of councils. The external validity of the estimates also appears substantial, given the heterogeneity in the states studied and the fact that village councils are sampled from states with a collective population of 473 million people – about 64% the population of Europe.[8] The data suggest a preponderant role of government-welfare schemes in the lives of the rural populations of these states. For example, Figure 11.1 shows the proportion of our survey respondents who received any government benefit in the previous year by state (we did not ask the question in this way in Karnataka); the proportion who have received a job from the village council in the previous year (a category that may be understood narrowly by respondents); and the proportion who benefited from the employment guarantee scheme MGNREGA in the previous year, a scheme that is substantially under the control of the village council (but that had not yet penetrated surveyed areas of Karnataka at the time of our surveys there, in 2009). On average between 60 and 80% of respondents received government benefits, and MGNREGA is a substantial source of benefits as well (e.g., more than 30% of respondents in Rajasthan).

---

[8] Karnataka: 64 million. Rajasthan: 74 million. Bihar: 99 million. Jharkhand: 32 million. Uttar Pradesh: 204 million.

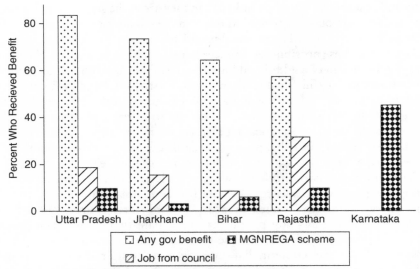

FIGURE 11.1 Benefit Receipt across Indian States

To implement the design, I first sampled blocks at random in Jharkhand (33 blocks) and Uttar Pradesh (150 blocks). Within each block, after obtaining village council information on reservation histories from the respective State Election Commissions or district officers, and the proportion of Scheduled Caste, Scheduled Tribe, and other covariates from the census, I followed the procedure outlined in Dunning and Nilekani to select pairs of village councils within each block: one assigned to an electoral quota in the most recent village council election and the other not. This resulted in a sample of 118 council constituencies in Jharkhand and 300 in Uttar Pradesh.[9] My survey firm then conducted detailed household surveys in each of these village councils; the protocol called for sixteen interviews per village council, with the houses selected using a random start point and interval sampling, and the individuals selected using the next birthday method.[10] This resulted in a sample of 1,888 citizens in Jharkhand and 4,800 citizens in Uttar Pradesh. Combining these data with the three states included in Dunning and Nilekani, the study group is comprised of 13,680 citizens living in 930 village council constituencies. To account for clustered assignment to treatment, our main analysis is at the level

[9] In Jharkhand, due to very fine-grained differences in the proportion of Scheduled Castes or Scheduled Tribes at the relevant thresholds, it was sometimes possible to select two pairs within a block.
[10] In cases where respondents did not know their birth date and no identity card with this information could be produced, enumerators asked who in the household had a birthday closest to the next major festival.

of the council constituency mean when using individual survey data. Evidence suggests balance across the treatment and control groups on a wide range of covariates, consistent with random assignment of the 930 councils to quotas.

What is the impact of reservation of the council presidency in these two additional states? Essentially, the results track our (Dunning and Nilekani) findings in the states of Karnataka, Rajasthan, and Bihar. In both Uttar Pradesh and Jharkhand, quotas have some impact on perceptions that the village council prioritizes the needs of marginalized groups (Figures 11.2 and 11.3). For example, quotas significantly increase the proportion of respondents who say that Scheduled Castes or Scheduled Tribes are "influential." In Jharkhand (though not Uttar Pradesh), reservation also increases the proportion of respondents who say the council gives "priority" to these groups. Yet, despite these perceptions, there is no evidence of impact on the material benefits received by marginalized castes or tribes. For example, among Scheduled Caste and Scheduled Tribe respondents, quotas do not affect the proportion of them who have received a government benefit, a job or benefit from the village council, or a benefit from MGNREGA in the previous year. We also asked respondents what they think the most important spending priority of the council should be and what it actually is, with a list of five response options.[11] In Uttar Pradesh, reservation of the council presidency does not increase the proportion of Scheduled Caste or Scheduled Tribe citizens for which the answers to these two questions agree; there is some evidence of impact in Jharkhand. However, when pooling data from five states, including the three reported in our 2013 article (Dunning and Nilekani 2013), I find evidence of impact on perceptions of council priorities – but very precisely estimated null results on the effect of quotas on benefits received by the groups the quotas are intended to help.

Why does sharing the caste or tribe category of the council president not result in a bigger increase in benefits received by citizens from the Scheduled Castes and Scheduled Tribes? As in the previous three states, the salience of party is striking in both Uttar Pradesh and Rajasthan, with knowledge of the party of council members as widespread or more widespread than knowledge of caste. Caste and party are not especially strongly related at the local level in Uttar Pradesh, especially among council members. This makes sense in some ways, despite the strong connection between caste and party in state elections (where fewer seats are reserved, and those that are remain permanently frozen between delimitations): to run candidates for council presidencies that are reserved in a particular term, parties must recruit them from among the caste categories eligible for quotas. Mobilization of voters may therefore occur among party lines, as fieldwork suggests it does in Karnataka, Rajasthan, and

---

[11] The match between responses to these two questions is similar to the outcome variable in Chattopadhyay and Duflo (2004), who find that female reservation increases spending on public goods desired by women citizens.

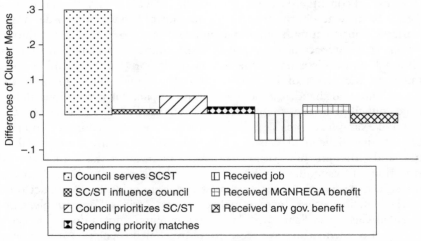

SE of the difference of means ~= 0.05;~= 0.18 for Council Serves SCST

FIGURE 11.2 Effects of Quotas (Uttar Pradesh)

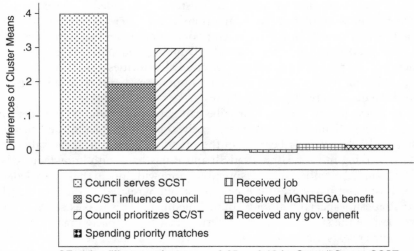

SE of the difference of means ~ = 0.05;~ = 0.18 for Council Serves SCST

FIGURE 11.3 Effects of Quotas (Jharkhand)

Bihar (Dunning and Nilekani 2013). Again, crosscutting party and caste ties at the local level could account for the relative lack of change in distributive targeting when there is a quota.

To investigate the influence of partisanship more systematically in Uttar Pradesh and Jharkhand, I embedded a survey experiment in our household survey instrument, in which the caste (*jati*) and political party of a hypothetical candidate for village council president were varied at random.[12] In both states, respondents were exposed at random to a candidate from the Yadav or the Chamar caste. The former is a dominant group classified as part of the Other Backward Classes in most states (and is the caste of Uttar Pradesh's current chief minister, Akhilesh Yadav). The latter is a Dalit (formerly "untouchable") Scheduled Caste comprised traditionally of leather workers (and is the caste of Uttar Pradesh's former Chief Minister Mayawati). I code the caste relationship between the respondent and the candidate using three indicator variables: (1) the respondent–candidate pair is coded 1 if the respondent and candidate are both Scheduled Caste or Scheduled Tribe, or both not Scheduled Caste or Scheduled Tribe (this is a "broad caste category" coding that potentially includes all respondents); (2) it is coded 1 if the respondent and candidate are both classified as Scheduled Caste or both Other Backward Classes (a "narrow caste category" coding, including only respondents from the Scheduled Castes or Other Backward Classes groups and therefore omitting Scheduled Tribes and Forward Castes, who cannot be exposed to a candidate from their own narrow caste category in the experiment); and (3) the pair is coded 1 if the respondent shares the candidate's *jati* or does not (a caste coding, which only includes respondents from one of candidate's potential *jatis*, i.e., Yadav or Chamar). Note the difference between caste categories (such as Scheduled Caste and Scheduled Tribe) and the individual castes (or *jatis*) that are included in those classifications.

The experiment also randomly varied the party of the hypothetical candidate. In Uttar Pradesh, the candidate's party was assigned as one of four relevant partisan options in that state (BSP, BJP, SP, and Congress); in Jharkhand, I used just two party options (JMM and BJP). To measure partisan ties between the respondent and candidate, I coded the respondents' partisanship in two ways: by the party in which the respondent professes membership (so this measure includes only professed party members), and by the party to which the respondent feels closest (which includes all respondents). Here, I report only analyses using the second measure, since the sample is very substantially larger in that case; however, results are similar using only professed party members. Note also that I exclude respondents who report closeness to a party other than one of the hypothetical candidate's four (in Uttar Pradesh) or two (in Jharkhand) possible parties, since such respondents are assigned with probability zero to co-partisanship. This excludes only a small number of respondents from the experimental study group.

---

[12] This parallels our (Dunning and Nilekani) approach in Rajasthan and Bihar (we did not embed a survey experiment in the Karnataka questionnaire).

The survey experiment thus exposes respondents at random to a candidate from their caste or not, and from their party or not. The co-partisan and shared caste conditions were fully crossed in a 2 x 2 factorial design; eligible respondents were exposed with equal probability to any combination. Using the broad definition of shared caste category, the study group size in Jharkhand and Uttar Pradesh is 4,826 respondents; with the narrow definition, it is 3,629; and using the definition based on caste (*jati*), it is 1,325. After reading respondents a short speech by the hypothetical candidate, we asked them to rate on a 1–7 scale (1) their likelihood of voting for the candidate; (2) their expectation of receiving a job from the village council if the candidate were elected; and (3) their expectation of receiving any other benefit from the village council if the candidate were elected. In the analysis, we sum the job and benefit responses to form a single measure; we then normalize both the vote and job/benefit measures to lie between 0 and 1.

The evidence suggests the salience of both party and caste ties, but suggests that the influence of partisanship on vote choice and expectations of benefit receipt is at least as important as is caste (Figures 11.1–11.6). In each figure, the effect of shared partisanship on vote intention – and crucially, expected benefit receipt – is about as large or larger as the effect of shared caste. Indeed, the effect of shared partisanship is about the same size whether or not the candidate is from the same or different caste as the respondent. As one would expect, both vote intentions and expectations of benefit receipt increase directly in response to sharing the caste, or sharing the partisanship, of the candidate. And those exposed to a candidate who shares both their party and their caste have the strongest vote intentions and expectations of benefits. Yet sharing a party nearly cancels, in each of the three figures, the negative effect of caste difference. The survey's experimental results therefore suggest the important of partisanship in

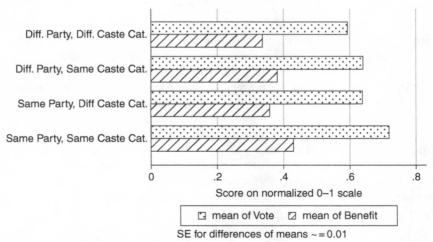

FIGURE 11.4 Effects of Shared Partisanship and Broad Caste Category

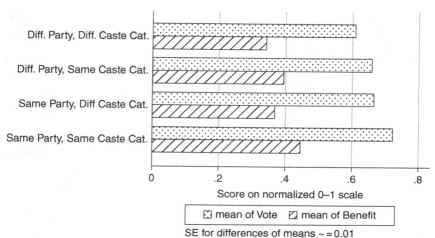

FIGURE 11.5 Effects of Shared Partisanship and Narrow Caste Category

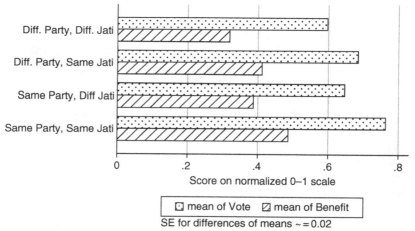

FIGURE 11.6 Effects of Shared Partisanship and Caste (*Jati*)

driving distributive outcomes (e.g., as measured by expectations of benefit receipt), even in a context in which local caste relations are the subject of explicit political interventions such as electoral quotas.

CONCLUSION: IMPLICATIONS FOR EVALUATION AND PROGRAMMING

Devolution could conceivably produce welfare gains from greater local cooperation, as well as policy outcomes that are more aligned with the preferences of the local population. This is arguably more often the case when the regions governed by devolved governments are more ethnically homogeneous than the national population as a whole. However, devolution to local governments that are themselves ethnically heterogeneous may duplicate many of the governance problems experienced at the national scale. Certainly, efforts to redress ethnic inequalities through quotas or other instruments may be more feasible to implement at the local level, and their potential symbolic impacts provide an important rationale for their adoption. However, their mixed success in promoting policy outcomes favorable to marginalized groups suggests that further scrutiny is warranted as well. The null effects of one policy intervention – caste-based electoral quotas in India – for increasing material benefits received by marginalized groups is a cautionary tale against the assumption that devolution and related interventions can solve problems of governance, and more particularly points to the importance of understanding the nature of links across government levels in the wake of decentralization.

Overall, the experiences of devolution raise the question of what it means for governments to be "closer to the people." To be sure, community councils elicit citizen candidates who make governance decisions at a small scale. Yet it is also important to recognize that devolution not only requires sustaining ties between levels of government. It can also create novel opportunities for top-down penetration of national actors at the grassroots. Particularly noteworthy is the way that local elections may allow state or national leaders to identify promising brokers, influential local leaders who can deliver services to people and votes to parties. The logic of partisan brokerage can deeply impact efforts to promote equity or accountability along ethnic lines, as in the case of devolution to Indian village councils analyzed in this chapter.

What are the possible implications for development programming? One natural possibility is that the set of prescriptions should differ in settings with local ethnic homogeneity and heterogeneity. And in both cases one should pay special attention to the nature of local–national linkages – for example, the influence and importance of local brokers empowered through subnational elections. Donor agencies such as USAID as well as groups such as NDI or IRI often focus on political party strengthening at the local level, but the evidence presented here suggests the multiple implications of strengthening parties – not all of them propitious from the point of view of governance outcomes. For town hall meetings and other efforts to promote programmatic politics, the identity of facilitators (for instance, whether they are local or national leaders) may be consequential (Fujiwara and Wantchekon 2013). Efforts to foment the political participation of marginalized groups may also have very different effects, depending on how ethnic and partisan affiliations line up locally. In this way, this chapter can contribute to USAID's thinking about the wide range of impacts that may emerge from decentralization under different circumstances – and perhaps move analysis away from an absolute normative preference for devolution.

REFERENCES

Allport, Gordon W. 1954. *The Nature of Prejudice*. Cambridge, MA: Perseus Books.

Auyero, Javier. 2001. *Poor People's Politics: Peronist Survival Networks and the Legacy of Evita*. Durham, NC: Duke University Press.

Baldwin, Kate. 2015. *The Paradox of Traditional Leaders in Democratic Africa*. Cambridge: Cambridge University Press.

Bates, Robert. 1983. "Modernization, Ethnic Competition and the Rationality of Politics in Contemporary Africa." In Donald Rothchild and Victor Olorunsola (eds.), *State Versus Ethnic Claims: African Policy Dilemmas*. Boulder, CO: Westview Press, pp. 152–171.

Bohlken, Anjali. 2016. *Democracy from Above: The Logic of Local Democratization in the Developing World*. Cambridge University Press.

Bruch, Elizabeth Eve. 2014. "How Population Structure Shapes Neighborhood Segregation." *American Journal of Sociology* 119(5): 1221–1278.

Bussell, Jennifer. 2012. *Corruption and Reform in India: Public Services in the Digital Age*. Cambridge University Press.

Camp, Edwin. 2017. "Cultivating Effective Brokers: A Party Leader's Dilemma." *British Journal of Political Science* 47(3): 521–543.

Chattopadhyay, Raghabendra, and Esther Duflo. 2004. "Women As Policy Makers: Evidence from a Randomized Policy Experiment in India." *Econometrica* 72(5): 1409–1443.

Chauchard, Simon. 2014. "Can Descriptive Representation Change Beliefs about a Marginalized Group?" *American Political Science Review* 108(2): 403–422.

Dixit, Avinash, Gene M. Grossman, and Faruk Gul. 2000. "The Dynamics of Political Compromise." *Journal of Political Economy* 108(3): 531–568.

Dunning, Thad and Janhavi Nilekani. 2013. "Ethnic Quotas and Political Mobilization: Caste, Parties, and Distribution in Indian Village Councils." *American Political Science Review* 107(1): 35–56.

Fujiwara, Thomas, and Leonard Wantchekon. 2013. "Can Informed Public Deliberation Overcome Clientelism? Experimental Evidence from Benin." *American Economic Journal: Applied Economics* 5(4): 241–245.

Grossman, Guy, Oren Gazal-Ayal, Samuel D. Pimentel, and Jeremy M. Weinstein. 2016. "Descriptive Representation and Judicial Outcomes in Multi-Ethnic Societies." *American Journal of Political Science* 60(1): 44–69.

Habyarimana, James, Macartan Humphreys, Daniel N. Posner, and Jeremy M. Weinstein. 2007. "Why Does Ethnic Diversity Undermine Public Goods Provision?" *American Political Science Review* 101(4): 709–725.

Horowitz, Donald. 1985. *Ethnic Groups in Conflict*. Berkeley, CA: University of California Press.

Kasara, Kimuli. 2007. "Tax Me If You Can: Ethnic Geography, Democracy, and the Taxation of Agriculture in Africa." *American Political Science Review* 1(1): 159–172.

Kasara, Kimuli. 2013. "Separate and Suspicious: Local Social and Political Context and Ethnic Tolerance in Kenya." *Journal of Politics* 75(4): 921–936.

Kasara, Kimuli. 2017. "Does Local Ethnic Segregation Lead to Violence? Evidence from Kenya." *Quarterly Journal of Political Science* 11(4): 441–470.

Koter, Dominika. 2013. "King Makers: Local Leaders and Ethnic Politics in Africa." *World Politics* 65(2): 187–232.

Krishna, Anirudh. 2011. "Gaining Access to Public Services and the Democratic State in India: Institutions in the Middle." *Studies in Comparative International Development* 46(1): 98–117.

Lierl, Malte M. 2015. "Essays on Informal Governance: Enforcement and Accountability under Weak Institutions." PhD dissertation, Yale University.

Manion, Melanie. 2016. *Information for Autocrats: Representation in Chinese Local Congresses.* Cambridge University Press.

Michalopoulos, Stelios. 2008. "Ethnolinguistic Diversity: Origins and Implications." Manuscript, Brown University.

Novaes, Lucas Martins. 2015. "Modular Parties: Party Systems with Detachable Clienteles." PhD dissertation, University of California, Berkeley.

Oates, Wallace E. 1999. "An Essay on Fiscal Federalism." *Journal of Economic Literature* 37(3): 1120–1149.

Padro i Miquel, Gerard. 2007. "The Control of Politicians in Divided Societies: The Politics of Fear." *Review of Economic Studies* 74(4): 1259–1274.

Posner, Daniel N. 2004. "The Political Salience of Cultural Difference: Why Chewas and Tumbukas Are Allies in Zambia and Adversaries in Malawi." *American Political Science Review* 98(4): 529–545.

Rodden, Jonathan. 2006. *Hamilton's Paradox: The Promise and Peril of Fiscal Federalism.* Cambridge: Cambridge University Press.

Rodden, Jonathan and Erik Wibbels. 2015. "Decentralization: Edited Volume for USAID's DRG Center." July 7, 2015.

Spolaore, Enrico and Romain Wacziarg. 2009. "War and Relatedness." NBER Working Paper No. 15095.

Stokes, Susan C., Thad Dunning, Marcelo Nazareno, and Valeria Brusco. 2013. *Brokers, Voters, and Clientelism: The Puzzle of Distributive Politics.* Cambridge University Press.

Szwarcberg, Mariela. 2015. *Mobilizing Poor Voters: Machine Politics, Party Rallies, and Social Networks in Argentina.* Cambridge University Press.

Wibbels, Erik. 2012. *Federalism and the Market: Intergovernmental Conflict and Economic Reform in the Developing World.* Cambridge University Press.

From Decentralization Research to Policy and Programs

A *Practical Postscript*

Derick W. Brinkerhoff, Anna Wetterberg, and Gary Bland

Around the world, scholars have studied decentralization, and a robust and ever-growing literature has emerged, containing a large degree of variation. Economists, for example, have focused on empirically testing hypotheses derived from the theory of fiscal federalism. Political scientists have addressed a wide range of decentralization issues, such as power distributions between central and subnational governments, the role of incentives and institutions, risks of local capture and clientelism, citizen empowerment, and political participation and voting, to name just a few. Not surprisingly, given the breadth and variety of the academic and practitioner literature streams, the benefits and downsides of decentralization are far from agreed. For developing countries and their international donor partners looking for advice, the lessons drawn tend to be equivocal, with camps of proponents citing the pluses, and of critics warning against the minuses, and both sides offering the caveat that "it all depends" on context.

This volume contains studies commissioned by the US Agency for International Development (USAID) to bring to bear the cumulative thinking of various current streams of academic research to address critical decentralization issues in the developing world, and to inform donor programming. As the introductory chapter summarizes, the studies provide an analytically rich menu of food for thought that can potentially inform donors' and country policymakers' choices in support of decentralization reforms. Each of the chapters concludes with some recommendations for additional research that could enhance the menu, but – with a few exceptions – stops short of considering how their findings could be integrated into the practical realm of donor program design and implementation. In this chapter, we seek to make that link, and offer some practical thoughts on how the book's decentralization research findings could usefully inform donor policy reforms and programs, with a specific focus on USAID.

Our discussion draws upon two analytic streams. To assess the potential uptake of the book's contents, we turn to analyses of policymakers' and practitioners' utilization of research and evaluation, a topic with a long history. Some of the classics include Weiss (1977), Patton (1978), and Lindblom and Cohen (1979). More recent sources focus on knowledge-to-policy processes and differential institutional incentives facing researchers and development practitioners (Court and Young 2006; Carden 2009; Sumner et al. 2009). To investigate where and how the decentralization findings might be applied, we pull from literature that addresses donor operating procedures, and explores process approaches to policy reform design and implementation that emphasize flexibility, adaptation, and learning. This stream too is long-standing, with early contributions from Rondinelli (1983) and Brinkerhoff and Ingle (1989), and later ones exemplified by Andrews (2013) and Valters et al. (2016).

DECENTRALIZATION RESEARCH UTILIZATION IN USAID

Our selective review of the factors identified in the research utilization literature highlights four key points that affect the potential for research findings' uptake among policymakers and practitioners.[1] First, the prospects for uptake are enhanced when prior researcher-agency collaborations are positive, and institutional incentives encourage openness to research. Second, utilization is more likely when researchers select topics relevant to the interests and concerns of policymakers and practitioners, and identify potential users of findings in government agencies prior to conducting studies. Third, a well-recognized factor concerns how findings are communicated. Researchers who can effectively communicate and disseminate analytic results, methods, and findings are more likely to see their work result in impacts on policy, programs, and/or practice. Fourth, the extent to which research findings suggest minor versus major changes in policies, programs, and operational practices can affect uptake. Those findings whose implications call for significant changes are generally less likely to be acted upon. In the following sections, we elaborate on these points as they apply to the contents of this volume.

USAID ENGAGEMENT IN DECENTRALIZATION RESEARCH

USAID has a long history of positive engagement in applied research and field support related to decentralization. USAID's central bureau that houses various research and analysis offices, which has changed names and modified its mandates over the years, began sponsoring research and technical assistance on decentralization in the late 1970s (Brinkerhoff 2012). Cooperative agreements with the University of Wisconsin examined regional planning and area development, while the University of California at Berkeley explored administrative decentralization for rural development. Through the Local

---

[1] For additional useful material, see www.researchtoaction.org.

Revenue Administration Project (LRAP), Syracuse University conducted analysis and country assistance focused on local government finance, with extended field activities in Peru, Bangladesh, Burkina Faso, and the Philippines. From 1988 to 1994, the Decentralization: Finance and Management Project (DFM), implemented by Associates in Rural Development (purchased by Tetra Tech in 2007) in cooperation with Syracuse University and Indiana University, concentrated on sectoral decentralization: rural roads maintenance, irrigation, community-based natural resources management, and health care and education service delivery. The research output from these cooperative agreements influenced programming in multiple country missions, and generated numerous books and journal articles.

In the late 1990s and early 2000s, USAID's democracy and governance (DG) office became the technical repository of decentralization programming guidance and technical support for the Agency. The office led the preparation of two handbooks on decentralization (USAID 2000, 2009). These documents distilled large amounts of research on decentralization topics into recommendations for program design, implementation, and evaluation, with an increasingly normative focus on the links between decentralization and democratization. In 2006, the office commissioned a set of decentralization studies intended to inform the revision of the 2000 handbook. These studies were later published as an edited book (Connerley et al. 2010). Then, in 2009–2010, the Africa Bureau and the DG office commissioned a series of cases studies on decentralization in Africa (USAID 2010), which also was subsequently published in book form (Dickovick and Wunsch 2014).

This current volume is the latest expression of USAID's long interest in the structure and effects of decentralization, and of an ongoing commitment to research. It suggests that: a) there are staff members within the Agency who remain committed to pursuing decentralization programming informed by research-grounded evidence; and b) the book's chapters have the potential to find a receptive audience among democracy and governance specialists, both in Washington, DC, bureaus and in USAID field missions.

INSTITUTIONAL INCENTIVES WITHIN USAID

Increasing research utilization by public agencies calls for the recognition that agencies are not monolithic, and thus interest in research findings and uptake will vary across categories of staff and across agency offices and business units. As a study of USAID's incorporation of systems thinking into its programs noted:

Within its boundaries, USAID comprises multiple types of organizations. Mostly closely resembling the mechanical bureaucracy of popular perception, USAID is a contracting and procurement entity. As an instrument of US foreign policy, USAID is a planning, programming, and service delivery organization. As a technical agency, USAID is a repository of expertise, experimentation, and learning in a range of international development sectors (Brinkerhoff and Jacobstein 2015, 23).

Technical staff members in the offices that commission and/or conduct research, and that offer training and assistance to country missions based on those studies, are the prime supporters and consumers of research. In the case of decentralization, these staff members are located in the Center of Excellence in Democracy, Human Rights, and Governance (DRG). Within the Center, the Learning Division is charged with developing and pursuing a DRG learning agenda, and supporting research efforts to address the analytic questions that the agenda lays out. USAID's Bureau for Policy, Planning, and Learning (PPL) is another supporter of research, with a focus on integrating learning into Agency operations. PPL staff have taken a leadership role in developing policy related to renewed attention to assessing country contexts, referred to as local systems, and integrating programs more explicitly into those contexts to enhance ownership and sustainability (USAID 2014).

The latest version of Agency policy guidance and requirements for country strategy and program design includes these elements, along with a focus on evidence and learning, thus reinforcing institutional incentives for research and analysis (USAID 2016). PPL's 2016 update of the Agency's evaluation policy places a heavy emphasis on the use of impact evaluation – experimental design with randomized controlled trials – to examine project effects. As one might expect, experimental approaches to analyzing decentralization are frequently referenced in the chapters in this volume and repeatedly advocated by the authors for future work. As noted later in this chapter, USAID's support for more rigorous evaluation of its projects, particularly decentralization and local governance programs, has already provided some initial lessons for consideration.

Outside the DRG Center and PPL, sector specialists' receptiveness to decentralization research – and governance research more generally – is related to the extent to which they see credible findings that establish a link to the sector outcomes that they are mandated to contribute to and report on. Congressional earmarks are a key source of incentives for USAID managers to think narrowly about programming so as to target investments specifically to sector performance indicators. As USAID's DRG budget has declined over time, the Center has increasingly sought to promote its expertise to sector offices and programs, such as the Global Health Bureau, the Feed the Future initiative (agriculture, food security, and nutrition), and the Bureau for Economic Growth, Education, and Environment (E3). One of the four development objectives of the DRG Center's most recent strategy, released in 2013, is the integration of governance (as well as democracy and human rights) principles and practices across the Agency's development portfolio (USAID 2013). Governance specialists are under pressure to demonstrate a direct connection between investing in governance and achieving sector-specific results.

A growing portion of USAID's portfolio is focused on integrated programming, bringing together governance and sector interventions under a single conceptual and contractual "roof." To the extent that these connections can be effectively demonstrated, arguments in favor of paying some attention to decentralization has led to inclusion of decentralization reforms in sector program designs and associated theories of change. These features then find their way into requests for proposals from implementers and eventually into contracts and grants (more on this in what follows).

ALIGNING RESEARCH TOPICS WITH THE INTERESTS AND CONCERNS OF POLICYMAKERS AND PRACTITIONERS

This brief historical discussion of USAID's involvement in decentralization research and technical assistance attests to an ongoing pattern of alignment with a subset of the substantive concerns of the Agency's staff. In the case of decentralization research's relevance today, the existence of evidence that it does, or can, contribute to sector outcomes increases the prospects that decentralization studies will find traction within a broader USAID audience. Since many of USAID's sector programs focus on service delivery, research findings that explore decentralization's contributions to better services align closely with Agency priorities. Wibbels's chapter (Chapter 2) on decentralized governance and social accountability offers useful insights to program designers and implementers alike on engaging citizens and service providers at the local level. Another example of direct relevance to services is Carter and Post's chapter (Chapter 8), which discusses urban services: land regulation, and water and sewerage. Among the authors' contributions is highlighting trade-offs in addressing the needs of the poor and powerful private interests in urban land markets.

Besides sector service delivery, the other – and perhaps stronger – alignment of the book's contents and USAID priorities relates to the specification and analysis of the contexts that surround donor programs. Even if decentralization reforms are not a specified target of intervention, the features of political, fiscal, and administrative decentralization loom large as affecting the prospects for achieving and sustaining program objectives and impacts. These features are called out in USAID's work on local systems and in policy guidance for the Agency's program cycle (USAID 2014, 2016). Like many donors, moreover, USAID now considers political economy analysis an essential tool for improving governance program adaptability and effectiveness. All the chapters make this point about contextual influence in one way or another. For example, Dunning (Chapter 11), writing on decentralization and ethnic diversity, provides evidence that local ethnic and partisan affiliations strongly affect whether donor-supported efforts to empower marginalized groups can succeed. He challenges USAID's and other donors' normative preferences for devolution. Pierskalla, in Chapter 6, explores the dynamics of subnational government unit proliferation, a phenomenon that has touched USAID programs in Indonesia, Uganda, and the Philippines, to name a few.

Given USAID's operational mandate, staff members are not simply interested in understanding contextual factors such as decentralization but also want to know what can be done about them, either to work around them or to change them. Here, understandably, a volume containing academic analysis of decentralization topics is less aligned with the practical realm. The one exception is Cristia's chapter (Chapter 9) on decentralization, community-driven development, and post-conflict countries, which pays the clearest attention of all the chapters to applying decentralization research findings in practice. She offers ten recommendations for donors and practitioners, most of which could be usefully applied across the range of topics covered in the book.

RESEARCH COMMUNICATION AND DISSEMINATION

The chapters in this book offer a wealth of information and analysis that illuminate ongoing debates in the decentralization literature. From a research-to-action perspective, where the intent is to achieve influence and impact, questions arise about content (what is being communicated), process (how it is being communicated), and relationships (who is communicating). On the *what* question, the chapters with the clearest answer are those that offer explicit practical recommendations – for example, Cristia's chapter mentioned previously – as well as suggesting where knowledge gaps remain.

A related answer on content as to where the decentralization research in this volume can help is to develop evidence-based assessment frameworks. These can inform donor strategies and project design, and associated program investments are a potentially useful way of communicating research and translating findings into policy-relevant tools. Many of the chapters suggest elements related to decentralization that could be assessed and questions that could be asked, though few develop these sufficiently to qualify as a framework. One example of a useful assessment tool comes from Malesky's chapter (Chapter 7) on decentralization and business performance, where he refers to work completed over more than a decade on a subnational economic governance competitiveness index for USAID in Vietnam. Indices can be helpful in establishing empirical baselines, tracking implementation progress on interventions, and determining impacts.

The *how* question concerns more than the choice of assembling research in book form, peer-reviewed articles, websites, blogs, and/or tweets. It extends to conceptions of the process of reaching the intended audiences that go beyond unidirectional information transmission. Feeding the contents of the book into communities of practice, research networks, and policy coalitions are all potential avenues for influence. USAID's DRG Center, PPL's Office of Learning, Evaluation, and Research, and the Learning Lab are engaged in a variety of knowledge exchanges, both face to face and virtual.[2] Beyond USAID, for example, the OECD's Development Assistance Committee's Network on Governance convenes donor agencies with interests in a variety of governance topics, including decentralization.[3]

The *who* question relates to whose knowledge counts. The fact that the authors commissioned for this volume are all academics indicates that the DRG Center values university-based expertise. Most of the authors have previous and in many cases ongoing relationships with USAID and other donor agencies, which provides a foundation for continued exchange on decentralization topics and for future opportunities to influence policy and programming.

DECENTRALIZATION RESEARCH MEETS POLICY AND PROGRAM OPERATIONS: LEARNING AND ADAPTATION

The point in the research utilization literature on the extent to which findings suggest major versus minor changes in agency policies, programs, and operational practices leads us to the second stream of literature we noted earlier. USAID, led by staff members in PPL, has made significant policy changes in how country strategies, programs, and individual projects are to be designed, implemented, and evaluated (USAID 2016). These changes have incorporated core principles of systems thinking, adaptive management, and organizational learning (Brinkerhoff and Jacobstein 2015). The latest version of the Agency's decentralization handbook refers to the need to adapt and update programs as a country pursues decentralization reform (USAID 2009). Several of the chapters in this book emphasize contextual adaptation. For example, as Wibbels (Chapter 2) notes in his discussion of social accountability and networks, donor programming that aligns with knowledge about social networks calls for adaptive design principles, highly specific theories of change, and relational data collection at program baselines to provide the evidence needed for adaptive decisions later on.

As a contracting organization under pressure to demonstrate tangible results to Congress, USAID has struggled with how to operationalize the principles of adaptation, learning, flexibility, and country ownership. To the dismay of researchers, decentralization programs too often reflect a standard package of interventions, and downplay or neglect underlying political and institutional dynamics (Smoke 2015). Likewise, to the dismay of practitioners, experimental research on decentralization or local governance programming can reflect a superficial understanding of development objectives and the practical requirements in their design and implementation. USAID's handbooks on decentralization offer nuanced guidance on context assessment and a series of

[2] See, for example, https://usaidlearninglab.org/about-usaid-learning-lab.
[3] See www.oecd.org/dac/accountable-effective-institutions/about-govnet.htm.

programming options as inputs to program design and evaluation (USAID 2000, 2009). Ultimately, however, programs need to choose an objective with solid chances of achievement given a time frame and a budget. Translation of research findings into programs that fit within Logical Frameworks and specify Intermediate Results and related performance indicators necessarily results in both oversimplification and over-specification. Programs are oversimplified in that, for purposes of design, they select an objective along with one or several components of decentralization that can be framed as discrete interventions, conceptually and operationally distinct from the vast array of relevant contextual factors. Further, given the contractual realities of implementation, they are over-specified in terms of performance indicators, time frames, and deliverables.

TARGETING DECENTRALIZATION AND DECENTRALIZATION-RELATED STRATEGY

In considering where decentralization research could prove useful, we can look beyond individual country-level projects to decision points at the start of the USAID programming cycle. A major one where the contextual factors that the research in this volume discusses could be useful is the Country Development Cooperation Strategy (CDCS). The CDCS is the five-year, interagency development strategy of each USAID mission, a reflection of the partnership with the host country for priority investments that can help ensure stability and prosperity. The chapters in this volume can help to determine the extent to which decentralization should be among the CDCS's development objectives. Monitoring, the establishment of a learning agenda, and evidence-based evaluation are also central to the CDCS process.[4] In this regard, in revisiting some issues, taking on others that have received less attention, and offering new research ideas, the chapters in this volume obviously have much to offer.

Further, USAID usually carries out sector assessments prior to the design of its programs. Several chapters in this volume provide both insights and a literature survey on a host of issues that can prove helpful to USAID decentralization assessment teams. In some instances, insights in these chapters could be of interest in project design. For example, Baldwin and Raffler (Chapter 4) discuss the ways that traditional leaders are subject to accountability and face differing incentives to participate in donor-supported local service delivery. They argue that the local governance system conditions the extent to which traditional leaders are embedded in their communities and may be more likely to respond to the needs and desires of local residents.

---

[4] For more information about the CDCS process, see http://usaidprojectstarter.org/content/cdcs-country-development-cooperation-strategy.

EXPERIMENTING WITH EVALUATION DESIGN

One clear recommendation of this volume, proposed in several of the chapters, is increased collaboration between researchers and practitioners on evaluating program impact. Practitioners surely need to better understand the variety of available evaluation methods, while researchers need to better appreciate what can be achieved given the developmental approaches of USAID and other donor programs. In the interest of scientifically rigorous evaluation, the authors variously propose clearer theories of change, less complex program designs, and more closely integrating impact evaluation into development programs. Rodden (Chapter 5), for example, suggests that in situations where country governments are contemplating intergovernmental financial reforms, donors can work with them to pursue phased rollouts of reforms with built-in experimental designs.

However, such collaboration faces practical challenges. Christia (Chapter 9) acknowledges the well-recognized limitations of impact evaluations and the challenges of designing rigorous evaluation around program activities (see, for example, Rao et al. 2017). RCTs can be costly, narrowly focused, insufficiently nuanced, and require short time frames. We know from recent experience that efforts to incorporate rigorous evaluation have created program implementation delays and RCT cancellations as the demands of sample size, random selection, and controlled treatments have come into conflict with development priorities and program designs that are grounded in USAID strategies and sectoral approaches. Integrated programming, for example, which is currently a major governance priority, tends to favor complex program designs with multiple operational components that call for correspondingly creative evaluation approaches. Effective incorporation of evaluations thus requires improved teamwork among donors, practitioners, and researchers to ensure that program and evaluation activities are complementary, are operationally feasible, and meet development and research objectives simultaneously.

DEGREE OF EFFECTIVE DECENTRALIZATION

Decentralization is not only highly political; it is also a dynamic process subject to fits and starts depending on the set of objectives it pursues and the level of support it receives. Decentralization may at first advance quickly in line with a recent series of reforms. It might then stall after the election of a new, less interested government. A subsequent ministerial change could lead either to renewed support or to a reversal of prior efforts. Practitioners – particularly program implementers who are attempting to advance the objectives of a decentralization project – quickly become aware of the vagaries associated with their work.

The effectiveness of the decentralization process – its strength, the enabling environment, and degree of actual implementation across regions of a given country, as well as across levels of government and sectors – is thus a critical contextual variable for practitioners (Wetterberg and Brinkerhoff 2016). Researchers likewise must grapple with the implications of effective decentralization. While some of the chapters in this volume acknowledge that decentralization may not always progress as planned, the discussions generally center on distinct models and their implications. For researchers, variations in the degree of effective decentralization may, on one hand, offer natural experiments to test posited relationships between decentralization and other variables of interest (see, for example, Pierskalla, Chapter 6). On the other hand, such heterogeneity can preclude the use of standardized interventions and complicate controls for data collection (in much the same way that it requires practitioners to tailor program activities to local contexts). Working together, program implementers and researchers can address how to incorporate varying levels of effective decentralization in improved project monitoring and evaluation and research design.

DECISION POINTS

The chapters in this book do an admirable job of presenting the available evidence for a range of options possible for different aspects of decentralization. Program designers, however, must account for a combination of different levels of each dimension and design programs to fit these idiosyncratic constellations. The challenge is to incorporate lessons from academic research – as well as learning from other projects – while resisting pressures toward isomorphism (Fejerskov 2015).

This volume provides evidence that can inform guidance to help program designers navigate the multidimensional thicket of decentralization. Here we offer some suggestions as to where in the project development cycle practitioners might find the preceding chapters and findings useful.

Resource allocations: As discussed earlier, this volume's findings are most likely to prove useful in USAID's CDCS development. Further, some chapters provide useful pointers as donor country offices act on such strategies and seek to allocate funds between programs in different sectors or regions. For instance, Rodden's guidance on levels of revenue generation could inform decisions by identifying particularly conducive and challenging environments for program investments. Similarly, Grossman's (Chapter 3) exploration of the implications of different types of leadership arrangements could inform allocation decisions.

Program design: The frameworks and reviews of related evidence can also inform program design decisions. As Christia points out, development programs' theories of change are often aspirational, rather than empirically based. The chapters in this volume demonstrate whether assumed relationships between decentralization interventions and outcomes are supported by evidence. For example, Dunning challenges the notion that decentralization necessarily results in improved services and accountability, and indicates specific instances in which positive outcomes have not resulted.

Program start-up: As they begin program implementation, practitioners must consider supporting factors that need to be in place for theories of change to be borne out. Malesky provides helpful guidance on specific elements needed to improve the likelihood of achieving intended gains in business performance. As he points out, gathering the necessary information to assess whether such underlying conditions are met can be challenging, but worthwhile for practitioners to attempt. Program implementers should pay similar attention to Wibbels's observations on social networks to understand how they are likely to facilitate or hamper intended outcomes.

Design of monitoring, evaluation, and learning (MEL) activities: As discussed, USAID has placed increasing emphasis on monitoring program effects, evaluating impact, and learning during implementation. The chapters in this volume provide a wealth of suggestions for designing MEL activities that build on existing empirical research, produce reliable data, and result in acceptable levels of causal inference. For instance, Pierskalla makes suggestions for ensuring causal inference even in highly variable and changing environments. Rodden outlines a research agenda for programs involving local revenue mobilization that could be used as a starting point for learning questions in relevant programs. Christia highlights multimethod measurement strategies that can be utilized to assess outcomes of community-driven development programs and triangulate data across multiple sources.

Adaptive implementation: During implementation, researchers can continue to contribute substantially in terms of designing data collection systems and evaluation studies, as mentioned earlier. Practitioners are best placed, however, to judge how learning can be incorporated in and responded to within a specific set of program activities. As Christia suggests, encouraging both researchers and practitioners to "innovate while replicating" can lead to advances in scholarly knowledge, as well as guiding more effective program implementation.

Reflecting on results for broader impact: Many of the chapters in this volume conclude with unanswered questions and gaps in existing research that could be adapted to MEL activities in specific programs. They also highlight remaining empirical lacunae and unanswered questions in development debates that rigorously collected data from projects could help to answer. For example, León and Wantchekon's chapter (Chapter 10) on clientelism highlights a gap in the decentralization literature on how decentralization can change politicians' incentives for responding to citizens' needs as a function of how clientelistic practices create career advancement possibilities. Carter and Post's chapter on decentralization and urban governance examines findings on two key urban services: land regulation, and urban water and sewerage. They offer three avenues for future research: 1) basic country-level data collection on urban services availability, access, and quality; 2) stronger focus in research designs on effects of decentralizing reforms, along with greater collaboration between donor agencies and researchers prior to investigation; and 3) fill gaps in topics that have received insufficient attention.

CONCLUSION

Academic research can provide a useful reminder that achieving donors' objectives is subject to large measures of uncertainty, complexity, and unpredictability. In USAID's political climate where results-based management predominates, this reminder is not always welcome. As the chapters in this volume demonstrate, decentralization is multifaceted and context-specific, a political process of institutional reform that is difficult to measure. Although the challenge of comparative decentralization analysis is long-standing, and faces both practitioners and academic researchers, the book provides concrete suggestions for advancing our knowledge and is itself a strong argument for continued collaboration.

This volume signals that dialogue between donors and academics is ongoing, vibrant, and mutually beneficial. The available evidence and delineated arguments on each side of different decentralization debates that researchers provide can serve as input to policy discussions. However, academically informed guidance needs to accommodate the bureaucratic realities of donor programming and country politics. Development practitioners are often better placed than researchers to undertake this accommodation and to engage with national governments, civil society, and local governments on decentralization. Researchers can usefully support this engagement with evidence and recommendations, while retaining the humility to recognize that their studies will rarely be determinant.

REFERENCES

Andrews, Matt. 2013. *The Limits of Institutional Reform in Development: Changing Rules for Realistic Solutions*. Cambridge and New York, NY: Cambridge University Press.
Brinkerhoff, Derick W. 2012. "A Selective Review of USAID-Funded Development Management Research and Practice: Relevance for Strengthening Country Systems." Background paper, Experience Summit on Strengthening Country Systems, US Agency for International Development, Bureau for Policy, Planning, and Learning, Washington DC, November.

Brinkerhoff, Derick W. and Marcus Ingle. 1989. "Between Blueprint and Process: A Structured Flexibility Approach to Development Management." *Public Administration and Development* 9(5): 487–503.

Brinkerhoff, Derick W. and David Jacobstein. 2015. "Systems Thinking and Institutional Performance: Retrospect and Prospect on USAID Policy and Practice." Research Triangle Park, NC: RTI International, International Development Group Working Paper 2015–02, April.

Carden, Fred. 2009. *Knowledge to Policy: Making the Most of Development Research.* New Delhi: Sage Publications India, for International Development Research Center.

Connerley, Edwin, Kent Eaton, and Paul Smoke, eds. 2010. *Making Decentralization Work: Democracy, Development and Security.* Boulder, CO: Lynne Rienner Publishers.

Court, Julius and John Young. 2006. "Bridging Research and Policy in International Development: An Analytical and Practical Framework." *Development in Practice* 16 (1): 85–90.

Dickovick, J. Tyler, and James S. Wunsch. 2014. *Decentralization in Africa: The Paradox of State Strength.* Boulder, CO: Lynne Rienner Publishers.

Fejerskov, Adam M. 2015. "From Unconventional to Ordinary? The Bill and Melinda Gates Foundation and the Homogenizing Effects of International Development Cooperation." *Journal of International Development* 27: 1098–1112.

Lindblom, Charles and David Cohen. 1979. *Usable Knowledge: Social Science and Social Problem Solving.* New Haven, CT: Yale University Press.

Patton, Michael Q. 1978. *Utilization-Focused Evaluation.* Beverly Hills, CA: Sage Publications.

Rao, Vijayendra, Kripa Ananthpur, and Kabir Malik. 2017. "The Anatomy of Failure: An Ethnography of a Randomized Trial to Deepen Democracy in Rural India." *World Development.* http://dx.doi.org/10.1016/j.worlddev.2017.05.037

Rondinelli, Dennis. 1983. *Development Projects As Policy Experiments: An Adaptive Approach to Development Administration.* New York, NY: Methuen.

Smoke, Paul. 2015. "Managing Public Sector Decentralization in Developing Countries: Moving beyond Conventional Recipes." *Public Administration and Development* 35 (4): 250–263.

Sumner, Andy, Nick Ishmael-Perkins, and Johanna Lindstrom. 2009. "Making Science of Influencing: Assessing the Impact of Development Research." IDS Working Paper No. 335. Sussex: University of Sussex, Institute of Development Studies, September.

USAID. 2000. *Decentralization and Local Democratic Governance Programming Handbook.* Washington, DC: US Agency for International Development, Center for Democracy and Governance, Bureau for Global Programs, Field Support, and Research, May.

USAID. 2009. *Democratic Decentralization Programming Handbook.* Washington, DC: US Agency for International Development, Center for Democracy and Governance, Bureau of Democracy, Conflict, and Humanitarian Assistance, June.

USAID. 2010. *Comparative Assessment of Decentralization in Africa: Final Report and Summary of Findings.* Washington, DC: US Agency for International Development, September.

USAID. 2013. *Strategy on Democracy, Human Rights, and Governance.* Washington, DC: US Agency for International Development, June.

USAID. 2014. *Local Systems: A Framework for Supporting Sustained Development.* Washington, DC: US Agency for International Development, Bureau for Policy, Planning, and Learning, April.

USAID. 2016. *ADS Chapter 201: Program Cycle Operational Policy.* Washington, DC: US Agency for International Development, Bureau for Policy, Planning, and Learning, June 20.

Valters, Craig, Claire Cummings, and Hamish Nixon. 2016. "Putting Learning at the Centre: Adaptive Development Programming in Practice." ODI Report. London: Overseas Development Institute, March.

Weiss, Carol, ed. 1977. *Using Social Research in Public Policy Making.* Lexington, MA: Lexington Books.

Wetterberg, Anna and Derick W. Brinkerhoff. 2016. "Cross-Sectoral Social Accountability in Practice: Findings from Six Cases," in Anna Wetterberg, Derick W. Brinkerhoff, and Jana C. Hertz, eds., *Governance and Service Delivery: Practical Applications of Social Accountability across Sectors.* Research Triangle Park, NC: RTI Press.

Index

CPSIA information can be obtained
at www.ICGtesting.com
Printed in the USA
BVHW031743050422
633465BV00002B/4